The Crimean War

War, Armed Forces and Society

General Editor: Ian F. W. Beckett

Andrew D. Lambert

The Crimean War

British grand strategy, 1853–56

Manchester University Press
Manchester and New York

Distributed exclusively in the USA and Canada by St. Martin's Press

Published by Manchester University Press
Oxford Road, Manchester M13 9PL, UK
and Room 400, 175 Fifth Avenue,
New York, NY 10010, USA

Distributed exclusively in the USA and Canada
by St. Martin's Press, Inc.,
175 Fifth Avenue, New York, NY 10010, USA

Reprinted in paperback 1991

British Library cataloguing in publication data
Lambert, Andrew D.
    The Crimean War: British grand strategy, 1853–56.—
    (War armed forces and society).
    1. Crimean War
    I. Title II. Series
    947'.073

Library of Congress cataloging in publication data
Lambert, Andrew D., 1956–
    The Crimean War: British grand strategy, 1853–56/Andrew
    D. Lambert.
        p.   cm.—(War, armed forces, and society)
    Includes bibliographical references.
    1. Crimean War, 1853–1856—Campaigns—Soviet Union, Northern.
2. Crimean War, 1853–1856—Naval operations, British.   3. Great
Britain—History, Naval—19th century.   I. Title.   II. Series.
DK215.L32   1989
947'.073—dc20   89–12701

ISBN 0 7190 3564–3 *paperback*

Photoset in Linotron Sabon
by Northern Phototypesetting Co, Bolton

Printed in Great Britain
by Billings & Sons Ltd, Worcester

Contents

Figures and tables

This book is dedicated with thanks to Geoffrey Dimock and Bryan Ranft, two historians who, in their different ways, made it all possible. What we attempt is nothing without such encouragement and advice.

Acknowledgements

I wish to acknowledge the gracious permission of Her Majesty the Queen to make use of material from the Royal Archives at Windsor, and the Royal Correspondence included in the Broadlands Archive. In addition I should like to thank Sir Robin Mackworth-Young and the staff at the Royal Archives for their assistance during my research.

Sincere thanks are also extended to His Grace the Duke of Norfolk for permission to use and quote from the papers of Vice-Admiral Lord Lyons; to Sir Charles Graham both for permission to use the papers of his ancestor, and for making them available at Netherby; to the Earl of Clarendon for permission to use the collection relating to the Fourth Earl held at the Bodleian Library, Oxford. For the use of manuscript sources in their care I am indebted to the trustees and staff of the British Library; the Scottish Record Office, the National Register of Archives; the Bodleian Library; The Borthwick Institute of Historical Research, York; the Manuscript Department of the Nottingham University Library; Wiltshire Record Office; Sussex Record Office; Rear-Admiral Morriss and staff at the Hydrographer's Department, Taunton; The National Army Museum; Colin White and the Staff at the Royal Naval Museum, Portsmouth; Alan Pearsall ISO, Dr Roger Knight, Dr Roger Morris, David Lyon and the staff of the Reading Room and Draught Room at the National Maritime Museum; Dr Nicholas Rodger and the staff at the Public Record Office. All those named above have made valued contributions to this work.

When presenting a work of this scope it is a pleasant duty to acknowledge the assistance of so many of those who have helped to make it possible as the author's failing memory enable him to recall.

Many have had the 'Russian War' inflicted upon them at some stage, none more often than Prof. Bryan Ranft. As a Ph.D. supervisor he had the Herculean task of overseeing the first round; his efforts were indefatigable, providing me with advice, encouragement and the freedom to make my own mistakes. I can only hope this book will repay some of the faith he demonstrated in taking on such a task. Other members of the Department of War Studies, King's College have been ready sources of advice and encouragement, notably Professor Brian Bond and Dr Michael Dockrill. In addition they, with Dr David French, have provided more than one opportunity to place my work before the Military History Seminar at the Institute of Historical Research, London. Similar debts of gratitude are owed to Professor Bourne, Dr Alan Sked and Dr David Stevenson for a welcome invitation to address the 19th and 20th Century International History Seminar, and to Professor Geoffrey Till with respect to the Modern Seapower Seminar at King's College.

I am also profoundly grateful for the help given by fellow scholars, both in this field and in others, notably Dr Iain Hamilton, Eric Grove and William Blair. Dr Basil Greenhill and Ann Giffard were for many years fellow-travellers in Baltic waters; I was privileged to read their work, the only modern study devoted to those campaigns, in MS. I hope our efforts will produce a better understanding of the theatre. My good friends Richard Billows, John Ferris and Sebastian Cox were members of a memorable MA programme, and not infrequent victims of the war. Among my colleagues and students, past and present, many have helped to make this book possible; they will know how grateful I am. Much appreciated financial assistance for research and travel was provided by the Twenty-Seven Foundation of the Univerity of London at a crucial stage in preparing this book.

It is another happy task to record my appreciation of the valuable advice and assistance from Manchester University Press, and to Ian Beckett and the Editorial Board of the War and Society Series. I hope the result will justify their faith.

Outside the world of scholarship my primary debt is to my parents; without their support and understanding it would not have been possible to bring this work to completion. Sadly my grandparents did not live to see this book, but I will never forget the pleasure it gave me to present them with a copy of my first work. Many members of my family have offered encouragement, for which I am indebted. In addition I have acquired three godchildren, to remind me there are other long-term commitments in life. I remain uncertain if Simon and Dianne and Peter and Patsy made a wise decision, but I will do my best. Finally I owe much to Zohra who, having to share her husband with a book, has done so with a rare appreciation of a complex relationship.

It only remains to emphasise that any errors or omissions in this book remain in spite of the best efforts of all those named above; they are the sole responsibility of the author.

Andrew Lambert
Norfolk, 1988

Abbreviations

HTN	Papers of Captain Sir Henry Keppel, National Maritime Museum
LYONS	Papers of Vice-Admiral Lord Lyons, Sussex Record Office, Chichester
MCM	Melville Castle Muniments, Papers of Rear-Admiral Sir Richard Saunders Dundas
MILNE	Papers of Rear-Admiral Sir Alexander Milne, National Maritime Museum
NAPIER	Papers of Vice-Admiral Sir Charles Napier, National Maritime Museum
NeC	Papers of the Fifth Duke of Newcastle, Nottingham University Library
NRS	Publication of the Navy Records Society. Unless otherwise indicated the reference is always to the relevant volume of the Russian war series
PANMURE	*The Panmure Papers* (London, 1908), 2 vols.
PRO	Public Record Office, cited for private collections, Napier and Lord John Russell
R.A.	Royal Archive, Windsor Castle
RAGLAN	Papers of Field Marshal Lord Raglan, National Army Museum
SPR	Papers of Captain T. A. B. Spratt, National Maritime Museum
WALKER	Papers of Rear-Admiral Sir Baldwin Walker, University of Cape Town
W.O.	War Office
WOOD	Papers of Sir Charles Wood at the India Record Office (F78)

Abbreviations used in the text

RE	Royal Engineer
RM	Royal Marine
RMA	Royal Marine Artillery

Note. Official Admiralty letters always passed through the office of the Secretary, and were addressed accordingly. This convention has been abandoned here to save space, but all official letters are, in the original, addressed in the proper form.

Books and articles are cited in full the first time they are used, and then by the author's name, unless there is more than one work by any particular author, in which case they are distinguished by an abbreviated title.

It is important to stress the difference between official and private correspondence, a distinction which is crucial to this work. Official correspondence between Government agencies, Commanders in the Field, Diplomats and Foreign Governments should always be referred to as dispatches. Private correspondence, letters, did not carry the same authority as dispatches, but were invariably more informative. Sir Charles Wood's letter to Sir Edmund Lyons of 12 March 1855 provides the contemporary understanding of the distinction. The point is important, particularly where the relationship between politicians and officers were on the verge of collapse, as they were in both theatres toward the end of 1854.

While every effort has been made to consult the original correspondence there are cases where this has proved impossible. For example, although Napier kept copies of his dispatches to the Admiralty, many of the originals were destroyed during the infamous 'weeding' process early in the twentieth century. Similarly the record of correspondence between Sir Charles Wood and the Admirals in 1855 is more complete in the Halifax archive than in the papers of Lyons or R. S. Dundas; therefore I have used the Halifax copies. In all cases where letters, cited as coming from the archive of the writer, are copies, I have pointed this out where significant.

The 24-hour clock has been used throughout for clarity, although this was unknown at the time. Similarly all dates have been reduced to common Western practice; old-style Russian dating would add unnecessary complications and involve some confusion.

All Russian, Turkish, Swedish and Finnish place names have been given essentially as they were used by allied officers during the war. Where there were alternatives the most commonly used, and clearest, have been selected. For the Baltic theatre the most important variations from modern usage are:

Old style	Modern usage
Abo	Turku
Brahestad	Raahe
Danzig	Gdansk
Dager Ort	Hiiummaa

Old style	Modern usage
Eckness	Tammisaari
Elgsnabben	Alvsnabben
Gamala Carleby	Kokkola
Helsingfors	Helsinki
Kioge Bay	Koge But
Konisberg	Kalinningrad
Libau	Liepja
Memel	Klaipeda
Nargen	Naissar
Osel	Saaremaa
Port Baltic	Paldiski
Reval	Tallinn
Sweaborg	Suomenlinna
Uleaborg	Oulu
Viborg	Viipuri
Wingo Sound	Vinga

In the Black Sea theatre there are very few significant differences, the substitution of Constanta for Varna being the most important, although alternative spellings have been adopted.

Introduction: A Crimean War?

The intention of this book is to demonstrate that the 'Crimean War' so familiar to twentieth-century historians has no historical reality; the conflict discussed under that label has been created by misguided and derivative scholarship. This assertion is based upon a fresh approach to the development, execution and impact of British strategy between 1854 and 1856. This theme demands an examination of politics, grand strategy, allied co-operation and diplomacy before and during the largest war in which Britain was involved between 1815 and 1914. To compound the difficulty there was never an agreed strategy, merely a collection of shifting perceptions lacking the co-ordinating unity of the more formal twentieth-century cabinet structures. However, the most serious obstacle to any understanding of the conflict remains the label 'Crimean War'. Starting from the narrow position implicit in this term has distorted the perception of a war that was fought on a larger scale, and for grander objects, than has hitherto been assumed. It is hoped that a new understanding will encourage a return to the original usage of a Russian War. In this connection it should be noted that the title of this book reflects the pressures of publishing, rather than the intentions of the author.

Initially, Britain and France conducted a limited war against Russia; this phase of the war ended when British statesmen accepted the need for an unlimited effort directed at the seat of Russian power on the Baltic coast, rather than peripheral campaigns on the Black Sea littoral. This was a maritime war; the decisive threat involved a large-scale naval assault on Cronstadt, the seaward fortress of St Petersburg, as the culmination of two years spent re-learning the basics of war and strategy. It marked the most complete combination of technological, economic and intellectual effort yet achieved by a major power in wartime, using over 300 warships and 40,000 men. The government had no doubt it would succeed, even though nothing like it had ever been attempted before. When Austria made a bid for a compromise peace this plan was adopted as the centrepiece of British attempts to secure an effective treaty by armed diplomacy. More significantly, the Russians were convinced that they could not withstand this assault. After the fall of Sevastopol the briliant engineer Totleben was recalled to work on the defences of Cronstadt/St Petersburg. Large earthworks were thrown up and numerous gunboats built, yet the Russians were not prepared to accept the chance of battle. The force prepared for the operation was paraded around Spithead on St George's Day 1856 and paid off, having served to end one war, and exercised a considerable influence over the troubled post-war relationship between Britain and France.

Without a reliable appreciation of British strategy diplomatic historians, troubled by the apparently inconclusive manner in which the war ended, remain divided. Some persist in linking peace with the fall of Sevastopol, others give more emphasis to the process of diplomacy. A study of the Baltic theatre would provide a very different view. Hitherto the Baltic had been treated as a sideshow, dismissed in the same cursory manner as allied efforts in the White Sea and Pacific. This cannot be justified when dealing with campaigns involving 35,000 allied personnel which threatened the Russian capital and detained an army of some 200,000 first-class Russian troops. Treating the Baltic as the second major theatre of war places the Black Sea in a much clearer context.

The only British cabinet minister with the commitment and ability to prepare a policy before the outbreak of war was Sir James Graham, First Lord of the Admiralty. From March 1853 Graham developed a maritime strategy for war against Russia; unwilling to take the political and financial risks of realistic pre-war preparations, he relied on two set-piece operations at the outbreak to destroy Russian seapower. These, he hoped, would help build up alliances to carry on the land war while Britain conducted a maritime war. The first plan resulted in the invasion of the Crimea, the second was thwarted by the timely withdrawal of the Russian battlesquadron from Reval. Graham was uncommonly secretive, never discussing his plans with anyone; consequently his role in the war has never been understood. Historical studies have been dominated by the heroism and sacrifice of the Crimean campaign to such an extent that the object of the allied invasion has been obscured. Graham's Black Sea strategy was based on a grand raid against Sevastopol. This would prevent Russia launching a surprise attack on Turkey by sea, hamper her operations in the Balkans and open the Russian coast, particularly in Asia Minor, to a wide-ranging maritime campaign. He secured the consent of his colleagues and the French Emperor for this plan before the declaration of war. Black Sea strategy was dominated by naval concerns and implemented by naval/maritime methods. The failure of Graham's strategy before Sevastopol forced the allies to rely on their logistics back-up, on their courage and command of the sea. The work of the Navy in destroying the logistics base of Russia's Crimean army, primarily by occupying the Sea of Azov, was a major factor in securing the fall of Sevastopol. Indeed, without command of the sea the allied armies would have remained at Toulon and Portsmouth.

The war has been approached at the level of strategic and operational planning, examining the politicians' attempt to form British war aims and strategy, the theatre commanders' handling of operations and the relationship between the two seats of decision making. In this the role of France, along with Austria and other neutrals, was vital. When considering operations the emphasis has been placed on strategic decision making and, to a lesser extent, the development of new tactics and technology in the light of war experience. The linkage between the two theatres requires clarification; major decisions in one theatre had a direct effect on the other. In this respect the structure of the book should be noted. Chapters 1 to 7 examine the pre-war origins of British and allied strategy against the background of the Eastern Crisis; 8 to 11 are concerned with the Black Sea theatre in 1854; 12 and 13 deal with Baltic operations in 1854. Chapter 14 examines the impact of diplomatic and political developments on British strategy during the winter of 1854–55, 15 to 18 complete the study of the Black Sea theatre, 19 and 20 that of the Baltic. Chapters 21 to 23 examine the blending of diplomacy and strategy in the pursuit of peace between December 1855 and March 1856, while chapter 24 attempts to draw some conclusions from the war.

It is almost a contradiction of the objects of this book to disclaim any attempt to study the campaigns in the White Sea and Pacific. These were an integral part of British war policy, but the small-scale and limited objects of both campaigns, in the light of the extensive material available, make them better suited to separate treatment. To have included any meaningful examination in this book would have distorted the work to an unacceptable degree. The White Sea and Pacific demonstrated the problems of making war on an evasive enemy in a vast theatre, and of defeating him once found. The strategy was that of attacking the enemy where he was weak; this was the major error of British strategists during the war, for until they were prepared to attack the centres of Russian power they could never force her to accept limits on her position, the only agreed war aim of the government.

A limited war

Britain and France fought a limited war against Russia; limited by the geography of the conflict, the German states prevented it becoming a Europe-wide conflict; in addition the allies would not make the financial and political sacrifices of an unlimited war effort because they were, at heart, more concerned with their own rivalry than fighting Russia. If allied aims had been suitable for a limited war against Russia this might have been adequate, but although they appeared limited in London and Paris they were still set far higher than Russia would concede short of a major defeat. Russia gave up the war because the allied aims were not sufficiently onerous to justify risking defeat in 1856, although British preparations fell far short of an unlimited effort. In combination the Cronstadt attack, the Swedish alliance, mounting pressure on Prussia and the Austrian Ultimatum left Russia with little option. Sevastopol, for all it might mean to British statesmen, was only a naval base on a distant shore of the Russian Empire, less important to the Czar than was Gibraltar to the British. Nicholas I went to war from pride, his son continued out of filial piety until it became obvious that the nature of war was changing. The inability, or unwillingness, of the allied statesmen to see the need for an unlimited effort gave Russia the chance to administer a severe check to their plans. Within a generation of the wars of 1793–1815 British and French statesmen were committing the same errors that characterised the early stages of those wars – failure to match war aims, level of commitment and strategy. It is undoubtedly trite to point out that the relevant part of Clausewitz's work *On War* was published in 1832–33. No British statesman or military commander had read this work, or obtained similar insight elsewhere; consequently when they made war plans they looked back to the French wars for inspiration and picked up anything that appeared to suit, from the lines of Torres Vedras to Nelson's Baltic plans of 1801. No attempt was made to link these plans with the level of commitment. Graham, for example, believed the right spirit would get round the lack of men and equipment; he did not understand that, without war aims, strategy could be no more than an academic exercise, one of Clausewitz's central themes. The point is valid because Clausewitz built his analysis on the experience of 1793–1815, experience which was available to anyone. Unfortunately the intellectual level of military writing in Britain in the years before 1854 was low, and the best of it focused on narrow, technical issues. Without a guide to the experience of the French wars British statesmen painfully and slowly re-learnt the old lessons and adopted some new tactics. By 1856 they were all wiser, but short of a painful defeat they had not taken to heart the real weakness of Britain in continental affairs. Significantly Clausewitz made no mention of seapower, and until Britain built a continental army she would remain at a discount in Europe.

The divergent claims of long-term planning and the needs of the moment created particular problems for the Navy. Nineteenth-century naval policy was dominated by the strategic threat of the French and Russian battlefleets. This had a profound influence on the campaigns of 1854. Ill-prepared for the war they had just embarked upon, Britain and France had to take extraordinary risks in the Black Sea and accept, albeit reluctantly, lesser objectives in the Baltic because they were not equipped to carry the conflict to an enemy content to remain on the defensive. As the dominant voice in strategy Graham led the risk taking, because he would not divert funds from the construction of a steam battlefleet required for the French war he believed to be inevitable in order to provide the flotilla craft his admirals and advisers requested. It was no coincidence that he placed his first major order for specialist coast assault craft after the failure of the grand raid against Sevastopol. Similarly the Great Armament for 1856 was not ordered until after the bombardment of Sweaborg had demonstrated what could be achieved and the fall of Sevastopol forced Britain to consider new methods of making war.

War aims

British aims in the crisis of 1853 remained essentially those that had conditioned her Turkish policy after 1833 – preserving the status quo with Turkey holding the Straits. Any other policy would open the way for her rivals to improve their position, adding to the strategic problems of the empire, forcing politically unpopular increases in defence spending. During early 1853 Britain opposed attempts by France and Russia to alter the balance; pressure on Turkey from Austria, which had no maritime pretensions, caused less concern. Despite this, British policy makers were planning to attack Russia in the Baltic, White Sea and Pacific, as well as the Black Sea, long before the war broke out, emphasising the imperial rivalry of the two powers. Palmerston, the most ambitious British statesman, wanted to force back the frontiers of Russia to remove the strategic threat to British interests. He believed this could be done with limited methods, and limited commitment. His colleagues had less grandiose schemes; they saw Russian seapower, particularly the arsenals at Cronstadt and Sevastopol, as the proper target for British efforts. These, they persuaded themselves, would both secure Turkey and improve Britain's position.

1

Great Britain and Russia, 1815–53

The accepted view is that the 'Crimean War' was fought to prevent Russia taking control of Turkey and entering the Mediterranean. This presupposes Russia had Mediterranean ambitions. Studies of Russian naval, commercial and diplomatic policy make it clear that under Czar Nicholas I, (1825–55), such aims were held for no more than a few days.[1] This should not obscure the central issue; between 1815 and 1854 Britain and Russia were the only world powers. Their economic and imperial rivalry was translated into strategic terms, making Russia Britain's most significant threat, even though her Navy was inferior in quality to that of France. Before considering the origins of the war it is necessary to establish the realities of Russian Black Sea policy.

The Russo–Turkish War of 1828–29 ended with a Russian army at Adrianople. The treaty signed there on 14 September 1829 was a model of restraint; Russia gained Georgia and Circassia, the Danubian Principalities of Moldavia and Wallachia were given a degree of autonomy under the Sultan. Russian commerce through the Straits was guaranteed, along with control over the mouths of the Danube. Russian policy was to maintain Turkey; the Imperial Conference of September 1829 accepted that a weak Turkey was the best guardian of the Straits, her downfall would cause a war among the major powers. Yet if Turkey collapsed Russia would not revive her and would not allow another power, even a resurgent Greece, to control the Straits.[2] If any such danger threatened, the fleet would carry an army to secure Russian interests at the Straits.[3]

The Mehemet Ali crisis of 1833 posed a serious threat to Turkey, forcing the Sultan to call for aid. Rebuffed by Britain, he turned to Russia. On 3 March 1833 a Russian squadron arrived in the Bosphorus, reinforced within fifty days by 10,000 troops. Britain and France sent their fleets to Besika Bay, just outside the Dardanelles. Despite this belated interest Count Orlov secured the Treaty of Unkiar Skelessi on 8 August 1833, including a secret article binding Turkey to close the Straits to all warships in time of war. The Russians then evacuated Constantinople. By the Treaty of Munchengratz, 18 September 1833, Nicholas secured Austrian co-operation to preserve Turkey, or partition her if she collapsed. Russia pledged herself to preserve the status quo. Hostile British reaction to Unkiar Skelessi marked the beginning of sustained interest in the Near East; Palmerston was unwilling to accept the honest Russian claim that the treaty did not give her the right to send warships through the Straits.

The resulting tension was manifested in an increased Russian fleet in the Black Sea, considered in Britain to be a sign of aggressive intentions. In fact Russia only claimed the same rights over the Bosphorus that Britain maintained at the Dardanelles. The Russian fleet, normally twelve battleships, was more powerful than that of Turkey, but could never threaten the Royal Navy. Its principal role remained the transport and supply of the army. The building yard at Nicolaiev was forty miles up the river Bug, while poor timber and construction methods promoted decay and structural weakness. Until the late 1840s there were no dry docks, preventing thorough repairs. These problems forced the Russians to keep up a considerable construction effort to maintain twelve effective ships. Visiting Sevastopol in 1829 Lieutenant Adolphus Slade found the Russian ships filthy, old fashioned and badly maintained; only the scale of corruption was impressive.[4] Captain Edmund Lyons formed similar views, and both men anticipated returning to more earnest purpose with some satisfaction.[5] In 1841 the Surveyor of the Royal Navy, Captain Sir William Symonds, inspected the fleet. Of thirteen ships fitted for sea only six were seaworthy, the rest crippled by dry rot: 'I think, upon the whole, that the Russian ships and naval establishments in the Black Sea have been overrated,' he concluded.[6] The defences of Sevastopol had been reinforced after 1833 to meet the danger that prompted the secret clause of Unkiar Skelessi, a British attack. Sadly Symonds' sane appreciation did not prevail, Slade's report of the poor state of the Bosphorus defences increased British alarm. Although Britain and Russia were status quo powers with regard to Turkey, both believed the other intended to take over at Constantinople. In truth neither wanted to transform their economic and political rivalry in the Near East into a clash of arms.

The second Mehemet Ali crisis of 1839–40, appeared to resolve the misunderstanding; Britain and Russia co-operated to maintain Turkey. However, the basis of their action was a common interest in keeping the Straits permanently closed. Mehemet Ali's challenge was ended by the brief Syrian Campaign of 1840. Palmerston's diplomacy united Britain, Russia, Austria and Prussia in forcing France to abandon her attempt to alter the balance of power in the eastern Mediterranean. The Straits Convention of 1841 confirmed the closure of the Turkish Narrows. This was a great relief to Britain and Russia, leading to a dramatic fall in Russian naval estimates. Between 1833 and 1839 these had averaged 37 million roubles. In 1840 they were cut to 11·6 million and did not rise above 20 million until 1853.[7] Reduction was also encouraged by the sharp fall in Turkish naval expenditure. The high water mark of Anglo–Russian *rapprochement* came with the Czar's visit to Britain in 1844. The resulting Nesselrode Memorandum engaged the parties to preserve Turkey, and to consult if her collapse appeared imminent. Puryear considered this binding, and being broken by the British Government, made them responsible for the war. In fact the memorandum was only a record of conversation, at most a gentleman's agreement. It was not a binding treaty, the Czar's decision to treat it as one was self deception. He considered that with the Treaty of Munchengratz he had bound Britain and Austria to preserve Turkey, or divide her, excluding France.

After 1844 another facet of Russian interest in the Straits replaced strategic fears. An Imperial Committee examining Russian trade discovered that exports, dominated by Odessa, relied on free navigation of the Straits. Odessa had risen to prominence after the Treaty of Adrianople, the Russians having deliberately allowed the mouths of the Danube to silt up, redirecting trade to their port. Austrian and British protests went unanswered while Russian industrialisation was primed by the profits from the export of primary products. This affected the trading relationship with Britain. While British merchants still dominated primary exports, those were decreasing as Russian industry expanded. Russian export of finished goods began to supplant those of Britain, particularly around the Black Sea. In addition Russia maintained protectionist barriers. Turkey remained Britain's best trading partner in the region. Her imports from Britain rose from £1·1 million in 1825 to £8·5 million in 1852. Turkish exports, principally Danubian grain, ran at only one-quarter of these figures, the difference being made up in bullion, secured by the

Treaty of Balta–Liman, 1838. Early in 1853 the British charge d'affaires at Constantinople considered 'the safety of our vast commercial interests' more significant than 'European Policy and the maintenance of peace'.[8]

In 1848 Russian troops occupied The Principalities, under the terms of the Treaty of Adrianople, to forestall the threat of revolution. European diplomats, Palmerston included, accepted Russian explanations. The Refugees Crisis of 1849 engendered a very different response; Austro–Russian demands for the surrender of Hungarian and Polish refugees implied Turkish subservience to the two Emperors. Such blatant use of force in Turkish affairs ended the unwritten *entente* of 1841. Palmerston sent the Mediterranean fleet into the Dardanelles, deliberately violating the Straits Convention to demonstrate the level of British concern. When Austria and Russia backed down Palmerston blamed the Ambassador and pressed the Turks to reinforce the Bosphorus defences, sending two British naval officers to drill the Ottoman fleet. However this was not enough to revitalise a moribund service, riven by political strife and corruption. By 1853 work had commenced on three steam battleships, although they were delayed by the inability of the Turks to pay for the engines.[9] The Ambassador, Stratford, implied Britain should help as the new ships would give the Turks command of the Euxine.[10] In 1853 the Turkish fleet remained undermanned, badly trained and ill-armed; the first concern of the senior adviser, Captain Slade, was to find a secure anchorage.[11] The 1849 crisis demonstrated the limits of Anglo–Russian co-operation. When Turkey was threatened by another power they would work together to preserve a mutual interest; but if either party attempted to secure an advantage the consensus collapsed. A high level of mutual suspicion demonstrated that the two states were the greatest rivals in Turkish affairs.

When the crisis in the east first threatened the peace of Europe the initial thoughts of one British statesman, Lord John Russell, turned to the Baltic. During the seventeenth and eighteenth centuries British Baltic policy had been dominated by the supply of naval stores.[12] After the Great Northern War, 1699–1721, when Britain had been forced to intervene, attempts were made to reduce British dependence on this region. The Baltic campaigns of Lord de Saumarez, 1808–12, only concerned naval stores as a part of the general trade of the region. Post-war developments in the use of timber and revised tariff structures increased the use of non-Baltic materials.

Naval timber was no longer imported, and during the war alternative sources were developed for hemp and flax.[13] Russian commerce declined with that of Britain, emphasising the linkage between the two.[14] British purchases of naval stores made them a valuable export for Russia, but after 1815 the majority of Russian exports, primarily grain, went through Odessa. By 1853 British interest in the Baltic was predominantly political and strategic.

The Russian Navy was a forced growth. Relying on imported shipbuilding and navigational skills, it remained inferior to the western navies. Russian power was land based, the navy was only an adjunct.[15] Nicholas I appointed Prince Menshikov Minister of Marine in an attempt to create an effective battlefleet. The Baltic fleet, thirty battleships, with smaller craft and a large force of the unique Baltic oared gunboats, was divided into three squadrons, at Cronstadt, Sweaborg and Reval. Despite the interest of the Czar the ships and personnel were not of the first quality. In 1839 Symonds found the ships old fashioned and overcrowded with guns.[16] While the revitalised fleet caused alarm it was not built to attack Britain.[17] The function of Russian seapower was to overawe the second rate powers of the Baltic and Black Sea. During the war Russian ships never attempted to meet the western fleets at sea, only attacking the Turks at Sinope. For all the expense of creating a battlefleet the Russians had no understanding of oceanic seapower; with no colonies, little sea-borne trade and no direct access to the broad ocean there was little opportunity, and no necessity for such an understanding.

The major Baltic arsenals, Cronstadt and Sweaborg had a complex role, providing bases for the fleet and the seaward defences of St Petersburg and Helsingfors. For the latter role they were very heavily armed. Cronstadt, built in the Russian style, consisted of numerous tiered granite casemates; Sweaborg, a Swedish construction, comprised numerous open batteries. In the event of a war with Britain the ships would be used to reinforce the land defences: a 'Fortress Fleet'.[18] There was no attempt to employ the ships as a 'Fleet in being' to hamper the offensive use of the sea by the allied forces.[19] This lack of strategic purpose was not understood in Britain, nor in Russia.[20]

Russia's Baltic position had been improved during the Napoleonic War; the capture of Finland and the Aland Islands during the winter of 1808–9 made the Gulf of Finland a Russian lake, although the

Finns were exempt from conscription. The Treaty of Frederickshamn, 1809, stipulated that the Aland Islands would not be fortified. In the 1830s Nicholas built a large fort at Bomarsund in response to the spirit of 'Scandinavianism' that might alter the balance of power and place the Baltic narrows in the hands of a single, strong power.[21] Taking exception to the more active foreign policy of the Swedish King Oscar I, (1844–59), further works at Bomarsund were started in the early 1850s.[22] Sweden remained silent, despite British prompting. Persistent rumours suggested the Czar would follow his work on the Alands by capturing Gotland, placing a Russian squadron within a day's sail of the Sound.[23] Other reports indicated that the Russians were intent on creating a naval base in the Warranger Fiord on the Northern Ocean.[24] While such developments might damage British interests, nothing could be done unless Sweden would act. The Schleswig–Holstein crisis of 1848 indicated the major themes of Russian Baltic policy. As the guardian of the Straits, Denmark, like Turkey, was too weak to deny them to Russia. In consequence Nicholas would not allow her to be destroyed by the powerful Prussian-led North German Confederation, or absorbed into a united Scandinavia.[25] Britain and Russia had a considerable degree of common ground over Denmark; both preferred to maintain Denmark against Prussia. However, in Britain Nicholas's concern was treated a part of his expansionist policy, presaging an attempt to seize the Straits. The French took a more favourable, and more accurate view, treating Russian policy in the Baltic and Black Sea as essentially similar. The Czar would not permit any great power to control the Straits, but he had no desire to hold them.[26] Russian policy was misunderstood in Britain primarily because of the heavy-handed fashion in which it was conducted.

War provided Britain with an opportunity to halt Russian expansion in the Baltic, without it it is difficult to see how this could have been achieved. Those in Britain who feared Russia had no doubt that once war broke out a fleet would be sent into the Baltic to sink the Russian fleet.[27] Palmerston had always been more hostile toward Russia than France. His Baltic policy had aimed at containing Russia, favouring the reunion of Finland with Sweden, and urging Sweden to resist pressure over the Warranger Fiord.[28] Consequently when the war began he had a policy for the Baltic, but little conception of practical strategy.

Notes

1 CURTISS, J. S., *Russia's Crimean War* (Ithaca, 1979); PURYEAR, V. J., *England, Russia and the Straits Question: 1844–1856* (Berkeley, 1931).

2 PURYEAR, pp. 10–13.

3 MOSELEY, P. E., *Russian Diplomacy and the Opening of the Eastern Question in 1838 and 1839* (New York, 1934), pp. 7–30.

4 SLADE, Lt. A, *Record of Travels* (London, 1833), vol. 1, pp. 487–9.

5 EARDLEY-WILMOT, Captain S., *Life of Vice Admiral Lord Lyons* (London, 1898), pp. 46–50.

6 SHARP, J. A., *Life of Rear Admiral Sir William Symonds* (London, 1858), p. 286.

7 MITCHELL, D. W., *A History of Russian and Soviet Seapower* (London, 1974), p. 138.

8 Rose to Clarendon 25 Mar. 1853: F.O. 78/930 f365–9; more generally, BAILEY, F. E., *British Politicians and the Turkish Reform Movement* (Harvard, 1942 and 1970).

9 Slade to Stratford 12 Oct. 1853: encl. in fn. 10.

10 Stratford to Clarendon 15 Oct. 1853: No. 298, FO 78/939.

11 Slade to Foster 4 Oct. 1853: R.A. G5 f119.

12 SEELEY, J. R., *The Growth of English Policy* (London, 1896, two vols.), vol. ii, p. 40.

13 ALBION, R. G., *Forests and Seapower* (Harvard, 1926), pp. 182, 343, 355.

14. PURYEAR, pp. 1–200 on Russian economic policy; TAYLOR, A. J. P., *The Struggle for Mastery in Europe, 1848–1918* (London, 1954), p. 12.

15 ANDERSON, R. C., *Naval Wars in the Baltic, 1522–1850* (London, 1910).

16 SHARP, pp. 218–24.

17 GLEASON, J. H., *The Genesis of Russophobia* (London, 1950), pp. 173, 200.

18 MAHAN, Capt. A. T., *Naval Strategy* (London, 1911), p. 441.

19 COLOMB, Adm. P. H., *Naval Warfare* (London, 1891), pp. 123–32.

20 GLEASON, pp. 159, 215–19; BARTLETT, C. J., *Great Britain and Seapower, 1815–1853* (London, 1963), pp. 103–11.

21 HATTON, R., 'Palmerston and "Scandinavian Union" ' in BOURNE and WATT, eds., *Studies in International History* (London, 1967), pp. 120–1.

22 HALLENDORF and SCHUCK, *A History of Sweden* (New York, 1970), pp. 376–7; Grey to Clarendon 3 Mar. 1854: F.O. 73/260 f38.

23 Grey to Clarendon 16 Jan. 1854: *ibid* f5.

24 KNAPLUND, P., 'Finnmark in British Diplomacy, 1836–1855', *The American Historical Review*, 1925, vol. 30, pp. 478–90; Grey to Clarendon 30 Jan. 1854: F.O. 73/260 f11.

25 SUMNER, B. H., *Survey of Russian History* (London, 1947), p. 411.

26 CURTISS, p. 101.
27 MALMESBURY, Earl of, *Memoirs of an Ex-Minister* (London, 1884, two vols.), vol. ii, p. 35.
28 WEBSTER, Sir C., *The Foreign Policy of Palmerston* (London, 1951, two vols.), vol. i, p. 319.

2

The crisis in the east

The Russian War developed when the affair of the Holy Places exposed the fragility of the 1841 Straits Convention as a means of binding the powers to act in concert over Turkey. By the outbreak of war four of the five guarantors had broken the convention while attempting to influence Turkish policy. The Holy Places in Palestine had long been objects of Christian pilgrimage. The Turks had no objection to this, according the various sects small privileges based on the power of their protector. Orthodox pilgrims outnumbered all others, providing the Czar with a powerful grip on the shrines. France, protector of the Latin party, had shown little interest until Louis Napoleon Bonaparte, President of the Second Republic, realised action over the shrines would gather Catholic conservative support for his *coup d'état*.

In mid 1850 the French Ambassador to the Sublime Porte opened the issue of the Holy Places; in 1851 LaVallette demonstrated a more flexible approach, demanding joint access to the shrines. His Russian colleague, Titov, reminded the Sultan that the Czar wanted no changes. When rebuffed in October 1851 LaVallette threatened to call up the French fleet, but the overthrow of the Republic on 2 December removed the urgency.

Throughout the crisis the Turks demonstrated commendable objectivity, relying on Byzantine duplicity to reconcile the demands of Latins and Greeks. They had no desire to become involved in a war with a great power over some schism in heathen dogma. LaVallette returned to Constantinople in May 1852 aboard the new steam battleship *Charlemagne*, breaching the Straits Convention and producing a profound effect on the Turks. As the first steam battleship in the Mediterranean, *Charlemagne* raised French prestige, made necessary, as LaVallette declared, by the position of Louis Napoleon. Britain protested this blatant use of force. The real purpose of the

French was to increase their influence at Constantinople and throughout Europe for internal political reasons. The Czar, acutely aware that French/Latin success involved a corresponding Russian/ Orthodox defeat, made a vigorous response based on the imprecise Treaty of Kutchuk Kainardji of 1774, manipulated to claim a protectorate over the Sultan's 12 million Greek Orthodox subjects.

On 2 December, as the Czar prepared to act, his rival declared himself Emperor, reducing the political pressures on French policy. Louis Napoleon had begun the process of breaking down the restraints placed upon France and the Bonaparte family by the Treaty of Vienna. It was in this context that Nicholas protested the use of the legitimising numeral III and refused to call the new sovereign his 'brother'. On 30 December Russian forces were alerted; Nicholas contemplated a rapid amphibious descent on the Bosphorus from Sevastopol and Odessa. His advisers persuaded him to rely on diplomacy to isolate France and secure Russian interests in Turkey. Feeling certain of Austria and Prussia he played for British support through the 'Seymour Conversations' with the British Ambassador. The Russian minister in London, Brunnow, informed Foreign Secretary Lord John Russell that Russia intended to move, although he realised that if Russia pressed Turkey too hard she would call for British aid. Unfortunately he relied on the Prime Minister, Lord Aberdeen, for information on British policy. Aberdeen was pro-Russian and had only a limited control over his cabinet. The Czar wanted to arrange a policy with Britain to cover the eventuality of Turkey collapsing, hinting that if nothing was settled beforehand he would occupy Constantinople. Russell's reaction was only in part what the Czar desired. While protesting the French use of menaces he informed Russia that if sincere she should not threaten Turkey and would not discuss partition; neither Britain nor Russia could gain from such an eventuality.

While the Czar considered how to recover his influence the Austrian Government indicated a suitable method. Disturbed by Turkish pressure on Montenegro and fearing disturbances among her Slavic subjects and their Serbian neighbours, Austria sent Field Marshal Count Leiningen to Constantinople in late January 1853, backed by military mobilisation. The Turks eventually accepted part of Leiningen's brief, but significantly would not give Austria a protectorate over the Christians of Bosnia, or stop using Cattaro as a naval base. The Turkish Government was not prepared to give way on issues they considered vital, a lesson that was lost on Russia. Russian policy developed from the legitimate, if minor, grievance over the Holy Places; her prestige at Constantinople had been reduced. The other great powers considered it essential that it be recovered, and for this reason Russell found little to complain of when Russia mobilised. By late 1852 the Czar was determined to have a settlement; he favoured pushing Turkey into Asia, leaving Constantinople a free city. Austria and Russia would hold the Dardanelles and the Bosphorus; Serbia and Bulgaria would be Russian clients while Britain, and perhaps France, took compensation elsewhere. The object was to preserve the Straits as a barrier against British warships and a free passage for commerce. The Russian Chancellor, Count Nesselrode, persuaded the Czar to rely on a diplomatic mission to recover Russian influence.

The Czar's mistake was to assume he had the support of Austria. This depended on Austrian perceptions of her interests, and they did not favour partition of Turkey. In the 'Seymour Conversations' of 9, 14 and 20 January Nicholas claimed he spoke for Austria when he called on Britain to agree a policy for the collapse of Turkey. Only later could Seymour reply that the British Government would not plot the destruction of Turkey and read a dispatch to Nesselrode praising Russia's hitherto moderate policy. Even this was misunderstood. Nicholas believed Britain supported his claims to protect the Sultan's Christian subjects. In the fourth conversation of 22 February, the Czar attempted to sweeten the pill by referring to commercial advantages. Seymour was certain he intended to partition, with Austrian support. In adopting Brunnow's assessment of British policy Nicholas committed another error, for Aberdeen did not represent a united cabinet and would ultimately be overruled by his colleagues. Consequently Nicholas considered genuine British support on the Holy Places also covered the partition of Turkey. When Clarendon took up the seals at the Foreign Office the lines of British policy became clear. Britain supported Russia over the shrines, as the instructions given to Stratford demonstrated, but she had no desire to see Russian influence at the Porte increased. This was an entirely British perception of Turkish independence. The Seymour conversations mark the beginning of a gradual shift in British policy over the next nine months, from supporting Russia to supporting France. France had disturbed the status quo in Turkish affairs, but was not planning the destruction of Turkey. After

February 1853 many in the British Government believed Russia would destroy Turkey, and with her the European status quo.

The Aberdeen ministry developed from the political disturbances of the previous decade and was created with a large degree of Royal influence.[1] Aberdeen, Foreign Secretary 1841–46, made an excellent peacetime Premier, but could do little to resolve the internal contradictions of the Whig/Peelite coalition.[2] Russell, with the support of disappointed Whigs, continually pressed him to hand over the Premiership. In resisting these demands Aberdeen allowed some ministers an unusual degree of freedom from cabinet control, notably Sir James Graham, First Lord of the Admiralty and a close political and personal friend. The Foreign Office, briefly held by Russell, went to Earl Clarendon. While contemporaries considered Clarendon an excellent choice he was too sensitive of public criticism and lacked the moral and political courage to take the lead in policymaking.[3] His shift from Aberdeen's policy to that of Palmerston changed the direction of British policy.

The Seymour conversations were only one facet of the Czar's Turkish policy. The intention was to leave France diplomatically isolated while Russia recovered her influence through the Sultan renouncing all recent pro-Latin measures. For this mission Nicholas selected Prince Menshikov, although Nesselrode preferred Orlov, architect of Unkiar Skelessi.[4] Menshikov was no diplomat and violently anti-Turkish; delayed by illness, he lost the chance to combine his mission with Leiningen. His instructions were dominated by religious questions. He was to persuade the Turks to act up to their earlier promises over the Holy Places, avoiding all contact with Fuad, the supposedly pro-French Foreign minister. Nicholas sent an autograph letter for the Sultan, hinting at grave consequences should the Turks reject Menshikov's proposals. The deeper purpose of the mission was to place the relationship between Russia and Turkey on a sound basis for the future in a convention of treaty force; in return Russia would provide support against French demands. If these terms were rejected Menshikov would issue an ultimatum and leave.

The Czar also considered a military solution. His memorandum of 19 January anticipated an early rupture with Turkey for which primary responsibility would rest with France. Russia would respond with a rapid seizure of the Straits; 16,000 troops, thirty-two guns and a few Cossacks would be sent from Sevastopol, and possibly a similar force from Odessa. Vice-Admiral Kornilov of the

Czar's staff listed twenty-eight warships and thirty-three transports capable of embarking twenty-six battalions of infantry, six batteries and 200 Cossacks. A detachment would pass down to seize the Dardanelles, while 100,000 men marched through the Balkans once the campaign season opened. This outline was sent to the Czar's military mentor Prince Paskevic, Governor of Poland. Kornilov accompanied Menshikov to Constantinople. Noting Turkish efforts to reinforce the defences of the Bosphorus he persuaded the Czar that a naval attack would now be difficult, if not impossible. In a note of 5 April the Czar planned an amphibious descent on Varna and the Gulf of Burgas to provide a forward base for the land army on the road to Constantinople. Both plans indicate the real role of the Russian fleet. The original plan would secure command of the Black Sea, the second version risked the entrance of British and French squadrons and was therefore both less bold and more dangerous.

Paskevic advised against both plans, in view of the high cost in troops, arguing for an occupation of the Danubian Principalities to put pressure on Turkey and increase Russian influence with the Balkan Christians. This was cautious advice. Paskevic was dominated by Poland, fearing attacks from Austria or Prussia and a Polish insurrection. Although Nicholas agreed, it appears certain he would have attempted Constantinople if France attacked Turkey.[5]

Military plans were dependent upon the outcome of Menshikov's mission. Diplomatic success would avoid the need to use force, although blatant preparations increased the pressure on the Turks. Those preparations indicated the scale of the Czar's interest. That the failure of the mission did not lead to the occupation of Constantinople reflected operational considerations. The underlying policy was reflected in the planned amphibious descent on the Straits, if Turkey would not accept Russian demands she would be driven out of the Straits region. The Holy Places had raised the question, Nicholas was determined to achieve a permanent solution. France and Austria had already raised the level of violence, albeit implied rather than actual, in great power negotiations with Turkey. Their success reduced Russian prestige and influence in the region. When Nicholas tried to recover that prestige his demands, unlike those of France and Austria, could not be conceded without a fundamental reduction in the authority of the Sultan, something neither the Czar nor his chancellor understood. The dangers of their policy were increased by the delusion of Austrian and British support. Preparing

to overthrow Turkey in Europe ran counter to the interests of both
Austria and Britain, rather than those of France. When Nicholas
realised this he was committed and could not pull back without
losing even more prestige.

Menshikov arrived in Constantinople on 2 March, accompanied
by a large military and naval staff reflecting both the status of his
mission, and an interest in the defences of the Bosphorus. The staff
departed on the 24th, their curiosity satisfied.[6] Kornilov went on to
Athens, reportedly to incite a Greek attack on Turkey.[7] The military
display proved counterproductive, encouraging the Turks to resist.
On landing, Menshikov deliberately ignored Fuad, and signalled his
contempt for the Turks by attending court in civilian clothes.[8] Fuad
was replaced by Rifaat, considered 'Russian' by western observers.
The following day Menshikov had an audience with the Sultan.
Fearing a Russian amphibious attack the Grand Vizier, Mehemet
Ali, called on the British and French representatives to send their
fleets to Vourla Bay, just outside the Dardanelles. Colonel Rose, the
British representative in the absence of Stratford, believed the
Russians would impose another unequal treaty, if nothing worse.
The senior naval officer in the Bosphorus, Captain Lord John Hay,
reported that as the fleet would leave Malta on the 20th for the Greek
Archipelago this would be only a minor inconvenience. Benedetti,
the French chargé, agreed.

The steamer *Fury*, bearing Rose's dispatch and other important
correspondence, arrived at Malta on the 14th. The Commander in
Chief, Vice-Admiral Sir James Dundas, refused to move. Holding his
squadron ready for sea he sent the dispatch to London, despite Rose
warning of a Russian *coup de main*, and Hay arguing that the crisis
was 'infinitely more important' than 1849. The Admiralty confirmed
Dundas's wisdom by return.[9]

During the nineteenth century the Mediterranean fleet occupied
the central position in the defence of empire. While it varied in
strength, depending on the level of tension, it remained the premier
seagoing command in the Royal Navy. The main body of the fleet,
five battleships, four large steamers and a sailing frigate, arrived at
Malta on 2 February 1853 after wintering at Gibraltar. Six smaller
steamers were detached to the east, including *Wasp* at Constantinople. Graham had wanted to reinforce Dundas in the spring to equal
the slightly larger French fleet of seven battleships.[10] Dundas had
some grounds for satisfaction: 'I have a *small* but splendid set of

ships, officers and people – all of them I like much, a good spirit prevails.' This peace time *esprit de corps* was maintained throughout the war.

Table 1: The Mediterranean Fleet, March 1853[11]

Sailing ships	Guns	In command
Britannia	120	Captain T. W. Carter, Flagship
Trafalagar	120	Captain H. Greville
Albion	90	Captain S. Lushington
Rodney	90	Captain C. Graham (brother of the First Lord)
Bellerophon	80	Captain Lord George Paulett
Arethusa	50	Captain T. M. C. Symonds
Steamers		
Retribution	16	Captain J. Drummond
Tiger	16	Captain H. W. Giffard
Wasp	14	Captain Lord John Hay
Niger	14	Captain L. G. Heath
Sampson	6	Captain L. T. Jones
Vulture	16	Captain F. H. Glasse
Fury	6	Commander E. Chambers
Spitfire	2	Commander T. A. B. Spratt
Oberon	2	(Station tender)
Triton	3	Lieutenant H. Lloyd

The squadron was too small to act alone. Russia and France held significantly larger forces to the east and west. The British remained weak in numbers of battleships throughout the year, affecting the diplomacy of the crisis, making the British Government appear irresolute, particularly in comparison with France. Furthermore it limited the diplomatic options open to Britain, making the dispatch of reinforcements a major issue.

Dundas had been a Naval Lord on the Whig Boards of 1841 and 1846–52 and Senior Naval Lord from 1847 before taking up the command. At sixty-eight he was not particularly elderly, although Lewis considered him too old, both in age and character, for war. This is hardly just; Dundas had not been selected for a war command, but as a peacetime Admiral more concerned with diplomacy than combat. Dewar noted he was 'something of a martinet', although on balance 'an officer of sound judgement, anxious to do his utmost for the achievement of the common task'.[12] As an ex Senior Naval Lord Dundas had many friends at the Admiralty,

notably the permanent Secretary Captain Baillie Hamilton. Despite
their warnings he could not bring himself to believe that war would
break out.[13] By late 1854 Graham was reminding his colleagues that
he had not selected Dundas, but that reflected problems not
anticipated in 1853 and had nothing to do with the Admiral's
abilities. Dundas's reputation has suffered from inaccurate comparisons with his second and successor, Edmund Lyons. Dundas was an
able officer. His long experience of politics enabled him to appreciate
the primacy of statecraft over strategy, a rare quality in the mid
nineteenth century. His only serious failing was the bad-tempered
sensitivity toward criticism, real or implied, that he shared with all
contemporary officers. He spent the last six months of 1852 in
dispute with the Duke of Northumberland, the Tory First Lord. His
relations with Stratford and to a lesser extent Raglan and Lyons were
also affected. Dundas's direction of the fleet in peace and war can
only be criticised for lack of genius; he did all that could be expected.
The wearing nature of his work sapped his strength, reinforcing his
natural caution.[14] Dundas was an example of the second rank of
British naval officers; able, reliable and experienced – a safe man. His
response to Rose's summons demonstrated this quality, vital in
peace time.

Dundas's telegraph arrived via Marseilles on 19 March; it was not
entirely unexpected. Rumour spread faster than hard news in this
period. Clarendon, recently installed at the Foreign Office, believed
Rose's action would prevent Stratford calling for the fleet; Graham
considered war would be the end of Turkey; Aberdeen was not even
aware that Dundas had left Gibraltar. The most serious problem for
the British Government was the French decision to send a fleet to
Salamis, made public on the 20th. This left Britain standing between
France and Russia, and both had supporters in the cabinet. Dundas's
telegraph arrived at the Admiralty late on the 19th. Graham called
on Clarendon and arranged a meeting for 15.00 the next day.
Aberdeen and Russell were summoned, and at the last minute
Clarendon persuaded Aberdeen to call Palmerston. Even before
hearing of the meeting, Russell believed Russia was preparing to
destroy Turkey; the Seymour Conversations merely fulfilled the
proviso of the 1844 memorandum concerning prior consultation. If
Russia invaded Turkey Britain had to demand an immediate evacuation, sending fleets into the Black Sea and the Baltic in concert with
France. Once aware of Rose's dispatch he was more trenchant.[15] At

the inner cabinet Clarendon did not raise the Baltic, preferring to follow Aberdeen's pacific line. Palmerston and Russell were outvoted. Their colleagues considered that as the interests of Britain and France were secondary there was no *casus belli*. This left the French in an embarrassing position. Awaiting the departure of their fleet on the 23rd they tried to draw Britain into an anti-Russian alliance which had been proposed in February, but this was rejected. To cover their embarrassment the French made a critical comparison with British policy during the 1849 crisis.[16]

After the meeting Aberdeen laid down Government policy; Turkey should be preserved through the 1841 treaty, and he opposed collaboration with France. After Brunnow had shown him a document purporting to be Menshikov's instructions Aberdeen believed that once the French calmed down the affair would blow over. Russell wanted to reinforce the battleline to equal that of France; Clarendon agreed, wanting to keep the squadron at Malta to avoid any appearance of support for either France or Russia. Dundas was praised and ordered to remain alert at Malta. To cover their humiliation and put pressure on Britain the French threatened Belgium. Puryear suggested this secured British support, exaggerating the effect on British freedom of action and ignoring the relative importance of Belgium and Turkey in the scale of British interests. In fact the British reacted by increasing the fleet in home waters. Puryear did not understand that Britain would not submit to French menaces over Belgium, or Turkey. British policy remained independent, and suspicious of France.[17] This first crisis revealed the attitudes of the cabinet ministers: Russell and Palmerston preferred co-operation with France; Aberdeen, at heart a Tory, favoured Russia. Clarendon, although a Whig, supported Aberdeen, while Graham remained hostile to France. More significantly Russell had raised the question of the strategy required to put pressure on Russia. He favoured a bold response, sending fleets into the Euxine and the Baltic. Clarendon considered this 'wild', and did not raise it on the 20th.[18] Russell continued to argue for this policy and it became the basis of British strategy, although it is not clear how far Russell's advocacy was responsible for a belated acceptance of the obvious. Ultimately pressure in the Baltic did persuade Russia to renounce her ambitions in the Black Sea, but in 1853 the Royal Navy was in no condition to carry Russell's demands to St Petersburg. Furthermore his erratic intellect was out of step with his more pedestrian colleagues. An attempt to end the crisis by armed diplomacy was premature because events in Constantinople, of which no-one was entirely certain, were far from warlike. Yet the limited horizons of the majority of Russell's colleagues should be noted. Because the problem had arisen in the near east they looked no further afield for a solution. This limited outlook led to the Crimean descent, and crippled the effective development of British war power throughout the conflict.

Existing studies of the 1853 crisis give a leading role to Lord Stratford de Redcliffe, British Ambassador the the Sublime Porte. Stratford Canning owed his early advancement to his cousin, George Canning; between 1812 and 1856 Stratford was five times ambassador at Constantinople, giving him an unrivalled expertise, and making him the popular choice in time of crisis. However Stratford was no ordinary diplomat. His powerful intellect, vanity and over-bearing character made him intolerant of other opinions. The Ministers of Aberdeen's Government were not alone in finding him difficult to deal with.[19] This side of his character exercised a baleful influence over the fleet during the last months of peace, but thereafter he receded into the background. In reappointing Stratford in February 1853, Russell and Aberdeen hoped to use his talents in a short mission to solve the two outstanding issues in Turkey: Montenegro and the Holy Places. They were also unwilling to see him join the opposition in the House of Lords. Stratford's instructions specifically witheld authority to call up the fleet; the problems at hand did not require such action, neither concerned the Straits, nor the independence of the Turkey.[20] Montenegro was settled before Stratford arrived and he agreed with the Government that France, not Russia, was in the wrong over the Holy Places. Aberdeen wanted to retain British freedom of action, as neither issue threatened British interests.

This comfortable view of Turkish affairs was being overturned even as Stratford made a leisurely progress to Constantinople, calling at Paris and Vienna. On 16 March Menshikov presented a memorandum to the Turks, calling for an alliance against France. On the 22nd he presented the draft of a *Sened* (convention) to establish a lasting basis for Russo–Turkish relations. It called for the election for life of the four Greek Orthodox Patriarchs of the Ottoman Empire, a dangerous proposal in view of their significant civil powers. Foreign Minister Rifaat realised that the *Sened*, by securing effective protectorate over the Sultan's 12 million Greek Orthodox subjects, would give Russia the right to interfere in Turkish internal affairs. It was also incompatible with the 1841 Five Power Treaty, threatening British interests, as the cabinet demonstrated once they were informed of the terms. Rifaat called on Menshikov to moderate Russian demands. Menshikov agreed, informing his master on 10 April that he would hold back the *Sened* until the Holy Places was settled; he would then force the Turks into an alliance to keep the British and French out of the Straits, and by implication, their influence out of the Porte.

Stratford reached Constantinople on 5 April. Unaware of Menshikov's wider designs he resolved the Holy Places issue by urging the Turks to concede Russia's just claims. By the 24th he considered the matter closed, yet he sensed Russia had ulterior objects, especially as the Turks where making strenuous efforts to reinforce the defences of the Bosphorus. Rifaat finally confirmed his suspicions, claiming Russian demands amounted to more than Unkiar Skelessi. The Turks' real fear was of a Christian rising, incited by Russia.[21] On 5 May the Holy Places was definitively settled. Menshikov then demanded Turkish acceptance of the *Sened*, giving five, later nine, days for a reply. The demand coincided with the maturing of Russian military preparations and the opening of the campaign season. At Sevastopol and Odessa two divisions were prepared for amphibious operations, the 5th division in Bessarabia was ready to enter the Principalities, although the 4th was delayed in Galicia by poor roads.

Stratford, unable to discover the terms of the *Sened*, reluctantly informed the Sultan that the fleet would be available if Constantinople were threatened. He specifically advised allowing the Russians to occupy the Principalities. The British Government approved. Menshikov, in his contempt for the Turks, fell into a plot of Byzantine complexity. Reshid, a disgraced minister, promised he could obtain the convention if Menshikov could return him to power. Menshikov agreed, pressing the Sultan on the 13th to dismiss Mehemet Ali and Rifaat. However, both remained in positions of power, ensuring the Sultan and the Grand Council rejected Reshid's half-hearted attempt to concede. Menshikov refused minor concessions and the mediation of the other signatories of the 1841 treaty. Demanding the complete *Sened* he boarded his yacht; Reshid then told him that the 'inexorable' Stratford had prevented his meeting the Russian demands. Reshid was lying, but Menshikov, Nesselrode and the Czar accepted his account, which Russian historiography has followed.

At noon on 21 May Menshikov steamed up the Bosphorus, his mission a complete failure. When he first arrived the Turks had been nervous and irresolute, but he failed to press the advantage. After Stratford's return there was little chance of securing an unequal treaty; British policy was firmly opposed, and Stratford too alert. Having made such blatant use of force it was now impossible for Russia to retract. The British Government had no opportunity to react before Menshikov's departure; until Stratford's telegraph of 16 May reached London the ministers had not expected trouble. Graham had been more concerned to laugh at the chaotic return of the French fleet from Salamis after a series of collisions crippled the hastily assembled symbol of French prestige.[22] The whole affair had been deeply embarrassing; France would not act again, without British support.

Aberdeen believed Russia was only interested in the shrines, which could not be a cause of war. Clarendon considered the situation to be more serious; agreeing with Stratford and the French Ambassador, de la Tour, that the *Sened* would be fatal to Turkey, he anticipated Russia would have problems withdrawing from her extravagant claims. Aberdeen did not see the danger, trusting to Russian good faith. Further information on Menshikov's demands arrived at the end of May. On the 29th Walewski, the French Ambassador, went to the Foreign Office with intelligence from Constantinople. French policy was dominated by a desire to secure British co-operation. Clarendon, swayed by Walewski and influenced by Russell and Palmerston, feared a Russian *coup de main*, openly regretted following Aberdeen on the 16th, in view of the political repercussions of the crisis and wished Stratford had authority to call up the fleet. Russell feared that if France did not secure British co-operation she would support Russia in return for Crete and Egypt. To prevent this the fleet must be sent east, but not enter Turkish waters.[23] This was a gesture, not a commitment. Palmerston came to dominate Clarendon with his view that Russia was hostile and only a new Five Power Treaty could settle the issue. After Menshikov's departure he urged a more determined response. At the cabinet of the 28th Palmerston called for the fleet to be sent with the French into Turkish waters, but Aberdeen persuaded the majority to wait on details of Menshikov's departure before acting. Graham argued that a fleet outside the Dardanelles could do no more to prevent a Russian *coup de main* than one at Salamis or Malta, while it would absolve the Czar from his engagement to keep the peace.[24] The latter was Aberdeen's argument and very weak; the former relied on the evidence of the Surveyor of the Navy, Captain Sir Baldwin Walker, effectively Commander of the Turkish Navy 1839–44. Walker reported that a squadron in the Bosphorus would be trapped by a Russian army seizing the Dardanelles. Palmerston considered this inaccurate, doubting Walker's geographical knowledge. The Dardanelles remained a source of concern right up to the outbreak of war. Palmerston argued that the fleet should go as close to the Dardanelles as possible, with Stratford having the power to call it up, which the French Ambassador already had. If Britain did not act, France would go alone, a rather debatable analysis based on conversations with Walewski. Graham feared Palmerston looked for some domestic political advantage. Walker's paper persuaded Clarendon that Stratford should have the authority to call up the fleet. Graham argued that the Government should either proceed directly to war, including sending fleets into the Black Sea and the Baltic, or hold still. A forward policy relied on co-operation with France, which Graham could not support, therefore he called for another cabinet. This struck Palmerston as 'twaddle' and he secured Russell's support for moving the fleet to the entrance of the Dardanelles, with power to Stratford. Faced with a decision Clarendon preferred to send the fleet cruising, without giving authority to Stratford. However, something had to be done to 'save the Government from shame', Aberdeen agreed.[25]

The cabinet meeting of 31 May granted Stratford power to call up the fleet, although Palmerston had called for it to cruise close to the Dardanelles. Aberdeen regretted the decision for the same reason that Clarendon supported it – the effect on public opinion. The move would appear resolute, but would achieve nothing. If there were good reasons for expecting an attack on Constantinople the fleet should enter the Black Sea to prevent it, if not moving into Turkish waters would only annoy the Russians. Graham pressed these arguments on Palmerston. Admitting Constantinople was a 'primary' British interest and unwilling to act hastily he wanted to establish why Menshikov had departed and keep some control over France. When the details of the Russian Ambassador's departure arrived Clarendon wanted to send the fleet to the Dardanelles. Aberdeen still relied on the influence of the four powers; Russia was to be informed and Stratford must not call up the fleet short of war. This was a curious attitude, for on the previous day he had argued that the fleet could do nothing from the Dardanelles in the event of war, but he now contended that it should be kept there until the conflict erupted. Stratford's authority was dispatched on the the same day and on 2 June the fleet was ordered to Besika Bay. Naval preparations were also in hand in case a Baltic fleet was required. Palmerston discussed Anglo–French co-operation with Walewski, ostensibly unofficially, confirming his suspicion that French coolness stemmed from the stationary position of the squadron at Malta. Once Britain indicated her policy, by moving east, France would support diplomatic pressure on Russia.[26]

The significance of the cabinet decision of late May cannot be overstated. Britain was morally committed to Turkey by the movement of the fleet; Admiral Dundas's ships were the guarantors of good faith, they could not be withdrawn without a tremendous loss of prestige. This marked the shift from interested observer to participant. At the Admiralty Graham was developing strategic options to support the new policy, althouh he had begun his preparations before news of Menshikov's departure reached London. This long term approach equipped him to dominate British strategic policy making during the first year of war. French policy remained more urgent, seeking a quick triumph for internal/political consumption; the objects were to humiliate Russia and secure a British alliance.[27] Both nations were committed before they knew the Russian response to the failure of Menshikov's mission. It was fortunate that Russia reacted as anticipated, albeit in a gradual and calculated manner.

On 28 May Nesselrode informed Seymour that if Turkey did not accept Russian terms the Principalities would be occupied. Paskevic's plan had replaced the Czar's *coup de main*. Nesselrode dispatched an ultimatum on 8 June to accept Menshikov's terms or suffer occupation as a 'material guarantee' of Turkish concession. The Turks rejected these terms, uninfluenced by the movement of the fleets. Russia was more cautious. While her threats to occupy the Danubian basin caused Britain and France to move their squadrons, Russian troops did not enter Moldavia and Wallachia until 2 July, a fortnight after the fleets arrived at Besika. Furthermore Prince M. D. Gorchakov's army, four infantry divisions and two cavalry, was only suitable for an uncontested occupation. It was not strong enough to cross the Danube, or keep the Turkish army out of the Principalities.

Notes

1 HENDERSON, G. B., *Crimean War Diplomacy* (Glasgow, 1947).
2 See generally: CONACHER, J. B., *The Aberdeen Coalition, 1852–1855* (London, 1968); CHAMBERLAIN, M. E., *Lord Aberdeen* (London, 1984).
3 STEELE, E. D., 'Palmerston's foreign policy and the Foreign Secretaries, 1855–1865' in WILSON, K. M., ed., *British Foreign Secretaries and Foreign Policy: from the Crimean War to the First World War* (London 1987).
4 TEMPERLEY, H. J., *England and the Near East: The Crimea* (London, 1936), p. 305.
5 CURTISS, pp. 81–3.
6 Slade to Dundas 25 Mar. 1853: DND/9 f33–4.
7 SAAB, A. P. *The Origins of the Crimean Alliance* (Charlottesville, 1977), p. 31.
8 TEMPERLEY, p. 309.
9 Dundas Journal 14 Mar. 1853: ADM 50/252; Dundas to Admiralty 14 Mar. 1853: ADM 1/5617; Rose to Dundas 8 Mar. 1853: DND/9 f22–3; Hay to Dundas 13 Mar. 1853: DND/9 f25–6; Slade to Dundas 25 Mar. 1853: *ibid.* f33–4; Admiralty to Dundas 21 Mar. 1853: ADM 2/1697 f33.
10 Graham to Russell 15 Feb. 1853: PRO 30/22/10H f81–2; Graham to Clarendon 19 Mar. 1853: Cl. Dep. C4 f150.
11 Dundas to Walker 10 Mar. 1853: WALKER BC356; Dundas Journal 1 Mar. 1853: ADM 50/252.
12 LEWIS, M., *The Navy in Transition, 1815–1865* (London, 1965), p. 123; DEWAR, Capt. A., *The Russian War 1854: The Black Sea*, Navy Records Society (London, 1943), p. 210.
13 BRIGGS, Sir J., *Naval Administrations 1827–1892* (London, 1897), p. 115.
14 Captain Baillie Hamilton to Graham 18 Jun. 1854: Gr. B.120; Raglan to Lyons 12 Dec. 1854: RAGLAN 6807–299.
15 Clarendon to Aberdeen 18 Mar. 1853: Add. 43,188 f34; Graham to Clarendon 19 Mar. 1853: Cl. Dep. C4 f150; Aberdeen to the Queen 17 Mar. 1853: Add. 43,047 f25; Dundas to Graham 27 Mar. 1853: Gr. CW1; Clarendon to Aberdeen 20 Mar. 1853: Add. 43,188 f38; Russell to Clarendon 20 Mar. 1853: Cl. Dep. C4 f278; Russell to Clarendon 20 Mar. 1853: *ibid.* f275 (sent after f278).
16 Cowley to Clarendon 20 Mar. 1853: F.O. 519/304; TEMPERLEY, p. 312; Cowley to Clarendon 21 Mar. 1853: F.O. 519/304.
17 Aberdeen to Clarendon 21 Mar. 1853: Cl. Dep. C4 f1; Aberdeen to the Queen 22 Mar. 1853: Add. 43,047 f32; Graham to Dundas 21 Mar. 1853: DND/9 f28–31; Russell to Clarendon 21 Mar. 1853: Cl. Dep. C4 f280–1: Clarendon to Graham 18 Apr. 1853: Gr. B.113; CONACHER, p. 143; PURYEAR, pp. 242–55; Graham to Aberdeen 27 Mar. 1853: Add. 43,191 f34; Clarendon to Cowley 30 Mar. 1853: F.O. 519/304.
18 KINGSLEY-MARTIN, B., *The Triumph of Lord Palmerston* (London, 1924), p. 103.

19   LANE-POOLE, R., *Life of Stratford Canning, Viscount Stratford de Redcliffe* (London, 1887, two vols.); Clarendon to Graham 9 May 1853: Gr. B.114.

20   TEMPERLEY , p. 314; Aberdeen to Russell 15 Feb. 1853: CONACHER, p. 145.

21   Slade to Dundas 27 Apr. 1853: R.A. G2 63.

22   Clarendon to Aberdeen 16 May 1853: Add. 43,188 f105; Dundas to Graham 25 Feb., 2 Apr., 2 May 1853: Gr.CW1; Graham to Dundas 9 May 1853: DND/9 f49; Graham to Clarendon 9 May 1853: Cl. Dep. C4 f163–4.

23   Aberdeen to Clarendon 17 May 1853: Add. 43,188 f110; Clarendon to Aberdeen 18, 21 May 1853: *ibid.* f111–6; Clarendon to Cowley 19 May 1853: F.O. 519/304; Aberdeen to the Queen 21 May 1853: Add. 43,047 f101; Clarendon to Aberdeen 29 May 1853: Add.43,188 f125; Russell to Clarendon 29 May 1853: Cl. Dep. C4 f306–7.

24   Palmerston to Clarendon 10 Apr., 22, 24 May 1853: Cl. Dep. C3 f9–38; Aberdeen to the Queen 28 May 1853: Add.43,047 f126–7; Graham to Palmerston 29 May 1853: Bdlds. GC/GR f76.

25   Aberdeen to Graham 30, 31 May 1853: Gr. B.113, Add.43,191 f63; Palmerston to Graham 29 May 1853: *ibid.* f50–4; Graham to Aberdeen 29 May 1853: *ibid.* f48–9; Clarendon to Graham 29 May 1853: Gr. B.113; Graham to Palmerston 30 May 1853: Bdlds. GC/GR f77; Palmerston to Clarendon 30 May 1853: Cl. Dep. C3 f40–52; Clarendon to Aberdeen 30 May 1853: Add. 43,188 f131.

26   Palmerston to Graham 31 May 1853: Bdlds. GC/GR f93–5; Aberdeen to Graham 31 May 1853: Gr. B.113; Graham to Palmerston 1 June 1853: Bdlds. GC/GR f78; Clarendon to Graham 1 June 1853: Gr. B.113; Aberdeen to Clarendon 1 June 1853: Add. 43,188 f134; Clarendon to Palmerston 2 June 1853: Bdlds. GC/CL f75; Palmerston to Clarendon 2 Jun. 1853: Cl. Dep. C3 f54–6.

27   Cowley to Clarendon 2 Jun. 1853: F.O. 519/304.

3

National strategy and naval policy

Despite the long-term threat from Russia British strategic policy after 1841 was dominated by France. Diplomatic struggles in the near east and the Iberian peninsula were only the most public indications of a rivalry that reached new heights in 1846, prompted by the Prince de Joinville's pamphlet calling for a French steam fleet to overthrow British maritime supremacy. In fact the Royal Navy was more than keeping pace with the French in the development of steam warships, so invasion was never a real danger. After 1848 the panic abated, the Second Republic was less hostile than the Orleans Monarchy. The temporary calm was shattered by Louis Napoleon's first *coup d'état* and the appearance of the steam battleship *Napoleon*.

This second invasion scare was still a major issue when the Aberdeen ministry took office. Defence policy was left to the ministers with a real interest in the subject. The Duke of Newcastle, Secretary of State for War and the Colonies, took little interest in the first half of his portfolio until 1854. Graham and Sir Charles Wood used their election speeches to attack the French Emperor.[1] Once in office Graham and Palmerston, at the Home Office, controlled a defence policy dominated by concern for the security of the British Isles. Both were influenced by recollections of the later stages of the French wars.[2] The Government was preparing for a war against France in 1853, which explains many of the strengths and weaknesses of the war effort. Palmerston formed the Committee on National Defence, comprising Graham, Sidney Herbert, Secretary at War, Lord Hardinge, Commander in Chief, Lord Raglan, Master General of the Ordnance and Sir John Burgoyne, Inspector–General of Fortifications. He argued that additional funds released by the invasion scare should be spent on fortifications and steam machinery, 'permanent additions to our defensive means', rather than 10,000 extra troops. Aberdeen merely called for some system to be imposed upon expenditure.[3] The forts Palmerston wanted were to protect the major dockyards, Portsmouth, Plymouth, Chatham and Pembroke, with the new Harbours of Refuge at Dover and Portland. Fortifying the Channel Islands, a measure adopted in 1846, presented the new ministry with a considerable dilemna. Much work had already been done, but Graham began by considering the whole business a 'job' and doubted the wisdom of continuing. Secure, fortified harbours in the Channel Isles would provide bases for British steamers to blockade Cherbourg. Burgoyne favoured Alderney, only twenty-five miles from the French base; Graham agreed that the other two islands were not worth the expense. The adoption of steam made it necessary to find new bases, for existing dockyards had been built to support a sailing fleet and were no longer ideally placed. Palmerston and Graham remained suspicious of France throughout 1853, having considerable common ground, notably on the need for forts. The Army viewed forts as a substitute for the manpower it could never raise in peacetime. Palmerston wanted to fortify everywhere, but Graham only looked to those points that were essential to the efficiency of the fleet.[4] He was happier with the existing policy of his own department, with good reason.

Graham had been a dynamic First Lord between 1830 and 1834, restructuring the Admiralty by absorbing into it the functions of the Navy and Victualling Boards, hitherto responsible for the civil administration of the service. In addition a system of individual responsibility gave each Naval Lord responsibility for a specific area of business; the Board advised the First Lord and he was responsible to Parliament.[5] This was controversial, party political and, in combination with low estimates, destroyed the long term basis of postwar naval policy. Only after 1848 was some order given to the Admiralty, and by 1853 the department had recovered from the effects of Graham's reform. Graham left office and the Whig party on a religious issue in 1834, joining Peel's government in 1841. He maintained an interest in the Navy; his work on the 1847–48 Committee on Naval Estimates revealed a solid understanding of naval administration. When the Aberdeen ministry took office Graham claimed, not entirely honestly, that the Admiralty was his first choice. His policy, based on distrust of Imperial France, did not alter during the Russian War. This was important because his relationship with Aberdeen allowed him to avoid cabinet supervision. For all his talents Graham was not popular. Outside a small group of political friends no-one trusted him, he was too cold and distant to attract the admiration of his contemporaries.[6] One biographer concluded: 'he was unpopular, snobbish, aloof, quick to find fault with others, he was disdainful of men's opinions, [and] suspicious of their motives'. Yet Graham was not immune to the pressure of public opinion.[7] In late 1854 the newspapers attacked his senior officers, and he used this to damn them as failures to cover his own shortcomings. Graham's autocratic tendencies led him to retain the sick Vice-Admiral Sir Hyde Parker as First Naval Lord, insulating himself from the Board. The other Naval Lords, Rear-Admiral Berkeley and Captains Richard Dundas and Alexander Milne, were talented administrators but not policy makers. With these junior Lords Graham completed the work of the preceding ten years, resolving the great issues of the post-war years, steam and manpower. To meet the French challenge the Navy was coming to terms with the industrial age.

The French challenge was the only constant factor in British naval policy between 1815 and 1853. Steam power and shell-firing guns had been adopted in response to French developments, and in 1853 both nations were at work on steam battleships. In time of war these ships would require large crews, making the issue of reserve manpower vital. The strategic requirements of war with France remained constant; the French fleets would have to be blockaded or destroyed, her colonies and commerce captured, anything more would depend on political circumstances. The invasion scare of 1852 produced a refreshing awareness of naval requirements in political circles, securing the funds for a steam battlefleet and continuous service for ratings. Both measures came into effect during the Russian War. However naval officers and politicians gave little thought to strategy; the prospect of war with France reduced strategy to the massing of a large force in the Channel.

The development of the steam battlefleet has been examined elsewhere. In outline Captain Sir Baldwin Walker, the Surveyor of the Navy, 1848–61, decided in late 1852 that the period of experiment with steam had ended, proposing a long term programme of construction and conversion to create an all steam battlefleet. Coming into office shortly after the adoption of this programme Graham supported Walker, accepting the Surveyor's view that a steam battlefleet would have to be 'a work of time'.[8] This anti-French slant to defence policy was also evident in the development of naval artillery. Following trials at Shoeburyness in 1852 the design of

heavy guns was improved to permit sustained firing at high elevation, to bombard the French Channel Ports. Significantly mortars
were not included. The leading gunnery officer of the day, Captain
Sir Henry Chads, was particularly impressed with the new Lancaster
oval bore rifled 95-hundredweight gun firing a 68 pound shell out to
6,500 yards, double the range of existing guns of the same calibre,
allowing bombardment from outside the range of any French reply.
Graham urged Aberdeen to develop the gun with secret service
funds.[9] Despite the technical success of the Lancaster gun and the
improvement of standard artillery, no plans were prepared for bombarding fortified harbours. The ability of the Navy to solve complex
technical problems was not matched by an understanding of strategy
and specialist tactics.

In the 1840s the problem of naval manpower had appeared insol-
uble. There were two separate issues: first, there were never enough
men to fit out ships in peacetime; second, a large reserve was required
for a war with France. Contemporary opinion believed a fleet of 700
vessels manned by over 140,000 men would be necessary. While the
solution to both problems was simple, all concerned insisted on
viewing them in isolation, making the discovery of an effective policy
largely fortuitous. Evidence for the 1847–48 Committee on Naval
Estimates supported impressment as the only reliable method of
manning the fleet in war. With improved legislation after 1835 the
system was still legally enforceable; in the event of war the liberties of
the individual would be less important than national security. By
1851 the First Lord, Sir Francis Baring, convinced impressment
would not work, prepared a committee on manning. The Parker
Committee decided to increase and regulate the peacetime fleet and
create a large reserve. On the latter issue they called for a naval
militia, the Royal Navy Coast Volunteers, 10,000 men, to be available for twelve months' service within 100 miles of the British coast.
Quite what use such a force would be the Committee did not state,
but as they sat during the invasion scare it is clear how they arrived at
this curious solution. When the French reinforced their Atlantic
Squadron and threatened Belgium, Graham adopted the Parker
Committee Report, on 1 April 1853.[10]

In fact the solution adopted for the peacetime fleet solved both
requirements. With continuous service for naval ratings, men entering at eighteen for an initial period of ten years would provide both a
regular force of seamen and, after twenty years, a large reserve, the

naval pension being in part a retainer for emergency service. Recent commentators have claimed that this measure did not create a war reserve.[11] It did not create one in time for the Russian War, but in the long term it did solve the problem. The war demonstrated the futility of non-professional reserves. Graham had hoped that ex-naval seamen would enter the reserve occupations he set up in 1831, the Coastguard and the Dockyard Riggers. However they were no substitute for able seamen. When war broke out only two permanent forces were available, the marines and the seamen gunners trained aboard HMS *Excellent* since 1832.[12] New ships were manned around a nucleus of these men, of whom there were never enough, and then filled up with Coastguard and landsmen. Additional men had been voted in 1853, but they could not be raised, seamen being in short supply with the merchant service paying high wages. The surprise of the politicians was unjustified, for nothing had been done since 1815 to alter the effective reserve strength of the Navy. Had the war been against France there can be little doubt impressment would have been used. By 1914 continuous service had built up a large and effective reserve, but in 1854 even a limited war effort found the Navy seriously short of seamen.

From the first rumour of Rose's summons to the fleet Graham placed the Navy on alert. The international situation forced him to consider a war with Russia, but the French were never far from his thoughts. Before the departure of Menshikov Graham, following Aberdeen, kept the fleet at Malta and prepared reinforcements to wait until France and Russia made their respective positions clear. *Vengeance*, 84 (guns), would proceed quietly, without indicating support for France or Russia. In preparing four battleships and four large steamers to reinforce Dundas, Graham was still looking to the French fleet. When the tension abated he wanted Dundas to undertake a training cruise, but a suitable opportunity never arrived.[13] When Constantinople appeared quiet the French were making their sorry way back from Salamis, and Dundas stayed in harbour to avoid a humiliating encounter. Graham's strategic horizons were not limited to the movement of ships and keeping a balance between the need to support British policy with a show of strength and avoid giving encouragement to either France or Russia. He began to collect information on the problems of a war with Russia, both in defence of Turkey and on the wider scale. He prepared for the worst – simultaneous Russian attacks on Constantinople and the British coast. In

securing advice Graham consulted very few men, for he did not want
to spread even a rumour of war, and both seats of Russian seapower
were little known to British officers.

After the cabinet of 31 May Graham turned to Walker for a
statement on the danger to Turkey. Graham's central theme was the
defence of Constantinople from an amphibious attack, an attack
that Walker believed the Turks could not resist. The Bosphorus forts
were weak and the tide and current favoured the attackers. While an
Anglo–French fleet in the Bosphorus could prevent a naval attack,
30,000 Russian troops landed a few miles north of the European
shore of the Bosphorus would capture the forts even if the Anglo–
French marines were sent ashore. Furthermore it would take no
more than three days for the Russian fleet to reach the Bosphorus
from Sevastopol. If the western powers entered the Black Sea they
could prevent any landing, but if they remained at Besika the
Russians would be well established before they reached Constantinople. The only disposition that would prevent a Russian success
would also be a clear violation of the 1841 treaty, providing Russia
with *casus belli*, the one thing above all else the cabinet wished to
avoid. Aberdeen's response was to advocate a policy of extremes: the
fleet should either proceed to Constantinople or remain at Malta;
Besika would be worse than useless.[14] This explains why Aberdeen
agreed to send the fleet to Constantinople in October.

Graham knew the Bosphorus was not the only point at which a
war between Britain and Russia would be fought. Dundas pointed
out that 'Russia, if determined on war, will have begun to fit her
Baltic fleet'. The French were also concerned. Foreign Minister
Drouyn de Lhuys pressed for an assurance that Britain would guard
their Channel ports. Intelligence from St Petersburg was reassuring,
the fleet was making the usual annual preparations, only thirteen
battleships were effective, 'the others being rotten tubs, tho' well
painted'.[15] For strategic analysis Graham turned to Admiral Sir
Thomas Byam Martin, the senior survivor of de Saumarez's campaigns. Hitherto relations between Byam Martin and Graham had
been anything but amicable, Byam Martin had led Navy Board
resistance to Graham's reforms in 1832. However, he sent a memorandum written in 1835 and a covering note on the impact of steam.
Martin hoped, rather than believed, the Russians might be brought
to battle in the Skaggerrack. He accepted that to mount an effective
blockade the British must enter the Baltic, calling for a fleet of large

battleships, with mortar vessels and rocket frames. Even with this equipment Cronstadt could not be attacked, the attempt would be dangerous, but with another squadron at Helsingfors ready to attack the damaged ships it became impossible. Navigational difficulties, lack of reliable pilots and bad weather were more likely to destroy ships than the Russians. With two sons pioneering the introduction of steam the Admiral made some significant points in his covering note; twenty-five steam battleships would be the minimum force, sailing ships would be almost useless. Coal should be carried in the screw steam colliers already used in the Newcastle–London trade. The fleet should remain in the Skaggerrack, making a brief sortie into the Baltic to offer battle. Because the major arsenals could not be assaulted, seapower in the Baltic would not deter Russia.[16]

For additional information Graham turned to the Hydrographer, Admiral Sir Francis Beaufort. Beaufort dispatched Captain John Washington with instructions to examine Bomarsund. Despite the international tension Washington was shown round Reval, Sweaborg and Cronstadt; only the last two were well defended. At Cronstadt he inspected the Russian paddle steamers, and preparations for constructing steam battleships although there was no machinery. Cronstadt's granite casemates were heavily armed and well drilled, but Washington believed they would fill with smoke during sustained firing. To end his visit the Russian ships staged an impressive target practice. Washington did not realise that the Russians had deliberately kept him away from their outdated battlefleet and other unsatisfactory equipment. Consequently his report was little less pessimistic than Byam Martin's memorandum. Graham believed he had all the Baltic information he required.[17] From St Petersburg the Ambassador reported the Russians, alarmed at the prospect of a British fleet entering the Gulf of Finland, were preparing ten battleships to reinforce Cronstadt and called for a camera. One of his juniors, Strachey, discovered a passage round the north of the island that might allow naval forces to attack the fortress in reverse. Belatedly rediscovered in late 1855, this became the key to the 1856 campaign.[18]

The impact of these reports on Graham was limited, for he was more concerned to keep the Russians in the Baltic than to attack Cronstadt. A fleet was kept in home waters until October, and only when the Baltic began to ice up was Graham prepared to send the *Queen*, 116 *London*, 90 and the new steam battleship *Agamemnon*,

91 to the Mediterranean.[19] By that time Seymour was reporting rumours the Russians would seize Gotland. He was ordered to provide weekly reports on the Russian fleet; Graham developed his Baltic strategy during the winter, aware that nothing could be done until March.[20] Until then his real concern was to avoid causing alarm.[21]

While his strategic enquiries were bearing fruit Graham prepared reinforcements for the Mediterranean and increased the force available at home without exceeding his estimates. This was not helped by the stop-go nature of the crisis between March and November.[22] The Western Squadron, the only effective force at home, was based at Lisbon for experiments with large screw steamers. Rear-Admiral Sir Armar Corry had been in command since May 1852.

Table 2: The Western Squadron, March 1853

	Guns
Battleships	
Prince Regent	92
London	90
Screw steamers	
Impérieuse	51
Highflyer	26
Amphion	36
Cruizer	17
Archer	15
Paddle frigates	
Leopard	16
Valorous	16

This force, with Guardships to a total of ten battleships and ten steamers, assembled at Spithead for a review in early June. Corry was soon reinforced by the battleships *Duke of Wellington* 131 steam, *Agamemnon* 91 steam, *Blenheim* 60 steam blockship, *Queen* 116, the steam frigates *Arrogant* 47 and *Tribune* 31 and the paddle frigates *Sidon* 16, *Desperate* 16 and *Vulture* 16. He could also call on three steam blockships and three steamers within easy reach at Lisbon, Cork and the home ports. The Western squadron was now noticeably stronger than the Mediterranean fleet. The material reserves of the Royal Navy in the mid nineteenth century were far larger than those of other navies, primarily because British ships were better built and maintained. Graham did not fit out more sailing battleships than required to relieve those overdue on the Mediterranean station and they were kept, for diplomatic reasons, with the Western Squadron. He preferred to wait for the completion of the steam battleships ordered in October 1852. Several ships being converted to steam were hurried, to the detriment of work on new construction. Walker made a clear distinction between new and converted ships; the second-class converted ships would be adequate to contain the sailing battlefleet of Russia, new ships would be needed to meet the French when crisis in the east ended. No reinforcements were sent to the Mediterranean after early June. The relief ships remained with the Western Squadron which served as a strategic reserve, as a squadron of evolution and as the nucleus of a Baltic fleet if one were required. In late July the crisis appeared to be settled by the Vienna Note, Graham staged a Royal Review at Spithead on 18 August. Thereafter Corry, joined by the new steam 101 *St Jean d'Acre*, cruised around Ireland and into the Tagus; unfortunately he was a sick man and did little to prepare the ships for war.[23]

Much criticism of the performance of the Navy during the Russian War concerns the failure of the senior commanders, largely due to advanced age. In 1853 the senior officers of the Royal Navy were over age, a problem dating back to the creation of an outsize permanent officer corps between 1793 and 1815. Without effective retirement these men only left the Navy List at their death, and many good officers only reached flag rank when too old or infirm for command.[24] The problem only disappeared when mortality caught up with the war generation, but professional competence had nothing to do with age. After forty years of peace there were few officers with any significant experience of European war. The problem was particularly serious among the junior officers.[25]

Graham's first flag appointment was a Rear-Admiral to be second in command in the Mediterranean. Soon after taking office he had been asked for a small act of patronage by Rear-Admiral Sir Edmund Lyons, Minister at Stockholm; Graham expressed the hope that Lyons was not lost to the Navy. Lyons, then sixty-three, had seen considerable service, including a famous cruise around the Black Sea in 1829, before leaving the Navy to be Minister at Athens in 1835. He had remained on the Navy List, and he stressed his experience of the Black Sea and a willingness to serve as second. Clarendon was interested in a useful vacancy at Stockholm. Dundas urged Graham to send a Rear-Admiral or a commodore's commission 'in case active operations should begin'. Graham delayed until he believed war was a distinct possibility, only requesting Lyons' recall in late September. Lyons reached London on 16 October meeting Brunnow at the Admiralty, purely by chance, the following day. Graham was delighted, while Clarendon reported Brunnow 'seemed to think it disagreeable evidence of earnest purpose' which 'made a deep impression'.[26] Lyons was a popular, energetic and outgoing man; believing he resembled Nelson, he attempted to imitate the great man. Lacking the reflective genius of his idol he was a worthy, if second rate officer, without the mental equipment for complex tasks. He did not originate a single worthwhile operation during the war, carrying out other men's plans with more courage than wit. For such a simple campaign Lyons was adequate, but his failure to divide the fleet in 1855 illustrated the weakness. He also suffered from unbounded vanity. For all that, he attracted the loyalty of the Mediterranean fleet, helping it to maintain an *esprit de corps* the Baltic fleet never matched.

Graham's next appointment was of a senior Admiral to command a Baltic fleet in 1854. He required a combination of experience and rank when few men could offer either quality. The obvious choice was Admiral Sir William Parker, nephew of St Vincent and a favourite of Nelson. Parker had just completed an unprecedented double term as Commander-in-Chief Mediterranean, 1846–52. Graham sounded him out privately in the autumn of 1853, but Parker, then seventy-three, felt worn out and unequal to the task of training a new fleet.[27] This was a serious loss. Possessed of unrivalled experience as a sailor /diplomat, Parker had the loyalty of almost every officer in the Navy, and of all the flag officers, most closely matched the qualities displayed by de Saumarez between 1808 and 1812. This left Graham without an entirely satisfactory alternative. Earl Dundonald, seventy-nine, offered his services and a plan to take Cronstadt by poison gas and smokescreen. Age and a reputation for eccentricity bordering on insanity saved the Russians from his sulphurous schemes. The only other officer of reputation and a touch of genius was Vice-Admiral Sir Charles Napier. During his life Napier's public fame was unequalled, although historians have dismissed him as an eccentric warrior, hopelessly inadequate for the Baltic command. Napier was a pioneer of steam warships and tactics, had a deep humanitarian concern for the lower deck and was an outstanding exponent of coastal and amphibious warfare.[28] His services during the Syrian campaign of 1840 were brilliant and insubordinate. Graham, who had known him since 1814, described him in 1841 in terms which reveal much of both the subject and the writer: 'Napier has the courage of a lion and should be held in a leash, ready to slip, when war is declared; but a more dangerous man was never employed when obedience to orders, moderation and good conduct are required.' A similar opinion would colour his handling of the Admiral in 1854. Napier's parliamentary career, 1841–46, ended with command of the Western Squadron. By mid-1853 Napier realised war was a distinct possibility, pressing for the North Sea command. While Aberdeen had no desire to see him employed, Graham had already granted him a Good Service Pension and knew he was keen. After Parker's refusal he considered no-one else. In late November, when he hinted Napier would have the Baltic, Napier knew exactly what was implied.[29] Despite his unpopularity with politicians and senior naval officers Graham considered he was the right man: 'I hope, even still, that the "Nelson Touch", will not be necessary: but if unhappily it should be so, Charley Napier is the boy to administer it.'[30] For all his public pessimism about the Baltic, Graham believed Napier could open the campaign with a great victory, the 'Nelson Touch', planned in 1801, destroying the Russian battlesquadron at Reval.

The selection of Napier appeared controversial, but in reality reflected Graham's caution. Napier, the most experienced officer available was, at sixty-seven, still relatively young. Public disappointment with the 1854 campaign had its' origins outside the Baltic. The Napier of popular legend might have done more, the man of flesh could not. Throughout 1853 Graham claimed he had not made any selection for the command, denying Napier any influence in the selection of captains. As a result he went to war in 1854 with inexperienced, if well connected, officers who distrusted him; their limited competence hampered the campaign, while their complaints helped Graham to secure Napier's dismissal. There were good men available, but Graham only turned to them after filling up the senior posts.

Graham used the September recess to tour the dockyards and coastal fortifications. This has been condemned as 'preparing for the last war rather than the next', 'anomalous' in view of the Anglo–French alliance then being forged. Graham realised that co-operation with France was a temporary anomaly in the long term rivalry between the two nations, refusing to be side-tracked by the crisis in the east. He found the steam battlefleet moving quickly to fruition while the new works at Alderney would check Cherbourg.[31] The fortress/arsenal on the Cotentin peninsula dominated his strategic focus. When Russia took centre stage he quickly transferred this role to Sevastopol.

The more immediate danger was of a Russian fleet in the North Sea which kept the relief battleships with the Western Squadron. After the squadron entered the Straits, *Agamemnon* was added to the list and the role of the relief ships altered. If necessary they would reinforce the existing ships, creating a force of ten battleships; if the crisis abated they would relieve *Trafalgar* and *Albion*. If those two ships did not come home, Graham would be forced to commission more to cover the Channel. The additional ships were only released from the Western Squadron in late October, arriving in December just in time for active operations. Graham did not want to fit out more sailing ships, commissioning the steam battleships *Princess Royal* and *Royal George* in October, months before they were complete. This balancing act, preserving a powerful force in the Mediterranean and in the Channel on peacetime estimates, has been commended.[32] The folly of not calling for more money, to fit out extra ships and recruit crews, did not become apparent until the Baltic fleet went to sea. Graham's failure to prepare in the autumn of 1853 ruined the Baltic campaign of 1854, the fleet still required three months' drill before it could be used.

Notes

1   BARTLETT, pp. 289–90; PARTRIDGE, M. S., 'The Russell cabinet and national defence, 1846–1852', *History*, No. 72, 1987, pp. 231–50.

2   Graham to the Queen 7 Oct. 1853: R.A. G6 f9.

3   Palmerston to Aberdeen 10 Jan. 1853: Add. 48,578 f1–2; Aberdeen to Palmerston 10 Jan. 1853: Bdlds. GC/AB f291.

4   Graham to Raglan in Graham to Palmerston 25 Jan. 1853: Bdlds. GCGR f73; M. S., 'The Defence of the Channel Islands, 1814–1870', *The Army Historical Quarterly*, Spring 1986, pp. 34–42; Graham to Palmerston 29 Jan. 1853: Bdlds. GC/GR f74; Palmerston to Graham 1 Feb. 1853: Add. 48,578 f2–3; Palmerston to Herbert 5 Feb. 1853: HERBERT F461; Graham to Palmerston 3 Apr. 1853: Bdlds. GC/GR f75; Burgoyne to Raglan May 1853, in WROTTESLEY, G., *The Life and Correspondence of Field Marshal Sir John Burgoyne* (London, 1873, two vols), vol. 1, pp. 484–9;

Palmerston to Graham 19 Apr. 1853: Gr. B113. STRACHAN, Hew, *The Reform of the British Army, 1815–1854* (Manchester, 1984), pp. 196–221; Graham to Gladstone 10 Apr. 1853: Add. 44,163 f86–7.

5 PARKER, C. S., *The Life and Letters of Sir James Graham* (London, 1907, two vols.); ERICKSON, A. B., *The Public Career of Sir James Graham* (London, 1952) WARD, J. T., *Sir James Graham* (London, 1967). These works contain no appreciation of Graham's naval policy or long-term interest in the navy.

6 PARKER, vol. ii, pp. 167 and 202; BARTLETT, pp. 289–90; Graham to Captain Milne 14 Nov. 1853: Milne /P/A/ia.

7 BRIGGS, pp. xxi, 107 ; ERICKSON, pp. 402, 320.

8 LAMBERT, Andrew, *Battleships in Transition: the creation of the steam battlefleet, 1815–1860* (London, 1984 and 1985); Graham to Dundas 12 Jan. 1853: DND/9 f15–7.

9 Chads to C-in-C Portsmouth 23 Dec. 1852: W.O./502; Graham to Aberdeen 26 Jan. 1853: Add. 43,191 f16.

10 Parliamentary Papers 1847–8, vol. XXI; Baring to Russell undated (early 1852): PRO 30/22/10ai f1–16; PHILLIMORE, Sir A., *The Life and Letters of Sir William Parker* (London, 1878–80, three vols.), vol. ii, pp. 710–14; BARTLETT, pp. 304–10; Parliamentary Papers 1852–3, vol. IX, pp. 11–15; TAYLOR, R. I., 'Manning the Royal Navy, 1852–62' in *Mariner's Mirror*, vol. xiiv, 1959, pp. 302–13; Graham to Aberdeen 27 Mar. 1853: Add. 43,191 f34; Graham to Clarendon 4 Apr. 1853: Cl. Dep. C4 f155.

11 BARTLETT, p. 309.

12 *Ibid.*, pp. 306–7; TAYLOR, p. 310.

13 Graham to Dundas 21 Mar. 1853: DND/9 f28–31; Clarendon to Cowley 1 Apr. 1853: F.O. 519/304.

14 Graham to Dundas 2 Apr., 6 May 1853: DND/9 f36–8, f45–8; Graham to Palmerston 29 May 1853. Bdlds. GC/GR f76; Graham to Prince Albert 2 Jun. 1853: R.A. G3 f33; Walker/Graham memorandum on the Defence of Constantinople, 2 Jun. 1853. A similar paper was circulated in late May: Gr. CW.19; Graham to Palmerston 30 May 1853: Bdlds. GC/GR f77; Aberdeen to Graham 31 May 1853: Gr. B.113.

15 Dundas to Graham 1 Jun. 1853: Gr. B.114; Cowley to Clarendon 16 Jun. 1853: F.O. 519/304; Graham to Stratford 8 Jul. 1853: Gr. B.114; Seymour to Clarendon 28 Jun. 1853: F.O. 65/428 no. 323.

16 HAMILTON, Adm. Sir R.V., *Journals and Letters of Admiral Sir Thomas Byam Martin, 1774–1854* (London, 1899–1901, three vols.); T. B. Martin to Graham 11 Jun. 1853: Add.41,370 f210–234;

17 Graham to Clarendon 6 Oct. 1853: Cl. Dep. C4 f216–7.

18 Seymour to Clarendon 22 Jun., 16 Aug. 1853: F.O.65/429 no. 307, 428; Seymour to Graham 26 Jul. 1853: Gr. B.114.

19 Graham to Clarendon 20 Oct. 1853: Cl. Dep. C4 f221.

20 Seymour to Clarendon Oct.–Nov. 1853: F.O. 65/431–2.

21 Graham to Clarendon 30 Jan. 1854, 8 Dec.1853: Gr. B.116, B.115;

22 BRIGGS, pp. 108–9.

23 Graham to Prince Albert 2 Jun. 1853: Gr. B.113; LAMBERT,

pp. 39–40; H. B. Martin to T. B. Martin 23 Dec. 1853: Add. 41,466 f320;
24 LEWIS, pp. 113–130.
25 CARLYLE, T., *On Heroes and Hero Worship* (London, 1840);
HAMILTON, C. I., 'Naval hagiography and the Victorian hero' in *The
Historical Journal*, 1980.
26 Graham to Lyons 12 Feb. 1853: LYONS L507; EARDLEY-WIL-
MOT, Capt. S., *Life of Vice Admiral Lord Lyons* (London, 1898): a reliable
and informative biography based on Lyons' papers, but lacking any insight
into his character. Lyons to Graham 10 Apr., 6 Jun. 1853: EARDLEY-WIL-
MOT, p. 123–5; Clarendon to Graham 13 Jul. 1853: Gr. B.114; Dundas to
Graham 4 Sept. 1853: Gr. CW2; Graham to Clarendon 25 Sept. 1853: Cl.
Dep. C4 f210; Graham to Herbert 17 Oct. 1853: HERBERT F4/59; Clarendon to Palmerston 17 Oct. 1853: Bdlds. GC/CL f537/2.
27 PHILLIMORE, vol. i, p. xiii.
28 ELERS-NAPIER, General G., *The Life and Letters of Admiral Sir
Charles Napier* (London, 1862, two vols.); WILLIAMS, H. N., *The Life and
Letters of Sir Charles Napier, 1786–1860* (London, 1917): unsatisfactory
books based on Napier's papers, lacking any treatment of his intellectual
achievement; KEMP, P., *The Oxford Companion to Ships and the Sea*
(Oxford, 1976), p. 572; Napier, Sir C., *The Navy* (London, 1851); LAING,
E. A. M., 'The introduction of paddle frigates into the Royal Navy',
Mariner's Mirror, vol. lxvi, 1980, pp. 331–50.
29 Graham to Charles Arbuthnot 1 Jan. 1841: *The Correspondence of
Charles Arbuthnot*, ed. A. ASPINALL (Camden Society, 1941), p. 224;
Aberdeen to Napier 9 Jul. 1853: Add. 40,023 f406; WILLIAMS. pp. 240–3;
Graham to Napier 22 Nov. 1853: Add. 40,023 f420; Graham to Clarendon
6 Oct. 1853: Cl. Dep. C4 f216–7.
30 Graham to Clarendon 8 Dec. 1853: Gr. B.115; PHILLIMORE, vol.
iii, p. 723.
31 CONACHER, p. 17; Graham to Herbert 15 Sept. 1853: HERBERT
F4/59; Graham to Wood 19 Sept., Graham to Prince Albert 23 Sept. 1853:
Gr. B.114.
32 Graham to Clarendon 21, 25 Sept. 1853: Cl. Dep. C4 f208, 210;
Clarendon to Graham 27 Sept. 1853: Gr. B.114; Dundas to Graham 29, 30
Sept. 1853: Gr. CW2; BRIGGS, pp. 106–9.

4

The strategic balance

Dundas remained in Valetta harbour while the crisis developed, for although Stratford had hinted at something more serious than the Holy Places in April this was primarily to justify having a faster steamer in the Bosphorus. A month later he revealed more, but only after Menshikov's departure did he even hint that Dundas should prepare to move to forestall a Russian attempt to seize the Dardanelles, again requesting a faster steamer. Graham was more concerned with the French. Dundas was ready when the Government decided to move his squadron, Graham supported the public orders of 2 June with a full statement of Government policy, stressing the limits on Stratford's authority to call up the fleet. The primary object, securing Constantinople, was conditioned by the second, that of avoiding a rupture with Russia. Graham's personal contribution was a warning to avoid trouble with Stratford or the French. The dispatches and letters reached Malta from Marseilles at 19.30 on 7 June aboard *Caradoc*.[1] After a brief examination of his correspondence Dundas ordered the squadron to prepare for sea, and *Arethusa* was towed out of port by *Niger* at 21.00. After refuelling with all haste, *Caradoc* cleared the harbour at 03.00 carrying dispatches for Constantinople. The squadron followed at day-break, being towed for much of the 10th.

The British squadron reached Besika Bay, seven miles south of the Dardanelles, at 07.30 on 13 June. *Tiger* went to the Consul in the Straits to organise a supply of coal. The French were sighted before midday on the 14th, Admiral LaSusse anchoring at 18.30. The junction of the squadrons indicated the resolve of the two Governments to resist Russian pressure on Turkey. Diplomatic historians suggest that placing them at Besika forced the western powers to act because, after October, the anchorage would be untenable. If they did move they must either retreat, reducing the influence of the two

Table 3: The French fleet at Besika Bay, 14 June 1853

	Guns	
Battleships		
Ville de Paris	120	Flagship
Valmy	120	
Montebello	120	limited steamer
Napoleon	90	steam
Charlemagne	90	steam
Jupiter	80	
Bayard	80	
Steamers		
Mogador	16	
Sane	16	
Caton	16	
Labrador	16	
Narval	16	

countries, or advance into the Dardanelles in breach of the 1841 treaty. Graham soon discovered Besika was safe throughout the year.[2] Therefore British diplomacy during the autumn, despite Palmerston's urging, was not directly affected by the location of the fleet. The French were in a more difficult position, their freedom of action being circumscribed by the inferior quality of French seapower. Stratford had not called for the move and did not anticipate a Russian *coup de main*, but was relieved to have the fleet close and requested a reliable officer to inspect the Bosphorus forts. Dundas sent his favourite steamer captains, Drummond, *Retribution* and Heath, *Niger* to relieve the unreliable *Wasp* as duty ship on the 15th. Sending two ships was a clear breach of the 1841 treaty. Dundas and LaSusse planned to pass the Dardanelles in the event of war; the French would lead, LaSusse being the senior officer. Dundas was concerned at the prospect of having to retire with the Straits in enemy hands.[3] This reflected Admiral Duckworth's problems in 1807 and a general reluctance to engage forts. Preparing for action was only one requirement; food and coal had to be brought up from Malta. Malta remained the principal depot for both services throughout the war. To add to the difficulties, the French had anchored so close to the British ships that neither could exercise their guns.

While still at sea LaSusse had proposed a reconnaissance of the

Russian ports, but this was rejected by Graham and Stratford. Russell favoured keeping a steamer off the Dardanelles to warn of an attack, but this would be diplomatically contentious and offered no significant strategic advantage.[4] Graham was unhappy at the prospect of remaining in close proximity to the French, especially as LaSusse was senior to Dundas and had a larger battleline, and reacted strongly when Stratford complained on both points. This delicate balancing of naval forces to support diplomacy was an irritating game when his naval policy was based on mistrust of France. LaSusse was replaced by Vice-Admiral Hamelin on 11 July. Graham discovered Hamelin was considered a better officer, did not outrank Dundas and had the confidence of the Emperor; LaSusse was unpopular, ill-tempered and his term had expired.[5] The arrival in July of the steam battleship *Sans Pareil* 70, gave Dundas seven of the line.[6] *Montebello* returned to Toulon for her engines, being replaced by *Friedland* 120 on the 15th. On the 27th *Friedland* attempted to shift her berth, went out of control and ran aground to the north of Rabbit Island. Refusing British assistance, the French took four days to refloat her and as long again before she could be sent up to Constantinople for repairs, where she fell over in dry dock.[7] As a battleship, *Friedland*'s entrance into the Straits violated the 1841 treaty, but was excused by the circumstances. Similar incidents in the Black Sea and Baltic during 1854–55 demonstrated the weakness of French seapower. Louis Napoleon increased the size of the navy, but lacked the experienced seamen and officers for an effective fleet. During the next nine months the poor order of the French ships, cables and rigging had more impact on western diplomacy than has been realised.

The strategic position of the western powers was not, as Walker and Graham anticipated, improved by the move to Besika. The squadrons were still 190 miles from Constantinople, and the opening third of their passage would be hampered by the adverse winds and currents of the Dardanelles. While the speed of communication had been improved, the benefit was only relative for the Bosphorus was eighteen miles long, and had a favourable current and poor defences. Russian troops could be in Constantinople within hours of entering the Bosphorus, but allied steamers would not arrive inside two days of being summoned. Viewed in this light it was not surprising that Palmerston and Russell urged sending the fleet into the Bosphorus, particularly when the Russians entered the Principalities.

The Turks were in a serious position while they remained passive; however, Islamic fervour and the expertise of Slade improved their defences. Consulted by Rose and Benedetti in March, Slade's work persuaded the Czar to abandon the *coup de main*, although British observers were less impressed.[8] Later Slade had to rely on Stratford's influence to keep the Turks moving, and while Stratford did not expect an attack he considered Slade's work a valuable deterrent. The defences of the Bosphorus were made up by a combination of ships and forts. In May the ships included four battleships, five frigates, four smaller vessels and two powerful steamers. Although they carried 800 guns they did not have heavy shell guns and even with 1,000 new raised men aboard they remained short-handed. The situation was not improved by their being moored off the Sultan's Palace where the Russians could double on them. Slade considered the Russians had two options for an amphibious attack – landing at Killia as Walker suggested, or passing down the Bosphorus after dark. To cover both threats he instituted daily gunnery drill, called for more blockships and requested that the ships should be moored further north on the European shore between Buyukedere and Therapia. Here they would enfilade a naval attack or be towed into the Black Sea to counter a landing at Killia, using steamers to report Russian movements. A flotilla returning from the Albanian coast would provide trained men. Stratford persuaded the Turks to adopt Slade's programme.[9]

Stratford's concern for the forts, shared by Clarendon, had already seen the garrisons reinforced with troops from the Dardanelles. The Bosphorus, between one-and-a-half and half a mile wide was covered by eight forts on the European shore and five on the Asiatic, with 3,800 men and 305 guns. Captain Drummond reported the guns were old, of many calibres and without sights. Badly corroded iron pieces were useless, the brass guns were better but short of ammunition. Nearly one third pointed down the Straits, only half faced north and they had narrow embrasures restricting their arcs of fire. All were open to the rear, offering no resistance to a land attack, for which eventuality there were 20,000 troops covering the forts on the European shore and 4,000 on the Asiatic. Drummond concluded the forts should be cut down to allow the guns to traverse as the ships passed. Another fifty heavy guns were available and sights were being made. By this stage the Turks had four battleships and eight frigates moored to Slade's satisfaction with almost all their upper deck guns replaced by British 32-pounders. The Sultan also received help from two of his nominal subjects: the Viceroy of Egypt sent 10,000 men, three battleships, four frigates and two steamers in mid August; the Bey of Tunis offered four frigates and a steamer. Finally a small squadron went into the Euxine to drive off the Russians and warn of any attack. With little help the Turks had made the Bosphorus defensible after two centuries of neglect.

By contrast the ten forts of the Dardanelles were already in good order; with 300 guns they would prove costly to pass. Only the Asiatic forts had defences on the land side. Dundas was worried they might be captured while the squadrons were in the Straits. Russell's suggestion that they be occupied by western forces was the direct genesis of the Crimean operation.[10]

By late June the danger of a Russian amphibious attack had passed without the western powers being in a position to prevent it. This allowed them to turn their attention to diplomacy and watch Russia move into the Principalities. However, both countries were committed to Turkey, and it would be morally impossible for the squadrons to leave Besika before Russia evacuated the Principalities, making the search for a diplomatic solution a matter of urgency for the western powers, particularly France. Russia could afford to wait on events. French precipitancy and British weakness had given them the first round. The squadrons had been committed to a position they could not maintain forever, without gaining any significant strategic or diplomatic advantage.

News of the Russian decision to occupy the Principalities reached London on 6 June. Although not unexpected, this produced another round of notes between the ministers. Aberdeen, concerned to provide the Czar with a means of escape that did not compromise his honour, accepted the Russian argument that occupation was not an act of war, although he feared Stratford would call up the fleet when the Russians crossed the Pruth. Clarendon and Russell had already agreed Turkey must be persuaded not to declare war, and the French concurred. Anticipating this, Stratford secured Anglo–French policy even before it had been communicated to him. That was the extent of Turkish flexibility, and they rejected Nesselrode's terms. At this juncture Stratford made a serious error, creating a linkage between the squadrons at Besika and the Russian army in the Principalities by offering to withdraw the former if the latter would move back.[11] Not only did he do this directly, writing to Seymour without going through the Foreign Office, but he appeared to abandon the western position of reacting to a Russian breach of the status quo. While this was a genuine attempt to reduce tension, removing the armed forces and allowing the Vienna Conference to settle the issue and would also improve the strategic position of the allies by returning them to the situation before the crisis, Stratford's initiative only encouraged Russian intransigence.

All that was in the future when the cabinet discussed how to react to the Russian occupation. Palmerston wanted the squadrons to enter the Euxine, because Russian action, whatever it was called, constituted *casus belli*. He was outnumbered and had to accept the majority view that the Turks should be persuaded not to declare war. Aberdeen and Clarendon argued this would preserve hope of a diplomatic solution, Palmerston accepted because Turkey could not hope to recover the territory even with the western fleets. Palmerston spoke a different language from his colleagues, more concerned with the realities of power than the niceties of diplomacy. The round of letters ended with a series of memoranda. Russell opened by enlarging on Britain's strategic and economic interests in Turkey, interests that had to be defended by force. Lansdowne agreed, calling for a tough ultimatum. Palmerston considered Britain and France could coerce Russia without Austria and Prussia. In concluding, Aberdeen stressed that preserving peace was the paramount consideration.[12] In May Aberdeen's primary consideration had been the security of Constantinople, but with war much closer he preferred a less dangerous position.

Clarendon was the key element in the cabinet, continually looking for a lead from the more experienced men and morbidly concerned with public opinion. His support was the prize in the struggle between Palmerston and Aberdeen. Conacher concludes that Palmerston's pressure 'probably' influenced Clarendon. Palmerston dominated Clarendon by late 1853, securing critical influence over the implementation of foreign policy. Outvoted in cabinet throughout June, Palmerston worked on Clarendon, arguing that if the Russian occupation was *casus belli* the 1841 treaty had been abrogated and the squadrons were free to enter the Straits. Forewarned by a wavering Clarendon, Aberdeen skilfully rebutted the argument, although his letter was marred by a sarcastic conclusion. When Nesselrode's memorandum attempting to justify the occupation appeared, Palmerston tried again. Still trusting to the Czar's good faith Aberdeen reasoned that if Turkey had not declared war it was not for Britain and France to do it for her; only an attack on Constantinople could justify entering the Straits, an eventuality covered by Stratford's instructions. Palmerston conceded gracefully; with a majority in cabinet Aberdeen could not be moved. Russell tried to find a middle ground, arguing that if the Russian fleet appeared in the Euxine the western squadrons should enter the Straits and occupy the Dardanelles forts.[13] Aberdeen had no trouble smothering this spark. Leadership of the war faction had passed to Palmerston. Palmerston's policy promised to bring the issue to a head when the western powers were ill prepared, but his deterrence would ring hollow in St Petersburg without British and French troops to support the squadrons.

In mid June the western governments made a joint approach to Austria, calling for a conference on the crisis to be held in neutral, but profoundly concerned, Vienna. This process was used by Aberdeen to parry Palmerston's demands, because the only deterrent gesture available, sending up the squadrons, would alienate Austria as well as Russia. The conference of Ambassadors opened on 24 July, chaired by the Austrian Chancellor, Count Buol. In three days the 'Vienna Note' was prepared from a French draft and dispatched to St Petersburg and Constantinople. Russian acceptance could be relied upon, as the French proposals had already found favour with the Czar. When this was formally announced Aberdeen believed the crisis settled. The single greatest error of European statesmen during the crisis was to ignore the wishes of the Turks. Aberdeen and Clarendon decided they 'must' accept the note, a view that should be conveyed '*in strong terms, privately to Stratford*'. Stratford anticipated problems, finding the earlier draft of the note open to a harsh pro-Russian interpretation. The final draft remained ambiguous on the vital issue of religious privileges granted to the Greek Church. On 20 August the Turks rejected it. Having ignored the opinions of the Turkish Government Aberdeen, Clarendon and Russell suddenly realised the 'stupidity' of the Ottomans might lead them to reject the note. When this was confirmed they blamed Stratford and the Turks for their own failure. Believing Stratford had the power to coerce the Turks, but had not done so, they made him the scapegoat. Graham argued that Stratford was deliberately disobeying the Government, encouraging the Turks to resist.

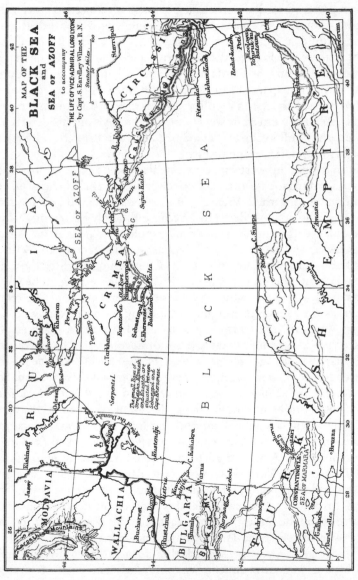

1 The Black Sea and Sea of Azov, 1854–56. From the *Life of Admiral Lord Lyons*

Essentialy Stratford and the Government adopted very different views of the crisis. Stratford properly saw it as an issue between Russia and Turkey; the ministers treated it as a European problem, to be settled by, and for the great powers. Britain only interfered to protect her own interests; those of Turkey were secondary. Stratford more sensibly tried to settle the issues between Russia and Turkey, guaranteeing the results in a Four Power Treaty. He saw blatant threats from Britain and France as counter-productive. This difference of emphasis, with Stratford trying to settle the crisis from Constantinople, encouraged Clarendon and Aberdeen to adopt the French view that Stratford himself was responsible for Turkish intransigence. For all that, no-one had the courage to dismiss Stratford. The Turks were even more difficult; it was easy to talk of withdrawing western support, but that would not make Constantinople any less a British interest.[14] Having recognised the independence of Turkey as an issue to be defended, the Turks had to be supported once the Russians crossed the Danube. Here again the cabinet lacked the courage to act decisively. If they believed in the Vienna Note they should have made a public committment, and the attempt to secure it by unofficial means was an admission of weakness. Failure returned attention to Besika.

Although French policy remained at odds with that of Britain, the clear linkage with Palmerston's minority view alarmed Graham. He believed that the Home Secretary's conversations with Walewski were encouraging the French to act ahead of Britain. As France had no real interest in preserving Turkey he anticipated her support being thrown open in return for a share in partition. Fear of French duplicity dominated his understanding, so he took no comfort from the growing community of western policy. Clarendon, supporting Aberdeen's view, spent much of July deflecting French calls to move up the squadrons, their urgency conditioned by fear for the ships so carelessly sent to Besika.[15]

Moving the squadrons to Besika was a diplomatic gesture which effected little in strategic terms. No sooner had the ships arrived than the problems of the open roadstead became obvious. While diplomatic historians have examined the politicians' fears for the winter weather, the climate was far from easy in the summer, malaria breaking out within a month. By August Captain Wardle, *Inflexible* had died along with several seamen, and Lord Edward Russell, *Vengeance* was seriously ill. Later *Bellerophon* and *Vengeance* were sent south of Tenedos for periods of isolation. A year later Graham, *Rodney* and Symonds, *Arethusa* were still suffering the after-effects of 'Besika fever', symptoms that did little to help the squadron resist cholera at Varna. Graham wanted to divide the fleets, sending one to cruise or to the superior anchorage at Vourla. Dundas realised tenuous Anglo–French co-operation made such a division politically impossible.[16] This left the ships in enforced idleness unable to drill or even fire their guns for over four months.

The other problem with Besika was diplomatic. If Russia did not evacuate the Principalities Clarendon foresaw a time when it would be necessary to move the ships, but feared Aberdeen lacked the moral courage to withdraw to Malta. This was not vital in July, so he let the matter rest for a month. Russell realised the squadrons could not retreat from Besika while the Russians remained, and in early September he joined Palmerston in pressing Aberdeen to consent to the ships' entering the Dardanelles when the weather made this necessary. Aberdeen refused to do so without cabinet consent. By this stage Clarendon supported the Whig policy and pressed it on Graham. Aberdeen wanted Graham to prove the ships would not have to enter the Straits before 1 November, taking the official version of the 1849 breach of the 1841 convention that Admiral Parker's move was forced by the weather. Graham was better informed; Captain Richard Dundas had been with Parker and knew he had been ordered, and Newcastle, who had been anchored with the fleet throughout December 1849, weighed in with yachting reminiscences. In a memorandum wrongly attributed to Aberdeen Graham objected to entering the Dardanelles. As the Russians had accepted the Vienna Note he wanted to retire fifty miles to Myitilene, which would be more healthy. Aberdeen was relieved promising Graham, then at Balmoral, that the issue would not be decided without a cabinet.[17] Government policy was to stay at Besika leaving the initiative with Russia. However, exposing the fallacious dangers of Besika did not satisfy the French. Anxious to enter the Straits, de la Tour pressed the Turks on 18 and 22 August to issue the necessary firmans to cover the possibility of bad news arriving from the west. In Paris the more honest explanation was concern for the ships. This encouraged Clarendon to favour a partial entrance, far enough for the safety of the squadrons.[18] At Constantinople events were moving toward the entrance of the squadrons; the festival of sacrificial Bairam and the arrival of the Egyptian forces encouraged Turkish war fever. Taking advantage of this the Minister of War, Mehemet Ali, incited a serious riot on 11 September. De la tour wanted to call up the squadrons but Stratford wanted, *'more proofs of urgent peril'* and only agreed to summon four steamers. Once again French anxiety had more to do with ships than Constantinople, despite Drouyn's bravado that they might go up alone. Hamelin wanted Dundas to send *Sans Pareil* as one of his steamers, but Dundas rejected so flagrant a violation of the convention. The arrival of *Furious*, *Niger*, *Mogador* and *Gomer* on the 14th ended the insurrection as Stratford had anticipated.[19] The Government did not react so coolly.

When news of the riots reached London the ministers were familiar with. Nesselrode's 'violent' interpretation of the Vienna Note, leaked from the Berlin Embassy and published in the major German and British newspapers by 16 September. The western governments now accepted that Turkey had been correct in rejecting the note. The French once more tried to get the squadrons moved, and using the term 'revolt' to describe something Stratford viewed as a 'disturbance' indicated their anxiety. The French Government received news from Constantinople a day ahead of the British, giving them the chance to send their version of events to London before Stratford's dispatches arrived. This time the deception worked. On the day Walewski read his dispatch Clarendon and Aberdeen ordered Stratford to call up the squadron, without holding a cabinet, nor consulting their colleagues or the Queen and without waiting a day for Stratford's dispatches. It was weakness on Aberdeen's part; under pressure from Russell over the Premiership and Palmerston over sending up the squadron, he took the easy way out. Here was an excuse to move the ships that could be justified to Russia. 'Our main object is for the protection of British life and property, and if necessary, the person of the Sultan . . . it is not intended as a menace or hostile movement directed against Russia.'[20] Graham accepted this argument without enthusiasm, his hopes were placed on the instructions sent to the civil and naval authorities. Aberdeen suggested that Dundas would have supreme authority when carrying out Stratford's instructions.[21] The instructions actually sent were ambiguous on this vital point, authorising Stratford to use the squadron in concert with the French to defend Turkish territory, or instruct the Russians they were empowered to do so should they appear ready to leave Sevastopol. The whole was qualified by

Clarendon's observation that the Russian fleet was not to be considered as hostile if it was moving supplies between Russian ports. Graham reinforced the cautious slant to the instructions by stressing that only a Russian attack would justify entering the Black Sea. If Stratford acted outside these instructions Dundas was to protest, but obey. Aberdeen still hoped for peace, Clarendon was preparing for war.[22] Palmerston condemned Aberdeen's justification for moving up the squadron, which provided Russia with an ideal precedent to occupy Constantinople in the future; the only secure ground for the move, which he had always urged, was the continued Russian occupation of the Principalities.[23] Stratford saw no need for the squadrons, particularly as his own measures had ended the danger. Privately he blamed the French who appeared to want to remain at Constantinople although he had already sent the additional British steamers back to Besika.[24] He had warned Clarendon about the French before. However there was little Stratford could do, for on the day his instructions arrived the Turks declared war and Reshid formally requested the presence of the fleets. Stratford resisted, hoping the Austro–Russian conference might provide a solution, but by the 15th he knew that that had failed, but even after warning Dundas he still tried to delay the inevitable. Pressure from de la Tour forced his hand, and late on the 20th orders were sent to Dundas and Hamelin. Stratford was disgusted. He had worked for peace and been outmanoeuvred by French pressure on London. Temperley observed how Stratford's influence with the Turks declined in October, but did not see how this had been caused by the Government. It was the tragedy of 1853 that the one man who might have been able to settle the crisis was feared and distrusted by the Government he served. In a last attempt to avert war Stratford tried to delay the onset of hostilities on the Danube. With the other three great power Ambassadors he persuaded the Turkish ministers to suspend hostilities at least until the end of October.[25] Stratford hoped to avoid any real fighting, leaving the winter clear for a diplomatic solution. This was his last throw, after which he would be forced into the background by military developments. Before the orders to avoid fighting reached Omer Pasha, the Turkish commander, at Shumla on the 23rd, two skirmishes had taken place, and fighting soon broke out on the Asian frontier. Only the Turks were satisfied.

At the Olmutz meeting on 20 September the Czar, the Austrian Emperor, Nesselrode and Buol produced a new postscript to the

Vienna Note, making the Four Powers joint guarantors. The French were initially enthusiastic, but they distanced themselves when Clarendon, who had no intention of accepting the Olmutz proposals, reasoned that the Turks would reject them anyway. The cabinet rejected the initiative on 8 October, publicly doubting Russian good faith in the wake of the 'violent' interpretation.[26] Clarendon knew public opinion would be hostile after the Turkish rejection, but he was still prepared for a peaceful settlement, urging Stratford to avoid annoying the Russians.[27] At this stage a Russian climbdown acceptable to the Turks and the British public was needed. Russia occupied the Principalities and until she evacuated there would be no guarantee of good faith. Furthermore, while she remained Russia had a major strategic advantage, so she could afford to wait knowing the western powers must move first.

At Besika Dundas had considered the possibilites of war. Although short of accurate information on the Russian fleet he had received the latest charts. When war broke out he wanted to enter the Dardanelles to secure the forts, unlike the French who were primarily concerned with the weather: '*Constantinople is nothing* if the power that has it cannot command the Dardanelles.' If Britain remained neutral the fleet would anchor under the Asian castles, if she joined the conflict only two battleships and two steamers would remain. The other steamers could operate all winter in the Black Sea leaving the battlefleet anchored off the Bulgarian coast. Despite good relations with Admiral Hamelin he did not believe the French were reliable and discounted the Muslim naval forces. Graham, while not particularly impressed with Dundas's views, did press Clarendon for more intelligence. When the squadrons were ordered inside the Straits he consulted Walker and Captain Dundas, favouring a small force at the Dardanelles and the main body at Constantinople. Significantly he appointed Lyons. Both Britain and France began to collect troops, the French to occupy the Dardanelles, the British to prevent any French occupation becoming permanent; neither anticipated moving before the spring. Russell favoured sending more marines for this task, but Graham had none to spare from fitting out the Baltic fleet.[28]

In early October Russell suggested the western powers should act as auxiliaries to Turkey. Graham, still anxious to preserve peace, was not encouraged by Aberdeen's view that such a position was untenable. In response Graham set out his policy, hoping Aberdeen would adopt it; the squadrons must stay at Constantinople, closing the Bosphorus and keeping the Dardanelles open, but they must not enter the Black Sea, the rubicon of Russia. When Aberdeen sent the fleet inside the Straits the Peelites unilaterally altered the rubicon from the Dardanelles to the Bosphorus. Herbert even urged that Dundas's instructions should be linked to a remonstrance against the Turkish declaration of war. The cabinet of 7 October agreed that the fleets could enter the Black Sea to defend Turkey. Aberdeen knew this posture could not long delay British involvement; Graham, having accepted Aberdeen's climbdown, was anxious to prevent Stratford or Dundas moving into the Euxine without authority. On the 8th the cabinet discussed the Admiral's instructions. Palmerston wanted to take control of the Black Sea in return for Turkey engaging to consult the western powers on the terms of any settlement; this would be using Turkey's quarrel to conduct a limited war against Russia to reduce her power and attack her naval arsenals. When Clarendon suggested using the squadrons to restrain the Turks he pointed out that this would be a breach of the very integrity they were attempting to uphold. Graham feared the squadrons would excite the Turks, and Stratford would drag the western powers into the war.[29]

In considering how to use the squadrons neither Russell's plan to act an auxiliaries, nor Graham's to hold hard short of war made much sense. Aberdeen knew war was all but inevitable. After Nesselrode's 'violent interpretation' of the Vienna Note, no Russian concession would satisfy Turkey. Russell was the first to realise that waiting at Constantinople was playing into Russia's hands. Palmerston condemned the lack of any decided policy, warning Aberdeen that the Government might be forced to resign. Graham realised Clarendon was moving to support Palmerston, but believed that while Aberdeen had a cabinet majority and the confidence of the Queen he would prevail. Yet Aberdeen had been giving way slowly over the preceding months, abandoning his own policy without adopting an alternative. Russell kept up the pressure for a decision on western strategy, wanting Britain and France to become principals in the war, with the passage of the Danube as *casus belli*.[30] This was an empty gesture in late October, for British forces would be unable to act in either theatre before the weather broke.

Notes

1 Stratford to Dundas 8 Apr., 25 May 1853: DND/9 f43–6, 58–9; Graham to Dundas 15 May, 2 Jun. 1853: *ibid.* f54–6, 61–3; Dundas to Graham 18 May, 7 Jun. 1853: Gr. CW1.
2 Dundas Journal 14 Jun. 1853: ADM 50/252; TEMPERLEY, pp. 333–4; Captain R. S. Dundas to Graham 7 Sept. 1853: Add. 43,191 f92–6.
3 Stratford to Dundas 13 Jun. 1853: Gr. CW1; TEMPERLEY, H., 'The alleged violations of the Straits Convention by Stratford de Reccliffe between June and September 1853', *English Historical Review*, vol. 49, pp. 657–72: while interesting this study is overly legalistic, obscuring the strategic issues and the conclusions are unreliable; Clarendon to Cowley 2 Jun. 1853: F.O. 519/304; Dundas Memo. 19 Jun. 1853: Gr. CW1.
4 Graham to Dundas 6 Jun. 8 Jul. 1853: DND/9 f65–8, f83–6; Dundas to Graham 6 Jul. 1853: Gr. CW1; Clarendon to Graham 3 Jul. 1853: Gr. B.114; Russell to Graham 4 Jul. 1853: Gr. B.114.
5 Stratford to Dundas 24 Jun. 1853: DND/9 f73–8; Graham to Stratford 8 Jul. 1853: Gr. B.114; Graham to Dundas 8 Jul. 1853: DND/9 f83–6; Clarendon to Cowley 30 Jun. 1853: F.O. 519/304.
6 LAMBERT, pp. 33–4, 138; Dundas to Graham 4 Jul. 1853: Gr. B.114.
7 Dundas Journal: ADM 50/252; Dundas to Graham 26 Aug. 1853: Gr. CW2; Slade to Dundas 25 Mar. 1853: DND/9 f33–4.
8 CURTISS, pp. 82–3; TEMPERLEY, p. 339.
9 Stratford to Clarendon 28 May 1853 no. 70: F.O.78/932 f387; Slade to Stratford 12, 25 May 1853: encl. in above Stratford to Clarendon 30 Jun. 1853: Cl. Dep. C10 f156–60.
10 Clarendon to Stratford 8 Jun. 1853: F.O. 352/36/1 f41–5; Dundas to Admiralty 5, rec. 21 July 1853 no. 219: ADM 1/5617; Stratford to Clarendon 7 Jul., no. 137 encl.; Slade to Stratford 30 Jun. 1853: F.O. 78/934; Stratford to Clarendon 20 Jun. 1853, no. 116: *ibid.* /933; Stratford to Clarendon 20 Jul. 1853, no. 164: *ibid.* /935; Dundas to Admiralty 12, rec. 31 Aug. 1853, no. 268: ADM1/5617; Dundas Memo. 19 Jun. 1853: Gr. CW1; Russell to Graham 4 Jul. 1853: Gr. B.114.
11 Aberdeen to the Queen 11 Jun. 1853: Add. 43,047 f138–9; Clarendon to Cowley 8 Jun. 1853: F.O. 519/304; Stratford to Clarendon late Jun. 1853, no. 161: F.O. 78/935.
12 Palmerston Memo. 20 Jun. 1853: PRO 30/22/11A f94; Cabinet memo late Jun. 1853: *ibid.* f94–105.
13 CONACHER, p. 161; Palmerston to Clarendon 18 Jun. 1853: Cl. Dep. C3 f85–7; Clarendon to Aberdeen 28 Jun. 1853: Add. 43,188 f204–5; Aberdeen to Palmerston 4, 13 Jul. 1853: Add. 43,069 f78–9, 85–6; Russell to Graham 4 Jul. 1853: Gr. B.114.
14 Aberdeen to Russell 9 Aug. 1853: PRO 30/22/11A f159; Aberdeen to Clarendon 16 Jul. 1853: Cl. Dep. C4 f55; Clarendon to Aberdeen 3 Aug. 1853: Add. 43,188 f268–9; Stratford to Clarendon 4 Aug. 1853: Cl. Dep. C10 f268–9; Graham to Aberdeen 9 Jun. 1853: Add. 43,191 f73; HERK-LESS, J. C., 'Stratford, the cabinet and the outbreak of the Crimean War',

The Historical Journal, 1975, vol. XVIII, pp. 497–523; Russell to Aberdeen 20 Aug. 1853: Add. 43,067 f100–1.

15   Graham to Clarendon 31 Jul. 1853: Cl. Dep. C4 f177–9, 187; Cowley to Clarendon Jul. 1853: F.O. 519/304.

16   Alison (Secretary to the Embassy at Constantinople) to Cowley 5 Aug. 1853: *ibid.*; Graham to Dundas 8 Jul. 1853: DND/9 f84–6; Graham to Stratford 8 Jul. 1853: Gr. B.114; Dundas to Graham 21 Jul. 1853: Gr. CW2.

17   Clarendon to Aberdeen 28 Jul. 1853: Add. 43,188 f204–5; Russell to Aberdeen 27 Aug. 1853: Add. 43,067 f109–10; Aberdeen to Graham 4, 6 Sept. 1853: Gr. B.114; Clarendon to Graham 3 Sept. 1853: *ibid.* Graham to Aberdeen 8 Sept. 1853, encl. Captain R. S. Dundas to Graham 7 Sept. 1853: Add. 43,191 f92–6; Newcastle to Clarendon 6 Sept. 1853: Cl. Dep. C4 f335–6; CONACHER, p. 181; Graham Memo. 9 Sept. 1853: Add. 43,191 f98; Aberdeen to Clarendon 12 Sept. 1853: Cl. Dep. C4 f90; Aberdeen to Graham 12 Sept. 1853: Gr. B.114.

18   Stratford to Clarendon 24 Aug. 1853, no. 238: F.O. 78/937; Cowley to Clarendon 1 Sept. 1853: F.O. 519/304; Clarendon to Cowley 2 Sept. 1853: *ibid.*

19   Stratford to Clarendon 15 Sept. 1853 no. 272: F.O. 78/938; Cowley to Clarendon 19, 20 Sept. 1853: F.O. 519/304; Dundas to Graham 16 Sept. 1853: Gr. CW2; TEMPERLEY, p. 351.

20   Aberdeen to Graham 22 Sept. 1853: Gr. B.114; Aberdeen to Clarendon 23 Sept. 1853: Cl. Dep. C4 f94.

21   Graham to Clarendon 25 Sept. 1853: *ibid.* f210; Aberdeen to Graham 24 Sept. 1853: Gr. B.114.

22   Clarendon to Stratford 8, 18 Oct. 1853: F.O.352/36/1 f221 and 230; Graham to Clarendon 1 Dec. 1853: Cl. Dep. C4 f249–54; TEMPERLEY, p. 354; Clarendon to Stratford 24 Sept. 1853: F.O. 352/36/1 f137.

23   Palmerston to Clarendon 29 Sept. 1853: Cl. Dep. C3 f151–2.

24   Stratford to Clarendon 6 Oct. 1853 no. 293: F.O. 78/939; Stratford to Clarendon 4 Oct. 1853; Cl.Dep. C10 f355–7.

25   TEMPERLEY. pp. 363–4.

26   SCHROEDER, P. W., *Austria, Great Britain and the Crimean War* (Ithaca, 1972), pp. 78–81.

27   Clarendon to Stratford 8, 10 Oct. 1853: F.O. 352/36/1 f149–56.

28   Dundas to Rear Admiral Sir Francis Beaufort, Hydrographer of the Navy, 3 Sept. 1853: H D216; Dundas to Graham 1, 4, 16, 28 Sept. 2 Oct. 1853: Gr. CW2; Dundas to Hamelin 3 Sept. 10 Oct. 1853: DND/5 pp. 32–5; Graham to Clarendon 25 Sept. 1853 encl. Walker memo.: Cl. Dep. C4 f210–15; Clarendon to Graham 22 Sept. 1853: Gr. B.114; Cowley to Clarendon 9, 18 Oct. 1853; Clarendon to Cowley 16 Oct. 1853: F.O. 519/304; Russell to Clarendon 16 Oct. 1853: Cl. Dep. C3 f460.

29   Graham to the Queen 7 Oct. 1853 R.A. G6 f9; Russell memo. 4 Oct. 1853: Add. 43.067 f153; Aberdeen to Graham 6, 8 Oct. 1853: Add. 43,191 f120, 135; Graham to Aberdeen 6, 8, 9 Oct. 1853: *ibid.* f122, 136; Herbert to Clarendon 7 Oct. 1853: Cl. Dep. C4 f216–7; Palmerston to Aberdeen 8 Oct. 1853: Add. 43.197 f122–3; Palmerston to Clarendon 7, 14 Oct. 1853: Cl. Dep. C3 f171, 187; Clarendon to Palmerston 13 Oct. 1853: Bdlds.

GC/CL f534; Graham to Herbert 14 Oct. 1853: HERBERT F4/59.
30 Russell to Clarendon 22 Oct. 1853: Add. 43,067 f166; Palmerston to Clarendon 14 Oct. 1853: Cl. Dep. C3 f187–92; Palmerston to Aberdeen 22 Oct. 1853: Add. 43,197 f134; Russell to Aberdeen 4 Oct. 1853: Add. 43,067 f157; Aberdeen to the Queen 24 Oct. 1853: Add. 43,047 f323; Undated memo. by Russell, all available evidence points to the last week in Oct. 1853: Add. 43,067 f183.

5

Sinope

In mid October Stratford advised Dundas that the long wait at Besika would soon end.[1] The orders of the 20th arrived aboard *Britannia* at 15.00 on the 21st. Although the squadrons would enter the Straits, only two sail and four steamers from each were required in the Bosphorus 'for the present'. The senior Captain, Lushington, *Albion* was detailed to take *Vengeance*, *Sampson*, *Retribution* and *Niger* to join *Wasp* and attend the Ambassador's requisitions.[2] While waiting three hours for the necessary firman, the wind to shifted to the north-west, preventing an early start. The battleships were finally towed out at 03.00 on the 22nd, followed by Rear-Admiral de Tinian, *Gomer* with *Henri IV*, *Jupiter* and two more steamers. The remaining ships departed under tow soon after day-break, making for anchorages in the Dardanelles. As they approached the Straits the NNE wind increased to gale force and the ships anchored off the European castles, although *Napoleon* towed *Ville de Paris* up to Lampsaki.[3] The British ships remained at anchor until day-break on the 29th, when *Britannia* and *Vengeance*, towed by *Furious* and *Inflexible* made for English Bay. The others followed under sail, but anchored after *Arethusa* and *Rodney* grounded. The following day *Retribution* towed *Vengeance* up to the Bosphorus, and the other ships assembled at English Bay. Dundas boarded *Furious* and pressed on to interview Stratford, leaving Captain Graham in command. Shortly after passing the French off Gallipoli *Furious* ran aground, forcing Dundas to shift into *Tiger*. He arrived off Therapia early on 1 November, hours before the advanced squadron, and Hamelin.

It had been intended that the advanced squadron would make a rapid passage of the Dardanelles to reinforce the Turks. The policy of leaving the squadrons at Besika had been reduced to a shambles by the weather. The British ships had been in some difficulty, although

Dundas still found time to laugh at French seamanship.[4] His first action on arriving off Constantinople was to recall Captain Spratt, *Spitfire* to assist *Furious*. Spratt had been surveying the Prince's Islands in the Sea of Marmora as a refuge for the local Christians in the event of a religious riot. Dundas excused the chaotic movement by referring to the lack of reliable charts above the entrance of the Dardanelles.[5]

The straggling advance of the squadrons demonstrated the central weakness of the western diplomatic position during the early stages of the crisis. Relying on naval forces as the symbol and potential executor of their policies required those forces to be a credible deterrent. If Russia intended an amphibious operation naval forces were credible, but only if they could reach the Bosphorus quickly. Most assumed it would take no more than forty-eight hours to summon the ships from Besika, and although Walker made it clear such a delay would be fatal, the risk had been taken to preserve the hope of a diplomatic settlement. Russia, by occupying the Principalities, indicated she had given up the amphibious plan, looking for prolonged occupation or an attack across the Danube. Against this the squadrons alone could effect little, indeed it was doubtful they could even secure their own retreat if the Turks were defeated. Troops had to be sent to preserve the credibility of western diplomacy. The move to the Bosphorus emphasised Walker's views; the advanced ships took nine days to reach Constantinople. Had they been summoned in an emergency they would have arrived to find the city in Russian hands.

Dundas, Hamelin and de la Tour met at Stratford's residence on the evening of 1 November and decided to call up the squadrons.[6] Shifting back into *Furious* the following day in Beicos Bay, the fleet anchorage in the Bosphorus, Dundas proposed sending a combined force of six steamers into the Euxine on the 13th.[7] He was already on bad terms with Stratford.[8] On the 7th Dundas sent four steamers back for the battleships at English Bay, keeping *Furious* and *Niger* at Beicos to tow *Albion* and *Vengeance* into the Black Sea if the Russians attacked.[9] The squadrons were at Beicos by the 13th, Lyons arriving aboard *Terrible* on the 24th.

With the squadrons of Britain, France, Turkey and Egypt at Beicos, Constantinople was safe from any naval attack, and western concern focused on the Dardanelles. Dundas proposed landing his marines to take the batteries in reverse rather than run down the channel under fire.[10] General Macintosh, with some experience of Turkey, convinced Stratford that the Gallipoli Isthmus could be fortified to hold the European shore.[11] While this became western policy Stratford and Clarendon, fearful the French would keep the forts after the crisis, wanted to send British troops.[12] Graham hoped this would not be necessary, at least until the spring.[13] On a more positive note Stratford had been encouraged to consider British strategic options. Although concerned by problems in Albania he believed it should be possible to blockade the Russian ports and, influenced by Slade, to attack Sevastopol and Nicolaiev.[14] Under pressure from Graham to obtain more intelligence on the Black Sea, Clarendon wanted to send a steamer, but renewed hopes for negotiations persuaded him to keep the squadrons in the Bosphorus. Having sent up the ships his only thought was to stop Stratford using them.[15] Stratford had been more concerned to keep the Turks quiet by threatening to withhold the ships, but once ordered to bring them up he agreed to have them all, although no force of western or Turkish ships should enter the Euxine. The Turks immediately decided to send their fleet into the Black Sea. As a concession to the season they would leave behind their three-deckers, but the remaining ships would cruise round the coast, attacking any Russians they might encounter. Stratford was furious. Knowing the Turkish ships were inexperienced and inferior in number to the Russians he sent his dragoman, Pisani, with a protest that spoke eloquently of Turkey's real independence:

I shall not order up the remainder of the squadrons, till I hear from Reshid that the intended enterprise, *insofaras sailing vessels are concerned*, is abandoned.
You must tell his Highness once and for all that we will not be drawn in the *wake* of the Porte, and that if they want our help they must be content to respect our opinions.[16]

The naval simile was, even if unintentional, a brilliant use of language, although wasted on Reshid. The distinction between steamers and sailing vessels was significant; steamers, needed to carry supplies, could avoid trouble. Stratford also secured a promise that Omer would not be allowed to cross the Danube again after his victories at Kalafat and Oltenitza. The weather had already stopped serious fighting.

Dundas's proposal to send six steamers into the Euxine on the 13th was declined by Hamelin, who had very few serviceable steamers after towing his battlefleet up the Straits. The Ambassadors wanted to retrieve their Consuls from Varna, but to avoid embarrassing Hamelin nothing was done.[17] Stratford's policy, and with the squadrons at Beicos his influence was decisive, still worked for peace. He would allow only a short sortie up the European coast of Turkey. When news of this proposed cruise to Varna reached London the ministers condemned him for trying to start a war. Graham was quick to apportion him the 'undivided responsibility', although Palmerston called for the entire fleet to be sent.[18]

This incident encouraged both governments to examine the orders of the Admirals and Ambassadors, a long overdue symbol of mutual trust that helped cement western co-operation. Graham, not alone in his suspicion of France, was alarmed by the appointment of General Baraguay d'Hilliers to replace de la Tour, briefing Lyons on the subject. Palmerston disagreed, but Clarendon found Graham's argument convincing, and more in line with Stratford's warnings of French attempts to occupy Constantinople. Realising the link between French internal problems and international policy, he was certain that if the price of bread kept rising Louis Napoleon would abandon Britain.[19] Worrying intelligence was coming out of France: 'The naval preparations of France are *prodigious*, there has been nothing like the present activity in their dockyards for a long time past. 80 gun screw steamers are the ships they are chiefly occupied with.'[20] The subject matter reveals the source of the concern. The French had their own grounds for complaint, primarily the casual manner in which the British advanced ships had sailed straight past them while they waited outside the Bosphorus.[21] Fortunately the incident blew over. To clear the atmosphere the French proposed a protocol establishing the status quo as western policy, and this was adopted on 26 November. Palmerston objected that Turkey might recover Circassia, while Graham refused to rely on French good faith, even after Sinope.[22] Anglo–French co-operation was an uneasy product of the Czar's inept diplomacy; the war was only a distraction for rivalry. The naval race continued throughout.

The cabinet consensus favoured using the squadrons to put pressure on the Turks to accept a diplomatic settlement. Palmerston observed that it would be impossible to bully them, but Aberdeen was desperate, clutching at straws to preserve the hope of peace, convinced Stratford and the Turks would bring on a war. Clarendon was disenchanted with Aberdeen and alarmed by public opinion;

Graham suspected Palmerston and Stratford were acting in collusion to start a war.[23] The Government was over-blessed with leaders. Palmerston and Russell both wanted to take over, while Graham would do anything to remain at Aberdeen's right hand, which was as near the top as his courage would allow.[24] There could be no harmony in such a cabinet. Aberdeen's inability to command, and his gradual retreat before Palmerston only increased the tension. Russell's new Reform Bill galvanised Palmerston to act. He pressed Aberdeen to send the squadrons into the Euxine, take control and warn the Russians not to send out a ship.[25] Aberdeen realised Palmerston wanted to use his popular position on the Eastern Question to snuff out the Reform Bill, and effectively invited him to resign, which he did on 13 December. Graham was anxious to replace him, before events in the Black Sea forced his policies on the cabinet, but Russell and Sir George Grey refused to take his place. Cabinet politics were profoundly altered when Sinope made Palmerston's analysis of Russian policy irresistible. Russian gunfire secured his return to office on Christmas Eve, modified the Reform Bill and united the cabinet.[26]

In the Euxine the naval war began in mid November with the capture of two Ottoman steamers and the bombardment of Batoum by a Russian squadron. However it appeared that the fighting would, as on land, be restricted to skirmishing. Encouraged by the presence of the western squadrons the Turks sent out a frigate squadron, despite Stratford's ban. This force, seven frigates, three corvettes and two steamers under Osman Pasha, reached Sinope on 13 November. A steam squadron passed through, returning from a supply run to Batoum. Sinope was a dangerous location, only 180 miles from Sevastopol and 350 from the Bosphorus. The Russians had suffered a series of attacks across their Asian frontier and, fearing the Turks would incite a rising in Circassia, decided to destroy the frigate squadron. Vice-Admiral Nakhimov, at sea with three 84-gun ships, located the Turks before recalling the remainder of his force from Sevastopol; three 120-gun ships and two frigates joined him off Sinope on 27 November. Osman made little effort to prepare his forces and did not try to escape. At 11.30 on the 30th the Russians moved in, overwhelming the Turkish ships, apart from one steamer which was ordered to escape. The Russians left the anchorage on 2 December. Sinope was a clumsy, brutal battle in which a frigate squadron was destroyed by battleships. Contemporary opinion fastened onto the imbalance of forces and labelled it the 'massacre of Sinope'. The Russians were at war, and perfectly justified in their actions.[27]

News of the battle, carried by the steamer *Taif*, reached the Bosphorus late on 2 December. While largely conjectural, it was clear that a disaster had occurred. Dundas wanted to sortie out and destroy the Russian fleet, but feared Stratford would not allow this and was alarmed at the idea of lying at Beicos when the Turks had been beaten.[28] Stratford initially agreed, but at the conference of the 3rd supported Baraguay's plan for two steamers to confirm the facts before deciding what should be done. If the reports were true he would send the entire squadron.[29] Dundas was annoyed, particularly when Stratford claimed that only a Russian landing would signal war. *Retribution* and *Mogador*, Hamelin's only serviceable steamer, left at 19.45 on the 4th with instructions to avoid hostilities. Later *Fury* and the despatch boat *Heron* went to Varna to recover the Consuls and report on the shipping.[30] Hamelin revealed that his force was not fit to cruise in the Euxine during the winter, although he would sortie to meet the Russians. As Baraguay supported Hamelin Stratford was annoyed; unless he could send the squadrons to sea, his influence with the Turks would be reduced.[31] At the conference of the 7th aboard *Britannia* both Admirals agreed to a sortie, but opposed cruising for no particular object. Dundas argued for the use of a steam squadron, to avoid the worst of the seasonal dangers. Lyons agreed it was dangerous to send ships for political, rather than military tasks.[32] Stratford was trying to impose an armistice, in the process he was starting a war with Dundas.[33] The steamers from Varna reported the fortress strong and well armed, but lacking a garrison.

Retribution and *Mogador* arrived at midnight on the 9th, crowded with wounded sailors. Drummond's report provided details of the battle, while the wounded sailors produced a powerful effect on the Turks.[34] Stratford ordered Dundas to cruise between Varna and Sinope on the 11th, something the Admirals had advised against. The order only reached Dundas on the 13th, and he requested 'clear and precise instructions as to the nature and extent of the service to be performed', so that he, as the senior naval officer, could judge how it should be conducted.[35] Stratford, thwarted by the proud Admiral, never again exchanged a civil word with him. His reasons for ordering the squadrons were 'moral and political', matters which should not concern Dundas, and he demanded a more detailed explanation of the Admirals' objections. Dundas sent Hamelin's letter of the 7th, and expressed himself willing to go when desired.[36] Stratford felt the move was justified under his instructions of 8 October, and believed Dundas was being obstructive. He was working for peace, forming a new proposal with Baraguay and Reshid which offered to confirm existing Christian privileges, in return for the evacuation of the Principalities. The Austrian and Prussian Ambassadors acceded to this on the 12th and the Turkish Grand Council debated it on the 17th and 18th. In an effort to forestall this plan the Sheikh ul Islam and Mehemet Ali inspired another religious riot on the 21st.

Stratford used the fact that the squadrons had not sailed to press the Turks to accept his peace initiative; his report suggested this had been his intention. In fact Dundas should have sailed before the peace proposal was presented to the Turkish grand council, and before the riots broke out. The calm at Beicos was first disturbed by rumours on the 21st; *Inflexible* with three Turkish steamers went down to the city, *Retribution, Fury, Gomer* and *Magellan* already lay in the Golden Horn. The western steamers only returned to Beicos on the 26th, after Stratford called the bluff of the Turkish war party. The peace proposal was published in the Turkish Gazette on the 22nd.[37]

Having secured another peace initiative Stratford considered the possibility of war. Slade argued that Sevastopol, at the centre of the Euxine, gave the Russians a major strategic advantage. He proposed to counter this by moving the squadrons to Sinope, without considering how they could cover the Bosphorus, or the European coast. Stratford wanted to send the ships into the Euxine for political reasons and was only too pleased to find a policy he could press on Baraguay.[38] The French Ambassador preferred the Admiral's plan to send a steam squadron. Aware of the poor state of the French fleet Stratford did not order Dundas to go alone, to avoid a rupture. Instead he requested Dundas's opinion if the steamers, or the British squadron could defend the Turkish coast.[39] The urgency for the squadrons to move reflected the desire of the Turks to reinforce their Asiatic garrisons, which could now only be done with western escort. Baraguay received instructions to send the French squadron on Christmas day; Stratford could now send the ships to support and thereby keep control over the Turks. If he did not send the ships the Turks would go alone.[40] Dundas had no desire to cruise, although he was ready to meet the Russians in battle alone and considered Sinope unsafe. Stratford was annoyed Dundas did not propose to take his entire force; his orders of the 27th pointedly avoided the issue. The fleet was to cruise along the Asian shore, assess Sinope as an anchorage, despite Dundas's objections, and deliver a notification of western policy – in effect, a warning to keep clear of Turkey – at Sevastopol. Coal and pilots would be provided by the Turks. Dundas asked the obvious question, should he take all his ships, leaving the Bosphorus unprotected; Stratford replied that he must send 'enough'. Dundas prepared a detailed statement demonstrating that a steam squadron would be more effective, leaving the battlefleet in the Bosphorus ready to sortie out to meet the Russians. If the main fleet went into the Euxine it would be damaged and miss the opening of the campaign season. The following day, the 30th, these objections became irrelevant when Baraguay ordered Hamelin to take a larger force. The two Admirals agreed on five battleships and six steamers each. Dundas used his minute to alert the Admiralty to the disastrous possibilities of Stratford's request. Stratford wanted the entire fleet; Dundas reinforced by *Queen*, *London* and *Agamemnon*, elected to leave the slow-sailing *Trafalgar*, with *Arethusa* and *Niger*. Stratford's real object was to escort a Turkish convoy to Trebizond and Batoum, claiming Constantinople no longer needed the security of the fleets, which was untrue. His overriding concern for the Asian coast could only be met by stationing the fleets at Sinope. He did not reflect on the equally exposed, and strategically vital, European coast where a Russian landing would outflank the Danube front. Dundas could see the influence of Slade, and pressed Graham to have him disciplined.[41] The entrance of the fleets on the 31st was prevented by a combination of gale force winds, thick cloud and rain, worsening after midday. The Turks failed to send pilots, because their ships were not ready. Eventually the ships left half full. The Admirals had no idea they were coming.[42]

News of Sinope reached London late on the 11th; Clarendon wished Stratford had sent the fleet immediately, Palmerston believed the time for war had arrived.[43] Graham anticipated a naval campaign had already begun and, having no faith in the French alliance, urged Aberdeen to replace Palmerston.[44] Aberdeen and Graham wanted to treat Russian troops crossing the Balkan mountains as the signal for war, whilst the Whigs preferred the strategically more secure Danube. The Peelite position made the fall of Constantinople almost inevitable, forcing the fleets back to the Mediterranean. Before the hesitant policy of Aberdeen could do any lasting damage the newspapers made it clear that Sinope was an affront that must be avenged. Peace and cautious measures were rejected by the nation. Palmerston's policy, now urged by Russell, was in the ascendant.[45] Russell wanted to take over as Prime Minister. When Aberdeen tried to delay active measures he threatened to resign unless Russia was officially notified that her ships would be intercepted.[46] Clarendon, having argued for Four Power co-operation as late as the 14th, agreed.[47] Louis Napoleon increased the pressure, realising he could turn Sinope to advantage to assert French military power and cement an alliance with Britain. Walewski read a dispatch demanding all Russian warships be intercepted and sent back to Sevastopol on the 19th; the French even threatened to act alone. Aberdeen caved in, lamenting the inevitability of war. Walewski then demanded Anglo–French protection be extended to Turkish shipping. The cabinet accepted this on the 22nd, in return for France supporting the latest peace proposals.[48] Palmerston returned to the cabinet in triumph, and resumed the leadership of the war party.[49]

With the commitment to enter the Black Sea it was vital to consider the strategic implications. Palmerston argued that the fleets should establish command of the sea, while the island of Karrack in the Persian Gulf be captured to prevent the Shah of Persia adding to Turkish problems. Diplomatic pressure sufficed to restrain the Shah, although instructions were sent to India.[50] Believing the Czar was committed to war Clarendon accepted Palmerston's advice, urging Stratford to take control of the Euxine.[51] Graham and Walker prepared a Black Sea strategy based on command of the sea, secured by an immediate attack on Sevastopol: 'the entire destruction of Sevastopol with its naval and military Establishments, and all their contents, before the Baltic opens in the spring, [is] an object of urgent and primary importance . . . so that we may have no more in our time at least, of Russian naval supremacy in the Black sea'. Other operations were to be subordinate. Dundas was to act on the outbreak of war, unless he considered it a 'desperate' venture. Significantly, Graham wanted the battlefleet to remain in the Bosphorus, unless the Russians were at sea, ready to strike the decisive blow.[52] Clarendon agreed, counselling Aberdeen not to inform Brunnow, or Stratford.[53] Granville wondered if there were any better targets and suggested leaving the decision to Dundas.[54] Dundas wanted to clear up the forts on the Circassian coast.[55] Aberdeen only wanted him to restrain the Turks.[56] To prepare for Sevastopol Graham and Clarendon agreed to send Engineer officers, and Clarendon even suggested informing the French.[57]

It would be wrong to credit Graham with the Sevastopol plan. Walker's hand can be seen in all aspects of Dundas's instructions; Graham accepted the plan as the centre of his strategy. Although much influenced by the Napoleonic war, Graham was not a student of strategy; his plans were based on assimilating the accumulated wisdom of others. The basic theme was the decisive blow as an alternative to prolonged war. Sevastopol was only a substitute for Cherbourg, indicating the strategic planning already in hand for a French war. It was the symbol and centre of Russian seapower, insofar as it related to the present crisis. At this stage Graham was the only man in the cabinet with a comprehensive view of the situation. Destroying Russian Black Sea power in time to switch resources to the Baltic for the spring reflected both breadth of vision and concern for scarce resources.

Despite the decision to send the fleets into the Black Sea the strategic position of the allies remained unsatisfactory. The time for active operations, particularly with sailing ships, had passed. Furthermore, seapower could do nothing to stop a Russian advance across the Danube, something most ministers believed the Turks could not resist. Although Sevastopol had been identified as the key to the theatre there was no reliable intelligence on the fortifications, garrison, or even the fleet. This made Graham's call for an early attack impracticable; no responsible officer would make the attempt, and Dundas was a very responsible Admiral. In addition the Baltic fleet had to be covered and Cronstadt was reported to be impregnable. Graham's confidence was little more than a facade, for he never had more than twelve battleships in home waters during 1853 to meet up to thirty Russian ships. Reluctance to call for more money and a shortage of seamen were in part to blame. The French could offer no help as they were equally short of men and had fewer effective ships. Louis Napoleon's interest in the crisis was European, rather than particular, he looked to increase French prestige and break down the 1815 system; every step toward war took Britain further from Austria, Prussia and the settlement of Europe they represented. By moving to Besika, under French pressure, the British made a moral commitment to Turkey that would only end when

Russia evacuated the Principalities. If Russia did not move in the spring the western powers would be forced to act, they could not wait forever at Beicos with Russia menacing Constantinople. The crisis was further from a settlement in December 1853 than ever, but Graham's strategy, the only set of ideas even remotely worthy of the name, was never going to force Russia to concede. Only when Sevastopol fell did the western powers realise they were committed to achieving a fundamental reduction in Russian power, something that the destruction of a naval arsenal could not justify.

Notes

1 Dundas to Graham 15 Oct. 1853: Gr. CW2.
2 Stratford to Dundas 16 , 20 Oct. 1853: DND/9 f102; Dundas Journal 21 Oct. 1853: ADM 52/243.
3 Dundas to Admiralty 22 Oct. 1853 no. 340: ADM 1/5617.
4 Dundas to Admiralty 31 Oct. 1853: DND/4 p. 373; Dundas to Graham 31 Oct. 1853: Gr. CW2.
5 Dundas Journal 1 Nov. 1853; ADM 50/243; Dundas to Graham 1 Nov. 1853; Gr. CW2.
6 Stratford to Clarendon 5 Nov. 1853 no. 330: F.O. 78/940.
7 Dundas to Stratford 4 Nov. in Dundas to Graham 5 Nov. 1853: Gr.CW2.
8 Stratford to Dundas, Dundas to Stratford 6 Nov. 1853: DND/9 f113
9 Dundas to Admiralty 7 Nov. 1853 no. 353: ADM 1/5617; Dundas to Admiralty 16 Nov. 1853: DND/4 p. 384.
10 Stratford to Clarendon 22 Oct. 1853: Cl. Dep. C10 f391.
11 Dundas to Graham 17 Nov. 1853: Gr. CW2.
12 Stratford to Clarendon 25 Oct. 1853: F.O. 352/36/1 f179–93; Stratford to Clarendon 18 Oct. 1853: Cl. Dep. C10 f169–77.
13 Graham to Clarendon 29 Oct. 1853: Cl. Dep. C4 f229–39; Clarendon to Graham 29 Oct. 1853: Gr. B.114.
14 Clarendon to Stratford 22 Aug. 1853: F.O. 352/36/1 f137; Stratford to Clarendon 22 Oct. 1853 no. 308: F.O. 78/939; Slade to Foster (Palmerston's office) 4 Oct. 1853: R.A. G5 f119.
15 Clarendon to Stratford 8, 10 Oct. 1853: F.O. 352/36/1 f149–64.
16 Pisani to Stratford 3 Nov. 1853 encl. in fn. 6; Stratford to Pisani 4, 5 Nov. 1853 encl. in Stratford to Clarendon 5 Nov. 1853 no. 331: F.O. 78/940.
17 Dundas to Graham 11, 25 Nov. 1853 encl. Stratford to Dundas 11 Nov. 1853: Gr. CW2; Stratford to Clarendon 24 Nov. 1853 no. 360: F.O. 78/940.
18 Aberdeen to the Queen 19 Nov. 1853: Add. 43,048 f26; Aberdeen to Clarendon 20 Nov. 1853: Add, 43,188 f323; Graham to Clarendon 1 Dec. 1853: Cl. Dep. C4 f249–254; Palmerston to Clarendon 25 Nov. 1853: Cl. Dep. C3 f322–3; Russell to Clarendon 28 Nov. 1853; *ibid.* f509–12.

19 Graham to Clarendon 27 Oct. 1853: Cl. Dep. C4 f227–8; Palmerston to Clarendon 27 Oct. 1853: Cl. Dep. C3 f209–11; Clarendon to Stratford 18, 29 Nov. 1853: F.O.352/36/1 f209, 233.
20 Clarendon to Stratford 8 Dec. 1853: *ibid.* f235.
21 Cowley to Clarendon 24, 28 Nov. 1853: F.O. 519/304; Graham to Clarendon 25 Nov. 1853: Cl. Dep. C4 f238.
22 STANMORE, Lord, *A Memoir of Sidney Herbert* (London, 1906, two vols), vol. 1, p. 215; Palmerston to Clarendon 2 Dec. 1853: Cl. Dep. C3 f234–5; Graham to Clarendon 13 Dec. 1853: Cl. Dep. C4 f270–3.
23 Aberdeen to the Queen 7 Oct. 1853: Add. 43,047 f301; Clarendon to Aberdeen 4 Nov. 1853: Add. 43,188 f301–4; Graham to Clarendon 25 Oct. 1853: Cl. Dep. C4 f225–6.
24 Graham to Russell 11 Dec. 1853: PRO 30/22/11B f454–7.
25 Palmerston to Aberdeen 10 Dec. 1853: Add. 43,069 f168–73.
26 Aberdeen to Graham 10 Dec. 1853: Gr. B.115; Graham to Aberdeen 13 Dec. 1853: Add. 43,191 f169; Aberdeen to Russell 19 Dec. 1853; *Aberdeen Correspondence 1852–5*, p. 418; CONACHER, pp. 215–32 on the cabinet crisis.
27 Dundas to Admiralty 9 rec. 27 Dec. 1853 no. 392: ADM 1/5626; Drummond to Dundas 8 Dec. encl. in above; Stratford to Clarendon 12 Dec. 1853 no. 380: F.O. 78/941b; ANDERSON, R.C., *Naval Wars in the Levant* (Liverpool, 1953), pp. 578–82; SLADE, Rear Admiral, *Turkey and the Crimean War* (London, 1867), pp. 139–51.
28 Dundas to Graham 3 Dec. 1853: Gr. CW2; Dundas to Walker 28 Dec. 1853: WALKER.
29 Stratford to Clarendon 4 Dec. 1853 no. 368: F.O.78/941b.
30 Dundas to Graham 4 Dec. 1853: Gr. CW2; Dundas to Admiralty 4 rec. 20 Dec. 1853 no. 387: ADM 1/5617.
31 Dundas to Graham 5 Dec. 1853: Gr. CW2; Stratford to Clarendon 5 Dec. 1853: Cl. Dep. C10 f475–9; Stratford to Clarendon 2 Jan. 1854: F.O. 352/37/2; Stratford to Clarendon 5 Dec. 1853 no. 371: F.O. 78/941b.
32 Dundas to Graham 7–9 Dec. 1853: Gr. CW2; Lyons to Admiralty 7 Dec. 1853: EARDLEY-WILMOT pp. 133–4.
33 Dundas to Graham 12 Dec. 1853: Gr. CW2.
34 Dundas to Admiralty 8–9 rec. 27 Dec. 1853 no. 392–3: ADM 1/5617.
35 Dundas Journal 13 Dec. 1853: ADM 50/243.
36 Stratford to Clarendon 15, 17 Dec. 1853 no. 382 and 392: F.O. 78/941b, encl. Stratford to Dundas 14 Dec. and Dundas to Stratford 16 Dec. 1853.
37 SAAB, pp. 124–5.
38 Slade to Stratford 15 Dec. and Stratford to Slade 17 Dec. encl. in Stratford to Clarendon 20 Dec. 1853 no. 395: F.O. 78/941b.
39 Stratford to Clarendon 23 Dec. 1853 no. 398: *ibid.*; Stratford to Clarendon 23 Dec. 1853: Cl. Dep. C10 f509–10; Stratford to Dundas 23 Dec. 1853 encl. in above.
40 Stratford to Clarendon 24 Dec. 1853 no. 400: F.O. 78/941b; Stratford to Clarendon 25 Dec. 1853: Cl. Dep. C10 f528.

41 Stratford to Clarendon 15, 17, 31 Dec. 1853 no. 383, 393, 412, 414: F.O. 78/941b encl. Dundas-Stratford Correspondence 25–30 Dec. 1853 especially Dundas's Minute of letter 29 Dec.; Stratford to Clarendon 26 Dec. 1853: Cl. Dep. C10 f530–1; Dundas to Graham 15–17 Dec. 1853: Gr. CW2; Dundas to Walker 28 Dec. 1853: WALKER.

42 Dundas Journal 31 Dec. 1853 and 1 Jan. 1854: ADM 50/243; SAAB, p. 129.

43 Palmerston to Aberdeen 10 Dec. 1853: Add. 43,069 f168–72; Palmerston to Clarendon 11 Dec. 1853: Bdlds. GC/CL f1375; Clarendon to Stratford 12 Dec. 1853 no. 322: F.O. 78/941b; Clarendon to Palmerston 13 Dec. 1853: Bdlds. GC/CL f548; Palmerston to Clarendon 13 Dec. 1853: Cl. Dep. C3 f246.

44 Graham to Aberdeen 13 Dec. 1853: Add. 43,191 f169; Graham to Clarendon 13 Dec. 1853: Cl. Dep. C4 f270–3.

45 Russell to Clarendon 14 Dec. 1853: Cl. Dep. C3 f559–61; Russell to Graham 15 Dec. 1853: Gr. B.114.

46 Aberdeen to the Queen 17 Dec. 1853: Add. 43,048 f80–1; Russell to Clarendon 18 Dec. 1853: Cl. Dep. C3 f567–8.

47 Clarendon to Russell 14 Dec. 1853: PRO 30/22/11B f221; Clarendon to Aberdeen 18 Dec. 1853: Add. 43,188 f359.

48 CASE, L.M., *French opinion on War and Diplomacy during the Second Empire* (Philadelphia, 1954), pp. 19–23; Aberdeen to Graham 19 Dec. 1853: Gr. B.114; Aberdeen to Clarendon 6 Dec. 1853: Cl. Dep. C4 f139; Clarendon to Graham 22 Dec. 1853: Gr. B.114; Aberdeen to the Queen 22 Dec. 1853: Add. 43,048 f99–100.

49 Palmerston to Aberdeen 23 Dec. 1853: Add. 43,0699 f189–90.

50 Palmerston to Clarendon 13 Dec. 1853: Cl. Dep. C3 f246; Graham to Newcastle 8 Jan. 1854: Gr. B.115; SAAB, pp. 122–3.

51 Clarendon to Stratford 17 Dec. 1853L: F.O. 352/36/1 f247–53; Clarendon to Aberdeen 18 Dec. 1853: Add. 43,188 f359; Clarendon to Graham 21 Dec. 1853: Gr. B.114; Clarendon to Palmerston 26 Dec. 1853: Bdlds. GC/CL f550.

52 Graham to Dundas 24 Dec. 1853: DND/9 f129; Graham précis of instructions to Dundas Dec. 1853: Gr. CW2.

53 Clarendon to Graham 25 Dec. 1853: Gr. B.114; Clarendon to Aberdeen 24 Dec. 1853: Add. 43,188 f366; Clarendon to Stratford 24 Dec. 1853: F.O. 352/36/1 f255–60.

54 Earl Granville to Clarendon 25 Dec. 1853: Cl. Dep. C4 f276.

55 Dundas to Graham 17 Dec. 1853: Gr. CW2.

56 Aberdeen to Graham 28 Dec. 1853: Gr. B.114.

57 Graham to Clarendon 28 Dec. 1853: Cl. Dep. C4 f276; Graham to Raglan 30 Dec. 1853: Gr. B.114; Clarendon to Graham 30 Dec. 1853: *ibid.*

6

Preparing for war

The conflict between Stratford and Dundas for control of the fleet during December 1853 reflected contrasting views of British policy. Stratford worked for a civilian/diplomatic solution to the crisis, using the squadron as an effective bargaining counter; Dundas looked to preserve his ships for a war which might open with an assault on Sevastopol. In correspondence the Ambassador adopted a tone of intellectual superiority which was both unjustified and offensive. Dundas fully understood the dominance of politics over strategy, and only required guidance on the policy objectives to control his fleet accordingly. However Stratford did not consider the senior seagoing officer in the Royal Navy capable of forming such judgements, preferring to make the decisions for him. Their relationship was not improved by the strict injunction to act in concert with their French colleagues. Essentially the Government intended that Stratford decide the policy, Dundas the method in which it should be conducted. Poor drafting of the instructions of 8 October gave Stratford some excuse for thinking he was the final arbiter on both points. The French instructions were similarly imprecise. This clash of wills was a problem peculiar to periods of armed diplomacy when neither peace nor war could claim primacy among the alternative methods of effecting Government policy. Stratford was Dundas's nominal superior, but the Government never intended that he should order the fleet into the Euxine against the stated opinion of the Admiral. The division of blame was simple; Dundas obeyed the letter and spirit of his instructions, Stratford the letter only. He escaped censure because the ministers still hoped his efforts would secure peace, and because to do so would only make matters worse for Dundas.[1]

The combined fleets moved from Beicos at 09.30 on 3 January, but were forced to anchor two hours later by thick fog. This allowed

Stratford to pass orders to protect the Turkish ships as well as their territory: 'It is only by obtaining the complete command of the Black Sea that the policy of Her Majesty's Government and that of France can be carried out.'[2] The fleets finally entered the Euxine on the 4th in overwhelming strength: eighteen battleships, one frigate and twelve steamers. One British frigate and three steamers remained in the Bosphorus. At daylight on the 5th the five Turkish steamers joined, carrying only 1,000 troops and 500 cases of powder for Batoum and Trebizond; Dundas and Hamelin were far from pleased.[3] *Retribution* parted company for Sevastopol at 07.00. The weather was not suitable for sailing ships to cruise in company: there were two collisions before the fleets arrived at Sinope on the 6th. A steam force under Lyons and de Tinian escorted the Turks: they were to use force as a last resort. *Sampson* and *Mogador* went ahead on the 7th, the remainder, *Agamemnon*, *Sans Pareil*, *Charlemagne*, *Terrible*, *Gomer*, *Descartes* and the Turks following on the 8th. Calling at Trebizond and Batoum on the 10th and 11th, the squadron returned to Sinope on the 13th.[4]

Drummond's mission, carrying notice of western policy to Sevastopol, proved the most productive part of the cruise. On the morning of the 6th he passed the Chersonese lighthouse in thick fog and entered the harbour, only stopping when Fort Constantine fired a blank gun. This left him in the fairway, midway between Forts Constantine and Alexander in ten fathoms. The Russians refused to accept his letter until he withdrew one mile; having done this Drummond waited ninety minutes for the quarantine officer, making inspections from the mast-head. He was informed that as Menshikov, Governor of the Crimea, and Nakhimov were absent there would be no reply. *Retribution* reached Sinope early on the 8th. With five battleships and one or two frigates in harbour Drummond concluded that Nakhimov, with ten battleships, lay in Kaffa Bay. The fortifications mounted 722 guns, 383 of which covered the seaward approaches, with 250 aboard Rear-Admiral Istomine's squadron anchored at the head of the harbour. Most were 32-pounders, although there were some larger pieces. 'I consider the fortifications so strong as opposed to ships that it would be impossible to enter the Harbour and destroy the ships at anchor without the almost certain destruction of the attacking force.' While the harbour could easily be blockaded, only a large land force could capture the city. 'The North Side presented some favourable points for the disembarkation of troops under the ship's guns, and I think that in carrying the position of F fort [the Star Fort] on the heights, the place would fall immediately.' This first accurate report reinforced Dundas's opinion that the place was 'a second Gibraltar'.[5]

Lying at anchor amid the wreck of the Turkish squadron Dundas received new instructions from Stratford, suggesting the fleets remain there for the foreseeable future. Dundas demanded clarification. Was he to use force if the Russians attacked the Turks? He also complained about the unannounced arrival of the Turks and the small quantity of powder they carried. Dundas and Hamelin decided to return to the Bosphorus, sending word with the returning Turkish steamers on the 13th.[6] The fleets finally left on the 17th, after a long wait for suitable winds, just as Stratford was responding to Dundas's letter. As the Turks had more stores and men to transport to Asia he declined any responsibility for the early return of the fleets. Baraguay agreed, although the only reason advanced was the 'impression' an early return would create at Constantinople.[7] Dundas received this letter as the fleets came in sight of the Bosphorus. His reply was conclusive; Sinope was entirely useless as a fleet anchorage from its distance to leeward and lack of supplies, while the weather would soon reduce the western forces to a lower level than those of Russia. The cruise of the steam squadron had demonstrated how to exercise command of the sea, and would escort the Turks again once it had coaled.[8] Stratford was furious: 'I cannot conceal from you that the impression remaining on my mind is one of dissatisfaction and regret . . . I have no reason to suppose that Her Majesty's Government contemplated the postponement of the service until a fair season.'[9] After these sneering taunts there could never be a reconciliation between the two men. Dundas replied, stressing his minute of 29 December. Refusing to comment on the points raised, he sent the correspondence to the Admiralty with Lyons' concurrence, only commenting on the Ambassador's 'unusual style'.[10] Further friction arose from Stratford sending *Fury* to Odessa in Dundas's absence; she returned with her bows damaged by the ice that still sealed the harbour. Stratford's humour was not improved by a mild rebuke from Clarendon, making it clear the Government preferred Dundas's policy. He was advised to rely on the Admiral's for operational decisions, as an attack on Sevastopol was planned.[11] Graham set out the policy for the fleet until war broke out: 'you should watch

Sevastopol and the movements of the Russian Fleet with your frigates and steamers, while the great body of the combined force remained within the Bosphorus ready to move at a moment's notice'.[12] The ministers condemned Stratford, only Russell argued that Dundas must share the blame: 'If, instead of firing pellets from his ship he had gone to the Ambassador and had shewn him Graham's letters, Stratford could hardly have persisted.'[13] In fact Stratford blamed Graham for much of Dundas's caution. Stratford attempted to justify his conduct; Dundas tried to resign, although Graham persuaded him to stay.[14] Nothing was resolved, only the outbreak of war reduced the tension by separating the two men's spheres of action. The one solid result was the Government's acceptance of Dundas's strategy: the sailing battlefleet would lay in the Bosphorus while steamers exercised command. The Ambassadors would provide clear instructions of the service to be accomplished and rely on the Admirals' judgement.[15] Graham was concerned to avoid further trouble with Stratford, but that proved impossible.[16]

The major theme of the new strategy was demonstrated within days of the fleet reaching the Bosphorus: de Tinian aboard *Gomer*, with *Sane*, *Sampson* and *Firebrand*, left on the 27th cruising to Varna, before inspecting Sevastopol and Kaffa Bay. He returned on 5 February, almost certain the Russian fleet was at Sevastopol, though the weather had been too rough for a closer inspection. *Furious* and *Vauban* followed the same route in late February. Although the Russian fleet did not leave harbour after late January, Dundas and Hamelin had to keep checking. Stratford reported the Russians were at sea on 16 March, but his information proved unreliable.[17] Stratford also made regular requests to escort the Turks, which Dundas granted, although he properly refused to tow. Lyons took *Agamemnon*, *Sans Pareil*, *Charlemagne*, *Terrible*, *Highflyer*, *Mogador* and *Descartes* as far east as Batoum between 7 and 21 February, convoying sixteen Turkish ships commanded by Slade carrying 7,000 troops. Leaving the Turks to disembark, Lyons ran up the coast to Redoubt Kaleh to examine the forts on the Circassian coast, where Dundas intended to open his campaign.[18]

Steamers also maintained communications between Constantinople and the Danube front, via Varna. Few days passed without allied steamers moving along the European coast. Stratford also requested steamers to carry Turkish troops to Thessaly, where a Greek-inspired insurrection had to be put down. Dundas refused. He was short of steamers and the Turks had ships enough of their own. Three steamers were sent to Athens, but once the situation cooled they were replaced by the sailing frigate *Leander*.[19] Dundas also tried to curb Stratford's use of steamers for dispatches, pointing out that a voyage to Marseilles cost £1,500 for coal alone. As there were regular mail boats Dundas believed they should be used, even in the Euxine. To overcome these objections Stratford secured Turkish coal from the mines at Heraclia. With British assistance the mines provided some of the coal required by the allies in the theatre during the war, saving on transport tonnage. As logistic support would be vital to any campaign Dundas wanted a Transport and Victualling Agent at Constantinople.[20]

While Graham made the fundamental error of equating mere numbers of men and ships with an effective fleet, he did appreciate that the diplomatic position of the Baltic powers would be crucial in that theatre. Clarendon pressed for Swedish neutrality. Denmark and Sweden issued a joint declaration of strict neutrality on 5 January, the principal result being to close all fortified harbours to belligerents. Russia demanded that all harbours should be closed, or some given up to Russian garrisons, encouraging the Swedes to prepare for war and favour the western powers.[21] Graham believed Sweden would be useful. To conciliate her he was prepared to make concessions on the old and contentious issue of belligerent rights at sea, as part of his wider policy of avoiding complications with neutrals. Government policy, framed by Graham and Clarendon, was dominated by a concern to avoid annoying the Americans and Scandinavians. In cabinet discussions Graham played down the Baltic, arguing the arsenals would prove invulnerable, while a blockade would only annoy neutrals.[22]

In private Graham had a bolder policy, using the Swedish army and flotilla to supplement his Baltic force. Realising it would require more than a liberal policy on neutral rights to bring Sweden into the war he wanted a display of British power, and the offer to return Finland, to launch his 'darling project of a Northern Maritime Confederacy against Russia'.[23] The Reval battlesquadron would be the target; the defences of the port were not as formidable as those of Cronstadt and Sweaborg, while the Baltic ice recedes from the west, leaving Reval open at least two weeks before the Gulf of Finland. Palmerston, also eager to strike a blow in the north after the destruction of Sevastopol, suggesting the battlesquadrons at Reval and

Helsingfors, was discouraged by Graham's gloomy cabinet memorandum just as the First Lord confessed he had 'a nice little naval exploit in view', although he would not commit his thoughts to paper. Nelson had drawn up a similar plan fifty years before, and Graham certainly referred to it as the 'Nelson Touch' that would justify the appointment of Napier.[24] It was no coincidence that the allied ultimatum to Russia was timed to expire at the earliest date a British squadron could expect to reach Reval. Within days of presenting his cautious memorandum Graham began covert preparations, detailing the screw corvette *Miranda* to examine Reval and Port Baltic and calling for intelligence from the Foreign Office.[25] He even tried to secure French assistance, sending Walker to Paris in late February, without result.[26]

At the cabinet of 9 February Graham and Palmerston secured the appointment of Napier, despite some difference of opinion. Napier was only officially appointed on the 23rd, indicating Graham's reservations. He knew that while the Government would earn praise for selecting the right man Napier's conduct ashore was always liable to cause embarrassment. He intended to keep Napier quiet until he could be sent to sea.[27] Dundas, with long experience of Napier's conduct, was appalled.[28] Graham began to assemble his 'North Sea Fleet' long before he appointed Napier. Rear-Admiral Berkeley, the Second Naval Lord, urged him to call out the Coastguard in early January, but Graham, knowing Napier would accept the command, was content to rely on his popularity to fill up the ships.[29] The first public announcement came on 6 February, with the appointment of Rear-Admiral Chads, and the belated mobilisation of the Coastguard and Dockyard Riggers.[30] Napier called for an efficient fleet, a bounty and laying up the Royal Yacht as an example before his appointment, hoping to have his post confirmed so that he could drill his fleet. Graham merely advised him to resign if he was not satisfied.[31]

Napier's concern was well founded. The men entered without a bounty were of a very low standard; hardly any were seamen. These landsmen and Coastguard were used to fill up the battleships, and their Captains soon discovered the latter were in many cases no better seamen than the former. Graham's naval reserve had failed. There was also a serious shortage of junior officers, forcing the Admiralty to reduce the official complements by one-third and recall officers from the Black Sea. This did nothing to promote the formation of good crews. Napier had an early indication of the problem; when he temporarily hoisted his flag aboard *Princess Royal* on 27 February she was hard aground at Spithead.[32] The vital post of Captain of the Fleet, responsible for the equipment and efficiency of the force, proved difficult to fill, Napier's nominee, the Earl of Hardwicke being rejected on political grounds. Several officers refused to work with Napier, and only the personal request of Graham secured Commodore Sir Michael Seymour.[33] The problems resulted from the late date at which Graham mobilised the fleet. The ships of the 1853 Western squadron were still below strength in February 1854. Graham would not create a fleet or employ an Admiral of Napier's reputation until war was inevitable, fearing the financial and political consequences of a major mobilisation in peacetime.[34] Preparing a fleet for war required more than just assembling ships and men; the need was for well-drilled ships, practised at fleet evolutions and gunnery. In peacetime this would take at least twelve months, in war six might suffice, but nothing less would produce an efficient ship.[35] Had Graham been serious about taking the initiative in early 1854 he should have mobilised in the autumn of 1853 and sent the ships to sea. Without such preparations Reval was a dangerous delusion; Nelson would not have attempted it with raw crews, and nor would Napier. Palmerston called for a bounty, but if he raised the matter with Graham he had no more success than Berkeley.[36]

The shape of the fleet also reflected Graham's desire to prepare at short notice. The decision for a steam battlefleet, taken in mid-1853, forced him to wait until early 1854 before the ships were completed, although that did not excuse the failure to have trained crews ready. However, battleships were not the only type required. They could control the deep water, but for offensive measures a flotilla was essential, as Martin had warned. Mortars were considered obsolete, there were no mortar vessels in the Navy and no orders were placed for gunboats or mortar vessels, although half-hearted attempts were made to buy some gunboats being built on the Thames for Brazil.[37] Graham expected these requirements would be met by a Swedish alliance, and in the Black Sea by purchasing local craft. Under Walker's influence he was reluctant to shift resources from the steam battlefleet. In addition the Navy generally had a low opinion of flotilla craft. Beaufort, anticipating the Russians would remove the navigational marks, called for two shallow draught surveying vessels to accompany the fleet. In an effort to find pilots Graham sent *Hecla* to the Great Belt with eight men from Trinity House, but their experience was necessarily restricted to the shipping lanes. This forced Napier to rely on local pilots, or Beaufort's surveyors. The Hydrographer's men, Bartholomew Sulivan, *Lightning*, and Henry Otter, *Firefly*, fully justified his faith. Later Captain William 'Nemesis' Hall was sent in *Hecla*.[38] While all officers had some experience of hydrographic work and Beaufort sent reliable Russian charts, it was necessary for the surveyors to check them, which inhibited offensive operations.

As the campaign season approached the Admiralty dispatched a large volume of intelligence to Napier unsorted, emphasising the value of a staff, but, in contrast to Dundas and Lyons, Napier was unable to delegate, revealing a weakness in his professional development. While still at St Petersburg Seymour reported new batteries and works at Cronstadt, but had no news of the Reval battlesquadron.[39] Graham sent *Miranda* ahead of the battlefleet and, on the eve of the fleet's departure from Spithead, directions for the attack on Reval. While Graham savoured the fruits of success, a Swedish alliance and the capture of Aland, one of Semour's juniors informed Napier that the Reval squadron had been withdrawn to Sweaborg in the autumn.[40]

Before his departure Napier was fêted at the Reform Club on 7 March, Palmerston and Graham making wild speeches. By contrast Napier was a model of restraint: *The Times'* claim that he promised to be 'in Cronstadt, or in Hell' within a month was pure invention. The editor of *The Times*, Delane, believed he had secured Napier's appointment and expected some reward. His own views were amateur, and bloodthirsty: 'Sir C. Napier is sent out to do all the harm he can to the Russians, and a dozen or two ships of the line and a few fortresses battered to pieces, and several thousands killed or wounded will be the probable, and indeed the wished for result.'[41]

The influence of such nonsense on strategic policy was greater than it should have been, as Napier realised. His reply to an heroic address by the Mayor of Portsmouth was to urge the people 'not to expect too much', hardly the sentiments of the man who had made the 'Cronstadt or Hell' speech three days before. His caution was only reinforced by a conversation with Byam Martin.[42]

The fleet left earlier than expected, because the Baltic Consuls reported the ice was breaking up a fortnight ahead of the normal season. This caused Napier to miss a Royal Levee, and Corry's new flagship, *Neptune*, to miss the tide. Although the allied ultimatum did not expire until the end of the month it was essential no Russian ship should leave the Baltic, although that was hardly possible.[43] It is more probable Graham wanted to be certain Napier was in place for the Reval attack. Napier led the first squadron out from Spithead on the afternoon of 10 March:

Table 4: The Baltic fleet, 10 March 1854

		Guns
Steam battleships		
Duke of Wellington	131	flagship
Royal George	120	
St Jean d'Acre	101	
Princess Royal	91	
Steam blockships		
Edinburgh	60	Rear-Admiral Chads
Ajax	60	
Blenheim	60	
Hogue	60	
Screw frigates		
Imperieuse	51	
Arrogant	47	
Amphion	34	
Tribune	30	
Paddle frigates		
Leopard	16	Rear-Admiral Plumridge
Dragon	16	
Valorous	16	

Cressy, an 80-gun steam battleship, and *Hecla* joined in the Downs that evening. Napier's instructions were to rendezvous at Wingo Sound, on the Coast of Sweden outside the Straits. The Foreign Office orders were to stop any Russian warships leaving, by force if necessary, and offer British protection to the Scandinavians.[44] Although Britain was not at war these instructions, and those issued in the Black Sea, reflected a political situation in which there was no longer any hope of peace, the timing of war being dependent only on the strategic necessities so apparent to Graham.

Allied policy on neutral rights at sea was based on liberal principles. A war against Russia did not justify attempting to uphold the contentious, extreme policy of the Napoleonic Wars. As Russian mercantile traffic was small, and largely coastal, Graham and Clarendon agreed to allow the neutral flag to cover all goods except contraband of war, without prejudice for the future. The definition of contraband was now believed to cover steam engines and possibly coal, although fortunately for Britain the latter was not conceded by Sweden. Graham considered that for the present conflict the temporary sacrifice of the old policy would be compensated by a strict and close blockade.[45] The value of economic warfare against Russia brought forth all shades of opinion. Clarendon thought it would be decisive, ruining merchants and forcing the Government to make peace; others argued dependence on Russian raw materials would make Britain suffer more than Russia. The principal items of trade – hemp, flax, linseed, tallow, bristles and wood – could all be replaced from other sources, and most continued to arrive through Prussia. Geography made this inevitable, although only Russell reached the obvious conclusion that vigorous military and diplomatic efforts would be needed to bring Russia to accept the allied terms.[46] Russia, an agrarian state, was not susceptible to blockade in the short term, with the exception of industrial products. This justified the sacrifice of maritime rights. Russian industrial backwardness was an important target; rifles, steam engines and other modern equipment had to be imported. Those on order from Britain were embargoed more than a month before war, including two screw corvettes, steam engines for battleships and woodworking machinery.[47] Other items, iron, chemicals, coal and machinery, were subjected to complex export regulations to prevent them reaching Russia. These were never going to be successful. With friendly neutrals on her land frontiers Russia imported Belgian rifles, gunpowder and steam machinery, despite allied protests.

Optimistic diplomats believed that the winter of 1853–54 would see a settlement of the crisis, that the Turkish declaration of war in October had only raised the stakes from a question of notes to one of treaties. The desire to avoid war was widespread; Count Orlov was sent to Vienna: Stratford pressed the Turks to try again. Buol approved the Turkish note, sending it to St Petersburg, while Aberdeen continued to pray. However, the warning carried by Drummond forced Russia to act. Ignoring the Turkish proposals

Orlov was sent to Vienna again, but his terms were incompatible with those of Turkey and he returned on 8 February. Louis Napoleon tried an autograph letter to the Czar, but this was rejected. Nicholas withdrew his Ambassadors on 4 February claiming the allies were not acting even-handedly in the Black Sea; three days later the allied Ambassadors were recalled.[48] The allied ultimatum demanded that Russia announce her intention of withdrawing from the Principalities by April; refusal would be equivalent to a declaration of war.[49] The courier arrived in St Petersburg on 13 March. When he read the document on the 17th Nicholas refused to reply. War was declared on the 27th, although all parties had been acting as if they were at war for the past two months.

The timing of the allied ultimatum was entirely dependent on strategic factors. It would bring on war just as the ice cleared at Reval and the weather in the Black Sea allowed large sailing ships to cruise in relative safety. It was also the earliest juncture at which the allied armies could hope to occupy Gallipoli. To delay would allow Russia to occupy forward positions in the Baltic and gain advantages on the Danube front. Russian occupation of the Principalities forced the allies to take the diplomatic initiative; it also allowed them to posture as upholders of the status quo, vital to the unity of the British government and to efforts to gain the support of the German powers.

Notes

1   Aberdeen to Graham 24 Sep. 1853: Gr. B.114; Clarendon to Stratford 8, 18 Oct. 1853 no. 221, 230 F.O. 352/36/1; Graham to Clarendon 1 Dec. 1853: Cl. Dep. C4 f249–54; Stratford to Clarendon 2, 5 Jan., 5 Feb. 1854: F.O. 352/37/2.
2   Stratford to Dundas 3 Jan. 1853: F.O. 78/988.
3   Dundas to Stratford 13 Jan. 1854: DND/1 f89.
4   EARDLEY-WILMOT, p. 149; Dundas to Admiralty 8 rec. 29 Jan. 1854 no. 8: ADM 1/5626;
5   Drummond to Dundas 7, 9 Jan. encl. in above; Dundas to Admiralty 12 Jan., rec. 1 Feb. 1854 no. 13: ADM 1/5626; Dundas to Graham 3 Jan. 1854: Gr. CW2.
6   Stratford to Dundas 9, 14 Jan. 1854 no. 2, 5: F.O. 352/38/1; Dundas to Stratford 12 Jan. 1854: DND/1 f87–9.
7   Stratford to Dundas 17 Jan. 1854 encl. in Stratford to Clarendon 17 Jan. 1854 no. 27: F.O. 78/989.
8   Dundas to Stratford 22 Jan. 1854: DND/1 f90–1; Dundas to Graham 23 Jan. 1854: Gr.CW3.
9   Stratford to Dundas 24 Jan. 1854: encl. in Stratford to Clarendon 24

Jan. 1854 no. 35: F.O. 78/989.
10   Dundas to Stratford 26 Jan. 1854: DND/1 f94; Dundas to Admiralty
27 Jan. rec. 13 Feb. 1854: ADM1/5626; Dundas to Admiralty 25 Jan. rec. 9
Feb. 1854 no. 30: *ibid.*; EARDLEY-WILMOT, pp. 152–5.
11   Clarendon to Stratford 7, 9 Jan. 1854 (private): F.O.352/37.
12   Admiralty to Dundas 9, 17 Jan. 1854 no. 44, 45: ADM 2/1697;
Graham to Dundas 7 Jan. 1854: DND/7 f1–10.
13   Clarendon to Graham 6, 7, 16 Jan. 1854: Gr. B.116; Graham to
Clarendon 6, 15, 23 Jan. 1854: Cl. Dep. C14 f128–9; Russell to Clarendon
15, 16, 22 Jan. 1854: Cl. Dep. C15 f306–9; Clarendon to Stratford 8 Feb.
1854 (private): F.O. 352/37.
14   Stratford to Clarendon 24 Feb. 1854 no. 80: F.O. 78/990; Stratford
to Clarendon 5 Feb. 1854 (private): F.O.352/37; Dundas to Graham 24 Feb.
1854: DND/9 f44–9.
15   Clarendon to Graham 24 Feb. 1854: Gr. B.116; Graham to Dundas
5 Feb. 1854: DND/9 f27–30.
16   Graham to Dundas 8, 22 Feb. 1854: DND/9 f27–34; Graham to
Lyons 24 Feb. 1854: Gr. CW9.
17   Dundas to Admiralty 5 Feb., 19 Mar. 1854 no. 54, 113: ADM
1/5626; Dundas to Graham 23 Feb. 1854: Gr. CW3.
18   Dundas to Admiralty 5, 21 Feb., 10, 23 Mar. 1854 no. 74, 98, 122:
ADM 1/5626; Dundas to Stratford 2 Feb. encl. in above; Stratford to
Dundas 1 Feb. encl. in above; Lyons to Graham 12 Mar. 1854: Gr.CW9.
19   SAAB, pp. 137–50 for details of the Greek problem; Dundas to
Stratford 19 Feb., 15, 18 Mar.1854: DND/1 f107, 120–7; Dundas to
Admiralty 15, 29 Mar., rec. 28 Mar., 19 Apr. 1854 no. 109, 130: ADM
1/5626.
20   Dundas to Admiralty 10 rec. 22 Mar. 1854 no. 99: ADM 1/5626;
Dundas to Stratford 16, 18 Mar., 5 Apr. 1854: DND/1 f123,126 139;
Dundas to Graham 21 Mar. 1854: Gr. CW3; Stratford to Dundas 17 Mar.
1854 encl. in Dundas to Admiralty 19 Mar. no. 113: ADM 1/5626.
21   Palmerston to Clarendon 17 Oct. 1853: Bdlds. GC/CL f137/2;
Clarendon to Lyons 13 Oct. 1853: Cl. Dep. C127 f113; Cowley to Clarendon 5 Jan. 1854: F.O. 519/304; Grey to Clarendon 16 Jan. 1854: F.O.
73/260.
22   ANDERSON, O, *A Liberal State at War* (London, 1967), pp.
248–74; Graham cabinet memo, 22 Jan. 1854: Gr. B.116.
23   Graham to Clarendon 28 Feb. 1854: Cl. Dep. C14 f215.
24   Palmerston to Clarendon 14 Jan. 1854: Cl. Dep. C15 f10–13; Graham to Clarendon 18 Jan. 1854; *ibid.* C14 f144–5; SOUTHEY, R., *Life of
Nelson* (London, 1830), p. 190; Graham to Clarendon 6 Oct. 1853: Cl.
Dep. C4 f216–17.
25   Graham to Admiral Sir Jamers Stirling (C-in-C, Sheerness), 25 Jan.
1854: Gr. B.116; Graham to Clarendon 6 , 7 Feb. 1854: Cl. Dep. C14
f171–5.
26   Graham to Cowley 6 Feb. 1854: F.O. 519/208 f1–7; Graham to
Newcastle 23 Feb. 1854: Gr. B.117; Cowley to Clarendon 27 Feb. 5, 9 Mar.
1854: F.O.519/212 f150–75.

27   WILLIAMS, p. 248; Graham to the Queen and Queen to Graham 4
Feb. 1854: Gr. B.117; Graham to Clarendon 7 Feb., 7 Mar. 1854: Cl. Dep.
C14 f175, 234.
28   Dundas to Sir Francis Baring 10 Mar. 1854: *Journals and Correspondence of Francis Baring* (London, 1905, two vols.), vol. ii, pp. 38–9.
29   Berkeley to Graham and Graham to Berkeley 8 Jan. 1854: Gr. Cw19.
30   BURROWS, M., *Memoir of Admiral Sir H. D. Chads* (Portsea,
1869); Admiralty Order 6 Feb. 1854: ADM 1/5632.
31   Napier to Graham 10 Feb. 1854: Add. 40,024 f2; Graham to Napier
24 Feb. 1854: *ibid.* f12; Minute of conversation with Napier, Byam Martin
5 Mar. 1854: Add. 41,370 f276–83.
32   WILLIAMS, pp. 251–3; H. B. Martin to T. B. Martin 25 Mar. 1854:
Add. 41,467 f84–5; OTWAY, A., *Autobiography and Journals of Admiral
Lord Clarence Paget* (London, 1896), p. 79; Admiralty Order 20 Feb.
1854: ADM 1/5632; Biddulph, Lady, *Charles Philip Yorke; Fourth Earl of
Hardwicke Admiral R.N. A Memoir* (London, 1910), pp. 283–7.
33   T. B. Martin to H. B. Martin 22, 27 Feb. 1854: Add.41,467 Graham
to Napier 27 Feb., 7 Mar. 1854: Add. 40,024 f3, 10.
34   H. B. Martin to T. B. Martin 16 Jan. 1854: Add. 41.467 f7–8;
Codrington Correspondence: COD/1; OTWAY, p. 78; RICHMOND, Adm
Sir H., *National Policy and Naval Strength* (London, 1928), p. 240.
35   TAYLOR, p. 303.
36   T. B. Martin to H. B. Martin 2 Mar. 1854: Add. 41,467 f92;
Palmerston to Clarendon 4 Mar. 1854: Cl. Dep. C15 f61.
37   Berkeley 27 Feb. 1854: HANSARD 3rd series CXXX col. 1979–93;
Graham to Clarendon 4 Apr. 1854: Cl. Dep. C14 f276.
38   Beaufort to Graham 23 Feb. 1854: WALKER WWL/1; F.O. to
Admiralty rec. 22 Feb. 1854 containing Seymour to Clarendon 11 Feb. 1854
no 136, 139: Adm 1/5634; Graham to Napier 16, 30 Mar. 1854: Add.
40,024 f71, 86; SULIVAN, H.N., *Life of Sir B. J. Sulivan* (London, 1896), p.
123.
39   F.O. to Admiralty various: ADM 1/5634 f1–153.
40   Washington to Napier rec. 9 Mar. 1854: Add. 40,024 f57; Graham
to Napier 12 Mar. 1854: *ibid.* f57; Strachey to Napier rec. 9 Mar. 1854:
ibid. f17–19.
41   Aberdeen to Russell 16 Mar. 1854: Add. 43,067 f322; Times 16
Mar. 1854; DASENT, A., *John Delane; 1817–1879* (London, 1908, two
vols.), vol. i, pp. 167–72; Times, Editorial 16 Mar. 1854.
42   Napier's Portsmouth Speech 10 Mar. 1854: Add. 40,024 f51.
43   Admiralty to Napier 8 Mar. 1854: PRO 30/16/1 f1; Graham to
Prince Albert 8 Mar. 1854: R.A. G11 f1; Graham to Clarendon 7 Mar.
1854: Cl. Dep. C14 f234.
44   Graham to Clarendon 1 Mar. 1854: Gr. B.118; Admiralty to Napier
8, 10 Mar. 1854, encl. F.O. to Admiralty 9 Mar. 1854: NRS 1854, pp. 43–5;
Admiralty to Napier 10 Mar. 1854 (Sealed Orders): PRO 30/16/1 f99.
45   Graham to Clarendon 3 Mar. 1854: ADM 1/5632.
46   Russell memo. 20 May 1854: PRO 30/22/11D f56.
47   Admiralty Proclamation 18 Feb. 1854: ADM 1/5634.

48   Graham to Clarendon 7 Feb. 1854: Cl. Dep. C14 f172–3.
49   Graham to Clarendon 13, 24 Jan. 1854: *ibid.* f132, 148; Aberdeen to the Queen 26 Feb. 1854; Add. 43,048 f268.

7

War aims and strategy

Although Graham's policy was never placed before the cabinet in a coherent form he dominated the formation of British strategy in 1853–54. His views were promoted by private correspondence, so that when the question of strategy came before the cabinet his opinions had wide support and he did not have to put them forward himself. As a result his name appears suspiciously infrequently in the records of decision making. After Sinope he outlined the broad issues of war with Russia, demonstrating an understanding of the unity of the theatres and the central position of Sevastopol. The contributions of his cabinet colleagues were restricted by inexperience and a failure to comprehend the scale of the task. Palmerston's war aims programme looked to restrict Russian power, but his grasp of practical strategy was weak. The political basis of Graham's policy was the need to keep Russia within the Turkish Straits, but for public purposes the maintenance of Turkey was the *sine qua non* of British policy.[1] The two objects were not identical, as the later stages of the war demonstrated. Graham believed the destruction of Sevastopol would secure the Straits, but he also prepared for the defence of Constantinople. In early January he believed it would be possible to destroy Sevastopol by a naval assault; Dundas was not impressed and Graham abandoned the idea after reading Burgoyne's paper on the possibilities of war with Russia, which pointed out the strength of Sevastopol against ships. A combined operation would be needed to take the city. Graham realised that a Russian advance to the Balkan mountains would force the fleets to leave the Euxine, unless British troops occupied Gallipoli as the French now refused to send any troops. Palmerston looked to Circassia and the Sea of Azov; Russell supported Graham in calling for troops to be held at Malta, Newcastle was prepared. Clarendon wanted a plan to put before the Emperor, but Graham was preparing a cautious memorandum on

the possibilities of war and discussing lines at Gallipoli to hold open
the passage into the Black Sea with Burgoyne. Later he favoured a
fortified camp at Adrianople, covering the Straits and the Ottoman
capital, or a force at Varna to turn the Russian flank if they crossed
the Danube.[2] While Burgoyne believed even 40,000 British troops
would not capture Sevastopol it remained central to Graham's
strategy:

My opinion from the beginning is in unison with the Emperor's. The
Dardanelleş must be secured; a position in front of Constantinople fortified
covering both the city and the Bosphorus; but *the* operation which will be
ever memorable and decisive, is the capture and destruction of Sevastopol.
On this my heart is set: the eye tooth of the Bear must be drawn: and 'til his
fleet and naval arsenal in the Black sea are destroyed there is no safety for
Constantinople, no security for the peace of Europe.

His copy of the letter was marked 'delenda est Sevastopol'.[3] Dundas
wanted to start with the Circassian forts and called for more steam
battleships. Sevastopol shifted in and out of the foreground of
Graham's policy as communicated to Dundas; on 5 February it was
not possible in the immediate future, on the 22nd it returned to
centre stage. There were no steam battleships available, the British
were sending theirs to the Baltic, the French to the Black Sea. Once at
war Dundas must take control of the sea and use an army to attack
the Russian coast.[4] War broke out a week later without further
development of Graham's plans. Those plans relied on French
troops, but when Cowley raised the possibility of attempting
Sevastopol with Louis Napoleon in early January, following Graham's suggestion that the combined operation sketched by Walker
could be carried out buy 25–30,000 French and 10–12,000 British
troops, the Emperor refused, fearing the domestic impact of a defeat
and proposed sending a few officers to assist the Turks. Cowley
urged that Walker be sent to Paris; Graham, now looking to fortify
Gallipoli, reluctantly agreed, and when the Engineer officer sent to
inspect the Dardanelles was taken ill at Lisbon Burgoyne volunteered to replace him. Graham dispatched him through Paris to
explain the need for troops and to take a French officer on his
inspection. Arriving in Paris late on 29 January Burgoyne had
several interviews over the two following days with the Emperor,
Marshal Vaillant, Drouyn, Prince Jerome and Cowley. Vaillant,
another veteran engineer, proposed a position ten to twelve miles in
front of Constantinople, to be held by 30,000 men, and sent Colonel

Ardant. The Emperor prepared to send troops from Algeria.[5] Burgoyne left the War Office to settle the details. Newcastle anticipated sending 25,000 British troops under Lord Raglan, with 35–40,000 French: 12,000 would remain at Gallipoli. The selection of Raglan reflected the paucity of experienced commanders; there were no other men of his rank fit to take the field.[6] Raglan, Lord de Ros, the Quartermaster-General, and Walker were in Paris between 26 and 28 February. Walker carried the outline of Graham's Black Sea and Baltic strategies. Raglan and Walker were unimpressed by the Emperor's plans for an assault on Sevastopol, which he pressed on Cowley after they left.[7]

This sudden shift, from refusing to send a man to pressing for an assault, reflected the primacy of *innenpolitik*. With war inevitable Louis Napoleon wanted a quick victory, which alarmed Graham. He considered fighting alongside France 'unnatural' and took comfort in the weaknesses in French maritime preparations. 'It may not be amiss to let them feel that armies in perfect fighting order are not carried across seas without immense difficulty and enormous cost.' It was obvious to which sea he was referring, his concern was not unique. Anglo–French rivalry had not ended; the decision to retain the old rules of commerce warfare, even if they were relaxed for the war against Russia, reflected their effect against France.[8]

Graham's Black Sea policy was based on the presumption that the Turks could not defend themselves, a view only Palmerston did not share. The Home Secretary wanted to attempt Sevastopol with Turkish troops, to preserve secrecy; Constantinople did not greatly concern him, he looked to carry the war to Russia. Colonel Rose's opinion that campaigning in the Danube basin would ruin the health of western armies, combined with a clear preference for the Crimea, encouraged Palmerston to outline his perception of British war aims:

This would be the result of our war with Russia.
1. Aland and Finland returned to Sweden
2. Poland re-established in its *antient* limits as an independent state.
3. The mouths of the Danube restored to Turkey unless some arrangement could be made for carrying Austria to the Black Sea.
4. Crimea taken and the Russian Black Sea fleet captured or destroyed. The Crimea given to Turkey in exchange for Moldavia, or else Sevastopol razed to the ground and the docks and arsenals destroyed.
5. Circassia independent and Georgia united with Circassia or annexed to Turkey.[9]

These aims presupposed a major war to defeat Russia, rather than upholding the status quo at the Straits, raising the fundamental issue of Austrian and Prussian attitudes, while presuming Turkey and Sweden, if not the German powers, would become catspaws for British grand strategy. Russell urged that Austria be persuaded, and Prussia coerced to join the allies, and instructions prepared for Dundas, Raglan and Napier. The two issues were inseparable; Russell believed it would only be possible to attack Sevastopol if the German powers joined.[10] In response Palmerston enlarged his aims, finding Russia's Baltic provinces an inducement for Prussia, and the offer of Moldavia and Wallachia in exchange for Lombardy and Venetia a reason for Austria to join the war. Such plans relied on major defeats for Russia, which he urged his colleagues not to discount. Lansdowne dismissed them as 'daydreams', the rest properly saw it as the recipe for a long war, yet these remained the basis of Palmerston's war aims programme until early 1856.[11] Only Louis Napoleon shared a belief that the war could be made to serve such wide ranging ambitions.

Allied Black Sea strategy, determined before the outbreak, developed from the 'occupation of Gallipoli as the base of all our operations'. Once the Turks signed the necessary convention the Dardanelles would be occupied, securing the basic British object, that of excluding Russia from the Mediterranean. The planned lines around Constantinople were abandoned, because of the terrain and scale of the undertaking. The main body of the allied army would camp on the shores of the Bosphorus, waiting for an opportunity to attack Sevastopol. The timing would be decided on by the theatre commanders, and a succesful operation would secure an 'honourable and durable peace'. While the armies moved into Turkey the fleets would be restricted to minor operations, possibly on the coast of Circassia, and intercepting Russian attempts to use the sea.[12]

Quite how the cabinet reached a consensus that the fall of Sevastopol would end the war is uncertain. There was no justification for such views in the history of war between major powers. Sevastopol was only an outpost of a large empire, intended to maintain a fleet that existed to aid the army; its destruction could not force Russia to make peace. In the eyes of many, notably Graham, Sevastopol achieved the same status as Cherbourg; as the base of a naval rival it had more significance to British statesmen than to the Czar. This fundamental error encouraged the policy makers to take risks because they saw an early end to the war. In late 1855 the Government was surprised that the fall of the city did not force Russia to treat for terms; yet this was never going to be decisive. The political object of the British Government, Palmerston apart, was to preserve Turkey as the best method of keeping Russia out of the Mediterranean. This could only be secured by altering the relationship between Russia and Turkey. British policy makers misguidedly believed Russian power to coerce Turkey was based on command of the sea, when the war of 1828–29 demonstrated that Russian power remained land based, with the fleet as a useful adjunct. Unless the state and the army were weakened and constrained by a binding treaty Russia would retain the power to attack Turkey whenever she wished, whatever happened to Sevastopol. Russia would have to be defeated in a major war, not a peripheral campaign, before she would concede such terms.

For Britain and France the Eastern Question was of limited interest, and they made the error of placing Russian interest on the same level. In reality the destruction of Sevastopol was the key to the Euxine, but no more. It would give the allies an absolute command of the sea, leaving them free to stage a wide ranging maritime campaign. Until it was destroyed, or completely masked, the Russian fleet would exercise a disproportionate influence on allied strategy because the British did not realise that, as a fortress fleet, it could be easily blockaded. Had they decided to blockade the Russian fleet the British lacked the necessary ships and seamen, forcing Graham to develop plans for both theatres to reduce Russian naval power. In the north his target was one battlesquadron, in the south the entire fleet. These operations would have permitted the development of a strategy more closely aligned to the military defeat of Russia, as the only method of forcing her to relinquish her pretensions toward Turkey. The problems of a war against France would have been similar, yet there had been no serious consideration of the strategic problems, or the specialist tactics required to deal with fortress/arsenals such as Cherbourg, Cronstadt and Sevastopol. The Navy was proceeding rapidly with the development of new instruments of war, but had no clear conception of how they should be employed. At the operational level the lack of flotilla craft to bombard forts mirrored this intellectual failure, and stemmed from the same inaccurate perception of war at sea.

Before any strategic policy could be adopted the issue of war aims had to be decided, at least as far as was required for diplomatic discussions with interested neutrals. Aberdeen's concept of the crisis had always been dominated by the need to secure European co-operation. Long before the outbreak the great powers had become split into three distinct groups; Russia, alone, was opposed by Britain and France, while Austria and Prussia remained neutral, with both sides canvassing for their support. The western powers believed Austrian interests in the Danube basin would force her to join them. Both German powers signed the Quadruple Convention of 9 April, declaring support for the Sultan, and the civil and religious liberties of his Christian subjects. On the 20th they signed an alliance guaranteeing their territories and deploring the continued occupation of the Principalities. Aberdeen considered Austria the key to an early settlement, and this dominated his war aims policy. Moving the allied armies to Varna was seen as an encouragement to Vienna, but before it could have any effect the Austrians issued an ultimatum to Russia on 3 June, demanding evacuation. On the 14th Austria concluded a convention with Turkey to occupy the Principalities for the duration of the war. This forced Austria to co-operate, although her object was to limit the scope of hostilities. The resulting discussions, largely carried on by the French, produced the 'Four Points' which remained the official statement of allied war aims into 1856. Inevitably Palmerston objected to any limitation. The cabinet, becoming increasingly bellicose, would not consider any suspension of hostilities until Sevastopol had been destroyed. Once Russia evacuated the Principalities Austrian enthusiasm for the alliance cooled. Having secured her only object, keeping Russia away from the Danube, there was no need to risk war. However, on 8 August the allied Ambassadors exchanged notes establishing the 'Four Points' as allied war aims. These were:

1. Replacing the Russian guarantee of the Principalities with a European guarantee.
2. The Danube to be a free river.
3. The Treaty of 1841 to be revised in the interests of the balance of power.
4. The Christian subjects of the Porte to be placed under European, and not Russian, protection.

These terms were urged at St Petersburg by Austria, but haughtily rejected in mid August. Austria did not join the war; her interests did not require such a sacrifice.[13]

Russell took the initiative, demanding the cabinet 'take some decided line upon the conduct of the war'. He anticipated Russia would advance to the Balkan mountains, outflanking Graham's lines and creating a Christian insurrection in Bulgaria. Therefore the allies must support Turkey close to the Danube and encourage Austria to act in the Principalities. He also wanted to reinforce both services, embodying 15,000 militia to relieve front line troops. On the following day, 28 April, the cabinet approved adding 15,000 men to the Army, and 5,000 to the Navy. There would soon be 80,000 allied troops to aid Omer Pasha, and encourage Austria. Aberdeen, considering the independence of Turkey to be the only war aim, objected to expanding the war by subsidising Sweden. Only Austria could assist the war he wanted to fight. The divergence between Aberdeen and Russell was fundamental, Aberdeen wanted the *status quo ante bellum*, Russell wanted to strike a blow at Sevastopol or Cronstadt; the former would solve the present crisis, while both would improve Britain's position in the long term. Palmerston wanted to bring Austria onto the north bank of the Danube, as a buffer between Russia and Turkey, which offered considerable benefits, and he adopted the same logic for the Asian frontier. When Russell's initiative did not produce the desired result – Aberdeen's retirement in his favour – he began to complain of the lack of leadership in an effort to secure Whig support for ejecting the Premier. Clarendon and Wood demonstrated the influence of Graham, calling for the destruction of Sevastopol as the key to a safe peace; Wood, as President of the Board of Control, was also anxious to act in Asia.[14] Russell's next attempt to secure the Premiership came with his memorandum of 20 May, calling for the division of the War and Colonial Offices and more active prosecution of the war, specifically in the Baltic. Aberdeen agreed to divide the Offices, but preferred to press Austria. He was supported by Gladstone. Molesworth shared his aims, although he wanted a success to secure the peace. Wood wanted to defend Turkey and rely on a maritime campaign, Herbert wanted to destroy Russian seapower in both theatres: 'such a blow could not be recovered because such arsenals and fleets could not be recreated during half a century and during that period Russia with her claws pared would give peace and quiet to her neighbours and to Europe.' Both the tooth-and-claw imagery and the strategy can be traced directly to Graham, who did not join the exchange of memoranda. Palmerston urged action in Asia, the Crimea and the Principalities to drive back Russian frontiers, condemning the narrow status quo view in favour of guaranteeing long term security. Lansdowne agreed with Herbert, adding the need to encourage Austria. Before Lansdowne's belated paper joined the circulating box, the cabinet of 27 May agreed to send the armies north to aid Silistria, which Graham and Newcastle believed had already fallen. Prince Albert pointed to Varna as a suitable base for 10,000 infantry, to relieve the Admirals from the lamentable alternatives of either remaining inactive spectators of its capture, or paralysing their fleets by having to land their marines for its defence.[15] When the armies went to Varna, their presence, rather than absence, paralysed the fleets.

The discussion, started by Russell, revealed a basic consensus on war aims and strategy; the defence of Turkey was the first requirement, there was no objection to móving the army to Varna. Only Aberdeen did not express a desire to destroy the Russian fleet at Sevastopol, considering the return of the Principalities a sufficient guarantee; but when his views became public he was obliged to shift.[16] Sevastopol was the dominant theme in Britain long before the *Times* editorial of 15 June, and Aberdeen could not prevent it becoming the centre-piece of allied strategy. War aims reflected a much wider divergence. Russell looked to replace Aberdeen and defeat Palmerston by conducting a popular war; Palmerston wanted to weaken Russia; Graham and his disciples, Newcastle, Herbert and Clarendon, along with Lansdowne and Wood, aimed their blows at Russian seapower. For Molesworth and Gladstone only Russian Black Sea power was a legitimate target. Excluding Russia from the Mediterranean, and in some cases restoring British influence in Persia and Central Asia, reflected a strand of strategic planning stretching back to mid 1853.

The singular feature of these discussions was the silence of Graham. The indecision of which Russell complained allowed him a free hand to develop and adopt his own policies; his private correspondence won over the support of many in cabinet. His influence with Newcastle was of particular significance. The major statements of Graham's war policy are to be found outside his cabinet correspondence; his Black Sea strategy was revealed to Raglan, Dundas and Lyons in letters of 8 May. To Raglan and Dundas he stressed the importance of securing Constantinople, leaving the point of attack to their discretion. Raglan was urged to move up to Varna, Dundas to sweep the Asian coast 'as a preliminary measure' not inconsistent

with moving to Varna. However, the real aim was the attack on
Sevastopol, if the Russians left the Principalities. Dundas was to
collect intelligence on a potential landing site and prepare a flotilla at
Constantinople. Lyons' role was to encourage the others. The continued reluctance to build a flotilla at home was typical. Graham
considered ordering gunboats at Malta, but as construction would
take fifteen weeks, preferred to rely on what could be found at
Constantinople.[17] This made plans to operate in the Sea of Azov
meaningless.

The campaign in the Black Sea unfolded exactly as Graham
intended. Gallipoli and then Constantinople were secured; the
armies moved up to the Danube and the fleets swept the coast of
Asia; everything moved inexorably toward Sevastopol. From the
beginning of the crisis Graham made use of the best available naval
and military expertise. His colleagues only read what he produced,
not one of them sent a detailed questionnaire to a senior officer. They
commented on the papers Graham secured from Burgoyne and
Walker, and read the private letters of Dundas and Lyons; most
offered strategic opinions, opinions shaped and conditioned by the
dominant will of Graham. The decision to adopt the Sevastopol
strategy was his, when Walker persuaded Louis Napoleon in early
1854 it became allied policy. Graham's contribution has not been
widely recognised.[18] He was a great lieutenant, and for all his ability
he feared to lead, dreading responsibility. Therefore he convinced his
colleagues by force of logic, to avoid setting his name to the plan for
which Louis Napoleon, Palmerston or even Newcastle are usually
given the credit. With the moral courage to match his talent Graham
would have been a great war minister, but he would not take the
lead. Newcastle, who had the courage, had little of his ability, merely
echoing Graham's views on Sevastopol, the Asian coast and the
political value of destroying the Russian fleet in his correspondence
with Raglan.[19] The decision to invade the Crimea, officially taken at
Kinglake's infamous sleeping cabinet on 28 June, only confirmed
months of discussion led and shaped by Graham. Lansdowne's call
for 'a prompt attack' only decided the day.[20] In public Newcastle
urged the operation, stressing that if the commanders felt unable to
attempt it the governments would regret their decision. In private he
emphasised that the Russian evacuation of the Principalities decided
the timing. The idea that only the destruction of Sevastopol would
secure 'an honourable and safe peace' provided the political

imperative. Graham sent an almost identical letter to Dundas, stressing Sevastopol as the 'grand object of the campaign'. Lyons would apply pressure to Dundas and Raglan.[21]

Graham, and under his tuition Newcastle, tried to control the Crimean operation to an extent hitherto unrecognised. Graham wanted an amphibious landing between Eupatoria and Sevastopol, followed by a combined arms assault in which the Star Fort, identified by Drummond, might be the key. He was also concerned to cut off Russian supplies and reinforcements across the Sea of Azov or the Isthmus of Perekop. The point of disembarkation should be disguised, and not too close to Sevastopol; once launched he was convinced the operation must succeed.[22] Prince Albert responded to the cabinet decision, supporting the move and reflecting on the dangers of a Danube campaign. He conceived an operation involving a tripartite army of 110,000 bombarding from a fortified base north of the city, with the Isthmus of Perekop blockaded. Newcastle, influenced by Graham and the Prince, adopted Graham's site for the landing, and suggested that Omer Pasha's army should hold Perekop. If it proved necessary to lay siege to Sevastopol the Sea of Azov would be a vital Russian artery of supply. Palmerston allotted six weeks to the operation, but believed that if it were put off the Russians would regain command of the Euxine in the winter. Russell shared Graham's view that capturing the north side of the harbour would enable the ships and the arsenal to be bombarded without having to take the city.[23]

The inspiration for the operation came from earlier British grand raids, most recently Copenhagen (1807) and Walcheren (1809). In all cases the object was the destruction of seapower, not the capture of territory. Once the operation was ordered Russell considered the destruction of the Russian fleet had become *sine qua non* for peace; Aberdeen, knowing the operation was far from certain and unwilling to let such a condition damage the chances of a negotiated settlement, was less enthusiastic.[24] While the Russian Black Sea fleet remained afloat it limited the allies' use of the Black sea, despite their overwhelming superiority.

After deciding to attempt Sevastopol several members of the cabinet turned their attention to the Russo–Turkish frontier in Asia. Russia had extended her power into the Caucasus during the early nineteenth cenmtury, largely at the expense of Persia, but her control was confined to fortified posts by Muslim zealots under Schamyl

Bey.[25] At the outbreak of war the Turks had 50,000 men around Kars, Baiazet and Ardahan, but they were demoralised by corruption, lack of food and pay. Several Polish exiles were sent by Palmerston and Stratford, but they proved an inferior collection, riven by their own jealousies. In late July 20,000 Russians under Prince Bebutov defeated the Turks at Kuruk-Dar, securing the frontier for the remainder of the season.[26] In Circassia Schamyl's guerrillas proved ineffective, despite British aid. Wood adopted an Indian approach, considering a blow in Asia would have a valuable effect on Persia. Palmerston had a long term interest in the Caucasus, hoping to push back the Russian frontier, following Sevastopol with a campaign in the Caucasus. Newcastle, Wood and Granville concurred. Clarendon acted, sending Colonel Williams to improve the Turkish army and calling on Stratford for information. Newcastle hoped to bring troops from India for 1855, warning Raglan to be prepared.[27] Within the cabinet a consensus was growing to favour an Asian campaign. Graham was not interested. Having cleared the coastal forts, only Kertch and the Sea of Azov concerned him, as part of the attack on Sevastopol. When Sevastopol finally did fall the new cabinet turned to Asia for the follow-up campaign. The inspiration was Palmerston, but the logic belonged to Wood.

The development of Baltic strategy during 1854 was crippled by the lack of an agreed programme of war aims, and of any clear understanding of what could be achieved in the theatre. The majority in cabinet had entered the war with narrow war aims, which did not include significant changes in the Baltic. Aberdeen saw the defence of European Turkey as the only war aim; Palmerston wanted to change the nature of the war to a wide ranging attack on Russian power in all theatres, drawing in new allies and creating unrest within the Russian Empire, notably in Poland and Finland. Poland was a difficult subject, for Polish nationalism also threatened Austria and Prussia. Clarendon continued to raise the subject into August, taking his lead from Palmerston, but the Prince Consort warned him of the dangers of provoking Prussia.[28] Finland posed different problems. The Finns were quite happy with Russian rule, but some credence was given to reports that they would fight to rejoin Sweden. Similarly most believed Sweden would join the war to recover Finland, Graham and Clarendon among them. During the first months of the war there was no cabinet discussion of the Baltic. Graham and Clarendon attended to their responsibilities and collaborated in developing a trade war policy, but this was not enough. With a powerful fleet in the Baltic it was necessary to formulate war aims and strategy, functions which Graham could not conduct without cabinet guidance. Palmerston's war aims programme, even before the outbreak of war, including Finland, the Baltic states and Poland, assumed Swedish support. This enlarged war did not generate any enthusiasm from his colleagues; only Russell admitted to a policy, wanting to encourage Sweden with a subsidy, to create a more effective Baltic strategy.[29]

The ambivalent attitude of the cabinet toward the Baltic was disturbed by the French. Two months before his fleet entered the theatre Louis Napoleon proposed an alliance to Sweden; on 5 April the French minister at Stockholm read a note to King Oscar. Crown Prince Charles had discussed the prospect of war with William Grey, the British *chargé d'affaires*, but believed the French had moved too soon. King Oscar made no reply, but his government condemned the French approach. This three-sided diplomacy, with the King, the Crown Prince and the government taking independent lines, frustrated the allies and appears to have been deliberate, at least on the part of Oscar. Clarendon was dismayed by the French action, telling Russell that any allied success 'must' have forced Sweden to join the war; he told Aberdeen it 'might'. The Crown Prince had hinted that a subsidy and a guarantee of Finland would bring Sweden into the war, but the King and government were more cautious. The French approach forced Clarendon to call for a cabinet and instruct Grey to accept no agreements. The cabinet of 22 April did not discuss the Baltic, but Russell, who had not been present, took up the issue. Clarendon used Russell's interest to press Aberdeen. Aberdeen did not object to a subsidy in principle, but he believed Sweden would only fight for her own objects, 'which would deprive us of all freedom of action'.[30] Russell returned with a more detailed proposal, suggesting that with a subsidy of £200,000 Sweden might be expected to employ 50,000 troops to support the allied fleet. This would cover the alarming lack of reserves and allow the allies to attack Cronstadt or Sevastopol. Aberdeen objected that the Baltic was a secondary theatre which could not help achieve the primary war aim, driving Russia out of the Principalities. He favoured concentrating all efforts on Austria. Palmerston argued for a subsidy, but against any guarantee. Aberdeen accepted that the Baltic must be discussed in cabinet, relying on Gladstone at the Treasury to frustrate any attempt to provide a subsidy. The cabinet of 6 May called for more information. Russell still urged Clarendon to act, but the Foreign Secretary was less enthusiastic, accepting Aberdeen's point about the importance of Austria. Wood called for a British policy, destroying Sweaborg and transferring the Aland Islands to Sweden, and objecting to a subsidy, which would be unpopular in Parliament. Newcastle sent an officer to inspect the Swedish army.[31]

Graham did not provide a concise statement of his Baltic policy. His letters to Napier urged restraint because there was nothing to be done; those to his cabinet colleagues varied, depending on the recipient. He shared his hopes for a major campaign with Clarendon, but in return for sending similar views to Gladstone he received a lecture on the moral issues of the war. Gladstone wanted to concentrate allied efforts in the Black Sea, as Sevastopol would be worth much more than any success in the Baltic, while Austria must be coerced to join the allies. In the Baltic a French army should be taken to capture Sweaborg.[32] These were Aberdeen's opinions, but Graham adopted and refined them, and in little more than a month they were the basis of allied Baltic strategy.

Anticipating major developments in the Baltic Clarendon sent Arthur Magennis to fill the vacant post of Minister, arriving at Stockholm on 20 May. On the same day Russell circulated his memorandum calling for Newcastle to be replaced as Secretary of State for War by Palmerston, and a treaty of alliance and subsidy with Sweden. He believed that only military success would force Russia to concede. The response of his colleagues illustrated the wide divergence of opinion on the Baltic; Molesworth saw the Baltic fleet as a defensive force, with the secondary advantage of preventing Russia concentrating all her resources in the south, while Clarendon accepted the need for troops to destroy Russian naval resources, but did not want to provide territorial guarantees for Sweden. Gladstone continued his objection to a Swedish alliance, considering Austrian involvement 'morally necessary'. Wood doubted the ability of the Swedes to affect much, while Herbert saw the Baltic as a diversion, looking to combine this with real British benefit. Destroying Cronstadt and Sweaborg would justify a subsidy to Sweden, but he did not believe it necessary to give guarantees. Herbert realised the war was limited, and capturing Finland would make it unlimited. Palmerston wanted to abandon the 'Four Points' in favour of a general attack on Russia to reduce her power; Finland should be returned, but without any guarantee, because Swedish troops and gunboats would be necessary to join the assault on the Russian arsenals. He was anxious to finish the war, anticipating trouble with the United States. This remained his policy until 1856. Lansdowne called for Napier's opinion on Cronstadt; if it could be destroyed it was worth any sacrifice, but Finland was irrelevant.[33]

The cabinet of the 24th could only decide that the French proposals were unsatisfactory, and that the Swedish offer on which they were based came from the Crown Prince. Two days later Russell confirmed that Oscar would only join the war after Austria, and the cabinet of the 27th effectively abandoned the Swedish question.[34] Oscar had conducted a devious policy, relying on hints from other quarters to test the value of a Swedish alliance. When the French appeared anxious to make terms he deliberately raised his conditions to include the most favourable circumstance for Sweden to enter the struggle – Austrian accession. This policy made him unpopular at home and abroad, but it served the allies well. Russia remained convinced he would join the war.[35]

The cabinet of 27 May ended any hope for a major Baltic campaign in 1854, as the season for amphibious operations was restricted by the weather to June, July and August. Swedish involvement had promised to solve the problems, providing troops and gunboats. Graham, having earlier looked for something significant in the Baltic, now argued the primacy of the Crimea in allied strategy, although he still hoped for Swedish help.[36] After the British abandoned the subject the French concluded a worthless treaty with Sweden, in which she engaged to enter the war after Austria, in return for £100,000 a month, the presence of 10,000 allied troops and the guarantee of Finland. The cabinet, at French insistence, agreed to the terms. This was an act of weakness by Aberdeen, and from his cabinet report it can be inferred he realised as much.

When this charade was played out the allies had already embarked on the one major strategic move of the year. After the prolonged, indecisive discussion of the Baltic the cabinet agreed to the Crimean descent. They accepted that the origin of the war lay in the east, and it must be settled there.[37] Operations in the Baltic were intended to further British aims, hence Gladstone's moral dilemma and Aberdeen's lack of enthusiasm. Oscar realised there was no benefit in playing the hired auxiliary in a limited war, he would wait until the allies were prepared to make an unlimited effort. Only then would

Sweden make sufficient gains to justify incurring the hatred of Russia. With Aberdeen as Premier, war aims would remain limited to the 'Four Points', whatever Russell and Palmerston attempted. Only Russell realised that Russia was not going to be brought to terms by limited methods, and therefore argued for major military efforts. Palmerston had long term aims, reducing the Russian challenge to Britain's world position, but he did not understand the need for an unlimited war to secure such major aims. The one issue that was not discussed during the debate on the Swedish alliance, or at any time in 1854, was the role of the Baltic fleet without a Swedish alliance. The cabinet majority believed nothing beyond a blockade could be hoped for, and when the public called for action it was too late for anything beyond a hurried attempt at the Aland islands. The blame belongs to Graham, who would not act or call for guidance. Behind his carefully contrived screen of secrecy he had no Baltic policy, after the Reval mirage burst. This was decisive, for without clear instructions from the Admiralty Napier could do very little; he had not been equipped for amphibious operations, or directed to any target. Without agreed war aims, strategy could not be formed.

Notes

1   Graham to Dundas 24 Dec. 1853: DND/9 f129; Graham to Clarendon 22 Jan. 1854: Cl. Dep. C14 f141–9.

2   Graham to Dundas 7 Jan. 1854: DND/7 f1–10; Dundas to Graham 3 Jan. 1854: Gr. CW3; GREVILLE, *Memoirs* (London 1938, 8 vols.), ed. STRACHEY and FULFORD; vol. vii, p. 123, 5 Jan. 1854; Graham to Burgoyne 25 Jan. 1854: WROTTESLEY, ii, p. 6; Graham to Clarendon 18 Jan. 1854: Cl. Dep. C14 f144–5; Graham memo. 18 Jan. 1854: Gr. B.116; Palmerston to Graham 19 Jan.1854: Gr. B.116; Russell to Graham 19 Jan. 1854: *ibid.*; Graham to Newcastle 19 Jan. 1854: *ibid.*; Newcastle to Graham 20 Jan. 1854: *ibid.*; Clarendon to Graham 22 Jan. 1854: *ibid.*; Graham memo. 22 Jan. 1854: *ibid.*; Graham to Burgoyne 21 Jan. 1854: WROTTESLEY, ii p. 3; Graham to Clarendon 31 Jan. 1854: Cl. Dep. C14 f162–3; Graham to Raglan 3, 10 Feb. 1854: Gr. B.117.

3   Graham to Clarendon 1 Mar. 1855: Cl. Dep. C14 f217–7 and Gr. B.116.

4   Dundas to Graham 14, 23 Jan. and 26 Feb. 1854: Gr. CW3; Graham to Dundas 24 Jan., 5, 22 Feb., 22 Mar. 1854: DND/9 f22–30, 44–9 and 54–8.

5   Cowley to Clarendon 13 Jan. 1854: F.O. 519/212 pp. 24–31; Graham to Clarendon 13 Jan. 1854: Cl. Dep. C14 f144–5; Graham to Burgoyne 25 Jan. 1854: WROTTESLEY, ii, p. 6; Graham to Raglan 26 Jan. 1854: Gr. B.116; Burgoyne to Col. Matson 31 Jan. 1854: WROTTESLEY, ii, p. 8;

Cowley to Clarendon 3 Feb. 1854: F.O. 519/212 pp. 87–8.
6   MUNSELL, F.D., *The Unfortunate Duke; Henry Pelham, Fifth Duke of Newcastle, 1811–1864* (Columbia, 1985), pp. 145–7; HIBBERT,C., *The Destruction of Lord Raglan* (London, 1961), pp. 20–38.
7   Newcastle to Clarendon 22 Feb. 1854: Cl. Dep. c15 f794–6; Newcastle to Raglan 23 Feb. 1854: RAGLAN 6807–282; Cowley to Clarendon 26 Feb., 9, 17 Mar. 1854: F.O. 519/212 pp. 149, 176–209; Newcastle to de Ros 13 Mar. 1854: RAGLAN 6807–283.
8   Graham to Clarendon 3, 19 Feb. 1854: Cl. Dep. C14 f168–70, 197–200; Graham to Dundas 24 Jan. 1854: DND/9 f22–6; Graham to Lord Heysterbury 2 Feb. 1854: Gr. B.117 ; The Queen to Aberdeen 24 Feb. 1854: Add. 43,048 f259–62; Graham to Clarendon 21 Mar. 1854: Gr. B.118.
9   Graham to Russell 17 Jan. 1854: PRO 30/22/11C f67–8; Palmerston to Clarendon 16 Jan., 4 Mar. 1854: Cl. Dep. C15 f10–13, 61.
10   Russell memo. Mar. 1854: PRO 30/22/11C f218–19; Russell to Clarendon 3, 5 Mar. 1854: Cl. Dep. C15 f395–8.
11   Palmerston memo. 19 Mar. 1854: PRO 30/22/11C f267; Lansdowne memo. 20 Mar. 1854: *ibid.* f271; Graham to Clarendon 20 Mar. 1854: Cl. Dep. C14 f246–7.
12   Newcastle to de Ros 13 Mar. 1854: RAGLAN 6807–283; Graham to Dundas 30 Mar. 1854: DND/9 f59–63.
13   Aberdeen memo. 5 May 1854: *Aberdeen Correspondence, 1854–55*, p. 121; Palmerston to Clarendon 25 Jul. 1854: Cl. Dep. C15 f138–9; CONACHER, pp. 429–36 and SCHROEDER, pp. 200–31.
14   Russell to Aberdeen 27 Apr. 1854: Add. 43,068 f37–42; Aberdeen to Russell 27 Apr. 1854: *ibid.* f44; Aberdeen to the Queen 28 , 29 Apr. 1854: Add. 43,049 f61–5; Palmerston to Clarendon 6 Apr. 1854: Cl. Dep. C15 f94–7; Russell to Aberdeen 5 May 1854: Add. 43,068 f57; Russell to Clarendon 12 May 1854: Cl. Dep. C15 f485–7; Clarendon to Russell 7 May 1854: PRO 30/22/11D f22–4; Wood to Russell 9 May 1854: *ibid.* f28–31.
15   Russell memo. 20 May; Aberdeen Memo. 20 May; Molesworth memo. 22 May; Gladstone memo. 23 May; Wood memo. 23 May; Herbert memo. 23 May; Palmerston memo. 26 May; Lansdowne memo. 29 May: PRO 30/22/11D f54–93; Aberdeen to the Queen 28 May 1854: Add. 43,049 f117; Graham to Clarendon 28 May 1854: Cl. Dep. C14 f358; Newcastle to Clarendon 28 May 1854: Cl. Dep. C15 f819–20; Graham to Newcastle 30 May 1854: NeC. 10,239; Prince Albert to Newcastle 20 May 1854: NeC. 9,689.
16   CONACHER, pp. 413–14.
17   STRACHAN, H., 'Soldiers, strategy and Sebastopol', *The Historical Journal*, 1978, p. 311; Graham to Dundas 8 May 1854: DND/9 f81–5; Graham to Raglan and to Lyons 8 May 1854: Gr. B.119; Graham to Stewart 13 Jun.; Berkeley to Stewart 8 Jul. 1854: LYONS B105/1.
18   PARKER and EARDLEY-WILMOT both give Graham the credit, without any evidence; Graham's own claim is in Graham to Cowley 26 Sep. 1854: F.O. 519/208 f65–70.
19   Newcastle to Raglan 3, 9, 18 May: 3,8,17 Jun. 1854: RAGLAN 6807–283.

20 Lansdowne to Russell 28 Jun. 1854: PRO 30/22/11D f169–70; Aberdeen to the Queen 29 Jun. 1854: Add. 43,049 f173:
21 Newcastle to Raglan 28, 29 Jun. 1854: MARTINEAU, pp. 145–7; Graham to Dundas 28 Jun. 1854: DND/9 f102–6; Graham to Lyons 2 Jul. 1854: Gr. CW9.
22 Graham to Dundas 12 Aug. 1854: DND/9 f145–7; Graham to Lyons 2 Jul. 1854: Gr. CW9; Graham to Clarendon 31 Jul. and 30 Sep. 1854: Cl. Dep. C14 f413–14.
23 Prince Albert memo. 29 Jun. 1854: NeC9,694b; Newcastle to Raglan 3, 29 Jul. 1854: RAGLAN 6807–283; Palmerston to Newcastle 16 Jul. 1854: NeC 10,039; Palmerston to Clarendon 25 Jul. 1854: Cl. Dep. C15 f138–9; Russell to Clarendon 25 Jul. 1854: Cl. Dep. C15 f574–5.
24 Russell to Clarendon 5 Jul. 1854: ibid. f517–20; Aberdeen to Clarendon 23 Jul. 1854: Cl. Dep. C14 f62–3.
25 SETON-WATSON, H. pp. 58–60, 183, 290–3, 416–17.
26 CURTISS., pp. 408–9 and 415–19.
27 Palmerston to Clarendon 13, 26, 27 Apr. 1854: Cl. Dep. C15 f98–111; Clarendon to Stratford 8 Jun. 1854: F.O. 352/37; Wood to Russell 9 May 1854: PRO 30/22/11D f28–31; Palmerston to Clarendon 30 Jun. 1854: Cl. Dep. C15 f120–1; Clarendon to Stratford 3 Jul., 4 Aug. 1854: F.O. 352/37; Newcastle to Clarendon 4 Jul. 1854: Cl. Dep. C15 f829–30; Newcastle to Raglan 29 Aug. 1854: RAGLAN 6807–283.
28 Palmerston to Clarendon 6 Apr. 1854: Bdlds. GC/CL f375; HENDERSON, pp. 93–5.
29 Russell memo. Mar. 1854: PRO 30/22/11C f218–19; Russell to Clarendon 13 Apr. 1854: Cl. Dep. C15 f445.
30 SCOTT, F.D., Sweden, (Minnesota, 1977), pp. 320–2; Grey to Clarendon 6, 13 Apr. 1854: F.O.73/261 f76–9; Clarendon to Graham 13 Apr. 1854: Gr. B.118; Clarendon to Russell 17 Apr. 1854: PRO 30/22/11C f388; Clarendon to Aberdeen 17 Apr. 1854: Add. 43,189 f38; Clarendon to Russell 20, 22, 23 Apr. 1854: PRO 30/22/11C f404–8; Russell to Clarendon 24 Apr. 1854: Cl. Dep. C15 f462; Aberdeen to Clarendon 23 Apr. 1854: Cl. Dep. C14 f37.
31 Russell to Aberdeen 27 Apr. 1854: Add. 43,068 f11; Aberdeen to Russell 27 Apr. 1854: ibid. f44–6; Palmerston to Clarendon 27 Apr. 1854: Cl. Dep. C15 f107; Aberdeen to Clarendon 29 Apr. 1854: Add. 43,189 f50; Clarendon to Russell 23 Apr. 1854: Cl. Dep. C15 f408; Aberdeen to the Queen 6 May 1854: Add. 43,048 f84; Russell to Clarendon 7 May 1854: Cl. Dep. C15 f472; Wood to Russell 9 May 1854: PRO 30/22/11D f28; Newcastle to Hardinge 6 May 1854: NeC 10,788.
32 Graham to Clarendon 31 Mar. 1854: Cl. Dep. C14 f68–9; Gladstone to Graham 17 May 1854: Add. 44,163 f137–41.
33 Russell to Clarendon 15 May 1854: Cl. Dep. C15 f489.
34 Aberdeen to the Queen 24, 28 May 1854: CONACHER, p. 427; Russell to Clarendon 26 May 1854: Cl. Dep. C15 f499.
35 SCOTT, pp. 320–2 ; CURTISS, p. 283.
36 Graham to Clarendon 28 May 1854: Cl. Dep. C14 f358.
37 Aberdeen to the Queen 8 Jul. 1854: Add. 43,049; Palmerston diary entry 28 Jun. 1854: Bdlds. D15.

8

The Danube front

After a brief flurry of activity in late 1853 the Russians and Turks settled to winter on opposite banks of the Danube. Logistical problems, exacerbated by the season, made a Russian offensive impossible. The Czar anticipated crossing the river in April, raising the standard of Christian insurrection, as Paskevic had advised. Paskevic was now more cautious, favouring an attack on Silistria to secure Bulgarian assistance before moving on to Adrianople. Far inland these operations would render allied seapower irrelevant. In a purely Russo–Turkish war strategic issues would have remained paramount, but Austria had no desire to see Russia increase her control over the Danube, the principal artery of her trade. Further, raising nationalist insurrection among the Balkan peoples would cause serious problems for the multi-racial Habsburg empire. These concerns were signalled by moving Austrian troops onto the Serbian frontier, which made Paskevic nervous. In early February he advised holding a strategic reserve in Poland against Austria or Prussia, and using Silistria to draw Turkish and allied forces deep inland, before crushing them. Initially Nicholas was more bellicose, but allied amphibious power led him to accept Paskevic's plan by the end of the month.

The Russian campaign opened on 23 March, crossing the Danube at Galatz in force. A fortnight later Paskevic was ordered to advance on Silistria, although he was prepared to retreat if Austrian forces intervened. He moved slowly, opening the siege on 4 May, six weeks after crossing the river, having originally planned to take the town inside three. Rumours of the Russian move reached Dundas at Beicos, and he urged Hamelin to move up to cover Varna once the weather broke. From his instructions he knew that a Russian crossing would mean war. Having checked that the Russian fleet remained inside Sevastopol the combined fleets weighed early on 24

March. Anchoring at Kavarna on the 26th Dundas discovered the Russians were across the river.[1] Interpreting this as an effective declaration of war, he planned operations on the Asian coast. *Sidon*, *Firebrand* and *Magellan* cruised along the European shore to the mouths of the Danube, with orders to capture any Russian vessels, prevent a landing and aid the Turks. This was nice judgement, it was possible to defend in Europe, but he would wait for the official declaration before Lyons' steamers opened the Asian campaign, covered by a steam squadron off Odessa and the battlefleet off Sevastopol.[2] This was not to be. On 1 April the fleet shifted into Baljick Bay, and was now tied to the Danube campaign. First reports from Captain Goldsmith, *Sidon*, suggested the Turks would be hard pressed. The cruisers had orders to stop vessels carrying supplies into the Danube, but not to capture them, as the Russians were allowing British merchant ships to clear the river.[3]

Realising war could not be long delayed Stratford requested Dundas pick up the Consuls at Odessa and Sulina. *Furious* went on 6 April, the fleet remaining at Baljick. On 9 April *Furious* rejoined, reporting her boat had been fired on at Odessa while under a flag of truce; at 16.10 *Niger* came into the bay, signalling the declaration, and bearing dispatches. The war orders bore all the hallmarks of Graham, confirming Dundas's policy and stressing the importance of battle.[4] The private letters to both Admirals had a similar import.[5] The propriety of keeping up a correspondence with the second-in-command did not trouble Graham; he felt secure discussing public policy behind the heading 'private'. At this stage there were no difficulties, Dundas showing all his letters to Lyons, although Lyons did not reciprocate. Lyons looked to attack Sevastopol. Dundas believed the place was too strong, wanting to reinforce Varna with elements of the Turkish fleet before moving to the Asian coast, using Lyons to secure Stratford's assistance to find Turkish ships. This disgusted Slade and the Capitan Pasha, who realised that to preserve their self-esteem the Turks must take an active role. Considering their ships unseaworthy and unfit for combat, Dundas wanted to restrict them to subsidiary duties off Varna, until Lyons had opened up the Circassian coast. Pressed by Slade the Turks prepared nine battleships, one frigate and seven steamers. Dundas urged Stratford to have this force sent into the Aegean, to combat piracy. He also requested Graham to discipline Slade, after a heated exchange aboard *Britannia*.[6] Graham wanted to recall him, but accepted

Clarendon's advice that he be forcibly reminded of his British rank. Dundas treated Slade as Stratford's creature, while Hamelin blamed him for hostile articles in the Turkish press.[7] The real problem was of divided loyalties. Slade was paid by the Turks, remaining in their service until his retirement. As with Stratford, he relied on his influence in British councils to secure his position with the Turks; when he lost the goodwill of Dundas and Hamelin, his Ottoman masters began to court the allied Admirals for themselves, leaving him no role.

Dundas attempted to control the theatre from Baljick, sending *Fury* to report on Sevastopol on 10 April, reinforcing the squadron off the Danube, and covering Odessa with three steamers. *Fury* returned on the 14th, having captured a merchant schooner off Sevastopol before being driven off by two Russian frigates. The merchant captain was taken prisoner, and revealed that there were twelve battleships, eleven smaller sailing ships and seven steamers ready for service, of which the British-built *Bessarabia* and *Vladimir* were fast. In addition he claimed 50,000 troops were at Sevastopol, expecting a naval attack, while 60,000 were reinforcing the defences at Odessa. The weather was still far from suitable for heavy sailing ships, with NNE gales, sleet and ice. This forced Dundas and Hamelin to keep several large steamers with the battlefleet, limiting the force available for independent operations. With the Russian fleet inside Sevastopol, the Admirals accepted their primary duty was blockade.[8]

Aware Russian troops were moving south of the Danube, Dundas elected to gain some satisfaction for the outrage at Odessa. Early on the 17th the fleet weighed. Not intending to divide the forces and give the Russians the advantage of interior lines, the battlefleet would mount a close blockade of Sevastopol while Lyons was away. The failure of the diplomatic service to obtain Crimean intelligence forced Dundas to rely on captured coasters; *Niger* took six off the Dnieper.[9] Late on the 20th the fleet anchored off Odessa, sending *Caton* into the harbour at 02.00 under a flag of truce to demand satisfaction from the Governor, General Osten-Sacken. An earlier exchange had not satisfied Dundas, this time Osten-Sacken did not reply. The Admirals ordered an attack on the shipping inside the Imperial Mole, taking care to avoid the commercial harbour where several allied merchant ships were held. The attack was carried out by a division of steamers under Captain Jones, *Sampson*: *Tiger*,

Retribution, Furious, Terrible, Vauban, Mogador, Descartes and *Caton*, with six rocket boats and the frigate *Arethusa*. Desultory firing began soon after 06.30 as the steamers closed in; *Arethusa* engaged a detached battery south of the mole between 07.40 and 09.10, being recalled just as the steamers came up. They anchored at 10.00, closing at 12.45; five minutes later the mole head fort blew up and the steamers ceased firing. A few field guns opened at 14.40, and they replied until 17.00 when the general recall was signalled. The rocket boats concentrated on the Man of War harbour and nearby government storehouses, to some effect. In the confusion several allied merchant ships escaped. The damage was substantial, all but one of the ships in the Man of War harbour were destroyed, fires burned through the night and the recently reinforced batteries were ruined. *Vauban* had to leave the action to dig two red hot shot out of her hull, losing two men killed and one wounded. *Terrible* also lost one man, although the other ten wounded suffered only minor injuries. The expenditure of ammunition was considerable, *Furious* alone using 600 rounds.[10] The bombardment of Odessa was a salutary lesson for the Russians; whatever had occurred to *Furious*'s boat the defences of the port were a legitimate target. Dundas had answered Graham's desire to make 'an early impression on the enemy's coast' before the troops came up from Malta.[11] Far from being content with this Dundas was about make the allied presence felt on the Asian coast.

Fury examined the port early on the 23rd, reporting the damage, and returned later with *Tiger* to blockade. Dundas proposed exchanging the sailors captured by *Niger* for allied merchant seamen held at Odessa, as his ships were all short handed. The weather off Odessa worsened, strong southerly winds blowing directly onshore. Before weighing for Sevastopol *Firebrand* and *Niger* were recalled from the Danube, where, with *Retribution*, they destroyed large quantities of wheat at Kustenjeh ahead of the advancing Russians. The fleet sailed on the 26th, arriving two days later to find fourteen Russian sail still at anchor. *Furious, Vauban* and *Caton* captured four vessels off Eupatoria while on passage; *Terrible* went down to Constantinople for interpreters to accompany Lyons' squadron, although they were refused as unbecoming to the dignity of the Turkish government.[12]

The Russian forces in Asia were outnumbered and exposed by their dependence on sea-borne logistics. This led to Sinope, and to

Paskevic's recommending the evacuation of the coastal forts. As early as September 1853 he knew they were open to attack in detail by superior naval forces, and once command of the sea was lost the Turks or Circassians could capture them. The latter point persuaded Nicholas to order the evacuation of the smaller forts in March, 3,849 men and many guns were withdrawn by sea.[13] Dundas appreciated the weakness of the Russian position, with a series of isolated forts intended to coerce the natives, not resist naval bombardment; he intended to open his campaign there. *Sampson* and *Cacique* carried out a thorough inspection between 9 and 19 March. Captain Jones reported the destruction of the smaller forts, anticipating the Russians would only hold the four largest, Soukham Kaleh, Gelenjih, Sanjak and Anapa. They encountered Russian troops at sea, before war had been declared.[14]

Dundas's orders to Lyons stressed the need to communicate with Schamyl and find a secure anchorage where Captain Brock and 100 marines could be put ashore. Forts were only to be attacked if they could be overcome without risk. The squadron comprised *Agamemnon*, *Sampson*, *Highflyer*, *Retribution*, *Firebrand* and *Niger*, with Captain de Chabannes' *Charlemagne*, *Mogador* and *Vauban*. The last three British steamers were to return to the fleet once Lyons reached the Asian coast, the rest would rejoin via Sinope.[15] The squadron left the fleet off Sevastopol on 5 May, steering along the southern coast of the Crimea and examining Kaffa Bay. *Highflyer*, *Firebrand* and *Niger* entered the straits of Kertch. *Niger* ran aground, although she was not damaged. Lyons went on to Anapa, which was too strong for an attack. Shortly after passing Anapa *Retribution* and *Highflyer* captured three coasters laden with troops and stores from the evacuated forts. Although the squadron anchored off Ghelendjick the Circassians were unwilling to join an attack, so Lyons moved on to land Brock at Berdan. All down the coast he discovered empty forts. Soukham Kaleh's 3,500-man garrison had decamped on 13 April, pausing only to spike their guns; further south the Russians still held Redoubt Kaleh, an important base for their Asian army. Lyons decided to attack, securing 600 Turkish troops from Batoum. The Turks were landed close to the town on the 19th. When the garrison rejected a summons the two steam battleships stood in, the Russians set fire to the fort and retreated inland. A Turkish garrison was left, with *Sampson*, which could burn the local anthracite, remaining in support. The only

problem was persuading the Turks to reinforce Redoubt Kaleh.[16]
They wanted to run their own campaign, not pick up crumbs left by
the allies. Slade was aware that this had a damaging effect on the
Asian theatre. Lyons coaled at Sinope, picked up a cargo of bullocks
and vegetables, and rejoined the fleet off Baljick on the 28th. The
allies had another task and would not allow the Turks to operate
alone. The Black Sea theatre was already suffering from the tunnel
vision of a Crimea dominated strategy. The Russian coast was open
from the Danube to Poti, but the opportunities were ignored.

After Lyons' squadron sailed for the Circassian coast Dundas and
Hamelin cruised off Cape Chersonese. Checking Sevastopol on 10
May, Dundas sent *Tiger*, *Niger* and *Vesuvius* to scour the Bay of
Odessa. Four days later *Niger* and *Vesuvius* returned, reporting the
loss of *Tiger* on the 12th. She had run aground in thick fog four miles
south of Odessa, and field guns on the dominating cliffs forced
Captain Giffard, already seriously wounded, to surrender. Shortly
after the crew reached the shore *Tiger*'s magazine blew up; *Niger* and
Vesuvius later shelled the wreck to prevent the machinery falling into
Russian hands. Dundas sent them back, to exchange *Tiger*'s men for
the troops captured near Anapa.[17] The combined fleets left the
Crimean coast on the 18th, anchoring at Baljick on the 20th. The
naval campaign had ended.

The defensive arm of Graham's Black Sea strategy was based on
Burgoyne's lines. Burgoyne still favoured trenches across the Gallipoli peninsula, holding the main army near Constantinople, ready to
build more lines. He believed the Russians would soon force the
Turkish position on the Danube, allowing the allies to meet them
south of the Balkan mountains at the greatest distance from their
bases. The object was to keep control of the Straits, enabling the
fleets to operate in the Euxine. Burgoyne viewed war as a siege, to be
conducted by gradual, cautious approaches from a secure base. A
visit to Omer Pasha's headquarters in mid March did nothing to alter
his attitude. Omer could not persuade him that moving the allied
armies up to Varna offered real advantages. He advised the Turks to
prepare to fall back on the Balkan passes, garrisoning Varna for a
siege, with naval support. It would be too great a risk to send allied
troops forward if Constantinople was not secure. For the offensive
Burgoyne looked to the Crimea, Georgia, or even the Danube, but
preferred small operations, particularly opening the Sea of Azov. On
his return he stopped in Paris, where Louis Napoleon and Vaillant

supported his plans. Back in London he realised the importance of taking the initiative.[18] Sevastopol had been accepted as the proper target, and expeditions were being prepared. When Raglan met his French colleague, St Arnaud, in Paris during April, instructions were already being sent for the Crimean operation. Newcastle also favoured sending some allied troops up to Varna. Raglan left Toulon on 23 April, arriving at Constantinople on the 29th a week before St Arnaud. Discovering that Scutari, selected by Newcastle, was filthy and the temptations of the town were damaging health and morale, he pressed the French to move to Varna. Newcastle's reasoning was simple. Securing Constantinople, or even liberating the Principalities 'without crippling their future means of aggression upon Turkey is not *now* an object worthy of the great efforts of England and France'. Sevastopol was the only target that appeared to promise an early peace; moving to Varna would relieve Silistria and prepare for the Crimea.[19] Burgoyne aligned himself with these developments, still convinced Sevastopol would be too difficult, preferring Anapa or the Sea of Azov, and anxious to base any offensive on secure lines at Constantinople.[20]

The siege of Silistria, which Paskevic conducted without enthusiasm, became the focal point of the war. Raglan saw the move to Varna primarily as opening the way for a relief, accepting the gauge thrown down by Paskevic. He secured French agreement on 19 May, Omer advising that Varna was a suitable base. St Arnaud quickly changed his mind, sending his Zouaves from Gallipoli to Adrianople on the 22nd; claiming Silistria was irrelevant, he wanted to keep the armies at Burgas, south of the Balkan. Raglan refused, sending part of the light division, with cavalry and artillery to Varna. This had nothing to do with Sevastopol, for Raglan accepted Dundas's view that it was a second Gibraltar. After meeting Dundas at Varna on the 22nd Raglan tried to damp down the Government's enthusiasm, but was never going to succeed. Dundas sent *Bellerophon*, *London* and *Arethusa* to assist the disembarkation of the troops, the fleet covered troop convoys on the European shore. Raglan quickly gained a moral ascendancy over St Arnaud. French troops were ordered to Varna on 9 June, almost three weeks after the original decision.[21] Events elsewhere moved more rapidly. The Austrian ultimatum was delivered on 18 June; three days earlier the Czar had ordered Paskevic to prepare to abandon the siege. On the 23rd Paskevic ordered the withdrawal, and two days later the

Russians recrossed the Danube.[22]

The Danube campaign ended before the allies were in a position to help the Turks. Raglan's rationale for moving to Varna had disappeared, leaving only Newcastle's offensive plans. Moving the army from Constantinople reversed Burgoyne's logic in sending troops to keep the Straits open for the fleets, allowing seapower to exert a decisive influence. With the armies at Varna the fleets were tied to their support, unable to adopt a maritime strategy.

Dundas's position was exacerbated by the ludicrous command structure. In late February Louis Napoleon discussed command with Cowley, proposing British command at sea, and French on land, with a good measure of discussion. The British Government refused, believing it would be undignified for French officers to send British troops into battle; they argued for simple co-operation. Burgoyne anticipated 'delays and weak measures', preferring to keep the armies separate except in battle, when the senior officer would command. His warning was ignored, although the problems soon became evident in both theatres. St Arnaud had authority over Hamelin, while Raglan and Dundas were equal and bound to co-operate. Dundas was also enjoined to co-operate with Hamelin, allowing St Arnaud to control the fleet through the co-operation of the Admirals.[23] The most severe effects of this plurality would be felt later in the year, but even in May it produced agreement only on cautious measures.

After the initial instructions to attack the enemy, the Admiralty waited until 4 April before directing Dundas to conduct a blockade, in collaboration with his French colleague. He acted quickly, declaring the coast of Russia from the Danube to Ghelendjik blockaded. Before the armies moved up to Varna the fleets had the strength to make this policy effective, but Hamelin would not join the declaration, having no instructions; the French Minister of Marine, Ducos, claimed not to understand this action, but Hamelin properly required positive authority. His refusal was still effective in late May, by which time the opportunity to set up a blockade had been lost. Instructions were finally sent on the 24th, but arrived after the armies began to move. Had the blockade been established before it might have been maintained, but once the Generals reached Varna St Arnaud would not agree to waste ships on what struck him as an irrelevant task.[24] Dundas proposed blockading the Danube as the Russians were already across it. The failure to provide a period of

grace for ships already in the river was a major error, when the
principal riparian power was neutral Austria. Hamelin allowed
Austrian vessels to depart unmolested, making the blockade of
doubtful legality.

Dundas's second proposal was novel; he wanted to employ the
geography of the Euxine to impose a distant blockade, not relying on
the classic requirement of physical ability to intercept shipping off
each port. The Ottoman government should stop every merchant
ship entering the Black Sea, notify it of the blockade, and seize any
attempting to reach Russian ports. Stratford objected, fearing
neutral opinion, but as the blockade would be conducted entirely by
the Turks his concern was unfounded. The Admiralty pressed for
this plan to be adopted. Unfortunately the Queen's Advocate, J. D.
Harding, adopted a narrow legalistic interpretation, claiming
Dundas's plan would only be justified in international law if a close
blockade had already been established. The Foreign Office adopted
this opinion, which the French accepted.[25] As Dundas pointed out, a
close blockade could not be established because of the demands of
the Crimean expedition. Even the Danube blockade was lifted when
the invasion took place, when in force it had only been a source of
conflict between Dundas and Stratford.[26] The blockade issue
remained a major frustration for the Admiralty, with merchants
complaining that the failure to impose one was causing them significant losses, adding to Whitehall's dissatisfaction. As a result Dundas
was repeatedly pressed to institute a strict blockade, even without
the French. All Dundas could achieve was advance notice of a
blockade for 1 February, 1855. He realised the French Generals
would not spare a ship. Paris preferred to blame Hamelin.[27]

The sixty-eight ships captured in 1854 totalled 2,343 tons, an
average of only thirty-five tons. This coasting trade was always
difficult to interrupt, even with steamers. The blockade issue was
badly handled in London, and as a result no effective measures were
taken. Dundas's distant blockade would have been effective, but the
government lacked the resolve to risk adverse comment from
neutrals, preferring to goad Dundas and ignore his explanations. As
Russia received most of her contraband through Prussia, and had
little grain for export in the south, the Euxine blockade was largely
irrelevant. The expedient attitude of the French was conditioned by
their very different experience of trade war.

Notes

1   Dundas to Stratford 19, 22, 23 Mar. 1854: DND/1 f129–32; Dundas to Admiralty 27 Mar. rec. 11 Apr. 1854 no. 124: ADM 1/5626.
2   Dundas to Stratford 27 Mar. 1854: DND/1 f134; Dundas to Captain Goldsmith 27 Mar. 1854: encl. in Dundas to Admiralty 27 Mar. rec. 11 Apr. 1854 no. 125: ADM 1/5626; Dundas to Graham 30 Mar. 1854: Gr. CW3.
3   Goldsmith to Dundas 1 Apr. 1854 encl. in Dundas to Admiralty 3 rec. 19 Apr. 1854 no. 137: ADM 1/5626.
4   Lyons to Graham 6 Apr. 1854: Gr. CW9; Dundas to Admiralty 8 rec. 21 Apr. 1854 no. 150: ADM 1/5626.
5   Newcastle to Admiralty 29 Mar. 1854: NRS pp. 246–7; Graham to Dundas 22, 30 Mar. 1854: DND/9 f54–63; Graham to Lyons 30 Mar. 1854: Gr. CW9.
6   Lyons to Stratford 28 Mar. 1854: F.O. 352/38/2; Dundas to Admiralty 24 Apr. rec. 11 May. 1854 no. 177: encl. Stratford to Dundas 6, 19 Apr. Dundas to Stratford 9, 22 Apr.: ADM 1/5626; Dundas to Graham 5 May 1854: Gr. CW3.
7   Dundas to Admiralty 13 May 1854: F.O. 78/1052; Foreign Office to Admiralty 3 Jun. 1854: F.O. 78/1052; Clarendon to Stratford 3 Jun. 1854: F.O. 352/37; Slade to Stratford 27 May 1854: F.O. 352/38/3; SLADE, pp. 293–4 and 226–234.
8   Dundas to Admiralty 14 Apr. rec. 1 May 1854 no. 164: encl. Captain Tatham to Dundas 14 Apr.: ADM 1/5626.
9   Dundas to Stratford 16 Apr. 1854: DND/1 f148; Dundas to Graham 19 Apr. 1854: Gr. CW3; Dundas to Osten-Sacken 21 Apr. 1854: DND/1 f149.
10   Dundas to Admiralty 21, 22 Apr. rec. 11 May 1854 no. 171, 172: ADM 1/5626 Logs of *Sampson, Terrible, Furious* and *Arethusa*; Dundas to Stewart 25 Apr. 1854: ADM 50/243.
11   Graham to Dundas 30 Mar. 1854: DND/9 f59–63.
12   Dundas to Admiralty 24 Apr., 1 May rec. 11, 21 May 1854 no. 178, 190: ADM 1/5626.
13   CURTISS, pp. 185–8.
14   Dundas to Admiralty 20 Mar., 25 Apr. 1854 no. 115, 179: ADM 1/5626 and NRS p. 256. Dundas to Graham 15, 17 Dec. 1853: 30 Mar., 19 Apr. 1854: Gr. CW2–3; Dundas to Stratford 27 Mar. 1854: DND/1 f134.
15   Dundas to Lyons 1 May 1854: NRS, p. 257.
16   Lyons to Dundas 9, 13, 20 May 1854: DND/9 f74–9, F.O. 352/38/2; Dundas to Stratford 8, 26 Jun. 1854: DND/1 f169 and 173; SLADE, pp. 205–240.
17   Dundas to Osten-Sacken 14, 16 May 1854: DND/1 f160–2.
18   Burgoyne to Cowley 12 Feb. 1854: F.O. 519/297; Burgoyne to Stratford 22 Mar. 1854: WROTTESLEY, ii, pp. 20–7; Burgoyne memo. on the state of the war 22 Feb. 1854 and Burgoyne to Raglan 30 Mar. 1854: F.O. 519/297; Burgoyne memo. of conversation 5 Apr. 1854: *ibid.*
19   Newcastle to Raglan 17, 22 Apr., 3, 9, 18 May 1854: RAGLAN 6807–283; Raglan to Newcastle 13 Apr., 5 May 1854: RAGLAN

6807–284; Newcastle to de Ros 13 Mar. 1854: RAGLAN 6807–283.
20   Burgoyne to Raglan 30 May 1854: WROTTESLEY, ii, pp. 37–42.
21   GOOCH, B.D., *The New Bonapartist Generals in the Crimean War*
(The Hague, 1959), pp. 82–3; Raglan to Newcastle 15, 17, 19, 25, 29 May,
10 Jun. 1854: RAGLAN 6807–284; Raglan to Cowley 30 May 1854: F.O.
519/297; Dundas to Raglan 10 May 1854: RAGLAN 6807–298A.
22   CURTISS, pp. 261–6.
23   WELLESLEY, F. A., ed., *The Paris Embassy during the Second
Empire* (London, 1928), pp. 43–4; Burgoyne memo. on divided authority
24 Mar. 1854: F.O. 519/297.
24   I have elected to deal, briefly, with the Black Sea blockade issue to the
end of 1854 in this section. Admiralty to Dundas 5 Apr. 1854 no. 162: NRS,
pp. 254–5; Dundas to Admiralty 1 May 1854 no. 189: NRS, p. 257; Dundas
to Graham 1, 29 May 1854: Gr. CW3; Cowley to Clarendon 24 May 1854:
NRS, p. 271;
25   Dundas to Admiralty 1, 10 , 22 Jun. 1854 no. 250, 266 and 296;
Stratford to Dundas 19 Jun. 1854 in Admiralty to Foreign Office 28 Jun.
1854: NRS, pp. 272–9; Admiralty to Dundas 3 Jul. 1854 no. 366: NRS, pp.
284–6.
26   Dundas to Graham 9 Aug. 1854: Gr. CW3; Dundas to Admiralty 8
Oct. 1854 no. 516: NRS, p. 331.
27   Foreign Office to Admiralty 18 Sept. 1854: NRS pp. 313–5;
Admiralty to Dundas 2 Dec. 1854 no. 783: NRS, p. 388; Dundas to
Admiralty 12 rec. 30 Dec. 1854 no. 664: NRS, p. 394; Dundas to Graham
23 Nov. 1854: Gr. CW4; Cowley to Clarendon 29 Oct. 1854; F.O. 519/214
f160–3.

9

The grand raid

The first task at Varna was to disembark the troops. Lacking harbour facilities, the majority came ashore over an open beach, valuable experience for the future; that this took over a month was ignored when deciding to invade the Crimea. The crews of four or five heavy ships assisted; the remainder kept to the north at Baljick, with steamers checking Sevastopol. Dundas now appreciated that if the Russian fleet did leave harbour it would be to land troops and stores south of the Danube. He also prepared to send steamers to support Turkish troops in the Sulina channel.[1]

Everything depended on the Danube campaign. The chance of Austrian intervention encouraged Dundas to hope for peace. He was furious when Stratford did not send him a copy of the Austro–Turkish convention of 18 June, especially as Hamelin was able to lend him one. Stratford did not consider him capable of assessing such information, preferring to explain it to him. Equally aware that strategy could not be formed in a political vacuum Raglan sent the Duke of Cambridge, a divisional commander, to interview Stratford and the Austrian internuncio on the policy of Vienna.[2] The Duke's report encouraged the commanders to offer aid to Omer at their 5 July conference. As a preliminary Raglan requested a naval party to bridge the Danube at Rustchuk. The Turks crossed on the 10th, and after giving battle at Giurgevo the Russians retreated.[3] *Firebrand*, *Vesuvius* and *Fury* captured the batteries at Sulina on the 8th, opening the river for a campaign just as Austrian intervention made the theatre irrelevant. Both allied armies made diversionary moves into the Dobrudscha, without affecting the Russians. Austria determined the pace of Paskevic's withdrawal, when her forces halted, allowing the Russians to retire unmolested. Raglan feared they would attack Omer. Dundas hoped this would delay the Crimean operation until 1855.[4]

While the armies disembarked the fleets were tied to Baljick. Dundas would have preferred to blockade Sevastopol, but St Arnaud ordered Hamelin to stay. Raglan appreciated Dundas's position, but could do nothing.[5] Ignorant of naval strategy St Arnaud preferred the simple comfort of a fleet near at hand to the more solid benefits of a close blockade. This prevented any significant detachments, paralysing the Asian coast, for unless the Russians were masked every naval movement had to be escorted by a force equal to their battleline. Placed in this subordinate role many officers favoured the Crimean operation, if only to leave Baljick.

Dundas was anxious for the Asian coast, detaching *Highflyer* and pressing for more troops. Lyons advised against further operations in that sector; pointing out that Anapa was neither the key to the Sea of Azov, nor a safe anchorage, he advised leaving the garrison in place. All efforts should be concentrated on the Crimea, for if Sevastopol were taken the whole Russian position on the Black Sea littoral would collapse. This was Graham's view. Dundas and Raglan accepted his arguments on Anapa, and although less enthusiastic for Sevastopol they persuaded the French to abandon a large scale reconnaissance of the Asian coast and press for Turkish troops to reinforce Soukham Kaleh. For all his advocacy of Sevastopol, Lyons was careful to tell St Arnaud that Anapa was better than nothing. Dundas wanted to send 10,000 men to reinforce the Turks in Asia and drive the Russians out of Georgia. He only secured 500 Turkish soldiers from Varna, and some from the now quiescent Greek frontier.[6] The divergence of opinion between Dundas and Lyons was clear; Dundas wanted to operate on the periphery, Lyons to destroy the theatre strength of the Russians, gathering the pieces later. Dundas's opinion was better attuned to the available resources and the political object of the war than the view Lyons had adopted from Graham. He saw Sevastopol as a gamble. Failure would destroy the allied armies, and he reminded Graham the Generals did not consider their forces sufficiently strong, an opinion his senior Captains shared.[7] However, both he and Raglan understood the primacy of politics. Their duty was to obey.

Newcastle's private letter of 28 June dismayed Raglan: 'The task we are to be called upon to undertake is of the most serious character and the information we have upon the Crimea generally and upon Sevastopol is as imperfect as it was when I left England.' While he had asked if landing boats should be built Raglan shared Dundas's lack of enthusiasm for the operation. Dundas called for a thorough inspection of the Crimean coast, sending Drummond to liaise with Raglan. The public dispatch of 29 June reached Varna on the 17th; Raglan called a conference to discuss the 'peremptory instructions'. The following day the commanders decided to prepare, 'more in deference to the views of the British government . . . and . . . the Emperor Louis Napoleon . . . than to any information in the possession of the naval and military authorities.'[8] Although ready to follow orders Dundas was alarmed by St Arnaud's sudden volte face. Earlier the French Marshal had opposed the operation; now, without any new information on landing sites and water supply, he was ready to begin. Dundas urged Anapa as an alternative, Raglan shared these anxieties. Lyons alone of the senior officers was not concerned by the lack of intelligence, although Rear-Admiral Bruat, the recently arrived French second-in-command, was less pessimistic than the others.[9] St Arnaud was dying from cancer of the stomach, but when the pain abated his optimism was unbounded. He had no fear of failure, he would hardly live to see success. No other French commander shared his optimism, and nor did St Arnaud when he suffered a crisis of his illness during the voyage to the Crimea. Underlying French caution was the fragile political position of the regime. The French commanders were committed to the Emperor, although many disliked him.

To conduct a strategic reconnaissance of the Crimea, the vicious disposition adopted by the Generals made it necessary to take the combined fleet to sea under Dundas and Bruat. General Canrobert, Colonel Trochu, General Sir George Brown and Lyons would examine the coast. The squadrons weighed at 04.30 on the 20th; by 10.00 adverse winds led Dundas to detach the sluggish *Trafalgar*; at 17.00 *Retribution* had to tow *Britannia* into the teeth of a westerly gale. Reaching the Crimea on the 22nd, Dundas pointed out the value of Eupatoria, a safe anchorage which would be essential for transports. On the evening of the 25th Canrobert, Trochu, Brown and Lyons boarded *Fury* for a closer inspection. At dawn she closed Sevastopol with *Terrible* and *Cacique*. The Russian battlefleet prepared to sail, until the allied main body came into sight. Lyons then ran north to Eupatoria, keeping close inshore to draw the fire of any batteries. Both British ships were hit but not damaged, there were no significant fortifications on the coast. The commanders selected the mouth of the river Katscha, which would solve Dundas's fear about water supply; Dundas was satisfied with Lyons' report, sending him back to Varna that day. The squadron then went round to Balaklava, detaching *Tribune* east to Kaffa on the 27th. Raglan and St Arnaud assembled a conference on the 28th to consider the reports. They continued preparations, recognising the final decision depended on circumstances beyond their control. When the squadrons reached Baljick on the 30th, Lyons was placed in charge of the amphibious force: *Agamemnon, Sans Pareil, Bellerophon, Leander, Highflyer, Diamond, Fury* and *Niger*, with the naval transports *Simoom, Megeara, Cyclops* and *Apollo*, and the tenders *Triton, Danube* and *Circassia* and the hired transports. Rear-Admiral Boxer would be responsible for collecting boats and shipping. The 'improbable' danger of a Russian attack would be covered by Dundas with the battlefleet.[10]

Two factors outside allied control threatened the operation – cholera, and the slow progress of the Austrians into the Principalities. The senior naval officer at Varna reported the disease ashore on 19 July, and by the 31st it had gained a foothold aboard his ship. The allies were helpless because they did not know the cause; it was still generally attributed to impure air, although experiments in London were demonstrating that it was water borne. This concern reflected a Europe-wide epidemic, particularly virulent at Marseilles and Toulon. French troops brought the disease to Gallipoli, and St Arnaud's refusal to quarantine the infected ships ensured it reached Varna by 10 July. Insanitary conditions in the camps, notably around the drinking water supply, promoted contagion. Sailors carried it back to their ships in their water tanks. The steamers, relying on distilled water, were hardly affected. The French ashore and afloat were the first to suffer, and had the worst of the outbreak. When *Valmy* shifted to Kavarna on 1 August she was already losing men. On the same day *Britannia* reported sixty-nine cases of diarrhoea, and mild symptoms had been increasing in ships connected with the armies, especially the large sailing ships. Dundas again believed he had found a reason to delay the operation until after his departure. Only on 8 August was the first case reported aboard *Britannia*. The fleet surgeon advised putting to sea, recently a successful palliative at Malta. *Trafalgar, Vengeance* and *London* weighed on the 11th, with the French fleet. The other British ships followed the next day. Aboard *Britannia* the infection reached a peak during her four days at sea. Meeting heavy weather she was forced to close her ports, reducing ventilation, ninety-three died causing panic among the crew which only ended after they returned to Baljick on the 17th and fumigated the ship with chloride of zinc. *Britannia* lost 139 men, out of 625 cases; in the fleet 4,500 suffered some form of diarrhoea, 760 were diagnosed as cholera and 411 proved fatal; the French lost more. Inadequate latrine facilities and the after-effects of the Besika fever of 1853 played a part in spreading the disease. During 1854, 734 men in the British fleet died of cholera, over half the total fatalities. Figures for the two armies do not exist, but they were far worse. Lyons' only concern was that 'exaggerated accounts' might cause the operation to be put off, (*Agamemnon* distilled her own water and had very few cases). By 19 August he was claiming the forces were much healthier. Lyons was urging reluctant colleagues to attempt the largest amphibious campaign of the modern age with troops weakened by a virulent disease. His only ground for optimism was that it appeared to have abated. But for massive doses of quinine, malaria would have finished off both armies, as it had General Diebitsch's troops in 1829. Just to add to the problems ashore, a large fire on 10 August destroyed 16,000 pairs of boots and 150 tons of biscuit.[11]

Placing Lyons in command of the amphibious operation was a wise election. Dundas provided his ostentatiously energetic second with a demanding task, keeping the critical escort role for himself. However, Lyons proving incapable, the detailed administration fell to his flag Captain, William Mends. Mends was inspired by recollecting the evacuation of 22,000 Russian troops from Constantinople in 1833 in twelve hours using only two small steamers and ships' boats. Lyons and Brown went to Constantinople on 1 August to confer with Admiral Boxer and use Stratford's influence to secure Turkish assistance. The Turks had already sent six battleships to embark their 7,000 man contingent. Lyons also consulted the Agent of Transports, Captain Christie, securing five small steamers and thirty-four pontoons. He considered his resources 'ample'. Malta sent thirty boats, fifty carts, mules, planks and nails. Dundas expressed his satisfaction with the plans, and the means to hand. Mends' plan provided steam power for every ship in the British force, and enough tonnage to carry the infantry, artillery and half the cavalry. By contrast the French were forced to leave their cavalry behind, and carry their infantry crammed into the battleships. The Turkish battleships were similarly crowded. Only Dundas's ships were capable of meeting a Russian attack.

After a conference ashore the four Admirals met aboard *Ville de Paris* on 20 August to decide the sailing arrangements. The French would embark at Baljick, the British at Varna, completing on 2 September. They would sail in two columns, the British to the north of the French and Turks. The transports would be towed if the wind failed, but the French battleships would have to fend for themselves. If a north east wind stopped the passage the Admirals would confer. Finally they considered forcing a passage into Sevastopol harbour, agreeing to consult before an attempt.[12] Dundas now believed the Russians would attack the convoy, as he would have done in their position.[13]

The dependence of the armies on the fleets grew as the time for embarkation approached. Short of artillery, Raglan checked the Turkish siege park before admitting he must rely on naval guns. His full establishment of guns arrived in time for the operation, but they proved totally inadequate.[14] The armies made some attempt to disguise the point of attack, sending forces into the Dobrudscha in July, and a small party under Captain Spratt along the coast, without producing any noticeable impact on Russian movements.[15] With the Austrians pressing one flank and allied seapower controlling the other they were hardly likely to risk action, while an allied attack along the Bessarabian corridor was equally improbable. Graham urged a more effective diversion, opening the Sea of Azov. However no sooner had Lyons identified Kertch as the key to straits, rather than Anapa, than *Highflyer* reported they were blocked with sunken ships and covered by new batteries. Troops were essential, and had they been spared, which was highly unlikely, they would have been wasted, for Dundas had no steamers to operate in the shallow sea. The purchased tenders were too flimsy for heavy guns, the other ships drew too much water. Graham later complained Dundas had ignored orders to enter the straits, but as he never sent such orders and did not provide the equipment, such strictures were dishonest.[16] After the decision to land at the Katscha had been published in *The Times*, Raglan persuaded Dundas to send another reconnaissance. *Terrible* and *Fury* left on 20 August, returning five days later with reassuring reports. Raglan would not send a spy, fearing he might be caught. Intelligence from London only indicated the extent of earlier neglect. Both Raglan and Dundas were certain the operation could not have started any sooner, whatever Graham might suggest.[17]

There is no indication of joint military planning, in contrast to the naval co-operation. General Bizot, the French Engineer, anticipated regular siege of the Star Fort; British plans were based on Graham's *coup de main*. Raglan's outline, discussed at British headquarters, involved landing under fire with naval support and moving to capture the Star Fort north of the harbour. General Tylden, the senior engineer, although not in Raglan's confidence, accurately predicted the course of the campaign. Raglan rejected his concerns, using Lyons' views.

Hearing Raglan had no confidence in Tylden, Newcastle decided to send out Burgoyne, although he had never agreed with the Sevastopol operation, as Newcastle and Graham intended it to be carried out. Newcastle had rejected Hardinge's proposal that Burgoyne be second in command, claiming he could not be spared; while Graham had only used him to outline the defensive arm of his Black Sea strategy. When the reports of the first reconnaissance of the Crimea reached London, Graham called for Burgoyne's opinion. The old engineer was horrified at the idea of landing over an open beach three hours' march from Sevastopol, and rightly deprecated the value of naval gunfire to support troops on broken ground. The plan struck him as 'impracticable' and he advised landing further north; the longer march would be no real disadvantage with the fleets to carry the stores. Graham passed these opinions to Newcastle, who interviewed Burgoyne on 7 August, and invited him to join the army on the 11th. Leaving the same night, Burgoyne had not requested, or been given, any status with the army.[18] The decision to send a man known to be opposed to the spirit of the operation, as well as the detailed plans which the politicians had ordered unwilling officers to carry out, to join an army on the eve of a major operation was an act of criminal irresolution on Newcastle's part. While the objections were sound, Burgoyne knew no more of the Crimea than those at Varna; furthermore, the *coup de main* was the only viable method of attempting Sevastopol with the available forces. The clash of his plans with the grand raid ensured the failure of both. Newcastle and Graham deserved to lose office for this single act. Had they shared Burgoyne's reservations they should have cancelled the operation. Instead they sent out Burgoyne, knowing that Raglan would defer to his opinion on questions of strategy.

As he crossed the Mediterranean Burgoyne sketched a plan of campaign. He wanted to land at Eupatoria and build a fort, in the meantime creating alarm at Balaklava, before collecting the allied forces, apart from 10,000 Turks who would simultaneously land on the south coast, and give battle. If defeated, the allies had a fort to fall back on; if successful they should turn the Russian defences by moving onto the south side of the city, using Balaklava and the bays of the Chersonese peninsula for supplies. Burgoyne had nothing to confirm the widely-held assumption that the south side was weaker than the north; Tylden anticipated it would prove far from easy. That so much of Burgoyne's plan was carried out, although he only reached Varna on 27 August, can be attributed to his relationship with Raglan and his influence with Dundas. Dundas's recently arrived guest, Colonel Brereton, 'an old friend' and great admirer of Burgoyne, convinced the cautious Admiral that the Engineer's plans were the most reliable. They already shared the conviction that Eupatoria was the place to land. Dundas was probably relieved to find a soldier who shared his low opinion of the grand raid, becoming increasingly cautious, notably in demanding a secure anchorage for the transports. Burgoyne's memorandum of 29 August contained two basic flaws. He believed it would be possible to bombard the docks and harbour from the south (the north was the better point) and that moving south was preferable to laying siege to the Star Fort. He shared Dundas's hope that the condition of the armies would ensure the operation was put off until the spring.[19] Every mile marched in the Crimea, and each added movement turned the allies away from the risk-laden grand raid toward Burgoyne's regular campaign. While this appeared to be more economical of manpower it exposed the troops to a winter under canvas that killed far more men than any *coup de main*, successful or failed. The friction of warfare would be increased by complex plans.

The embarkation arrangements were concerned to reduce the time between commencing and completing the process, to prevent an epidemic aboard the crowded ships. The conference of 20 August anticipated a five day loading, 28 August to 2 September. The allies loaded slightly over 50,000 men with 128 guns.

	British	French
Infantry	22,000	25,000
Cavalry	1,000	—
Engineers, etc.	3,000	2,800
Guns	60	68

The British forces were carried in fifty-two sailing and twenty-seven steam transports, with a small contingent aboard Lyons' ships; the French used 200 small sailing ships for their stores, guns and horses with 1–2,000 infantry aboard each battleship; the Turks used their battleships for men and stores. At first the embarkation went smoothly. Lyons anticipated sailing on the 3rd, but the need to load 1,000 cavalry and 3,000 other horses made his forecast optimistic. A heavy north-east swell set in on the 1st, but by the evening of the 4th all three forces were ready. Early on the 5th five large steamers arrived from Varna, short of coal and water. Dundas decided to delay until daylight to allow them to prepare. Raglan had to agree, but by day-break adverse winds prevented the convoy sailing. Without cavalry the French had been ready on the 4th, but only then did Hamelin discover he did not have enough steamers to tow all his transports, persuading Dundas to allow his ships to leave before the British and proceed under sail. Lyons and Raglan feared more delay.[20] The French and Turkish warships sailed on the 5th, but adverse winds and St Arnaud's irresolution ensured they made little progress.

The British fleet and the Anglo–French transports were under way by 10.00 on the 7th, meeting the French and Turkish warships early the next morning, thirty miles south of Serpent's Island. St Arnaud sent a message that he wished to see Raglan and Dundas aboard *Ville de Paris*. Stricken with a crisis of his illness the Marshal could not move, and Raglan, unable to climb the sides of the three-decker, sent his secretary, Colonel Steel, with Dundas. They reached the French flagship at 13.00 to find St Arnaud in bed, almost unable to speak. Admirals Hamelin, Bruat and Bouet-Willaumez, Colonel Trochu, believed to be the Emperor's agent, and General Rose were with him. The conference had been called to discuss an unsigned paper criticising the choice of the Katscha. The authors were reported to be Canrobert and the artillery and engineer Generals, the latter doubtless sharing Burgoyne's dislike of the whole scheme. The site had been published and *Terrible*'s last inspection revealed a large body of troops close by. The opinions were those of the Emperor, but St Arnaud was prepared to defer to Raglan. The conference shifted to *Caradoc*, and Lyons was summoned; Trochu read the paper, claiming to dissent. It suggested the Katscha, Eupatoria, Yalta and Kaffa as possible landing sites, favouring the last; all except Rose accepted that selecting Kaffa would prevent any attack on Sevastopol before the spring. The paper was claimed to arise out of the opinions of the Admirals, at which Lyons, Dundas and Bruat protested their innocence.

Raglan, in a difficult position, decided to inspect the coast himself. Clearly he shared some of the reservations expressed in the paper, and such doubts would have been increased by the arrival of Burgoyne. The conference broke up at 18.00. Burgoyne later joined *Caradoc*, Canrobert and Bizot boarding *Primauget*. Early on the 9th *Agamemnon*, *Caradoc*, *Primauget* and *Sampson* left the fleet, which anchored at the original rendezvous forty miles west of Cape Tarkan at 13.50. The detached force steamed to Sevastopol during the night, Canrobert, Bizot, Lyons and Brown then boarded *Caradoc*. Closing Sevastopol at dawn the allied ships passed south toward Balaklava, where the coast was too steep. Attention switching north, the mouths of the Belbec, Katscha, Alma and Bulganak were all rejected, the beaches being too narrow. Six miles north of the Bulganak Raglan found a wide beach with deep water at a point where the map indicated the now invisible remains of an old fort. He selected this, subject to St Arnaud's approval.[21] The ships reached the rendezvous at 07.10 on the 11th, and after consultation the fleet got underway at 03.50. The French warships lagged behind throughout the 12th. Even with assistance they were thirty miles astern by nightfall, forcing the convoy to anchor at 19.00, the escort at 20.00. The warships passed during the night and the convoy weighed at 05.30. Reunited by midday the entire force was anchored off Eupatoria by 17.30 after another day of very light winds. The town had been summoned and would be occupied on the following day. Dundas had not been informed of the decision to stop at Eupatoria and angrily demanded to know what was going on. Raglan replied in the same style, and although both letters were withdrawn an effect had been created.[22]

The fleet weighed at 03.00 moving down to the Old Fort. It had been intended that the allies would share the beach, but the marker buoy ended up at the north end, directing the British toward a cliff. Lyons noticed, securing Raglan's consent to shift the British landing to a separate beach a mile to the north. The French anchored at 07.00 and began landing. Lyons was annoyed that the British battlefleet remained two miles out, so that although the boats were sent away at 07.50 they did not begin landing troops until 09.00. Mends had planned a simultaneous disembarkation from every boat, 7,000 men at a time. Without opposition such precise plans were no longer essential, but by the end of the day the infantry were all ashore, without tents. Because the plans envisaged an opposed landing the cavalry, needed to scout inland, were kept until last. Unfortunately the next day, the 16th, a heavy swell set in from the south, ending attempts to land horses at 08.00 with 1,500 horses still aboard ship. The attempt was renewed at 03.00 and completed soon after midday on the 18th, the French being ready at day-break on the 17th. The lack of flexibility shown in the landing was significant. Lyons criticised Dundas for keeping the battleships and large steamers too far out, and doing nothing to aid the landing.[23] Although his comments achieved a wide circulation through Layard and Delane, aboard *Agamemnon* and *Britannia*, they were quite unjustified and reflected Lyons' overconfidence. Dundas expected a Russian attack, and with the other battleships disabled by troops he would have to meet the danger alone. This forced him to scout southward and keep his squadron to seaward of the transports. He could not reduce his already weakened crews as the Russians had fourteen sail, double his own force. While this prolonged the landing, to have acted as Lyons suggested would have been both unnecessary and dangerous.

Dundas's caution was also evident in his concern for the safety of the transports. Aware that anything other than a rapid and complete success would force the allies to depend on sea-borne supplies he wanted to hold Eupatoria, to prevent the enemy bringing up guns to command the only secure anchorage on the Crimean coast. The town would also be a useful source of fresh supplies and water. *Retribution* and *Vesuvius* went to prepare the town for defence on the 15th, and while Dundas must have been encouraged by Burgoyne and Brereton, Raglan would not send any troops. Captain Brock with 430 officers and men were sent up on the 18th, driving off a large body of Cossacks the following day. On the 23rd 300 French and 200 Turkish marines were landed, and on the 26th *Leander* was stationed in the anchorage. After the capture of Balaklava Raglan wanted the marines to defend that harbour, believing Eupatoria would be of little use. Dundas disagreed: 'Eupatoria is every day more useful to us and I cannot well withdraw the 400 marines'. Brock was instructed to forward livestock and vegetables at every opportunity. Raglan did not anticipate being long delayed before Sevastopol, so supplies seemed unimportant and no attempt was made to cut the Russian supply line, as Newcastle had suggested.[24] While the armies disembarked Dundas's steamers located the Russian army, camped by the Alma. On the 14th *Sampson* with six steamers drove the Russian ships into Sevastopol, shelling the Russian camp; *Terrible*'s report the following day established the size of the Russian force, which was of great value as Raglan would not commit his tiny force of cavalry out of sight. Aware the army would soon move Dundas detailed Lyons' division for inshore support. On the 18th seven transports and five French battleships went back to Varna, escorted by *Furious*.[25]

The Russians had been surprised. Menshikov had anticipated an attack, but by early September he and his master looked for a spring campaign. Russian intelligence in Bulgaria was clearly non-existent. When Engineer Colonel Totleben arrived at Sevastopol he found the land defences utterly inadequate, and, contrary to British reports stronger, in works and terrain, south of the city. When informed of the allied landing Menshikov did not send his fleet, properly believing defence on land would make the best use of Russian strength. The problem was that the backward army was incapable of meeting the allies in the field. Excessively rigid infantry and cavalry formations, failure to adopt the rifle, very low standards of musketry, with a complete lack of initiative at all levels made the much vaunted army of Nicholas I a blunt instrument. It had nothing to counter the long range fire of minié rifles, the *élan* of the Zouaves, or the disciplined courage of the British. Only in artillery and engineering could the Russians match their enemies.[26] It was hardly surprising they elected to defend Sevastopol rather than face the allies in the field, even in superior numbers. Menshikov's intemperate character proved as dangerous in the Crimea as it had been at Constantinople, although his strategy cannot be faulted. Had his army been adequate the allied effort would have ended in disaster. With complete authority over all Russian forces he had a major advantage over the allied commanders. Informed of the allied landing Menshikov marched his army up to the river Alma, established a strong defensive position on the south bank, and waited for a week.

The allies finally moved south early on the 19th, crossing the Bulganak before camping for the night. The next morning they moved up to the Alma before forming up in battle order, the French and Turks on the coast, the British inland. St Arnaud proposed turning both Russian flanks; Raglan did not commit himself. The battle started at 12.30 with the steamers helping the French to cross the river and capture the sea cliffs, achieving one of St Arnaud's flank movements. Raglan, unwilling to extend his line inland in the face of superior cavalry attacked the centre, driving the Russians off the field in disorder. He was convinced that if the French had continued the pursuit most of the Russian army would have been taken.[27] This failure had many causes, primarily the reluctance of the commanders to concert grand tactics before the battle. Afterwards an exhausted St Arnaud claimed his men had left their knapsacks north of the river. Raglan had one division and cavalry ready to advance, but would not act alone. The defeated army reached Sevastopol in disarray. A sustained pursuit might have collapsed the Russian position north of the city, achieving the sole British object. The battle secured Burgoyne's major prerequisite for success, the defeat of the enemy field army. It also gave the allies a moral ascendancy that would be reinforced in later battles.

Returning to Sevastopol Menshikov took a grim view. After a prolonged discussion with Vice-Admiral Kornilov on the 21st he rejected a naval sortie. Instead he ordered the harbour entrance, between the forts, to be blocked with ships as soon as the allies approached to prevent a naval attack. The seven ships positioned late on the 21st were the hulks Kornilov had not considered taking to sea. The seamen were turned over to the land defences, along with the resources of the naval arsenal, principally heavy guns. Some ships were moved to cover the north of the harbour, only 6,000 troops were to remain with this extemporised garrison. Menshikov had no intention of tying his army to the city, electing to move to Batschi Serai, re-form and threaten the allied flank and rear, wait for reinforcements and then take the offensive. While the allies moved across the Katscha Menshikov led his army inland. Elements of his rearguard clashed with allied troops on the Batschi Serai road on the following day.[28] This offered the allies another chance to finish the work begun on the Alma, or assault the city. However, Burgoyne's plans now controlled the armies, and no-one considered pursuing the enemy away from the city. Raglan allowed a beaten army to march across his line of advance, escaping in disorder up a narrow road. St Arnaud had no idea what was going on.

After the Alma Raglan intended to assault the defences north of the harbour, following the concept of the operation communicated to him by Newcastle and Graham. This explains his lack of concern for Eupatoria. Twice on the morning after the battle he pressed St Arnaud to advance for the *coup de main*, but the Marshal claimed his troops needed rest. He feared the Russians would make another stand on the Belbec, causing unacceptable losses.[29] The optimism of August had gone, for he was now very ill and increasingly cautious. Raglan requested naval assistance to pick up the wounded after the battle. Lyons anticipated a renewed march; promising support, Dundas was more concerned with the enemy, detaching *Sampson* and *Terrible* to follow them. Captain Jones reported a hasty retreat, and burning villages on the Katscha, and late on the 21st he noticed the Russian ships being placed to block the harbour. This persuaded Dundas that they would not make a stand outside the city.[30] However, the movement of the Russian ships caught the steamers out of position, and when the Turkish Admiral claimed some had escaped, Dundas wanted Lyons to meet them off Odessa. Lyons sarcastically demanded to know why the steamers watching the harbour had been out of position, although *Sampson*'s next report established the Russian ships were all in harbour. Dundas planned to attack the ships across the harbour 'at the first favourable opportunity', like Graham he anticipated a combined assault.[31] In this, as in all else, Dundas was dominated by the demands of inter-Service co-operation. The Navy properly sacrificed its independence to the success of the military operation.

Late on the 21st General Tylden was struck down by cholera, dying within twenty-four hours, and Burgoyne naturally took his place. His view of the campaign had not changed, he believed the Alma would be decisive. Having pressed his views on Raglan he was sent to St Arnaud on the 22nd. The two commanders had decided to move, but not how to attack the city. The French did not want to send their troops to assault fortifications. Raglan did not press them, nor did he agree with Burgoyne, and in this he was supported by Lyons, who remained ashore after the 22nd. Lyons emphasised that Burgoyne's plan would alter the nature of the operation, but Raglan was prepared to modify his plans to suit the French.

The armies crossed the Katscha on the 23rd, accompanied by the fleet, which anchored off the river, disembarking the Scots Greys. The Light Brigade moved on to the Belbec. When the fleets appeared off Sevastopol in the afternoon the Russians scuttled their ships. Dundas now looked to find a diversion south of the harbour to assist the assault, as he also wanted to shell the forts. A Polish deserter claimed the Star Fort was mined, and covered by the ships in the harbour, adding to St Arnaud's concern.[32] At 07.00 on the 24th he requested a three-hour postponement of the march, assuming the Russians had destroyed the harbour for the foreseeable future, which would alter the nature of the campaign. This unjustified supposition led him to consider finding a secure winter anchorage was his first priority, in line with a major element of Burgoyne's plan. More immediately, St Arnaud was troubled by a small earthwork covering the mouth of the Belbec. Therefore when the march resumed it avoided the Star Fort and the new earthwork. The armies halted on the ridge between the Katscha and the Belbec to look down on the city, but their line of advance had already taken them away from the fleet. At this point St Arnaud was stricken with cholera. He was already in favour of attacking from the south; Raglan, encouraged by Lyons, still favoured the north, because he believed the Star Fort was the key to the city. Although reinforced by Totleben, it was only formidable if held by an army. Burgoyne believed it would be, advocating a flank march round the city. St Arnaud, supported only by Bizot, agreed. On the evening of the 24th he refused to attack the Star Fort, except by regular approaches. Raglan accepted, and agreed to start the flank march the next morning. The only crumb of comfort he could derive from the decision was that Burgoyne had at least persuaded the French to act.[33] That night St Arnaud's illnesses took him beyond the ability to command. Handing over to Canrobert on the 26th, he died at sea two days later.

The descent on the Crimea was planned as a grand raid on a target of strategic significance. Without reliable intelligence on the Russian forces it was always a risk. Kinglake condemned it as an 'Adventure', Philip Colomb concurred. Yet Corbett pointed out: 'As a combined operation its opening movement, both in conception and organisation was perhaps the most daring, brilliant and successful thing of the kind we ever did.' One thing is certain: from the moment the operation began every modification to the original concept increased caution, and this exposed the allies to greater danger. The French review in mid passage caused Raglan to reconsider, shifting the point of landing under the growing influence of Burgoyne. This allowed the Russians to prepare a powerful defence on the Alma that should have ended the allied campaign. After the battle St Arnaud's prevarication allowed the Russians to recover and prepare, persuading him not to make an early assault, and effectively ended the grand raid.

The real failure was one of staff work and consultation. There was never any fixed plan of operations on which Raglan could base his opposition to delays and cautious measures, and in the interests of allied harmony he sacrificed his opinions. Avoiding the north side was an absurd decision. Only one commentator has ever argued it was too strong.[34] The value of the position was demonstrated the following autumn when Russian heavy guns commanded the harbour and the city. From the north side the allies could have destroyed the fleet, bombarded the city and reduced Fort Constantine. The only thing they could not guarantee was to occupy the city, which exposed a divergence of attitude between the allies. The French saw no value in destroying Russian seapower, to benefit Britain. They wanted to occupy the city, earn *la gloire* for the army and increase Louis Napoleon's prestige. At a lower level the French line regiments had shown a marked unwillingness to face artillery, and St Arnaud would not send them against the Star Fort. This, with his arbitrary decision that the harbour was ruined, made it easy to fall in with Burgoyne's plan, making a nonsense of landing north of the city and the Alma. Unknown to Burgoyne it also turned the attack onto the more heavily defended sector of the city. The north side could have been taken by assault, it was not particularly strong, and with naval support could have been turned on the coast. With a little preparation the Star Fort was vulnerable to guns on the overlooking heights. Raglan felt it could be stormed. The Russians were demoralised, and their lack of infantry firepower had been revealed – only twenty small guns stood between the allies and success.

Despite the delay Raglan should have called a full council of war and presented a coherent plan. He did not even consult Dundas. The difference of opinion on the 13th had soured relations. With Lyons at headquarters Dundas was left afloat, ill-informed and largely ignored. For all his caution he accepted the grand raid, and from his conduct on the 8th it must be argued he supported carrying it out. In a council of war Raglan and St Arnaud would have been joined by Dundas, Hamelin, Lyons, Bruat, Bizot, Canrobert, Brown, Burgoyne and the divisional Generals. Burgoyne's plan was supported by St Arnaud and Bizot, the others agreed with Raglan. His deference allowed St Arnaud to alter the nature of the campaign; characteristically, Raglan accepted a dangerous flank march and starting afresh, rather than quarrel with St Arnaud.

Notes

1 Raglan to Dundas 13 Jul. 1854: NRS, pp. 290–1; Dundas to Graham 19 Jun. 1854: Gr. CW3; Dundas to Raglan 26 Jun., 4 Jul. 1854: RAGLAN 6807–298; Raglan to Dundas 30 Jun. 1854: *ibid.*

2 Dundas to Admiralty 22 Jun. rec. 8 Jul. 1854 no. 295: NRS, pp. 275–6; Admiralty to Dundas 11 Jul. 1854 no. 390: NRS, p. 289; Raglan to Dundas 1 Jul. 1854: RAGLAN 6807–298.

3 Raglan to Dundas 5 , 10 Jul. 1854: *ibid.*

4 EARDLEY-WILMOT, pp. 178–9; Raglan to Dundas 21 Jul. 1854: Gr. CW4; Dundas to Graham 29 Jul. 1854: Gr. CW3.

5 Dundas to Graham 24 Jun. 1854: Gr. CW3; Dundas to Raglan 11 Jun., Raglan to Dundas 13 Jun. 1854: RAGLAN 6807–298; Dundas to Stratford 8 Jun. 1854: DND/1 f169.

6 Lyons to Dundas 10 Jun. 1854, copy to Stratford: F.O. 352/38/2; Newcastle to Raglan 17 Jun. 1854: RAGLAN 6807–293; Raglan to Dundas 3, 10 Jul. 1854: *ibid.* 298; Dundas to Raglan 3, 4 , 13 Jul. 1854: *ibid.*; Lyons to Graham 4 Jul. 1854: Gr. CW7; Dundas to Graham 8 Jul. 1854: R.A. G14 f105.

7 Dundas to Graham 8 Jul. 1854: Gr. CW4; Captain Eden (*London*) to Baring 27 Jul. 1854: BARING, ii pp. 39–40.

8 Raglan to Newcastle 14 Jul. 1854: RAGLAN 6807–294; Raglan to Dundas 13, 17 Jul. 1854: *ibid.*–298; Dundas to Raglan 11, 15 Jul. 1854: *ibid.*; SPIERS, E.M., *Radical General* (Manchester, 1983), p. 152; MARTINEAU, J., *Life of Henry Pelham, Fifth Duke of Newcastle* (London 1908), p. 149.

9 Dundas to Raglan 19 Jul. 1854: RAGLAN 6807–298; Raglan to Dundas 20 Jul. 1854: *ibid.*; Dundas to Graham 19 Jul. 1854: Gr. CW4; Lyons to Graham 19 Jul. 1854: Gr. CW7.

10 Dundas to Admiralty 20 Jul. 1854 no. 349: ADM 1/5626; Lyons to Dundas 26 Jul. 1854: EARDLEY-WILMOT, pp. 181–3; Dundas to Raglan 26, 31 Jul. 1854: RAGLAN 6807–298; Lyons to Stratford 29, 30 Jul. 1854: F.O. 352/38/2; Dundas to Lyons 27 Jul. 1854: EARDLEY-WILMOT, p. 184; Lyons to Dundas 30 Jul. 1854: LYONS B42.

11 Dundas Journal: ADM 50/253; Dundas to Raglan 2, 13 Aug. 1854: RAGLAN 6807–298; Dundas to Graham 3 Aug. 1854: Gr. CW4; LLOYD & COULTER, *Medicine and the Navy; 1200 – 1900* (London, 1963), vol. iv pp. 140–154; Lyons to Graham 14, 19 Aug. 1854: EARDLEY-WILMOT, pp. 190–2.

12 MENDS, B.S., *Life of Sir W. R. Mends* (London, 1899), pp. 31, 105; Lyons to Graham 4 Jul. 1854: Gr.CW7; Lyons to Stratford 30 Jul., Stratford to Lyons 1 Aug. 1854: F.O. 352/38/2; EARDLEY-WILMOT, pp. 188–9; Operational memo. 20 Aug. 1854: RAGLAN 6807–298.

13 BRERETON, Maj. Genl. Sir W., *The British Fleet in the Black Sea* (London, 1856); Dundas to Graham 13 Aug. 1854: Gr. CW4.

14 Raglan to Stratford 15 Jul., 2 Aug. 1854: F.O. 352–38/4.

15 Raglan to Stratford 21 Jul. 1854: *ibid.*; GOOCH , pp. 101–2; Spratt Notice of Service: SPR1/3

16 Dundas Journal 17 Jul. 1854: ADM 50/253; Dundas to Graham 3, 13 Aug. 1854: Gr. CW4; Graham to Lyons 19 Feb. 1855: LYONS L286–7.
17 Raglan to Dundas 19, 28 Aug. 1854: RAGLAN 6807–298; Dundas to Raglan 14, 27 Aug. 1854: *ibid.*; Raglan to Lyons 20 Aug. 1854: *ibid.* 299.
18 Tylden to Raglan 10 Aug. 1854: WROTTESLEY, ii pp. 53–6; Newcastle to Raglan 12 Aug. 1854: RAGLAN 6807–283; Newcastle to Graham 11 Aug. 1854: Gr. B.120; Hardinge to Newcastle 10 or 12 Feb. 1854: NeC. 10,060a.
19 Burgoyne memos. 22, 29 Aug. 1854: WROTTESLEY, ii pp. 64–73; Brereton to Burgoyne late Aug. 1854: *ibid.* pp. 68, 75; Burgoyne to Dundas 28 Aug. 1854: DND/9 f154–6; Dundas to Raglan 30 Aug., Dundas to Brown 22 Aug. 1854: RAGLAN 6807–298; Burgoyne letter to family 29 Aug. 1854: WROTTESLEY, ii p. 73.
20 Lyons to Graham 4 Sept. 1854: EARDLEY-WILMOT, p. 195; Dundas to Admiralty 4, rec. 18 Sept. 1854 no. 446: NRS, p. 305; Dundas to Raglan 5, 6 Sept. Raglan to Dundas 5 Sep. 1854: RAGLAN 6807–298; Lyons to Raglan 6, 7 Sept. 1854: *ibid.* 299.
21 GOOCH, p. 171 for Louis Napoleon's admission that he urged Kaffa; Dundas to Graham 9 Sept. 1854: copy in F.O. 352/38/3; Lyons to Dundas 11 Sept. 1854, encl.in Dundas to Admiralty 11, rec. 28 Sept. 1854 no. 460: NRS, pp. 305–8.
22 Dundas to Raglan, Raglan to Dundas 13 Sept. 1854: RAGLAN 6807–298.
23 Lyons to Dundas 17.30, 16 Sept. 1854: DND/11 f8–9; Lyons to Raglan 21, 22 Sept. 1854: RAGLAN 6807–299.
24 Dundas to Raglan 14, 27 Sept. 1854: *ibid.*–298; Raglan to Dundas 16, 26 Sept. 1854: *ibid.*; Dundas to Brock 17 Sep. 1854: NRS, pp. 310–13; Dundas to Brock 27 Sept. 1854: ADM 50/253.
25 Raglan to Dundas 14, 15 Sept., Dundas to Raglan 18 Sept. 1854: RAGLAN 6807–298.
26 CURTISS, pp. 302–4; CURTISS, J.S., *The Russian Army under Nicholas I, 1825–55* (Ithaca, 1965).
27 Raglan to Newcastle 24 Sept. 1854: RAGLAN 6807–284; For a more detailed account of the battle see; HIBBERT, C., *The destruction of Lord Raglan* (London, 1963), pp. 78–118.
28 CURTISS, pp. 311–13; GOOCH, p. 130.
29 Lyons' acount in KINGLAKE, A., *The Invasion of the Crimea* (London 1877, nine vols.), vol. iv.
30 Raglan to Dundas 21 Sept. 1854: DND/11 f16; Lyons to Raglan 21, 22 Sept. 1854: RAGLAN 6807–299; Dundas to Raglan 21, 22 Sept. 1854: *ibid.*–298; Dundas to Admiralty 21, 23 Sept. 1854 no. 485, 487: NRS, pp. 317–21.
31 Dundas to Raglan 24 Sept. 1854: RAGLAN 6807–298;
32 WROTTESLEY, ii pp. 88–93; Dundas to Admiralty 24 Sept. rec. 8 Oct.1854 no. 489: NRS, pp. 321–2; Dundas to Raglan 24 Sept. 1854: RAGLAN 6807–298.
33 GOOCH, p. 129; Lyons to Raglan 24 Sept. 1854: RAGLAN 6807–299; Raglan to Newcastle 28 Sept. 1854: *ibid.*–284.

34   COLOMB, p. 402; CORBETT, J.S., *Some Principles of Maritime Strategy* (London, 1911), p. 292; HAMLEY, Gen. Sir E., *The War in the Crimea* (London, 1891), pp. 66–77.

10

The siege

At 08.30 on the 25th the British began to march round Sevastopol. Finding the bridge at the head of the harbour heavily fortified, the cavalry led the army along a narrow track. After colliding with Menshikov's baggage train on the Batschi Serai road the British troops camped at the Traktir bridge by the river Tchernaya, the French arrived late in the evening. Dundas, unaware of the Army's plans, could only suspect they were marching to Balaklava; Raglan had only requested he pick up the remaining Russian wounded at the Alma. By contrast Lyons was well informed, preparing to meet the army at Balaklava.[1] The following morning the British reached the small harbour, and Canrobert offered it, with the exposed right of the aallied position, to Raglan. After consulting Lyons, Raglan accepted; he had only considered a brief operation, not a prolonged siege. The French moved across the Chersonese to use Kamiesch and Kazatch, which although less secure were better suited to landing stores. Raglan and Lyons still favoured an immediate assault, but Canrobert, no more willing to send his troops against artillery than his predecessor, wanted to subdue the Russian guns with a heavy bombardment before storming the city. The engineers agreed: Burgoyne claimed an immediate assault would cost at least 500 killed. By the evening of the 27th the arduous work of landing the heavy guns had begun. Once again the grand raid had been deflected. After taking the risk of the flank march to turn weak defences on the north side, it was curious to halt before those of the south and watch while they were improved. Burgoyne was still very sanguine, but the nature of the campaign had changed, and this was first apparent afloat.

The scuttling of five Russian battleships was decisive, ending any possibility of a naval battle. Dundas now saw no good reason to take on the stone forts guarding the harbour mouth. Lyons, allowed to

2   The Crimean Upland, showing the major events of the campaign. The Woronzov road led east to the plain of Baidar and Yalta. The mountain passes inland from the plain were heavily fortified by the Russians during 1855, limiting allied opportunities to penetrate into the heart of the Peninsula. The possibility that this was influenced by Louis Napoleon's strategy of field operations cannot be discounted. From the Navy Records Society Volume *Russian War 1854*, by permission

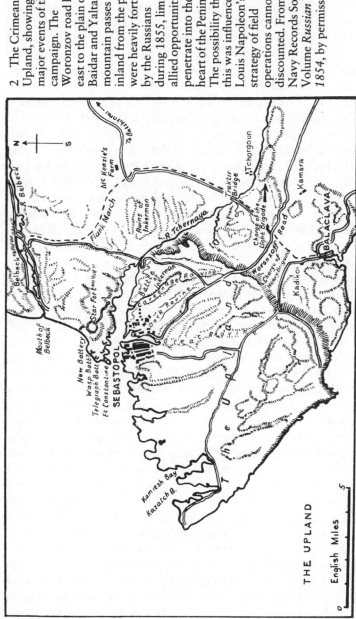

THE UPLAND

English Miles

0   5

read all his letters, became alarmed, hurriedly writing to Raglan to explain that Dundas only meant there would be no battle, and suggesting he could land 100–32-pounders, gun crews and 1,500 marines.[2] Had Lyons behaved properly Dundas's opinions would never have been communicated to Raglan, let alone required explanation. Still anchored off the Katscha Dundas, believing the campaign was almost over, was determined to take no risks. Rumours that the Russian steamers would run for Odessa occupied two or three allied steamers throughout the last months of the year. Lyons urged Raglan to call for naval guns, although Raglan's first concern was for marines to defend Balaklava. Dundas sent 1,000 ashore on the 28th, but refused to evacuate Eupatoria. The need for guns was obvious. Raglan requested fifty 44-hundredweight 32-pounders, with crews and hauling parties to drag them the ten miles to the front.[3] Captain Lushington, *Albion* landed with a Naval Brigade of 1,040 officers and men. *Diamond* was disarmed to provide guns and serve as a hospital, while the fleet's field guns went with the marines. Dundas also provided six 68-pounders.[4]

Dundas was careful to send ashore only what he could spare. The battleships were unlikely to see much action and gave up men and guns, the steamers were kept fully manned for inshore service. Dundas did not anticipate setting up a blockade until the city fell. The fleet had concentrated for the amphibious operation and would have to remain so while there remained a chance of the army having to re-embark. He left Lyons in charge of liaison, placing the forces ashore on *Agamemnon*'s books and refusing his requests to leave Balaklava. This kept Lyons busy and filled an important post; had *Agamemnon* not been vital for the winter patrol off Sevastopol Dundas would have kept Lyons in harbour. With coal from Heraclia and South Wales brought by *Supply* and *Industry* the fleet was dominated by logistic support for the Army. At first this was on a day-to-day basis, but once the siege began long term requirements became paramount. The French led a party to scour the southern coast of the Crimea for stores. Yalta yielded only miserable quantities of coal, wine and rye flour; Eupatoria provided cargoes of livestock, vegetables and timber. Dundas had the bay surveyed as a winter anchorage and secured 400 Egyptian marines in time to help to drive off another force of Cossacks on 12 October. Eupatoria should have been developed as a reconnaissance base, but Raglan and Canrobert allowed it to be shut up, relying on the Navy for early warning of Russian reinforcements, Dundas passed on reports from ships that fired on forces crossing Kinburn Bay, encouraging Raglan to make an early assault.[5]

Inside Sevastopol Kornilov and Totleben made good use of the time given them by the allies, building up new earthworks. Yet until the first week in October the garrison of only 16,000 men was incapable of defending the four-mile front. Menshikov returned to the city on 28 September, but only agreed to reinforce the town when Kornilov threatened to complain to the Czar. By 9 October another 28,000 troops had joined the defence. Menshikov wanted to build up an overwhelming superiority outside the city before attacking the allies, using Sevastopol to hold them in place for a decisive attack. Throughout this period the allies did nothing to hamper the Russians, electing to open with an overwhelming bombardment. Even the steamers were told to cease after dark as their fire upset the troops. Raglan, concerned at the length of time being taken, proposed pushing the guns forward at night without trenches, but this was rejected by the divisional commanders. Burgoyne discovered the rocky ground in the British attack would only allow him to support a French assault. Raglan was astonished, but Canrobert accepted. The following night the French built a massive earthwork, Mont Rodolph, less than 1,000 yards from the central bastion. The British were nowhere inside 1,500 yards.[6]

As the time approached for the bombardment Raglan requested the assistance of the fleet. Not expecting to be refused he stressed the lateness of the season, Russian reinforcements and public expectations as as the reasons for urgency. However, he only expected the fleet to occupy the attention of the defences, and at Lyons' urging suggested *Agamemnon* be recalled from Balaklava. Dundas was alarmed, but promised his aid and consulted Hamelin. Lyons, still at headquarters, believed the fleets could do more than merely occupy the attention of the forts. Dundas knew that the blockage of the harbour would ensure he could achieve nothing, and wrote accordingly to Graham.

My dear Sir James,

By a letter from Lord Raglan presented to me by his secretary Colonel Steele I find that his Lordship expects and strongly urges that the fleet should attack the batteries on both sides of Sevastopol and I am now going to the lighthouse harbour to meet the French Admirals and Sir E. Lyons on the subject.

I am quite sure this is an attack that will be of no service to the army and most likely destructive to many of our ships but I will not shrink from doing what is so looked upon by Lord Raglan as a means to effect the capture of Sevastopol. I have enclosed with this his Lordship's letter and my reply.

I shall put this in the hands of the chaplain in case I should be cut off in the approaching action.

The length of time in pressing the siege operations has caused the enemy to take courage after his defeat at the Alma and the sea front is now far stronger than ever, very commanding and I cannot see much probability of our making any impression on his works, if we did we have no force to land on the north side and that makes me regret the attack there – If our ships get disabled I see difficulty and danger should the army wish to embark and that I think will be the case after the south side of the harbour falls and the fleet I hope by that will be destroyed, however I may see things in too dark a colour and I will say no more than this, my object will be to carry out Lord Raglan's wish, altho' contrary to my own opinion, and the French Admiral shall only hear from me today that I consider the attack by the whole fleet absolutely imperative after the communication I have received, and no doubt the French Admiral has the same desire expressed by the French general. I shall add to this when I return after the conference with Admiral Hamelin.

Although Dundas never completed his letter, and never sent it, his caution was entirely justified. The whole operation depended on absolute command of the sea.[7] Meeting aboard *Mogador* on the 15th the Admirals agreed to support the land attack with a general bombardment of the sea forts, leaving the timing of their effort at the discretion of the Generals. This was significant, the fleets had already landed their reserve ammunition, keeping only seventy rounds per gun. The Admirals put forward three alternatives: they could open with the land batteries, wait for the assault, or use half their ammunition on each occasion. Raglan and Canrobert decided in favour of a joint bombardment to commence at 06.30 the following day, the fleets keeping half their ammunition for the assault. After conference Lyons consulted the battlefleet captains, who argued for supporting the assault only, not wanting to retire after expending half their ammunition. Lyons agreed, but still anticipated meeting Raglan inside Sevastopol on the following day. Soon after Dundas received the Generals' reply, at 20.30 on the 16th, a message arrived from Hamelin. The French Admiral shared the British captains appre- hensions about retiring from action. With his ships short handed and low on ammunition he would not open fire before 10–11.00. Dundas accepted, having little enough hope of achieving anything. His operational memorandum paid lip service to the bombardment as a serious attack, devoting most attention to keeping the ships safe and leaving the captains a discretion to retire. The battleships were to be lashed alongside a steamer, apart from *Agamemnon* and *Sans Pareil*, which would lead. All the ships would keep underweigh. Dundas was relying on the steamers to keep his fleet up to strength.[8] At 07.00 on the 17th, shortly after the firing ashore became general, Hamelin came aboard *Britannia*; under orders from Canrobert he urged that the fleets should fight at anchor at ranges in excess of one mile. The French and Turks would form a line to the south, the British to the north. Dundas protested, but Hamelin declared the French would follow this plan whatever the British did, forcing him to give way. The distance between the Katscha and the camp made any reference to the Generals impossible. British fleet tactics before Sevastopol were determined by General Canrobert, and forced on Dundas by the allied command structure.

Dundas called Lyons and the captains aboard *Britannia* at 08.30, aware that the armament of his ships would only marginally effective against stone casemates at the range selected. The French plan combined inability to inflict damage with risk. The captains anticipated serious damage, so Dundas placed *Britannia* in the most exposed position, the southern end of the British line. Lyons wanted to take *Sans Pareil* and other ships into a gap in the shoal within 800 yards of Fort Constantine, discovered the previous night. Dundas accepted, allowing *London* to join; *Albion* and *Arethusa* were detached to engage the cliff-top works. The steamers *Sampson*, *Tribune*, *Terrible* and *Sphinx* with *Spitfire* and *Lynx* were free to fire underweigh and to help disabled ships. *Sphinx*, loaded with reserve ammunition, would keep out of range.

The Russian defences were impressive. To the south the Quarantine Fort, an open battery, and Fort Alexander, a two-decker casemate, presented almost 100 guns. North of the harbour Fort Constantine mounted twenty that would bear on the fleet, supported by ten guns in the Telegraph and Wasp earthworks on the cliffs 100 to 130 feet above sea level. The barrier across the harbour restricted the allies to a diversion, although ten battleships and more forts were ready if they could enter the harbour.

Ashore the Russians anticipated the bombardment, opening a heavy fire on the French works; the main French magazine blew up at 10.30, battery practice ceased soon afterwards. The British, with heavier guns, kept up a rapid fire, demolishing the defences around

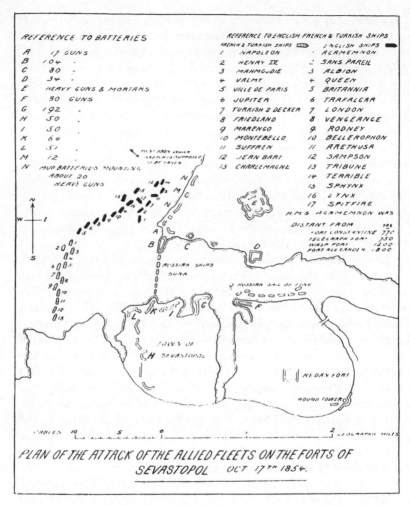

REFERENCE TO BATTERIES

A	17 GUNS
B	104 "
C	80 "
D	34 "
E	HEAVY GUNS & MORTARS
F	80 GUNS
G	192 "
H	50 "
I	50 "
K	64 "
L	51 "
M	12 "
N	MUD BATTERIES MOUNTING ABOUT 20 HEAVY GUNS

REFERENCE TO ENGLISH FRENCH & TURKISH SHIPS

FRENCH & TURKISH SHIPS

1	NAPOLEON
2	HENRY IV
3	MAHMOUDIE
4	VALMY
5	VILLE DE PARIS
6	JUPITER
7	TURKISH 2 DECKER
8	FRIEDLAND
9	MARENGO
10	MONTEBELLO
11	SUFFREN
12	JEAN BART
13	CHARLEMAGNE

ENGLISH SHIPS

1	AGAMEMNON
2	SANS PAREIL
3	ALBION
4	QUEEN
5	BRITANNIA
6	TRAFALGAR
7	LONDON
8	VENGEANCE
9	RODNEY
10	BELLEROPHON
11	ARETHUSA
12	SAMPSON
13	TRIBUNE
14	TERRIBLE
15	SPHYNX
16	LYNX
17	SPITFIRE

HMS AGAMEMNON WAS

DISTANT FROM   YDS
FORT CONSTANTINE   770
TELEGRAPH FORT   750
WASP FORT   1200
FORT ALEXANDER   1800

RUSSIAN SHIPS SUNK

9 RUSSIAN SAIL OF LINE

TOWN OF SEVASTOPOL

MUD DAY FORT

ROUND TOWER

CABLES   10   5   0   1   2   GEOGRAPHIC MILES

PLAN OF THE ATTACK OF THE ALLIED FLEETS ON THE FORTS OF SEVASTOPOL   OCT 17TH 1854.

3   The bombardment of Sevastopol, 17 October 1854. From the *Life of Admiral Lord Lyons*, drawn by Cowper Coles, Lyons's Flag Lieutenant

the Redan. By 15.00 the position was wide open, but Raglan could not order an assault; the French were not ready, the eventuality had not been anticipated and the Generals were on separate parts of the field. No-one thought to cancel the naval attack.

The fleets lay at anchor off the Katscha, the French began to shift 10.30; *Britannia* hoisted anchor at 11.00, and within thirty minutes the fleet was underweigh. The plan was for the battleships to form up from the south, running down past the harbour. The advance was hampered by calm, oppressively hot weather, forcing them to rely on the steamers. The forts south of the harbour opened on the French at 12.55, but received no reply for twenty-five minutes while Hamelin's ships took station. The Franco–Turkish force kept up a heavy fire for the next four hours, but they produced little effect; only eleven Russians were killed, thirty-nine wounded, and more significantly, only six guns were dismounted. The French suffered 200 casualties, 25 per cent of which were fatal.

At 13.07 Dundas signalled Lyons to run in directly from the north, the hired tender *Circassia* sounding the edge of the shoal. The battleships engaged the cliff-top works as they passed. At 13.55 *Agamemnon* anchored and opened on Fort Constantine, followed by *Sans Pareil* and *London*; *Albion* and *Arethusa* joined from the south-west. The Lyons' ships were covered by the steamers. At 14.14 the open barbette of Fort Constantine was wrecked by a shell from *Tribune*. The barbette was abandoned, and this, combined with the powerful fire from Lyons' ships forced the fort to cease firing for six minutes, before the casemates reopened. The main body came up and anchored between 14.25 and 15.20, continuing the arc of the French line. *Queen* had to unmoor after being fouled by *Mahmoudieh*. By this time Lyons' ships were heavily engaged, and sustaining casualties. Yet the first ship to be seriously damaged was *Retribution*; lashed to the disengaged side of *Trafalgar*, her mainmast was shot away at 13.25. Five minutes later *Albion* was hit by four shells which exploded on the orlop deck, setting fire to the ship and cutting the hawsers securing her to *Firebrand*. This forced her to close the magazines and cease fire. *Albion* slipped anchor and after a period under heavy fire while *Firebrand* re-established the tow, hauled out of action. She was seriously damaged, with eleven killed and seventy-two wounded. *London* left the action five minutes later, two shells exploding on the main deck. *Arethusa* had to abandon the unequal struggle after four shells burst on the main and lower decks, starting the planking on the starboard counter. In imminent danger of sinking, *Arethusa* hauled out at 15.50. All three had been hit by the cliff-top batteries, only *London* rejoined the action.

Sans *Pareil* kept station astern of *Agamemnon* using one anchor and her engines until 16.20 when a breeze and engine failure drove her ahead of the flagship. Lyons ordered her back, and although Captain Dacres realised he was powerless against the cliff-top batteries kept in position until 17.10. By then the ship was heavily damaged, with eleven killed and fifty-six wounded. *Agamemnon* had taken a fortunate position, few of Fort Constantine's guns could bear on her, and while the ships astern absorbed the fire from the cliffs, Lyons was happy to remain. *Sans Pareil*'s move exposed *Agamemnon* to the full weight of Russian fire, and Lyons called on *Bellerophon*, *London* and *Sans Pareil* to take station astern. Captain Jones, *Sampson* went aboard *Britannia* at 16.00 claiming Lyons was doing great execution. Dundas then ordered *Rodney* in; *Queen* closed at 16.10, but by 17.07 she had been set on fire twice and forced to withdraw. *Bellerophon* temporarily silenced the cliff-top batteries at 16.20, but had to withdraw at 17.50 after they reopened. *Rodney*, the last ship to join Lyons, anchored at 17.00 and drifted onto *Agamemnon*'s bow, forcing the flagship to back before tailing on the shoal where she remained until the action ended. *Agamemnon* ceased at 17.10, hauling out soon after *London* and *Sans Pareil*. The French began to withdraw at the same time, and within thirty minutes all were bearing up for the Katscha. Dundas signalled the recall at 17.30, although *Britannia* did not shift until 18.15. *Rodney*, being aground, did not cease fire until 18.30, having to call in *Lynx* and shift several guns before *Spiteful* could pull her clear. By then it was completely dark.

Every ship in the British fleet had been damaged, particularly the battleships. *Britannia* had been hit at least forty times, *Agamemnon* more than 200. As the Russian fire had been generally high all were were badly cut up aloft. With a large proportion of their men ashore the battlefleet captains had not fought the exposed upper-deck batteries, reducing casualties (*Niger*'s men fought *London*'s upper deck guns); despite this forty men were killed, 266 wounded. The Russian works facing the British escaped serious injury, although Fort Constantine lost eleven killed and thirty-nine wounded, but had five of the twenty-seven guns that bore on the fleet serviceable.[9] The battle centred around Lyons and *Agamemnon*. The ships that joined him suffered most of the damage and casualties; those remaining with Dundas had only twenty-one wounded and were ready for action the following day. By taking up an advanced position Lyons challenged the Russians to fire at his ships, which only the hope of a decisive result could justify. Once the cliff-top batteries found the range he should have withdrawn; Dundas's memorandum specifically enjoined the captains not to risk their ships. Lyons achieved the result Dundas had been at pains to prevent – two ships had to leave the fleet for repairs. Dundas had the option of recalling Lyons, but the precedent of Hyde Parker at Copenhagen was a bad one. His error was to sanction the original request at the morning conference, apparently as a reaction to the extreme caution of the French. Anchored before Fort Constantine the explosion on the barbette encouraged Lyons to remain, and Dundas sent in *Rodney* when he should have recalled Lyons. Like all British officers, Lyons' natural tendency was to close with the enemy; once battle was joined only the threat of imminent destruction caused any officer to leave the line. All senior officers were careful to display the cool courage so admired by their contemporaries.

The French had a better understanding of their role, being content to stay in line and act as a diversion. The British found the lure of close action irresistible. The gesture was futile, the Russians had enough men to man the forts, and now knew the allies could not force the harbour. They were careful to reinforce the line of ships after the storm of 14 November, and float two booms inside to entangle propellers and paddles. The lesson for the British was that they, like the French, were firmly placed in the role of army support. Dundas had appreciated this back in April, but Lyons and the majority others had not; consequently they saw the Admirals' caution and deference to the Generals as irresolution bordering on cowardice. Dundas knew the fleet was the junior partner in the amphibious operation, and the action of 17 October proved him right.

The other lesson of the attack was that the age-old view that stone forts far too strong for ships held good. Battleships could only hope for success inside 500 yards, where close quarters weight of metal would outweigh accurate fire with red-hot shot and shells. By contrast ships armed with a combination of shell and solid shot guns were badly equipped to deal with masonry. Leading gunners insisted that only the heaviest solid shot guns, preferably 95-hundredweight

68-pounders, would injure stone forts. Although the facings of Fort Constantine were heavily marked, the range had been too great for serious injury.[10]

Dundas's dissatisfaction was complete. Casualties and damage were more serious than he had anticipated, while nothing had been done to damage the enemy. He shared his views with Raglan:

I cannot repeat too often and with perfect sincerity that there is nothing in my power which shall not be done to assist your operations in the siege of Sevastopol.

I will land as many guns, with officers and seamen to work them, as you may desire to have – even though it may entail dismantling my ships. All this would be to act in a true position, the action of the 17th was a false one and one which I decline to repeat.

By all this I do not mean to say that even afloat I may not materially assist your Lordship on the day of your assault, and after a confidential conference with our mutual friend Sir Edmund Lyons I intend to propose to Admiral Hamelin as follows.

When we know from your Lordship and General Canrobert the day and hour you have fixed for the assault the united squadrons of France and England, should join here and make a feint of landing troops, at the same moment the steam vessels (certainly 20 of them) of the longest range should by divisions bombard the batteries on the north side.

This diversion may have the effect of withdrawing some troops from the southern shore to the north.

It has been suggested also to me by Sir Edmund Lyons that a repetition of our operations on the 17th would exhaust the ammunition of the two squadrons and leave them at the mercy of the Russian fleet – if they were wise and active enough to come out and attack us in that defenceless condition.

Raglan accepted that no diversion without troops could be effective. Lyons favoured another attempt at the forts, at close range. The fulsome praise of the French appears to have weakened his suspect judgement, and he complained about Dundas sending away *Arethusa* and *Albion*, which he believed would encourage the Russians and Turks to think the British had been beaten. Both were seriously damaged, had long been posted to pay off and were of little use off Sevastopol. Repairing them off the Katscha would have wasted the efforts of the fleet's carpenters, who had more important work in hand, repairing the other ships, and building siege gun platforms. *Albion*'s injuries required several months' work in Constantinople dockyard. Two French battleships joined her there, while the fleets spent the following days repairing their rigging, fishing damaged masts and plugging shot holes. *Sampson* kept watch off

Sevastopol.[11]

News of the action of 17 October arrived in Britain amid an atmosphere of mounting dissatisfaction. Early in September Newcastle and Prince Albert travelled to Boulogne to discuss the war with Louis Napoleon, although no decisions were reached. The war was delicately balanced. The Baltic campaign was closing indecisively, the Emperor's proposals related to the following season. In the Euxine the allies were embarking for the Crimea, causing deep despondency in the French high command. Only Louis Napoleon expressed any faith in the operation.[12] Graham was convinced success must follow, complaining bitterly of the prevarications that had ruined his grand raid. Promising Lyons the succession, he called for a more active prosecution of the war. Newcastle was more concerned about the French, warning Raglan not to demolish the city without Government sanction. His plans for 1855, notably in Asia and the Isthmus of Perekop, were already well advanced. Graham had persuaded him that the Sea of Azov was vital to success. When he heard the rumour of the fall of Sevastopol he wanted Lyons' opinion on attempting Nicolaiev. Clarendon, in a state of nervous excitement, revealed his deepest fears, admitting the Crimean operation was a leap in the dark forced on a reluctant Louis Napoleon, and on even more reluctant commanders, by the Government. The political future of the administration rode on it.[13]

Throughout September the more active members of the Government considered the fate of Sevastopol, sharing Graham's belief it must fall. The French Emperor agreed, proposing to winter in the Crimea, and demolish the sea forts and docks. This was accepted by all save Palmerston and Lansdowne; Lansdowne believed an undamaged city would be a better bargaining counter, indicating the type of warfare he thought was being waged. Palmerston wanted to give the city to the Turks; in geostrategic terms, returning Sevastopol to Russia would guarantee she would resume command of the sea. Graham fancied a quick election after the city fell would be useful.[14]

Already half convinced of success the cabinet was easily taken in by the rumours that followed the Alma. The nervous tension of the preceding months was released in a brief period of exultation. Aberdeen, cautious on 1 October, hoped that success 'cannot be long delayed', by the 4th he was 'strongly inclined' to believe. Russell's conversion came on the 3rd. Both were encouraged by Graham's belief the city had fallen to a combined assault on the 24th or 25th.

Clarendon looked for more, but Palmerston mocked the idea of easy victory. He knew the Russians would not give up the city without a struggle. Newcastle looked to occupy the whole peninsula, or raid Nicolaiev.[15] The bubble burst on the 5th. Chastened by his own gullibility Newcastle looked for scapegoats, Departmental loyalty prevented him selecting Raglan; the nature of the alliance made it impossible to place the blame where much of it belonged. Therefore he selected Dundas, who had already annoyed him. Dundas had enemies in the fleet, the Army and the newspapers; Layard, Delane and Kinglake all relayed low opinions, Layard's going straight to Russell. These ignorant letters achieved undue weight in *The Times*. Newcastle to hope for divine intervention: 'If a Russian gun should be so pointed by a good angel as to removed from this world's pains Dundas and Layard I for one should be in favour of a testimonial to both the maker and the angel. I strongly urged Graham last night to *relieve* Dundas immediately if Sevastopol is taken.' When he realised Sevastopol had not fallen Newcastle redoubled his efforts to have Dundas removed, but the only evidence of incompetence was the reported escape of the Anapa garrison by sea, 'a disgrace to the fleet'. On his way to attend the Queen at Balmoral, Graham was followed north by the opinions of the amateurs, and Newcastle's outburst. While sharing their anxieties he had sound political reasons not to recall Dundas. To avoid responsibility he asked for Aberdeen's opinion, stressing that as there were no good reasons for relieving Dundas he preferred to let him serve out his time. The escape of the Anapa garrison was unfortunate, but recalling the Admiral just as the city fell would be even more serious. Dundas, a long serving Whig MP, was not without influence, furthermore Graham knew he was ill and would not stay beyond his term. Aberdeen agreed, relying on Lyons to infuse some spirit into proceedings.[16]

In this affair Graham treated Dundas as he would Napier, leaving him command, while attacking his character and reputation at home. Almost overnight Clarendon linked the Admirals in mutual disgrace. Newcastle was less circumspect, instructing Raglan: 'If Admiral Dundas gives orders which unnecessarily imperil your army, and you can induce Sir Edmund Lyons to do so gallant an act as to disobey such orders, you and he shall have every support that I can give you.' Two days later he called on Aberdeen, but the Prime Minister found good reasons to support Dundas, notably his prompt landing of the marines at Balaklava.[17] The charges against

Dundas were that he had disapproved of the Sevastopol operation, failed to show any enthusiasm in its execution and allowed the Anapa garrison to escape by sea. The last point was based on entirely inaccurate information – the garrison only left in May, 1855 marching overland after the capture of Kertch. As for the Admiral's lack of enthusiasm, he had shown a consistent and laudable deference to the wishes of Raglan on any question relating to the Army, leaving the liaison role to Lyons while he attended to the naval requirements of the campaign. Few Admirals have gone so far to assist combined operations, yet Dundas was blamed for not taking risks and winning great victories which the political fortunes of the Government made necessary. The conduct of the largest amphibious operation of modern times was no substitute for a battle, either at home or in the fleet. Before his term was up Dundas would be subjected to further attacks, arising from exaggerated expectations.

Even after the Sevastopol hoax had been exposed Graham and Newcastle were certain success was imminent. For Graham the scuttling of the Russian ships appeared, as it did to Dundas, to end the chances of naval action. He sent out special equipment to blow up the ships and open the harbour, once the city fell. He also urged Dundas to act against other parts of the Russian coast, Azov, Perekop and Odessa, to prevent the Russians concentrating their resources in the Crimea. The dissatisfaction evident in his letters to Lyons was mirrored in the official dispatches; on 13 October he demanded to know why the harbour had not been attacked on the 19th or 20th to distract the enemy. Unlike Graham, Newcastle's plans stretched to Asia, although the two men were otherwise in agreement. On the day the armies opened their bombardment of Sevastopol the cabinet considered the best methods of crippling the resources of Russia.[18] The realisation was dawning that the methods adopted so far would not be enough. The Crimean operation would not force Russia to make peace.

Notes

1   Dundas to Raglan 25 Sept. 1854: RAGLAN 6807–298; Lyons to Raglan 25 Sept. 1854: *ibid*. 299; Dundas to Admiralty 28 Sept. rec. 8 Oct. 1854 no. 498: NRS pp. 323–5.
2   Dundas to Graham 24 Sept. 1854: Gr. CW5.
3   Dundas to Raglan 26, 27, 28, 30 Sept. 1854: RAGLAN 6807–298.
4   Raglan to Dundas 26, 30 Sept. 1854: *ibid*.; Dundas to Raglan 27

Sept., 1 Oct. 1854: *ibid.*
5   Lyons to Graham 13 Oct. 1854: Gr. CW8; Rear Admiral Boxer to Rear Admiral Stopford 4 Oct. 1854: RAGLAN 6807–299; Dundas to Admiralty 8 rec.23 Oct. 1854 no. 517: NRS pp. 332–6; Dundas to Raglan 5 Oct. 1854: RAGLAN 6807–298.
6   Dundas to Raglan 2 Oct. 1854 (21.00): *ibid.*; Raglan to Newcastle 8 Oct. 1854: *ibid.* 284.
7   Raglan to Dundas 23 Oct. 1854: *ibid.* 298; Dundas to Raglan 14 Oct. enc. in Dundas to Admiralty 18 Oct. rec. 6 Nov. 1854 no. 527: NRS pp. 339–45; Lyons to Raglan 15, 16 Oct. 1854: RAGLAN 6807–299; Dundas to Graham 15 Oct. 1854 'In case of my death'(never sent): DND/11 f76–7.
8   Resolutions adopted by the Admirals of the three alllied fleets respecting the attack on Sevastopol, 15 Oct. 1854: NRS pp. 339–45; Lyons to Raglan 16 Oct. 1854 (22.00): RAGLAN 6807–299; Dundas to Raglan 16 Oct. 1854: *ibid.* 298; Dundas to Lyons 16 Oct. 1854: KINGLAKE, vol. iv, p. 335; Dundas to Graham 16 Oct. 1854: Gr. CW5.
9   EARDLEY-WILMOT, pp. 238–51; KINGLAKE, vol. iv, pp. 334–419; BRERETON, p. 26; MENDS, pp. 358–64; Dundas to Admiralty 18 Oct. 1854 no. 544: ADM 87/50; Lyons to Graham 23 Oct. 1854: LYONS B66; Ships' Logs, Admirals' Journals (Dundas, Lyons and Stopford); Slade to Stratford 22 Oct. 1854: F.O. 195/441.
10   Dundas to Raglan 18 Oct. 1854: RAGLAN 6807–298; Lyons to Graham 18 Oct. 1854: Gr. CW8; MENDS, pp. 362–4.
11   Dundas to Raglan 18, 19, 20 Oct. 1854: RAGLAN 6807–298; Raglan to Dundas 2 Oct. 1854: *ibid.*; Lyons to Graham 18, 21 Oct. 1854: Gr. CW8; Lyons to Berkeley 18 Oct. 1854: in F.O. 352/38/3; Lyons to Berkeley 23 Oct. 1854: LYONS B66.
12   Cowley to Clarendon 8 Sept. 1854: F.O. 519/304.
13   Graham to Dundas 4 Sept. 1854: DND/11 f1–3; Graham to Lyons 4 Sept. 1854: EARDLEY-WILMOT, pp. 197–8; Newcastle to Raglan 13, 28 Sept. 1854: RAGLAN 6807–283; Newcastle to Russell 21 Sept. 1854: PRO 30/22/11E f451–4; Clarendon to Stratford 29 Aug., 18 Sept. 1854: F.O. 352/37.
14   CONACHER, p. 463; Graham to Aberdeen 30 Sept. 1854: Add. 43,191 f243–6.
15   Aberdeen to the Queen 1, 4 Oct. 1854: Add. 43,048 f298–320; Russell to Clarendon 1, 3 Oct. 1854: Cl. Dep. C15 f660–7; Graham to Clarendon 1 Oct. 1854: Cl. Dep. C14 f454–6; Clarendon to Stratford 3 Oct. 1854: F.O. 352/37; Clarendon to Palmerston 4 Oct. 1854: Bdlds. GC/CL f577; Palmerston to Clarendon 1 Oct. 1854: Cl. Dep. C15 f204.
16   Layard to Russell 16 Sept. 1854: PRO 30/22/11D; DASENT, A. I., *John Thadeus Delane* (London 1908, two vols.), vol. i, pp. 186–95; Newcastle to Clarendon 3, 5 Oct. 1854: Cl. Dep. C15 f853–6; Newcastle to Graham 5 Oct. 1854: Gr. B.121; Graham to Aberdeen 7 Oct. 1854: Add. 43,191 f254–9; Osborne (Secretary to the Admiralty) to Graham 18 Aug. Graham to Osborne 20 Aug. 1854: Gr. B.121; Aberdeen to Graham 8 Oct. 1854: *ibid.*
17   Graham to Gladstone 6 Oct. 1854: PARKER, ii, p. 253; Graham to

Clarendon 8 Oct. 1854: Cl. Dep. C14 f463–7; Clarendon to Stratford 13 Oct. 1854: F.O. 352/37; Newcastle to Raglan 9 Oct. 1854: RAGLAN 6807–283; Newcastle to Aberdeen 11 Oct., Aberdeen to Newcastle 15 Oct.1854: MARTINEAU, pp. 167–9.
  18 Graham to Dundas 13 Oct. 1854: DND/11 f61–3; Admiralty to Dundas 13 Oct. 1854 no. 622, 628: NRS pp. 337–9; Graham to Lyons 13 Oct. 1854: Gr. B.121; Newcastle to Raglan 28 Sept., 3 Oct. 1854: RAGLAN 6807–283; Aberdeen to the Queen 17 Oct. 1854: Add. 43, 048 f309–10.

11

The Russian response

After nightfall on the 17th the ruined works of the Redan were rebuilt and rearmed; although they were battered down again the following day, Russian resistance delayed an allied assault. The French batteries on Mont Rodolph only rejoined the action on the 19th, and were quickly silenced by another magazine explosion. Burgoyne at last understood: 'It is not a fortress we are attacking, but an *army* deeply entrenched in strong ground, and with an immense provision of heavy artillery.' The roads north of Sevastopol remained open for troops and supplies, and the co-operation of Menshikov's reinforced field army was assured. For another week the allies prepared for an assault, French trenches closing on the Russian works. Totleben ensured the defences were never completely silenced, although morale suffered with the death of Admiral Kornilov on the 17th. He was replaced by the uninspiring General Moller and the fatalist Vice-Admiral Nakhimov. The defence became a grim business under continued heavy bombardment. Without action by the army the city would fall.

Reinforcements from Odessa; the 12th division, under General Liprandi, reached the army shortly after the bombardment opened. From the 20th a large force assembled at Tchorgun, five miles east of Balaklava, and much closer to the allied flank than hitherto. On the 23rd Menshikov called a conference to consider the crisis in the city. He proposed attacking the right flank of the British batteries, on Green Hill, to disrupt the bombardment; Liprandi, who would be in command, rejected this in favour of a move against Balaklava, accepting that the available force was too weak for a decisive move. Although several formations were marching into the Crimea, the 10th and 11th divisions arrived only ten days later, Menshikov could not wait. He had used Sevastopol and the fleet to preserve his army as a field force rather than being bottled up in the city. The strategic withdrawal to Simpheropol retained the freedom to manoeuvre and moved the Army closer to reinforcements and supply depots. Pressure on the city forced him to move before he was ready; as he could only stage a diversion, he accepted the Balaklava plan. The British position east of the harbour was only intended to delay the enemy until the army could come down from the heights. General Sir Colin Campbell commanded 4,000 newly raised Turkish militia, 1,100 marines and the 93rd Highlanders strung out along a three-mile front. The Turks were in six small redoubts on the Causeway heights and Woronzoff road; the marines held the immediate defences of the port with the Highlanders and cavalry camped mid-way between. This position covered the roads to the front, and the rear of the attack, ensuring Liprandi created the maximum dislocation with the least risk to the 25,000 of all arms available on the 24th. That evening a Turkish spy gave a warning, but Raglan, who had responded to earlier reports, did nothing.

At 06.00 on the 25th Liprandi's infantry and artillery moved up to the Woronzoff road, taking the four easternmost redoubts after a brief, but bloody struggle. Raglan ordered the 1st and 4th divisions to leave the heights, but the leisurely response of the commanders allowed two hours to pass before they reached the plain. In the interval Lord Lucan attempted to hold up the Russian advance with the cavalry. The remaining Turks fled past the camp of the 93rd, but Campbell's men beat off a force of Russian cavalry trying to reach the harbour. As the main body of Russian horse retired they were charged uphill by the far smaller British Heavy Brigade and driven off the field. This gave Raglan time to position his infantry, and order Captain Dacres, *Sans Pareil*, to clear the harbour. The misdirected charge of the Light Brigade, instead of retrieving the guns abandoned by the Turks, completed the confusion of the Russian forces. Raglan failed to take advantage of this with the infantry, leaving the Russians across the Causeway heights, closer to Balaklava than before and, most significantly, on the Woronzoff road. Liprandi was justifiably satisfied; the pressure on Sevastopol had been relieved, and the British would have to reinforce their flank before returning to the bombardment. French troops under General Bosquet moved onto the British right. Dundas landed 500 marines from Eupatoria on 3 November, 200 had landed from the newly arrived *Algiers* on the 24th, just before the battle. The French pressed on with the siege, hoping to assault on 6 November.[1]

Within days Menshikov, reinforced to a total of 90,000, against 71,000 allies, including 11,000 of the discounted Turks, decided to renew the attack before the expected allied reinforcements arrived. The field army assembled on the Inkerman heights, to attack the high ground just south of the head of the harbour and drive the enemy into the sea. However, the battle orders were badly drafted and the plans placed too much reliance on forces marching from separate points and combining on the field of battle. The attack was launched during the early hours of 5 November. A diversion to pin down Bosquet's troops was unconvincing, a sortie from the city ineffective. The main attack was reduced to a series of frontal assaults on the weakly held British line, with powerful artillery support. Allied reinforcements held the ground, until a pair of 18-pounders from the British siege park drove the Russian guns off the field. The attack then ceased, ending Menshikov's attempt to drive the allies out of the Crimea. Casualties in excess of 12,000 made the battle too costly to repeat, and with winter approaching it would be difficult to keep men in the Crimea. Logistics would dominate the remainder of the campaign, and ultimately decide its outcome. The Russians would keep their field army close to Sevastopol, to counter allied pressure on the city, as long as they could feed the men and horses. The allies would keep up their bombardment while they received fresh troops and stores. These problems emphasised the role of the Navy.

Inkerman prevented the allies assaulting on the 6th; at the conference on the 7th Canrobert and Raglan postponed any assault until the right wing had been strengthened; logistics had become a major influence on their decision. They refused Dundas's request to bombard Odessa on the same grounds, wanting to keep every ship close to the beachhead, making a mockery of allied command of the sea. As the original intention had been to capture Sevastopol quickly little thought had been given to the winter; the governments assumed an intact city would provide winter quarters. Raglan only accepted that the Army would have to remain on the Chersonese plateau on the 7th. A week later a storm destroyed the British ammunition, winter clothing and the road from Balaklava to the camp. The superior Woronzoff road had been lost on 25 October. With the only road reduced to a knee-deep quagmire, the transport horses soon died. The resulting shortage of supplies stopped the bombardment, destroyed the cavalry and finally wreaked havoc in the ranks of the tired and sickly Army. Accustomed to rely on the regiment for everything the troops showed little resource, in contrast to the French and the Naval Brigade. The lack of organisation at Balaklava was lamentable, but it should be stressed this was a crisis of control, not supply; even before the rail line to the camp was completed in March the position had improved. Raglan's requests, and Newcastle's considerable forethought, provided the necessary huts and clothing. Once the road was repaired, and better use was made of the cramped harbour, supplies were abundant. The French at Kamiesch and Kazatch had a better anchorage, and with less distance to their camp built a metalled road; their only problem was finding the mercantile tonnage to keep up supplies. Recent campaigns in North Africa ensured they had a well organised camp, with bakeries, a slaughterhouse and hutted hospitals. When the Admiralty, albeit reluctantly, helped find ships there were no serious difficulties.

The Russian position was less satisfactory. The administrative structure in the Crimea had been designed for a small, peacetime garrison. It lacked the magazines and land transport for a major campaign, while the Crimea produced little but grapes and cattle on any scale, depending on the Don basin for grain and forage. Prince M. D. Gorchakov, commander in Bessarabia, sent 6,000 wagons but by late December two thirds of the teams had died of overwork. Forage for the cavalry and artillery horses was the largest single item, and the teams could never carry enough for themselves, forcing the Russians to reduce those arms. Even when the grass began to grow and 125,000 wagons were drafted in, the army and garrison could not be built up as quickly as the allies. This proved the weak link in Menshikov's position.[2]

The attack on 17 October reinforced Dundas's conviction that while the armies remained ashore his first duty was to secure the supply line and support the Army. This attitude had always been enshrined in the French command structure. French steamers were turned over to transport duties, leaving only *Cacique* off Odessa on detached service. Dundas's calls for a blockade and offensive measures were met by a polite refusal, dictated by Canrobert. This did not trouble Dundas greatly, as he was more concerned by the problems of winter, particularly finding a secure anchorage. At sea his first concern remained the surviving elements of the Russian fleet – ten battleships, two frigates and seven paddle steamers. He knew steamers were essential to blockade Sevastopol in winter, so the arrival of the 91-gun steam battleship *Algiers* on 23 October, with the paddle frigates *Gladiator, Stromboli* and *Sphinx* was particularly welcome. Dundas was also troubled by rumours of Russian fireships, possibly steam driven. To meet the danger he kept two steamers off the harbour at night, four more with steam up, and the battleships anchored with springs on their cables. The Russians did prepare fireships after the Alma, but never attempted to use them. A more mundane concern, water, led him to recall *Agamemnon* from Balaklava to prevent the Russians building batteries at the mouth of the Katscha where the fleet sent its boats for water. There was no other local supply, although with a steam fleet the problem disappeared in 1855.[3] With the French dominated by army supply Dundas was responsible for watching Sevastopol, a task he took seriously. Army co-operation was left to Lyons, logistics support to Boxer. He also attempted to conduct offensive operations, principally Graham's plan for the Sea of Azov. Dundas pressed Hamelin, but the need for 2,000 troops to take Kertch ensured Canrobert's veto. The French commander preferred to send a steam squadron as far as Kertch; *Tribune, Highflyer* and *Lynx* went in early November, demolishing a martello tower on the Anapa-Kertch road and inspecting the straits. Elsewhere Dundas was content to shift his forces, relieving *Inflexible* off Odessa with *Gladiator*, and consider the chances of the Russian Danube flotilla running for Nicolaiev. Concern for the Army prevented anything more.[4]

This did not satisfy the Admiralty, which continued to press for a blockade, opening the Straits of Kertch and investigating the Gulf of Perekop. A complete lack of understanding was demonstrated when the Board complained about the manner in which Dundas had landed seamen and guns. By 28 October there were 1,786 officers and men ashore, with 1,930 marines and seventy-four guns, and Raglan requested more marines for Balaklava. The initial landing of men and guns had been approved, but the Admiralty claimed that having so many men ashore destroyed the efficiency of the fleet. Graham preferred to see some ships dismantled. The value of Eupatoria declined as winter approached. On 17 October Russian troops burnt the outlying villages, preventing the collection of livestock, and tested the defences. The Turkish garrison was reinforced by the battleship *Mahmoudie* on the 28th. When the marines were withdrawn Dundas sent *Bellerophon* to join *Leander, Megeara* and *Cyclops*. With no supplies forthcoming and less need for the anchorage, he believed the place should be abandoned.[5]

Between 09.00 and 13.00 on 14 November, a hurricane, with hail, rain and snow blew across the Crimea from the south-west, followed by a westerly gale. Off the Katscha five transports were wrecked, *Sampson* was fouled by two transports and dismasted, *Terrible* was damaged by a blow on the stern. *Queen, London* and *Trafalgar* all suffered damaged rudder heads, while *Britannia* was run down by a French battleship. Three French battleships, including Hamelin's flagship, lost their rudders. The tender *Danube* was wrecked on Cape Kherson, although the crew were saved. Off Balaklava seven transports were driven ashore and destroyed, including the *Prince* and *Resolute* containing winter clothing and reserve ammunition, and *Retribution* was dismasted. At Eupatoria *Henri IV, Mahmoudie*, the steamer *Pluton*, five British and seven French transports were wrecked. The Turkish battleship *Peyk-i-mesenet* was lost at sea with all hands. In the confusion the Russians attacked Eupatoria, but were driven off. Dundas immediately dispatched *Valorous* to Constantinople for clothing and forage. *Danube* and a transport were salvaged, along with many stores, off the Katscha.[6] The loss of shipping off Balaklava was severe because the harbour had been partially cleared during the battles. Many officers believed something should have been done, preferably sending the transports to sea. Captain Christie, the Principal Agent of Transports, was exonerated at the enquiry; Dacres, the harbour master, was sick and about to invalid home. When Heath took over, and Boxer replaced Christie, the handling of transports improved, and those unable to enter Balaklava were held at Sinope. Dundas's part in the disaster was confined to the selection of Dacres, Christie being a Board appointment. The disaster only reinforced Dundas's desire for steamships off Sevastopol and a secure anchorage.

Hamelin had been nervous about the inadequate cables of his sailing battlefleet before the storm, suggesting to Dundas that three sail from each fleet should winter in the bays near the Chersonese lighthouse, with three steam battleships to patrol off the harbour. Dundas sent Spratt to survey before giving his qualified assent on 15 November. With five steam battleships and ten frigates to keep up the blockade, and six ships in the bays, the other sailing ships could be sent down to Beicos. Lyons would have preferred to remain at the Katscha. The disabled French ships sailed for the Bosphorus on the 18th, leaving *Montebello* and *Jean Bart* at sea, with *Alger* and *Marengo* in Kamiesch and Hamelin aboard *Montezuma*. *Rodney* and *Vengeance* were to enter Kazatch with Dundas in *Furious*. *Queen*, *Trafalgar* and *London* would wait for *Britannia* and *Albion* in the Bosphorus, leaving *Bellerophon* and *Leander* at Eupatoria. *Agamemnon* and *Algiers* remained off Sevastopol, where three more steam battleships were expected.[7]

With the French in winter quarters Dundas could not establish a blockade and felt obliged to land more guns. Raglan requested forty 56-hundredweight 32-pounders, which were removed from the damaged *Trafalgar*, and the gun crews came from *Queen* and *London* once they reached Beicos. He tried to reduce his commitments by evacuating Eupatoria, but Canrobert reinforced the Turkish garrison with 20,000 men, assuming the British would provide transport and provisions. Newcastle wanted Omer at Eupatoria, to attack Russian communications, but Raglan had no faith in Ottoman troops. In consequence the army at Eupatoria was never directed to any task, only adding to the logistics burden.[8] Winter also brought a crop of officers invaliding home, sick or bored. Dundas let them go without comment; he was only anxious to leave when his time was up. The storm created a gap in the Russian barrier, leading them to scuttle another two-decker on the 18th. With fewer active ships off the harbour, Dundas relied on Lushington to provide advanced notice of any sortie. The Russians did not disappoint. At 13.15 on 6 December *Vladimir* cleared the harbour standing out to the west. *Terrible* and *Valorous* went after her; the Russian ship turned for home at 14.30 and the British steamers hauled off at 15.00 before coming within range of the batteries. Dundas believed the object had been to determine how many ships were in the bays, a mission which must have failed. The French, reflecting their priorities, thought it was an attempt to bombard their batteries. Dundas still feared a large scale sortie, especially after four British battleships and a steamer left for the Bosphorus on 29 November. Two more went to help the Turks disembark at Eupatoria, leaving only four steam battleships off Sevastopol, but *Hannibal*, *Napoleon* and *Royal Albert* arrived between 5 and 18 December. Lyons and Bruat, now in command, were convinced the danger had passed. *Rodney* went into Kazatch on the 12th, *Bellerophon* and *Vengeance* left for Beicos. Dundas's justified concern hampered the development of offensive plans, but the measures proposed were not always practical. The Admiralty suggested the Gulf of Perekop might be deep enough to allow the new gunvessels inshore. Spratt went with the gunvessel *Lynx*, but his surveying gig grounded fourteen miles from the head of the Gulf. However, he did discover that the Isthmus of Perekop was not the only route into the Crimea – another road crossed the Putrid Sea by the Tchongar bridge, a pre-war military precaution kept secret from the British consul at Kertch. Raglan was impressed.[9]

Within the fleet many had lost faith in Dundas, finding his cautious policy of watching the Russian fleet and securing the supply lines tedious and unrewarding. Apart from the Naval Brigade, 17 October had been their only taste of action. Boredom and despondency turned to complaint, and Lyons' popularity increased as the campaign slowed. During the landing Dundas's policy had been misconstrued, and now every act was treated with suspicion. As Lyons explained: 'No-one for a moment doubts Dundas's personal courage . . . but he is too careful of other men and ships to suit the occasion'. Lyons finally joined the critics when the Admiral decided to send the disabled *Retribution* to Constantinople. The ship required dockyard attention, but Drummond, highly regarded by Lyons and Raglan, was desperate to stay. Once one of Dundas's favourites, he lost his position by over-anxious urging of offensive measures. Lyons and Raglan wanted *Retribution* sent into Balaklava, giving Drummond a major role in running the port, or, if the ship had to leave, he should be moved into the vacant *Tribune* or *Sans Pareil*. Dundas's motives were clear to Lyons:

The Admiral seems to have placed himself entirely in the hands of his guest, Colonel Brereton of the Artillery . . . little adapted in my opinion as well as that of all whom I have heard speak on the subject to be the adviser of a naval commander in chief as any man we ever saw – and yet appears to *think* for Admiral D., to speak for him, and, if I am rightly informed, to *write* for him on important matters relating to the fleet.

Lyons never saw Dundas without his guest, even when briefing the captains on the morning of 17 October, 'tho' many a glance of surprise was cast towards him'. Lyons only sent his letter on 7 November; Graham quickly ordered Drummond into *Tribune*. Within days Dundas earned more of Lyons' ill-feeling, accidentally opening Graham's private letter of 25 October. Lyons accused him of irresolution during the invasion, which did nothing to raise his credit at home. On shifting from *Britannia* into *Furious* on 28 November, Dundas elected to keep his guest and send away the almost superfluous Captain of the Fleet, Rear-Admiral Stopford.

This provoked further acid comment from Lyons, and Raglan. To complete the picture Lyons claimed Dundas would send away all the heavy ships, allowing the Russians to disarm their sea batteries. This was both malicious and unjustified, furthermore Lyons had no scruple in speaking his mind to all who would listen.[10]

Admiralty pressure reflected the disappointed hopes of early October. When Sevastopol did not fall the temptation to find a scapegoat on the scene, rather than accept that the nature of the operation made success a matter of chance, was irresistible. Graham was particularly dissatisfied with the apparent inaction on the day of the Alma, and the unmolested closure of the harbour, arguing that an attack on the forts might have been justified to aid the Army. In private he was less combative, only calling for diversions in the future. Dundas explained that, with Hamelin, he was committed to providing transport and a safe retreat for the Army, which could not be done if the ships were badly damaged attacking the forts. While specific complaints were refuted, Dundas could do little to silence the carping comments on the need for a blockade and on his policy on landing seamen, marines and guns. These were often linked to hints that he had neglected opportunities to attack. The answer to all this lay in his appreciation of what was being attempted. Up to Inkerman he treated the operation as a grand raid, not a siege. This distinction, which had great significance lying off Sevastopol, was not apparent to those in Whitehall, who wanted the best of both worlds. Hoping for a *coup de main* they now wished Dundas had acted as if a siege had been the object all along, keeping the fleet at full strength and setting up a blockade. Dundas's solution had been to leave all major decisions to Raglan, accepting the position of the Army was more difficult than that of the fleet; this also avoided problems with the army-dominated French. The blockade issue was resolved by securing Hamelin's signature on a statement of intent for February, 1855. Manpower was more difficult, as any spare men were needed to fit out the Baltic fleet for 1855. The loss of the *Prince* and *Resolute* on 14 November, and the conduct of Boxer and Christie caused more complaint. Boxer, replaced by Stopford, was moved to Balaklava.[11]

Dundas had been ill all year. The strain of high command and a series of bitter disputes stretching back to 1852 undermined his health and weakened his resolve. This allowed Brereton improper influence, exacerbating his pessimism and his temper. By late November he was also showing early symptoms of cholera. Raglan met him ashore on 3 December, for the first time since the landing, and found him thin and worn. As he prepared to leave Dundas revealed to a confidante that he had never believed in the operation, while he believed capturing the south side would prove indecisive. Although his opinions were sent to Newcastle it is unlikely the Duke gave them any credit. Dundas's term ended on 17 January, Graham was careful to avoid problems, giving permission to come home when he wanted. Realising the importance of serving out his time Dundas left the anchorage on 20 December, with his flag up. Lyons ordered *Agamemnon* to fly 'happiness attends you', but 'hanging attends you' was flown in error, to the amusement of all afloat and ashore. Dundas rejoined *Britannia* in the Bosphorus on the 22nd, finally hauling down his flag at Malta on 17 January. In Paris a few days later Cowley found him 'anything but cheery'.[12]

The Admiral's reputation had been under attack for the last twelve months. Delane had not spared him, while Layard, who blamed him for Sinope, was reported to be intent on impeachment. Lyons hoped his departure would avoid a scandal, although after Graham's work Dundas had few friends. Graham and Newcastle were glad to send him away burdened with other men's guilt; Hamelin, Raglan, Lyons and others all shifted some of their load onto him.[13] With Napier ready to launch his attack Graham could not afford to have the other senior Admiral up in arms. In the event Napier handled his case badly, while Dundas made no effort to defend himself, retiring a broken man. Graham treated the two Admirals as convenient scapegoats, carrying the condemnation that properly belonged to his department, and himself. In his efforts to avoid Layard's furious attacks he was happy to defend Dundas's character, but only to avoid deeper and more damaging revelations.

After Inkerman Menshikov had no hope of victory; the storm and the onset of winter forced the allies to adopt the same policy, hanging on for spring. Raglan wanted to assault, but Canrobert would not agree. His guidance came from Marshal Vaillant, the French Minister of War. Like Burgoyne he wanted regular, safe operations, he anticipated a long campaign and opposed an assault. He advised Canrobert to build a fortified camp, and batter Sevastopol 'to powder', noting 'we may gradually advance into the place in this way with comparatively small loss'.[14] In the face of such opinions it was hardly surprising the grand raid failed. The winter placed the siege in suspended animation, giving the diplomats another opportunity, and the strategists a chance to relearn some old lessons. One thing was clear: the policy of looking for large results without adequate commitment had failed in both theatres. Russia would not be subdued by half measures.

Notes

1 See HIBBERT, pp. 164–232 on the battles. WROTTESLEY, ii, p. 106; Dundas to Raglan 3, 23 Nov. 1854: RAGLAN 6807–298; Lyons to Stratford 4 Nov. 1854: F.O. 352/38/2.
2 CURTISS, pp. 334–41.
3 Dundas to Admiralty 27 Oct. rec. 12 Nov. 1854 no. 541: NRS p. 351; Dundas to Graham 3 Nov. 1854: Gr. CW4; Dundas to Raglan 21, 25 Oct., 10 Nov. 1854: RAGLAN 6807–298; Dundas memo. 7 Nov. 1854: DND/2; SEATON, H., *The Crimean War* (London, 1977), p. 108.
4 Dundas to Admiralty 8 rec. 22 Nov. 1854 no. 541–2: NRS pp. 359–61; Dundas to Graham 13 Nov. 1854: Gr. CW4; Dundas evidence before Sevastopol Committee.
5 Raglan to Dundas 22 Oct., 3 Nov. 1854: RAGLAN 6807–298; Dundas to Raglan 3, 11 Nov. 1854: *ibid.*; Admiralty to Dundas 20 Oct., 7 Nov. 1854 no. 648, 692: NRS pp. 345–58; Dundas to Admiralty 23 Oct. rec. 6 Nov. 1854 no. 534: NRS pp. 347–8.
6 Dundas to Admiralty 17 Nov. rec. 2 Dec. 1854 no. 592: NRS pp. 366–70; Information supplied by Dr W. Blair.
7 Lyons to Graham 18 Nov. 1854: Gr. CW8 and LYONS B66; Dundas to Raglan 11, 15, 17 Nov. 1854: RAGLAN 6807–298; Raglan to Lyons 15 Nov. and Lyons to Raglan 16 Nov. 1854: *ibid.* 299; Dundas to Admiralty 23 Nov. rec. 11 Dec. 1854 no. 617: NRS p. 371.
8 Dundas to Admiralty 17, 22 Nov. rec. 2, 11 Dec. 1854 no. 596, 611: NRS pp. 371–5; Raglan to Dundas 17, 21 Nov. 1854: enc. in no. 611 above; Dundas to Graham 23 Nov. 1854: Gr. CW4; Dundas to Raglan 19 Nov. 1854: RAGLAN 6807–298; Stratford to Raglan 19 Nov. 1854: F.O. 352–38/4; Newcastle to Raglan 28 Nov. 1854: RAGLAN 6807–283; Raglan to Newcastle 8 Dec. 1854: *ibid.* 284.
9 Dundas to Lushington 24 Nov. 1854: DND/2 p. 72; Dundas to Raglan 7 Dec. 1854: RAGLAN 6807–298; Lyons to Stratford 12 Dec. 1854: F.O. 352/38/2; Admiralty to Dundas 13 Nov. 1854 no. 718: NRS pp. 364–5; Spratt to Dundas 12 Dec. enc.in Dundas to Admiralty 13 Dec. 1854 no. 667: *ibid.* pp. 401–5; SPRATT, SPR/3; Raglan to Lyons 9 Dec. 1854: RAGLAN 6807–299; Raglan to Newcastle 14 Dec. 1854: *ibid.* 284. Rear-Admiral Stopford had been sent by the Admiralty in July to restore discipline in the fleet. Dundas can hardly have been pleased by this mark of dissatisfaction, and this places an entirely different light on his decision to send Stopford away: Berkeley to Napier 25 Jul. 1854: Add. 40,025 f115
10 Lyons to Capt. W. A. B. Hamilton 28 Nov. 1854: LYONS B66; Lyons to Raglan 24, 30 Nov. 1854: RAGLAN 6807–299; Lyons to Graham 28 Oct., 27 Nov., 3 Dec. 1854: Gr. CW8; Lyons to Stratford 7 Dec. 1854:

F.O. 352/38/2; Graham to Clarendon 8 Jan. 1855: Cl. Dep. C30 f65–7; Raglan to Lyons 15 Dec. 1854: RAGLAN 6807–299; For Lyons' lack of discretion see, MENDS, p. 215.
11 Admiralty to Dundas 13 Oct., 2, 11, 18, 28 Dec. 1854 no. 628, 783, 829, 861, 893: NRS, pp. 338, 388, 394, 406, 414; Graham to Dundas 13 Oct., 11 Dec. 1854: DND/11 f61, 141–3; Dundas to Admiralty 27 Oct. rec. 12 Nov. 6, 12 rec. 23, 30 Dec. 1854 no. 540, 644, 664: NRS pp. 349, 388, 394–7; Lyons to Raglan 26 Nov. 1854: RAGLAN 6807–299.
12 Dundas to Raglan 20 Nov. 1854: RAGLAN 6807–298; Raglan to Lyons 3 Dec. 1854: *ibid.* 299; H. W. Ward to Newcastle 25 Dec. 1854: MARTINEAU, pp. 170–2; Dundas to Graham 13 Dec. 1854: Gr. CW4; Graham to Dundas 29 Nov. 1854: DND/11; MENDS, p. 228; WARNER, P., *The Fields of War* (London, 1977), p. 134; Cowley to Clarendon 30 Jan. 1855: F.O. 519/215 f101.
13 WATERFIELD, G., *Layard of Nineveh* (London, 1964), pp. 243–56; Lyons to Layard 18 Dec. 1854: Gr. CW8; Lyons to Graham 28 Dec. 1854, 16 Jan. 1855: *ibid.*; Lord Cranworth to Dundas 18 Dec. 1854: DND/11; Dundas to Baring 14 Dec. 1854: BARING, ii pp. 40–1; Raglan to Lyons 15 Jan. 1855: RAGLAN 6807–299; Lyons to Berkeley 9, 13 Jan. 1855: LYONS L507; Graham to Lyons 19 Feb. 1855: LYONS L286–7.
14 Cowley to Clarendon 29 Sep., 28 Nov. 1854: F.O. 519/212 f74, 245.

12

The Baltic campaign

Napier arrived at Wingo Sound on 17 March, waiting another two days for the rest of his fog-dispersed fleet. A brief visit to Copenhagen, meeting the King and the British minister, Buchanan, made him decide to pass the Great Belt at once. Admiralty orders to wait appeared to him to conflict with the later dispatch from the Foreign Office, requiring him to prevent any Russian ships leaving the Baltic. This could not be ensured while he remained at Wingo. As the fleet weighed on the 23rd it was joined by Corry, *Neptune*, *Monarch*, 84 and the paddle steamers *Vulture* and *Bulldog*. The Danes, under pressure from Russia, refused pilots, forcing Napier to send the small steamers ahead to mark the shoals. Passing the Belt took two days, the fleet anchored briefly at Kiel before moving to Kioge Bay on 1 April. Shortly before anchoring *Cressy* and *Princess Royal* collided, and although neither was badly damaged Napier's nerves were shaken. Rear-Admiral Plumridge's squadron went ahead, meeting *Miranda* late on the 25th. Captain Lyons reported there were no warships at Reval or Port Baltic, and the entrance to the Gulf of Finland was choked with loose ice.[1]

Napier's decision to pass the Belt alarmed the Admiralty, and he was ordered to justify acting without prior consent. Graham had always intended to order this move once Corry reinforced the original squadron, but had not discussed it with the Naval Lords. Napier pointed to the confusion of the double orders and the danger of the Russians escaping. Graham, fearing Napier might attempt something rash, wanted to keep him under control until the 'Nelson Touch' was required at Reval. The double correspondence – official dispatches and private letters – remained at variance throughout the campaign, where the proper function of the latter was to enlarge on matters too sensitive for the former. Criticising the passage of the Belt was an error, which the Board grudgingly conceded.[2]

4   The Baltic Sea. From the Navy Records Society volume *Russian War 1854*, by permission

Graham's hope for an early success was checked by the news from Reval, although he did not give up hope of a Swedish alliance based on territorial guarantees. He anticipated leaving the Swedes to fight on land, while the British conduced a blockade – a lack of reality common among his colleagues. These hopes encouraged his natural tendency to secrecy, avoiding cabinet discussion of war aims and Baltic strategy. When the French announced their Baltic fleet would include troops, the Emperor having heard this was Napier's wish, Graham wanted to hold back 5,000 men to do 'something' in the Gulf of Finland. He did not discuss what Napier might do, or how this related to the only agreed war aims, the 'Four Points', and concealed the troops from Napier. Newcastle warned Hardinge to select a commander capable of 'holding his own' as Napier 'thinks himself a great general'.[3] From his experience of combined operations Napier knew the dangers of divided command.

Three battleships joined the fleet at Kioge Bay; the sailing 70 *Boscawen* and the steam 91s *Caesar* and *James Watt*. The first should have been flagship on the North American station, but was sent to cover the shortage of steam battleships; four more battleships would join the fleet during the campaign, but only *Nile* 91, was a steamer; of the others, *St George* 120, and *Prince Regent* 92, were delayed by the shortage of men, while *Cumberland* 70, was sent direct from three years' service on the North American Station. The crew demanded leave, but, after failing with an appeal to their better nature, Berkeley had to tow the ship out to sea with the Admiralty yacht *Black Eagle* on 9 April. Warning Napier that the crew was 'mutinous', Graham urged him to use the same men to fill the vacant higher rates on the new manned ships the following day. Other ships returning from distant stations were paid off and the crews broken up to avoid a repetition of the *Cumberland* incident. Most believed the Admiralty had treated her crew badly. Berkeley admitted that the manning arrangements had not kept pace with the ability of the dockyards to fit out the reserve ships. Graham even suggested picking up Scandinavian seamen. He took considerable pride in getting so many ships to sea at short notice, and did not take kindly to Napier pointing out the flaws in his creation.[4]

The most obvious weakness was the badly manned battlefleet. The coastguard could only claim to be a naval reserve if they were experienced seamen. Recent commentators have treated them as 'fine seamen' or 'excellent, but often over-age seamen'; the captains of the battleships filled up with these 'Ancient mariners' were less enthusiastic. Henry Martin, *Nile*, reported his were 'quite worn out and worse than useless'. Of 2,000 borne in eleven of the largest ships, 10 per cent had never drilled at a heavy gun, 5 per cent had never been to sea; *Nile's* crew, among the last raised, and not included in these figures, was if anything worse. The old men began to die before leaving Britain and made up the majority of the cholera fatalities in the summer. Berkeley and Graham praised their 'steadying influence' in Parliament; indeed, most were too old for mischief, unless there was any rum to be had. After forty a seaman lost the agility to work aloft, and without naval experience had little value on deck. As Codrington observed, they were an inferior substitutes for seamen.[5]

A bounty would have secured young seamen, needing only gunnery drill to become effective; instead Graham sent men who could not meet the demands of the campaign. Their only virtue was to obscure the failure of his manpower policy.

From the first rendezvous at Wingo Napier spared no efforts to drill his ships, sending the junior Admirals and the Captain of the Fleet to each ship. However, he was not satisfied, losing no time informing Graham and Berkeley of the need for more seamen. Few ships in the first division could keep station under sail, and none of the later arrivals. Even gunnery drill had to be curtailed, because ammunition was short.[6] Napier had been sent to sea with a hastily collected agglomeration of ships, more or less badly manned, forcing him to spend the first three months of the campaign working them up into a combat-ready fleet. Nothing could be done until they were efficient, but this was only apparent in the Baltic; by then distance insulated the Admiralty from criticism. Few outside the Navy realised the difference between a well-manned ship and one filled up with landsmen and coastguard and sent out with a steamer to shepherd it through the Baltic narrows. Napier did, and it limited his perception of the theatre.

Napier's war orders were restricted to defensive measures and reconnaissance. Mercantile and naval blockades were the first priority. Thereafter, he was to investigate the Russian positions outside the Gulf of Finland, specifically the Aland Islands. All this confirmed the influence of Graham, who could now use private correspondence to amplify a document sufficiently vague to cover almost any eventuality.[7] Receiving the news of the outbreak of war on 4 April at anchor in Kioge Bay, Napier responded with a characteristic signal: 'Lads, war is declared, we have a bold and numerous enemy to meet. Should they offer battle, you know how to dispose of them. Should they remain in port, we must try to get at them. Success depends on the quickness and precision of your fire. Sharpen your cutlasses, and the day is your own.' The signal excited much ridicule when the campaign ended without a suitable victory, but this ignored the essential purpose. It was not intended to be read by the Lords of Admiralty, or to be a statement of policy; if he was to move quickly Napier knew there was a need for immediate improvement in fleet drill. His signal was designed to keep up morale on the lower deck. Keppel's crew gave him three cheers, and while Paget was unhappy at the lack of reference to the Almighty he believed Napier would be as good as his word. Napier sent Plumridge's squadron to the Gulf of Finland with orders to examine the state of the ice, avoiding contact with Russian forces. Byam Martin had hoped to catch the Russians unprepared, while Foreign Office intelligence and Baltic rumours suggested the Sweaborg division was icebound outside the port.[8]

When Plumridge reached Sweaborg, on the 8th, he observed the rigging of seven battleships and one frigate from a distance of fifteen miles. He was unable to give an accurate position for the Russian ships, but noted there was no ice. *Dauntless* brought his report to Kioge on the 11th, Napier immediately started for the Gulf with the bulk of his force, announcing his intention to impose a blockade. Graham read more into the dispatch than had been written, claiming the Russians were trapped in the outer roadstead, unprotected by batteries and unable to retreat because of adverse winds. Plumridge made no reference to the wind, and gave no position for the Russian ships. Moving east Napier detached ships to blockade; on the 14th *Cruiser* and *Conflict* went to cover Libau and the Gulf of Riga. The following day *Archer* took station off the Filsand light and *Desperate* off Dager Ort. Corry, with *Neptune, Boscawen, Hogue, Blenheim, Ajax* and three frigates would cruise between Dager Ort and the Hufoundskar beacon. The newly arrived *Lightning* was detached to Stockholm for Gulf of Finland pilots.[9] At this stage Napier had little time for surveying vessels, although he was desperate for pilots. Sulivan returned empty handed from Stockholm, fearing Russian treachery. In early May Napier read Sulivan's paper on organising seamen for land service, a subject close to his heart, and thereafter the two men worked closely. Sulivan blamed his early difficulties with Napier on the Master of the Fleet, George Biddlecombe, who feared the surveying officers would usurp his position; Keppel also criticised Biddlecombe, whose influence with Napier dated back to his service with the Western Squadron in 1847–49.[10] After detaching Corry Napier pressed on, passing Hango Head on the 17th. However, the wind was due east and the barometer falling, and without navigational marks or pilots he did not consider Plumridge's report justified pushing blindly into unknown waters; Plumridge agreed. Further support came from the journals of Saumarez's campaigns. While the Admiralty approved the decision not to enter the Gulf, they observed that steam made the journals irrelevant. Napier made the equally superfluous reply that steam had no effect on fog.

Byam Martin accepted that the campaigns of his old chief were more a hindrance than a guide in the changed situation. In accepting the withdrawal Graham feared Napier's rashness more than the Russians:

I by no means contemplate an attack on Sweaborg or Cronstadt . . . I have great respect for stone walls, and have no fancy for running even screw line of battle ships against them. Because the public may be impatient, you must not risk the loss of a fleet in an impossible enterprise. I believe both Cronstadt and Sweaborg to be all but impregnable from the sea, Sweaborg especially.[11]

These sentiments, and the impression they created, should be recalled when Graham called for an impossible attack on Sweaborg.

After leaving the Gulf Napier rejoined Corry and moved into Swedish waters. The fleet anchored at Elgsnabben, close to Stockholm on 21 April, after a second collision involving *Caesar* and *Royal George*, which led Napier to fear the loss of ships, or defeat in detail. The cruisers were spread for the blockade, surveying anchorages and watering places. The battlefleet was delayed at Elgsnabben by a succession of gales and fogs typical of the Baltic spring, although it impressed the Swedes. Napier met the King, who informed him Sweden had no desire to join the allies, even for the Aland Islands. This was in stark contrast to the views of Graham, who informed him even Sweaborg would be possible with the Swedes, although by implication the fleet could do nothing alone.[12] At Elgsnabben the fleet was reinforced by the French screw 100 *Austerlitz, Prince Regent* and *Cumberland*. After a fortnight of bad weather the fleet weighed on the morning of 5 May, but no sooner were the ships in the narrow, rock-studded passage than an exceptionally dense fog came down. The ill-manned *Monarch* broke her tow, and was only brought up by the skill and composure of Captain Erskine. Corry lost his nerve, retiring to his cabin. Napier, and others considered the complete escape of the fleet nothing short of a miracle.[13]

Dispatches and mail for the Baltic fleet were initially sent with reinforcements. Graham, anticipating delays, in early April arranged to send public correspondence with the Foreign Office courier to Berlin. A special courier would then make an exchange of dispatches at Danzig on Friday. This system was in operation from early June. Private letters were sent by the Post Office in naval transports at the fixed charge of 1*d*. agreed for both Black Sea and Baltic.[14] Concerned by Napier's relations with the press, Graham raised the subject of newspaper correspondents in the fleet. Finding their reports damaging he asked Napier to deal with them. Napier knew who they were, but dishonestly claimed they were in no position to obtain reliable intelligence, Napier himself was a correspondent of *The Times*, despite the standing order prohibiting communication with the press. Anticipating problems, Napier looked to Delane for support, providing a catalogue of the deficiencies of the fleet, which he blamed on the radicals. He enlarged on the subject of correspondents:

if you have any in my neighbourhood give them a letter to me and I will be able to give them news from time to time – and I wish you would give me a line occasionally.

Be cautious in alluding to this letter – the news you get can always come from your own correspondent. Direct to me for the present to Copenhagen under cover to Mr Ryan, for I believe my letters are opened.

Graham had earned a reputation for opening letters while Home Secretary, although there is no evidence he tampered with Napier's mail.[15] Delane remained a valuable ally; *The Times* provided a balanced commentary that only rarely betrayed its origins.

The steam battlefleet anchored off Hango Head on 20 May, leaving the sailing ships, with *Royal George*, *James Watt* and *Ajax*, near Dager Ort. Hango had been a gunboat station before the war, and Napier was looking for these craft. Although he had no intention of attacking he allowed *Dragon* to try the range on the 22nd. She had the worst of a short exchange of fire, being hit several times and losing one man. *Magicienne*, *Basilisk* and *Hecla* went to her assistance, but Napier recalled them. Several captains believed the batteries should have been silenced, if only because the men wanted a fight; Sulivan realised the engagement was too petty, risking damage for no advantage.[16] There were no gunboats at Hango, they were of no value against a steam battlefleet, and would only invite attack. Without gunboats Hango had no role for the Russians, and could not be held by the British. Napier delayed in Hango roads, waiting for strategic direction from London and the French. His cruisers remained active; the frigate squadron under Captain Watson, *Imperieuse* went up to Helsingfors, *Dauntless* going in on the 25th, covered by hazy weather. Captain Ryder noted that twenty-four gunboats had left the harbour, they were later discovered further down the Gulf at Viborg. The other cruisers attempted to capture merchant ships before settling down to the blockade. On the 20th

Arrogant and *Hecla* went twelve miles up river at Eckness, driving off Russian troops, to capture one ship. Two more were hard aground. Captain Cooper-Key, *Amphion*, senior officer on the coast of Courland, summoned the Burgomaster of Libau and received the surrender of all shipping in the harbour on 12 May.[17] These minor operations were important, impressing on the Russians the hopelessness of their position, and setting the tone for the rest of the campaign. The British forces had the initiative; the problem was how to exploit it. Napier knew there were few places open to attack without troops, and he had no instructions. By early June the campaign threatened to become a tedious affair of cruising and blockades. Several battlefleet captains blamed Napier for a situation beyond his control.

Plumridge demonstrated what should not be done. Napier had detailed his squadron to examine the Alands and blockade the Gulf of Bothnia. Unable to find a pilot for the Alands, Plumridge moved up the Gulf. On 30 May the ships' boats landed at Brahestad to investigate shipbuilding yards and storehouses. Assuming everything was the property of the Russian government the entire complex was burned. The squadron employed similar tactics at Uleaborg on the following two days, and again at Tornea on 8 June. A conservative estimate of the value of the materials destroyed came to £365,000, of which most had already been bought by British merchants. Plumridge had orders to look for gunboats, and destroy any being built; after consulting his flag captain, Giffard, he decided this included any shipbuilding materials. The junior officers who led the parties ashore adopted a similarly cavalier attitude. This had a considerable impact on the Finns, who had hitherto not been interested in the war. Neutral opinion was outraged, the ministers at Copenhagen and Stockholm forwarding complaints. Opinion in the fleet was equally hostile, leading Napier to stress that he was not responsible.[18] Giffard noted Plumridge's 'terrible fear' of gunboats, which he found inexplicable. In fact Plumridge knew a great deal about gunboats. On 23 May 1809 HMS *Melpomene*, a 38-gun frigate, was attacked by twenty Danish gunboats while becalmed. The action lasted for seven days before she could drive off her opponents. Five men were killed, twenty-nine wounded and the ship so badly damaged she had to be sold out of the service. Plumridge was one of her lieutenants.[19] On 10 June Plumridge reaped the harvest of his actions. The boats of *Vulture* and *Odin* went into the port of Gamla Careleby, where they were met by heavy fire from Russian infantry and Finnish militia, losing fifty men killed, wounded or captured, along with a boat, a flag and a gun. The whole campaign in the Gulf of Bothnia had been badly executed. Going into the harbour at Gamla Careleby broke the cardinal rule of such operations, attacking out of sight of the ships.[20]

Although they provided no strategic directions the Admiralty pressed Napier to institute a complete blockade; his first declaration, that he would sail for the Russian coast to impose a blockade, was inadmissible, as the Queen's Advocate informed the Admiralty. Later he codified his views on legally enforceable blockades. The blockade had to be imposed by a competent force at the time of declaration; if the declaration proved inaccurate, any seizures made under it were invalid, and the owners entitled to damages. While Graham believed the Tory Queen's Advocate was making unnecessary trouble, Harding wrote to Napier calling for an effective blockade. The Admiralty continued to press for blockades with a vigour that revealed the underlying political pressures. In late May Napier was able to declare the coasts of Russia as far east as Sweaborg and Eckholm blockaded. Unable to tolerate the least criticism, he urged that the Queen's Advocate be informed that steam had altered the nature of a *de facto* blockade as steamers were better suited to intercepting ships. As his dispatches took an unusually long time to reach London the Admiralty began to panic, calling for a declaration on consecutive days. The root cause of delay was the failure of the Board to issue instructions. Only in late May did he receive guidance, and even then there were ambiguities only resolved at the end of the year. Napier's declaration was published on 20 May.[21]

During a petty debate about when the fleet should enter the Gulf of Finland Napier, annoyed by the Board implying he was going too slowly, complained that several of his ships were 'perfectly unfit to go into action', which was serious as he only had twenty battleships to meet thirty credited to the Russians. The Board refused to accept his spirited reply, enquiring why he had not sent detailed reports with his assertion. Privately Berkeley informed him that he took offence unnecessarily and his dispatch had been unjustified. In truth the Board's correspondence on this and several other matters had been written in a manner and tone which was not conducive to satisfactory relations with the Commander-in-Chief. The Board was well aware which ships he considered unfit to fight, and having selected a man well known for his hasty temper it was also unnecessarily provocative. In addition the official correspondence did not sit at one with the private letters of Berkeley and Graham. Berkeley, who became First Naval Lord in June on the death of Hyde Parker, was dominated by manpower, whilst Graham continually urged restraint.[22]

Admiralty dispatches were far from the only problem facing Napier. His fleet was still unfit for action; drafts of warrant officers and bluejackets from the Black Sea and constant drill were improving matters, but time was short. After the two collisions in April Napier resorted to some unusual signals, publicly ridiculing the unfortunate captains. The Flagship, *Duke of Wellington* sailed 'like a witch', her next astern, the old *Royal George* was dangerously crank, badly rigged and had a poor crew. Napier decided to make an example of Captain Codrington, calling him aboard the flagship and giving him a strongly worded reprimand. Codrington, like his fellow battlefleet captains, had disliked Napier before the war, and now objected to the furious pace at which he worked them.[23] From experience in the French wars Napier knew what was required. His only desire was to put the ships in order, he had no time to put the fine feelings of his captains above seamanship and gunnery. When he first complained of lack of energy among his officers Graham and Berkeley promised to make examples. But when he wished to discipline Alfred Ryder, *Dauntless*, George Elliot, *James Watt*, and Codrington they refused; all three were too well connected. The criticism of Ryder was damning; he had ruined the engines of his ship and allowed a prize to escape, causing an incident with the Dutch. The Naval Lords' inaction deprived Napier's strong reproofs of any weight, while both corresponded with the Captain of the Fleet and other senior officers.[24] Napier was not slow to feel this want of confidence.

The battlefleet captains, bored and disillusioned by the routine of cruising and drill, blamed Napier, little realising the restrictions on his freedom of action. On first sighting Sweaborg, Keppel proposed taking *Cumberland* in tow behind *St Jean d'Acre*, and steaming into the harbour, where if sunk they would at least block up the Russians. Paget begged Napier not to allow this, as he had promised to follow! The arrival of the French made matters worse. Parseval was far more cautious than Napier. When the fleets went up to Cronstadt all urged plans to bombard the arsenal and wrote bitter letters.[25] Sulivan, who was constantly employed and spent more time with Napier, gave a favourable judgement on his chief.

Only as Napier left Stockholm did the cabinet give any thought to Baltic strategy. Hitherto the directions had been for a blockade and containing the Russian fleet, along with the restrained, private allusions of Graham, the whole was dominated by the call for caution. While the cabinet debated the Swedish alliance Napier and Graham considered the possibilities with or without the Swedes; Graham wanted a complete blockade of the Gulf of Finland, covering the Russian fleet. Thereafter Aland might be examined, but the Swedish terms were unacceptable and the task beyond the fleet alone. On inspecting the charts Napier declared Sweaborg 'unattackable'. His first sight of the fortress, on 3 June from the Renskar Lighthouse fifteen miles away, only confirmed his suspicions. He also noted eight battleships, three frigates and three steamers in the military harbour. The following day the steam battlefleet anchored at Baro Sound to watch the Gulf and resupply. Napier sent Sulivan to Aland to complete the task abandoned by Plumridge.[26]

Napier sortied down the Gulf again on 9 June, coming to an abrupt halt in thick weather off the Renskar Lighthouse. The fleet remained at anchor for three days before joining Captain Watson's frigate squadron outside Sweaborg. Napier and Chads inspected the position at close quarters. Chads considered Sweaborg might be bombarded from the outlying islands with Lancaster guns; this would not destroy the fortress, but it would ruin large parts of the naval arsenal without risking the fleet. Napier agreed. His error was to send the plan to Graham, rather than the Board. Graham had outlined a scheme to attack Sweaborg using dredgers, Napier responded with Chads' plan. Graham never placed this before the Board. In hindsight Napier considered this was to avoid having his own effort exposed to ridicule.[27] Having prepared for a detailed survey of the approaches the fleet was called away on 18 June by the arrival of the French at Baro Sound. Not anticipating any great delay Napier took the surveyors with him. He was never to return under such favourable conditions. This apart the French had an immediate, detrimental, impact on the campaign. *Austerlitz* had been an adequate squadron ship, but Vice-Admiral Parseval Deschenes' seven sailing battleships and six frigates were in poor order. Their untrained crews and inexperienced officers demonstrated that Britain was not alone in finding her naval reserves difficult to mobilise; Berkeley had at least given a warning. Graham must have realised the French would hamper Napier, but urged him to co-operate.[28] He was concerned to preserve the alliance from Napier, but in so doing he kept Napier away from the Russians, ruining any chance of offensive measures. Believing joint command worked well in the Black Sea, Graham urged it on the French.[28] Parseval insisted on accompanying Napier everywhere, fearing public reaction if he missed any action. Napier had wisely divided his battlefleet into steam and sail divisions from the beginning of the campaign; to accommodate Parseval he had to sacrifice his strategic mobility and tactical cohesion for the doubtful reinforcement of a sailing squadron in worse order than Corry's. The tactical problems of controlling two fleets of steam and sail under equal Admirals were insuperable. Given Napier's direct tactical ideas it can be assumed he would have signalled the general chase, leaving the French to follow. Until then he had to treat his allies as equals, which deprived him of any opportunity to display initiative, his finest quality.[29]

Sulivan returned from Aland on 10 June with a full report on the garrison, fortifications and navigational problems at Bomarsund. He considered the best method of attacking the fort, which mounted eighty guns facing Ledsound, the three smaller twenty-two-gun forts and the seven-gun battery at Transvig, would be a regular siege using 10,000 men. Sulivan also reported new foundations on the shore of Lumpar Bay, which should be destroyed before the season ended, if only by long range bombardment. Napier sent the report to Graham and the Board, assessing the situation in the Baltic now the French had arrived and in the light of Sulivan's report. Unfortunately he sent this to Graham. The Russian fleet was blockaded in the Gulf of Finland; Sweaborg would require heavy guns and troops, as set out in Chads' plan, a naval attack being impossible from the intricacy of the navigation. Merely keeping up the blockade would be unpopular at home, but Cronstadt was impossible and the Russian fleet would not come out; therefore he proposed landing 10,000 sailors and marines at Aland immediately, with Parseval's concurrence. However the French Admiral refused, believing his duty was to appear off St Petersburg without delay, which Cowley reported was Louis Napoleon's only object in the Baltic.[30] Graham revealed his views to Napier, insofar as he wished Napier to know them. He looked for a sortie down to Cronstadt, although the two divisions of the Russian fleet should not be allowed to unite. Without the benefit of Sulivan's report he saw no advantage in capturing Aland, unless Sweden joined. As for the major arsenals: 'It would madness to play her game and to rush headlong on her Granite walls risking our naval supremacy with all the fatal consequences of defeat in an unequal contest with wood against stone which in the long run cannot succeed.' The differences between Graham and Napier at this stage were minor. Napier would have preferred the entire Russian fleet in one place. If he went up to Cronstadt he had to cover Sweaborg with Corry's ships, the French being determined to visit the head of the Gulf. More significant was the First Lords' opinion on offensive measures; if Cronstadt and Sweaborg were 'madness' and Aland irrelevant that only left the blockade, which Napier knew would not be enough.

Graham's views on Aland were expressed more clearly during the cabinet discussions leading up to the decision of 28 June. Prince Albert urged the operation, if only for the impression of activity. Graham could see no point. They could not be held during the winter without Sweden, if she joined troops would be unnecessary: 'I am anxious that the concentrated military efforts of France and Britain should be directed to the Black Sea'. He bowed to the pressure; if Cronstadt was impossible he would plan an attack on Aland, with French troops. The British reserve, held back for possible Baltic operations, would be sent to the Crimea. Graham's dislike of the Bomarsund operation was clear. Transport for the French was organised from the reserve fleet.[31]

Napier left Baro Sound for Cronstadt on 21 June with the steam battlefleet and six French sail; Corry, with two French sail, was left to cover Sweaborg. With the combined fleet off Cronstadt on the 26th the blockade of the Russian coast was complete. On the 30th Napier reported the existing fleet could do nothing. He needed an army, or gunboats armed with long range (Lancaster) guns: 'I have thought it better to send all this and all the drawings to you privately'. He expected Graham to adopt the plans for Sweaborg and Cronstadt set out in his private letters, building gunboats and finding troops. The combined fleet left Tolboukin on 2 July, after an outbreak of cholera. Captain Watson went up to Biorko Sound, finding the shallow inshore passage between Viborg and Helsingfors that allowed the Russians to move gunboats along the northern shore of the Gulf unhindered by heavy vessels. Biorko, the one place where deep water interrupted this passage, was given more emphasis in

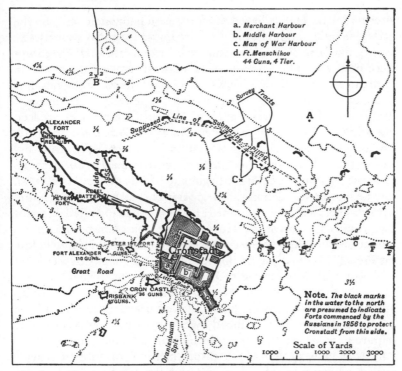

7 Cronstadt, the defences and the line of submarine piling. Figures on the dotted lines indicate depth of water in fathoms (a fathom equals six feet, or slightly under two metres). The Survey tracks are those of Sulivan. Note the site of the post-1856 batteries, indicating Russian awareness of the danger of an attack from the north side. It is worth noting that the piling was placed 3,000 yards from the island, indicating the range of attack expected. British mortars and Lancaster guns could exceed this range, but a close-range attack would have been required to capture the island. The line of blockships marked L(ine of battleship) F(rigate) and C(orvette) cover the weak eastern side of the island. From the *Life of Admiral Sir Bartholomew James Sulivan*

1855. Picking up Corry the fleets reached Baro Sound on 6 July and practised boat landings for the Aland operation.[32]

While the fleet lay off Cronstadt Captain Hall, *Hecla*, steamed up flying a signal that Bomarsund had been bombarded. Plumridge had come up to Cronstadt to confer with Napier, leaving Hall as senior officer. On 22 June, having obtained a pilot, *Hecla* led *Odin* and *Valorous* into Lumpar Bay at 16.30. They kept up a long range fire from their 10-inch shell guns, running out of ammunition shortly after midnight. Hall believed the forts were badly damaged, but he had done little beyond burning a store house for shells were useless against masonry. Napier was annoyed, particularly as all three ships were now without ammunition. Graham trumpeted the attack in Parliament, because any news was good news, although like Berkeley he must have shared Napier's opinion.[33] This incident demonstrated the tenuous nature of Napier's control over his fleet. Plumridge had exceeded his orders, an example followed by Hall. The other detached commands were in better hands; Watson and Key were excellent officers, while Corry was unlikely to do anything, let alone anything rash. At the beginning of July the Baltic fleet had, for the first time, a definite strategic object. Furthermore the entire Russian coast had been examined and Napier had prepared plans for Sweaborg and Cronstadt. However, the season for amphibious operations was slipping away. Another month would elapse before the French army arrived. During the interval Graham's view of what was possible before the end of 1854 began to alter. The reasons for this are uncertain, but his optimism was raised by the decision to attempt Sevastopol. During June his letters urged restraint, but from 2 July he repeatedly mentioned Sweaborg. Knowing Napier only required troops, and having told him on 27 June there were no Lancaster guns available, the casual mention of another scheme served no purpose. Unwilling to find the gunboats and troops required by Napier's plans, Graham ignored them. Even on 11 July his letter was dominated by caution: Sweaborg must not be attempted at any risk. Sevastopol was the 'principal operation' and he complained that the French army corps for Aland reduced the resources for the attempt. In part his return to Sweaborg was a reaction to newspaper attacks on Napier and the Admiralty. Berkeley promised to support Napier against 'a public who expect impossibilities' and 'who would hang us if we fail in anything we undertake'. He did not think any more could have been done.[34]

Notes

1   Napier to Admiralty 18, 22, 26 Mar. 1854 no. 2, 5, 12: ADM 1/5624.
2   Admiralty to Napier 24 Mar. 1854: BONNER-SMITH, D., *The Russian War: 1854, The Baltic*, NRS (London, 1943), p. 46; SULIVAN, p. 122; Graham to Clarendon 16 Mar. 1854: Gr. B.118; Napier to Admiralty 1, rec. 8 Apr. 1854 no. 21: ADM 1/5624; Admiralty to Napier 8 Apr. 1854: NRS p. 49; Graham to the Queen 31 Mar. 1854: R.A. G11 f91.

3 Cowley to Clarendon 29 Mar. 1854: F.O. 519/3 f109; Graham to Clarendon 30 Mar. 1854: Gr. B.118; Newcastle to Hardinge 4 Apr. 1854: NeC 10,781.

4 Napier to Admiralty 11 rec. 17 Apr. 1854 no. 46: ADM 1/5624; Berkeley to Napier 18, 28, 30 Mar. 9, 20 Apr. 1854: Add. 40,024 f74, 84, 92, 122; *Times*, 6 Apr. 1854; Graham to Napier 5, 10, 11 Apr. 1854: Add. 40,024 f114, 128, 134; Keppel to Captain Stephenson 23 Apr. 1854: HTN/52A; The Queen to Aberdeen 2 Apr. 1854: Add.43.049 f11.

5 TAYLOR, p. 312; HAMILTON, C. I., 'Sir James Graham, the Baltic Campaign and War Planning at the Admiralty', *The Historical Journal*, 1976 p. 97; H. Martin to T. Martin 25 Mar., 1 May, 13 Jun. 1854: Add. 41,467 f80, 121, 173; Codrington to Lady Bourchier 29 Apr. 1854: BOURCHIER, Lady, *Selections from the Letters of Admiral Sir Henry Codrington* (London, 1880), p. 369.

6 Napier to Graham and to Berkeley 19 Mar. 1854: PRO 30/16/12 f20–3; Napier to Graham 26 Mar. 1854: WILLIAMS, pp. 270–1; Berkeley to Napier 4 Apr. 1854: Add. 40,024 f112.

7 Admiralty to Napier 30 Mar. 1854. NRS p. 46, The London Gazette 29 Mar. 1854.

8 EARP, G.B., *Sir Charles Napier's Baltic Campaign* (London, 1857), pp. 96–7; OTWAY, pp. 87–8; Keppel to Capt. Stephenson 4 Apr. 1854: HTN/52A; Napier to Plumridge 4 Apr. 1854: PRO 30/16/9 f24; Foreign Office to Admiralty, enc. Seymour to Clarendon 23 Jan. 1854: ADM 1/5634.

9 Plumridge to Napier 8 Apr. 1854: PRO 30/16/12 f95–7; Napier to Admiralty 11 rec. 17 Apr. 1854 no. 46: ADM 1/5624; Graham to Clarendon 17 Apr. 1854: Gr. B.119; Admiralty to Napier 3 Apr. 1854: PRO 30/16/11 f16; SULIVAN, p. 128.

10 SULIVAN, pp. 135, 145.

11 Keppel to Capt. Stephenson 23 May 1854: HTN/52A; Napier to Admiralty 18 Apr.(missing) 20 May 1854 no. 53, 95: NRS p. 52; Admiralty to Napier 2 May 1854: *ibid.* p. 51; T. Martin to H. Martin 4 Sept. 1854: Add. 41,467; Graham to Napier 1, rec. 15 May 1854: Add. 40,024 f159; Graham to Clarendon 30 Apr. 1854: Cl. Dep. C14 f316–17.

12 Napier to Codrington 22 Apr. 1854: COD 113/2; Napier to Admiralty 24 Apr., 2 rec. 8 May no. 60, 72: ADM 1/5624; Napier to Clarendon 26 Apr. 1854: EARP, pp. 125–6; Graham to Napier 1 May 1854: Add. 40,024 f159.

13 Napier to Admiralty 27 Apr. 1854 no. 65: ADM 1/5624; GIFFARD, Adm. Sir G., *Reminiscences of a Naval Officer* (Exeter, 1892), p. 119; Keppel to Capt. Stephenson 13 May 1854: HTN/52A.

14 Graham to Napier 10 Apr. 9, 10 May 1854: Add. 40,024 f130, 183, 310; Col. Herbert and Graham 21 Mar. 1854: HANSARD 3rd series CXXXI 1069.

15 Graham to Clarendon 30 Apr. 1854: Cl. Dep. C14 f316–17; Graham to Napier 2 May 1854: Add. 40,024 f165–8; Napier to Graham, undated: EARP, p. 135; Napier to Delane 24 Apr. 1854: PRO 30/16/12 f158; WARD, p. 209.

16   Napier to Admiralty 20 May, rec. 2 Jun. 1854 no. 95: NRS, p. 52;
Keppel to Capt. Stephenson 23, 27 May 1854: HTN/52A; SULIVAN, pp.
152–7; EARP, p. 153.
17   Napier to Admiralty 23, 30 May 1854 no. 96, 107: NRS p. 55.
18   Plumridge to Napier 10 Jun. 1854: Add. 40,024 f237; GIFFARD, p.
120; OTWAY, pp. 96–7; BOURCHIER, p. 386; Buchanan to Clarendon 23
Jun. 1854: PRO 30/16/2 f195–7; H. Martin to T. Martin 18, 26 Jun. 1854:
Add. 41,467 f180–90; For the Finnish view of these operations, and the war
see; GREENHILL and GIFFARD, *The British Assault on Finland 1854–55:
A Forgotten Naval War* (London, 1988) which the author was privileged to
read in manuscript while completing this book.
19   GIFFARD, p. 115; JAMES, W., *The Naval History of Great Britain*
(London, 1902 edn.), vol. V, p. 39.
20   Napier to Admiralty 18 Jun. 1854 no. 152: ADM 1/5624; Graham
to Napier 2 Jul. 1854: Add. 40,024 f12.
21   Admiralty to Napier 5 Apr., 4, 29 May, 12, 13, 26 Jun. 1854 no. 85,
348, 354, 385: NRS p. 47, 60, 80. May corres. is no longer extant; Napier to
Admiralty 11 Apr., 28, 30 May rec. 15 Jun. 1854 no. 46, 101, 102: ADM
1/5624; Graham to Napier 30 May 1854: Add. 40,024 f218; Memo. by J.
D. Harding 11 Aug. 1854: ADM 1/5624; Harding to Napier 20 May 1854:
Add. 40,024 f220.
22   Napier to Admiralty 18 Apr., 16 Jun. 1854 no. 53, 144: NRS pp. 50,
62–3; Napier to Admiralty 20 May 1854: Add. 40,024 f203; Admiralty to
Napier 2 May 1854: NRS p. 51; Graham to Napier 1, 28 May 1854: Add.
40,024 f159, 214; Berkeley to Napier 6 May 1854: *ibid.*
23   Berkeley to Napier 18 May 1854: *ibid.* f199; Napier to Walker 30
May 1854: PRO 30/16/12 f323; Milne to Napier 30 May 1854: Add.
40,024 f226; Codrington to Walker 3 Sep., Codrington to Berkeley 16 May
1854: COD 109/2; H. Martin to T. Martin 5 May 1854: Add. 41,467 f135.
24   Graham to Napier 16 Apr. 1854: Add. 40,024 f44; Berkeley to
Napier 30 Mar., 30 May 1854: *ibid.* f93, 222; Napier to Admiralty 13 Jun.
1854: ADM 1/5624; Napier to Milne 8 Apr. 1854: Milne 166; Graham to
Clarendon 23 Jul. 1854: Gr. B.120; Admiralty to C-in-C Sheerness 27 Jul.
1854: ADM 1/5623 c905; Berkeley 8 Mar. 1855: HANSARD 3rd series
CXXXVII 307.
25   Keppel to Capt. Stephenson 9, 18 Jun. 1854: HTN/52A; H. Martin
to T. Martin 1 Jul. 1854: Add. 41,467 f195; Codrington to Lady Bourchier 1
Jul. 1854: BOURCHIER, p. 399; OTWAY, pp. 110–11; Capt. F. W. Grey
to General Sir Charles Grey (Prince Albert's Secretary) 18 Aug. 1854: RA
G14 f52.
26   Graham to Napier 15 May, rec. 8 Jun. 1854: Add. 40,024 f191;
Napier to Admiralty 30 May, 4 Jun. rec. 8, 15 Jun. 1854 no. 102, 108: ADM
1/5624.
27   Napier to Admiralty 12 rec. 19 Jun. 1854 no. 137: *ibid.* Chads memo
14 Jun. 1854: Add. 40,024 f271; Washington to Graham 20 Jun, 1854: *ibid.*
f333; EARP, p. 185.
28   H. Martin to T. Martin 27 Jun., 4 Jul. 1854: Add. 41,467 f195–8;
Berkeley to Napier 4 May 1854: Add. 40,024 f175; Graham to Clarendon

28 May 1854: Cl. Dep. C14 f358; Graham to Napier 27 Jun. 1854: Add. 40,024 f347; Graham to Rear Admiral Sir R. S. Dundas 14 Apr. 1854: M.C.M. GD 51/2/1088i f34.
29   Napier to Graham 20 Jun. 1854: PRO 30/16/12 f403; LAMBERT, p. 87.
30   Sulivan to Napier 10 Jun. 1854: EARP, pp. 333–6; Napier to Admiralty 12, rec. 19 Jun. 1854 no. 137: ADM 1/5624; Napier to Graham 12, 20 Jun. 1854: PRO 30/16/12 f348, NRS pp. 7–9.
31   Graham to Napier 20 rec. 27 Jun. 1854: Add. 40,024 f310; Albert to Graham 19 Jun., Graham to Albert 20 Jun. 1854: Gr. B.120; Graham to Napier 27 Jun., 2 Jul. rec. 4, 10 Jul. 1854: Add. 40,024 f347 and 40,025 f12; Aberdeen to the Queen 29 Jun. 1854: Add.43,049 f173.
32   SULIVAN, pp. 187–9; LLOYD and COULTER, vol. iv, pp. 151–2; Napier to Graham 1 Jul. 1854: Add. 40,025 f1; Napier to Admiralty 1, 7 rec. 10, 12 Jul. 1854: NRS p. 85, ADM 1/5624.
33   SULIVAN, p. 190; WILLIAMS, p. 310; Napier to Admiralty 22 Jun., rec. 19 Jul. 1854 no. 225: ADM 1/5624; Berkeley to Napier 11 Jul. 1854: Add. 40,025 f61.
34   Graham to Napier 2, 11 rec. 10, 17 Jul. 1854: *ibid.* f2, 63; Graham to Clarendon 2 Jul., 5 Aug. 1854: Cl. Dep. C14 f380, Gr. B.120; Delane to Napier 26 Jul. 1854: Add. 40,025 f124; Berkeley to Napier 11, 31 Jul. 1854: *ibid.* f61, 124.

13

Bomarsund

While on a smaller scale than the invasion of the Crimea the Aland operation also demonstrated the problems of alliance warfare. The cabinet decision of 28 June was made in haste and without strategic rationale, Graham later made a feeble attempt to justify it by reference to a possible Swedish alliance.[1] The British requested 6,000 men, Louis Napoleon added ten guns and fifty horses, the guns were superfluous when the fleet already had several thousand heavier weapons in the Baltic. Milne organised transport, using British warships and merchant ships, steam and sail, under Commodore Frederick Grey. The warships *Algiers* and *Hannibal* steam 91s, *St Vincent* 102 and *Royal William* 120 sailing three-deckers with the steamers *Termagant, Sphinx* and *Gladiator* landed their lower deck guns to embark troops. Graham was concerned they should return quickly, to join the reserve of ten battleships he intended to assemble by September. The transports *Belgravia, Edwin Fox, Herefordshire, Julia, Clifton* and *Colombo* were under the command of Captain Henry Chads, son of the Rear-Admiral, aboard the ill-fated steamer *Prince*. The British presumed the French would embark from Cherbourg, their only deep water harbour on the Channel coast, but the French claimed they could not, lacking a railway line to the arsenal. Clarendon and Graham accepted the alternative of Calais, while casting doubt on French good faith, and expressed reservations about embarking so many men in an open roadstead.[2] The troops would be victualled by the Admiralty, at the expense of the French War Ministry. Graham stressed that Napier was not to attempt the operation with his scratch force of seamen and marines, and instructed him to survey the islands and assist the transports, precautions he should have had the confidence to leave unmentioned.[3] Later the French increased their force to 9,000; Clarendon advised taking them, as they were reported to be of poor quality. Napier complained there were too many for Aland, and too few for anything else, particularly as he did not anticipate them wintering in the Baltic. Many of the French troops were raw recruits which, as Milne anticipated, encouraged cholera.[4]

To keep Napier away from General Baraguay d'Hilliers, Graham secured Colonel Harry Jones, RE as liaison officer. He hoped Napier would remain in the Gulf of Finland with Parseval, leaving Aland to Chads. Napier considered it would be unwise to leave the French in command at Bomarsund.[5] Graham's concern was well founded, Napier was already arguing with the victuallers, Rainals and Deacon of Elsinore, about the poor quality of the bullocks they were supplying. He condemned the contract as an Admiralty 'job', and told Rainals his services were no longer required, leaving Milne to smooth out the dispute.[6] The battlefleet left Baro Sound on 18 July, anchoring at Ledsound, close to Lumpar Bay on the 22nd. Corry, his nerve entirely broken, invalided home, and died early in 1855. Commodore Henry Martin, expecting his flag, took *Nile, Austerlitz, Royal George, Caesar, Cressy, Neptune, Prince Regent* and *Monarch,* to cover the Gulf of Finland and support Watson's frigates. Martin left Ledsound on 22 July, anchoring in Reval roads.

Plumridge's squadron surrounded the Alands before the main fleet arrived. On the 23rd Sulivan piloted Chads' four blockships and *Amphion* into Lumpar Bay; Chads lost no time, convinced the Russians would resist any landing. By the 30th the naval preparations were complete. Grey's warships arrived late that day, Napier having changed the rendezvous from Faro Sound. Only the non-arrival of French warships carrying their engineers' stores prevented an immediate start. Graham now believed Bomarsund would be 'no bad beginning'.[7] The most serious problem for the allies was, as Graham anticipated, the inevitable clash of personalities. Parseval found Napier coarse and abrupt, complaining he had assumed overall command. Graham could only point out the dangers of a breach with France; Berkeley hoped a fight would put the Frenchman in better humour. On 1 August Baraguay and Engineer General Niel, a favourite of the Emperor, arrived after a mission to Stockholm, where the King had rejected their proposals. They immediately went into Lumpar Bay with Parseval, followed by Napier and Jones in *Lightning.* Napier, a changed man once relieved of anxiety for the fleet, wanted to start at once, but the French refused to land until their equipment arrived, even with 8,000 troops and a large fleet.

Termagant brought in a transport on 2 August, but there was still no sign of the French ships. Napier was becoming despondent, hearing a rumour that 300 Russian gunboats would attempt to relieve the islands; *Locust* fired on a boat to the north of the island.[8] However, this was an isolated incident. The Russians made no attempt to assist the garrison.

The plan of operations was decided by Napier, Parseval and Baraguay; French troops would land to the south of the main fort, allied marines with British Sappers and Miners to the north, commanded by Jones, who had abandoned the liaison role. The French transports finally arrived on the 5th, the following day Biddlecombe took a sounding party within 600 yards of the fort and buoyed several shoals under fire. The French troops were placed in steamers during the evening of the 7th, and landed at day-break on the 8th. Jones met no opposition, but *Amphion* and *Phlegethon* spent forty minutes shelling the abandoned battery at Transvig that flanked the landing site. Napier shifted his flag into the small steamer *Bulldog* to get close inshore. Lack of roads hampered the siege operations; the French had fifty horses, but the British relied on the muscle power of the sailors. The artillery was landed on the 10th, the British using six 42-hundredweight 32-pounders from the upper deck of *St Jean d'Acre*. The first three were ashore when the men were called away.

The paddle frigate *Penelope*, Captain Caffin, crossed Lumpar Bay on the morning of the 10th, piloted by Biddlecombe. Napier reported she was to proceed between Presto and Tofto 'to watch the passage'; Caffin more accurately stated his orders were to anchor abreast the 11th embrasure of the main fort. Napier's desire to avoid publishing this can be understood, for, as Keppel reported, the purpose of this strange order was to 'draw the fire, if there were any guns mounted'. At 11.30 *Penelope* ran hard aground, with a rock under her port bilge, a hazard not indicated on any chart. She lay 1,900 yards from the main fort, abreast the 17th embrasure, which proved to be armed and opened fire. *Gladiator*, Captain Broke, and *Pigmy* came down from the end of the Presto Tofto channel, with the boats of *Trident* and *Duperre*, the shore party and *Hecla*. Hall took charge, attempting to pull *Penelope* clear, but she was stuck fast. *Gladiator* and *Hecla* were being hit by red hot shot. Napier, forced to act quickly for the first time in the campaign, ordered Plumridge down to get her off, throwing her guns overboard if necessary. Caffin unshipped fifteen heavy guns, 240 fathoms of chain cable, and 118 round shot, and finally blew out the boilers. *Penelope* floated at 15.15, after three and three-quarter hours under fire. She suffered only one killed and one wounded, the other parties lost one killed and four wounded. Damage was superficial, although her guns were ruined. She was fortunate the fleet was at hand. Keppel, using information supplied by *Bulldog's* captain, King-Hall, claimed Napier wanted to send the ships in to bombard the fort, but was dissuaded by Chads. Keppel had a strong prejudice against Chads, believing the Rear-Admiral to be responsible for the advanced position of the blockships, little realising Napier had been ordered to place the expendable old vessels before forts in place of the modern battleships. Embarrassed by the *Penelope* incident, Napier sent Paget to Reval when he expressed a critical opinion.[9]

On the 11th the remaining three British guns were landed. They were intended for the French, but they had brought their own guns and mortars and would not allow the French navy ashore. The French batteries facing Fort Tzee, four 16-pounders and four 8-inch mortars, were complete by the evening of the 12th. Baraguay told Jones he could not open before the 15th, but commenced battery practice at 03.00 on the 13th. While his mortars damaged the roof, the guns were ineffective, although accurate French rifle fire picked off the Russian gunners. Early the next morning the fort surrendered, the main fort then opened fire on it until the magazine exploded. The ships in Lumpar Bay occasionally joined in, more to disturb the Russians than from any hope of causing serious damage. During the 14th Jones turned his battery of three 32-pounders to face Fort Nottich, opening at 08.00 on the 15th at 800 yards. In the course of the next nine-and-a-half hours the guns fired 532 rounds, averaging eighteen per gun per hour. At the end of this tremendous battering a large section of the wall fell in and the fort capitulated. Baraguay spent the time shifting the front of his battery to face the main fort; Captain Pelham, *Blenheim* placed a 10-inch gun in the Transvig battery. At day-break on the 16th the French mortars and Plumridge's squadron opened on the main fort and Fort Presto. The Russian commander, General Bodisco, aware his position was hopeless, surrendered before the breaching batteries could get into action. Drunken Russian troops began looting their officers' quarters, until relieved by the French. All told, 2,255 prisoners went aboard the warships and transports, leaving on the 20th for Britain and France. The returns make it clear the garrison was of poor quality, including significant numbers of non-Russian and even convict troops. While Bomarsund had considerable strategic value against Sweden, as part of Russia's expanding Baltic position, it was hostage to a superior naval force. If eyewitness accounts are to be credited the Russian courage was largely drink-induced. The gunnery of the forts, adequate against *Penelope*, fell off once subjected to an accurate return.[10]

The Russians assimilated the lessons of Bomarsund. Small, isolated garrisons could not resist allied amphibious power. They hurriedly destroyed the works on Hango Head when the allies next passed that way, and redoubled their efforts to improve the major fortresses. As a military operation Bomarsund demonstrated the value of complete naval control. Like most sea forts Bomarsund was weak on the land side, making it logical to attack in that area. With so many troops success was inevitable, which was fortunate as the allies spent more time bickering than fighting.[11]

Once the fortress had fallen the allies had to decide what to do with it; that they had not considered this already indicated the lack of any realistic discussion of the campaign. Graham, like his colleagues, had only approved it to quieten the public. After Baraguay's visit to Stockholm the allies considered the Swedish terms 'too strong'. They also made the capture of the islands irrelevant; the only possible justification had been to bring Sweden into the war. They had no strategic value to the allies, and could be taken at any time. Graham still hoped for progress with the Swedish negotiations, arranging winter quarters at Carlscrona. Aberdeen wanted to destroy Bomarsund, believing Baltic operations should not be shackled to the possibility of a Swedish alliance which would 'greatly extend and complicate the objects of war, and render peace infinitely more difficult'. Napier, certain Sweden could not hold Bomarsund, pressed Graham, Palmerston, Clarendon and the Admiralty to prevent Russia refortifying a position he feared would 'eclipse Sweaborg and Reval and become the principal station of the Russian fleet'. Newcastle wanted to install a Swedish garrison; Graham was inclined to agree, a swing of opinion that said much about his desperation to achieve something. Palmerston, concerned Aberdeen would make peace on easy terms, wanted to attack Sweaborg with the Bomarsund force. This was to be a last throw, not part of his mature strategy.[12]

All these schemes depended on Sweden and France, Britain lacked the troops for an independent policy. Sweden would only occupy the islands if her terms were met, in full. The French would winter at Stockholm if the Swedes garrisoned Bomarsund, but this was rejected. Palmerston and Russell were reluctant to destroy the fortress, although they had no realistic plans. As Lansdowne pointed out, the Baltic was now subordinate to the Euxine. Aberdeen favoured acting without the Swedes. Graham anticipated bad weather, intending to withdraw the sailing battleships once Napier had destroyed the forts, and with them the Swedish illusion. The cabinet and the French Emperor shared his assessment. Aware the negotiations with Sweden had failed, Napier had been prepared.[13] Only Newcastle claimed any concrete results for the operation:

I am bound to say that what we *now* know of Bomarsund makes its destruction of higher importance than was anticipated when the expedition was planned. It is manifest that the Emperor intended this to be his great arsenal, and through its means to command the trade of both Gulfs, and either annex Sweden, or to make her an unresisting vassal. I hope we shall never allow this object to be attained.[14]

The allies had administered a severe check to Russian Baltic policy, and while Bomarsund was not a direct threat to Britain, it reduced Swedish independence and threatened to carry Russian power to the Sound, which were direct British interests. The Eastern Question provided an opportunity to check Russia in the Baltic as well as the Euxine. However, attempts to entangle the Swedes had again broken down; King Oscar played on the easily raised hopes of the allies to increase Sweden's value. The allies, unwilling to contemplate the unlimited war that Oscar required, preferred to destroy the forts, leaving the islands undefendable.[15] The British cabinet, learning from the earlier negotiations, lost interest in Sweden by early August. Palmerston still wanted a wider war, but his colleagues were intent on the Crimea. Aberdeen's analysis, that Baltic strategy should not be tied to Sweden, was by far the wisest. That chimera had persuaded Graham to ignore the obvious need of the fleet for flotilla craft. Although his enthusiasm waned as the year passed, yet the basic theme remained. After Aland he looked for a more spectacular success to encourage Sweden, in line with public demands for success, demands which he used in September when trying to force the pace of Baltic operations.

Before the forts were destroyed Napier directed Chads to conduct a trial against a section of the main fort. *Edinburgh* carried a powerful battery of heavy guns which Chads tried at 1,060 yards, firing 390 rounds to little effect. Closing to 480 yards, he fired ten rapid broadsides totalling 250 rounds which brought down large sections of the wall. Shells were confirmed as useless, the single Lancaster gun proved inaccurate. Chads claimed that at 1,000 yards 1,000 shot would be required to breach the works, and 500 at 500 yards. Napier was more concerned with the poor state of the fort, built of loose rubble faced with granite, persuading Chads to submit a second, less enthusiastic report. This stressed the dangers to *Edinburgh* had the fort been manned, and the leisurely process of getting into range. Martin, left to complete the destruction, was unimpressed with Chads' effort; Keppel took the opposite view, believing Chads had demonstrated 'what might have been done had our ships been near enough months before'.[16] Keppel, with the majority of captains, suggested that only Napier's lack of resolve prevented a successful attack on Sweaborg. Such views proved useful when Graham decided to dismiss Napier.

From the beginning of the Baltic campaign it became clear that Prussia would not assist the allies. The close relationship between the Czar and the Prussian King, and their mutual border in Poland, provided real common interest. However, Prussia valued her neutrality, secured by the treaty of 20 April with Austria. By acting in unison the German powers prevented the war spreading to central Europe; if they moved from their neutral stance the war would be decided. The allies objected to the hesitant attitude of Prussia, accepting Buol's claim that she was holding Austria back. While the wider issues of the war were being discussed Prussia's interpretation of neutral rights made the blockade largely ineffective, as Russell had anticipated. The government ignored the shipment of arms from Belgium, despite British complaints starting two weeks before war was declared. This placed British policy makers in a dilemma, for although they wanted to stop Prussia conniving at the breach of the blockade, they did not want her to join Russia. Prussia bowed to *force majeure*, allowing the British to sell captured Russian ships at Memel and the arms traffic. The Prussian economy received a considerable boost from the war, factories being set up to support Russia, or process Russian produce for export.[17] Clarendon considered extending the blockade to cover Prussia, but did little until mid August when it became known the Prussians were erecting new fortifications at Danzig, and abandoning work on land defences facing Russia. The French proposed taking action; Clarendon wanted to raise the Polish question, until the Prince Consort dissuaded him. This policy was then pressed on the French, although the British minister, Bloomfield, was instructed to watch the works at Danzig. Clarendon and Graham agreed that an effective blockade of Russia required the allies to take a stronger line with Prussia. The Admiralty had been arranging the exchange of two iron gunboats for some old sailing ships, to 'coax' Prussia, but the news from Danzig made this less urgent. In October the Treasury memorandum on the blockade pointed to the Prussian ports as a serious weakness, but concluded little could be done short of war. Graham hoped for a more effective blockade, but did not suggest how this could be achieved. In the last resort there was nothing the allies could do, short of force, to stop Prussia trading with her neighbour. This exposed the weakness of the blockade as a weapon in a limited war against a continental nation. In the short term a blockade could only be an inconvenience to Russia, making it wise not to alienate Prussia. The corollary was the need to achieve war aims by military success, not economic pressure. Only Russell realised this from the start.[18]

Sweaborg

Anticipating success at Bomarsund Graham began to hope for more, warning Napier to consult the French. However, he was concerned to avoid responsibility, pointedly leaving the choice of target to the commanders on the spot, in stark contrast to the Black Sea. A week later he looked for something at Abo or Reval, but shared Berkeley's concern to bring the ships home before the weather deteriorated.[19] These contrasting views caused a serious dispute between Napier and the Admiralty that overshadowed the campaign. Berkeley admitted that public pressure lay behind the new-found desire to take the offensive. His inadequacy as First Naval Lord was a major factor in the dispute. Berkeley filled a similar role to his sickly predecessor; his low rank, lack of significant sea service and narrow-minded jealousy all militated against his being able to provide sound advice. He had asked for the Baltic command in January, and offered to serve as a junior, but Graham preferred to keep him at the Board.[20] When Napier met problems Berkeley was quick to attack, and while Graham rejected his initial criticism he would later adopt similar views. Berkeley's bitterness increased when he realised Lyons, his junior, would have the Mediterranean command in 1855. It required all Graham's tact and flattery to keep him at his post. Berkeley later claimed Graham had promised him the Baltic fleet for 1855, but there is no evidence. Graham knew Berkeley's limits, and used him accordingly.[21]

In the Baltic Napier had anticipated Graham's reference to Abo, sending Captain Scott, *Odin*, with *Alban*, *Gorgon* and *Driver* on 18 August. Scott reported navigational difficulties and a strong garrison at Abo, the sea approaches were narrow, and enfiladed by batteries; he concluded a naval attack was not feasible. The French Generals, with Jones, went to Reval and Sweaborg in *Lightning*. Napier waited to consult them on using troops at Abo. The Generals saw Reval on the 24th, and Sweaborg on the 27th, while on passage between the two they watched the Russians blow up the forts at Hango Head. They shared Napier's view that neither place could be attacked with the forces at hand, but enclosed Jones' report, claiming Sweaborg could be attacked by landing 5,000 troops on Bakholmen with gun and mortar batteries. Napier commented on the similarities to his own plan of 14 June, but argued that men landed on Bakholmen would be captured. He wanted to attack Abo; Baraguay declined, for his troops were sickly and his Emperor believed the campaign was finished.[22]

The following day Baraguay requested transport for his army, leading Napier to conclude the campaign was over. Graham still hoped to bring in Sweden, wanting the French to winter in the Baltic. If they did not he would begin to withdraw the least seaworthy ships, the sailing three-deckers and the blockships. Yet Napier was ordered to call a Council of War, to decide if anything remained to be done. All was not well at home: 'My Lords have only to add that they have the fullest confidence in your coming to that decision which will reflect credit on the arms of the allied forces, and justify before the public the confidence placed in you.' The weakness of the Government was made obvious by the allusion to the wishes of the public. Where Graham had long urged caution, both in public and private, he now tried to goad Napier into action, without specific orders. The dispatch was dishonest, and with the French leaving, out of date even before it was sealed. The troops embarked at Ledsound the same day. Graham knew they were leaving on the 29th, but kept Berkeley in the dark until 5 September. The Board supported Graham because the public was demanding success, and although Parliament was in recess the Government desperately needed a victory. Therefore Graham, looking for a withdrawal in late August, was calling for major operations within a week.[23] *The Times'* view of the Baltic changed dramatically after the fall of Bomarsund. In late June the theatre had been reported as unlikely to produce significant results; Sweaborg and Cronstadt were 'unattackable', almost certainly a quote from one of Napier's letters to Delane. After Bomarsund the editorials called for more. Delane observed Napier would be well prepared for the following campaign, when Cronstadt and St Petersburg might be taken. Days later the editorial criticised both Napier and the Admiralty, but Delane had gone to the east, leaving Henry Reeve in charge. Other journals were more hostile.

The crucial evidence that changed Graham's view came from within the fleet. It explained why nothing had been done, and pointed to a chance for action. Graham pressed Napier because he believed he was being unduly cautious. Newcastle sent him some of Paget's harsh and inaccurate letters. Ignoring Bomarsund Newcastle looked for the destruction of Hango, so that the fleet 'might come home without disgrace'; this should be urged to show the Government had not restricted a willing commander (when in fact they had) and he must be given the widest latitude. Even so there should be 'no useless waste of life . . . even to please the British public'. The next Admiralty dispatch, on 4 September, contained vague orders to act, against unspecified targets, but took no responsibility. The closing allusion to public opinion was intentional. Berkeley wanted to pull back to Kioge, but he soon fell in with Graham.[24] Dissatisfaction was focused by receipt of the Jones plan, which appeared feasible to the amateurs at home, while Napier had not rejected it outright. Graham believed Napier was trying to stifle the plan, while the fleet wanted to make an attempt. After another discussion with Newcastle he ordered a second Council of War to consider Jones' plan, unaware that Jones had proposed the same plan in May, long before he entered the Baltic. He persuaded Aberdeen that Napier must be pressed. Yet the public, Graham and even Berkeley, knew the French troops, vital to the plan, were already at sea. Napier had been ordered to assist their departure![25]

Napier was creating further problems for himself, discussing Jones' plan with the French Generals. Baraguay believed the weather prevented any operations; Niel suggested Sweaborg could be ruined in a few hours by eight or ten battleships, although he stated that he was not competent to advise the attempt. Both agreed landing on Bakholmen was 'inadvisable'. Their opinions were undoubtedly influenced by their own imminent departure. Napier believed he had emphatically refuted Jones. The dispatch calling for a Council of War on Jones' plan arrived on 16 September, when the French fleet was preparing to follow their army out of the Baltic. The previous Council had declared that nothing could be done, on account of the lack of resources and the weather. Napier had the poor taste to include Jones' plan among the many 'absurd propositions' he had received. The second Council produced a similar result, without the acid commentary; Napier pointed to his letter of 18 July as the best method of attacking Sweaborg.[26]

The final stupidity came when the Admiralty ordered Napier to lay Niel's plan before his colleagues. By this they meant the opinion of a French General that Sweaborg could be destroyed by eight or ten battleships inside two hours. It was not a plan, or even the advice of Niel, merely an idea mentioned in passing, and specifically disclaimed. The dispatch stated that Niel regarded it as 'certain to succeed' when he had said nothing of the sort: 'It must be remembered that the destruction of Sweaborg has always been regarded as an object of great importance from the first commencement of the war.' This might have been true, but Graham, Berkeley and the Board had spent much time persuading Napier otherwise. The French, more concerned with their imminent departure, refused to attend the third Council. The British Admirals signed another paper stating that the lateness of the season and lack of resources prevented anything being done. Napier was disgusted and annoyed:

I hope I may be permitted to ask Their Lordships what reliance could be placed in the opinion of two military engineers on naval subjects when one decides that Sweaborg could be destroyed by 5,000 men, guns, mortars and rockets from the Island of Bak Holmen, combined with the allied fleets, in seven or eight days, and the other decides it can be laid in ruins in two hours by the fleets alone.

He enclosed a copy of his letter to Graham of 18 July, containing his views. The essential points of Napier's plan were the use of gunboats and mortar vessels for long range bombardment, followed up by the fleet when the defensive fire had been beaten down.[27] The only problem was the need to provide flotilla craft, which were not available, and would not have been, even if Graham had ordered them when Napier's letter arrived. Instead the First Lord wanted results before the end of the current campaign, forcing him to rely on the nonsense of the Generals in direct opposition to Chads, the Navy's leading gunner, Sulivan, who had seen more of Sweaborg than anyone, and Napier, the Admiral selected for the 'Nelson touch'. Graham's action was the more remarkable when set against his judicious remarks opposing the Aland operation. There was no better reason for attacking Sweaborg. The Russian ships could easily withdraw into the inner harbour, and without an army the arsenal could not be occupied. Even if successful, the attack had no possible strategic benefit. It would have been an empty, bloody gesture to prove that the Navy was doing something.

Graham knew Napier was correct, ordering the equipment he had called for only one month later, but he was determined to relieve him and employ a more pliable Admiral. To this end he conducted a subtle character assassination to deprive Napier of his powerful supporters, particularly Delane and Palmerston. This required only a hint, implying he was trying to leave the Baltic before it was safe, coupled with the news he would be dismissed. Clarendon soon relayed the story that he was responsible for the early return of the French to Palmerston, Napier's only friend in the cabinet. It can be assumed the information came from Graham. Napier's conduct was termed 'shabby' because he was not attempting an impossible task he had long been warned against. Graham also let it be known he was recalling Lyons for the Baltic command. Delane, sensing Napier's days were numbered, knew *The Times* could not afford to support a man accused of inaction, or worse, by public and Government, added his weight to Graham's purpose. Like Dundas, Napier was universally damned for a failure that no-one could actually describe.[28] Berkeley followed Graham, and kept up his correspondence with Napier, hoping to ride out the storm on two anchors. His letter of the 19th indicated that the Board no longer had any confidence in him, making the timing of any withdrawal 'a matter for the Government to decide'. The request that Napier treat all his correspondence as private was revealing: 'We shall have Blue Books and Parliamentary questions without end. The attack failing against you, will be level'd at the Board, or failing against the Board will be level'd at you.' He even pretended to believe a French claim that their fleet was not leaving; the official dispatch of the 26th expressed equal surprise. The purpose was obvious; Graham wanted to keep Napier in the Baltic until the season ended, he could then be dismissed.[29]

The attack affected Napier. Leaving Ledsound for Nargen on the 20th, he examined Reval on the 22nd and Sweaborg the following day, proposing a plan of attack for Sweaborg. In outlining a bombardment by heavy ships alone he failed to stress the dangers, or state that it would only succeed if the arsenal had first been bombarded by a flotilla. The deteriorating weather led him to send Plumridge's sailing battleships down to Kiel on the 26th. The Admiralty ordered Plumridge to reprovision and prepare to return, and announced the return of the French. Napier's new plan for Sweaborg reached London on 2 October, while the Sevastopol rumour was current at the Admiralty and Printing House Square. *The Times* made unfavourable comparisons between the quick success in the Euxine and Napier's unproductive campaign. The Admiralty dispatch of 4 October was more forthright: 'what are the obstacles to an immediate attempt? . . . Your second reconnaissance of Sweaborg opens a new view, and the presence or absence of a few guns of improved construction or even mortar vessels cannot make the whole difference between a possible and an impossible attack.' Knowing the attack would be a forlorn hope, Graham left the responsibility to Napier. Berkeley claimed this was because the Board had implicit confidence – curious when they wanted to decide the lesser matter of timing the withdrawal. The cabinet had taken responsibility, albeit hesitantly, for the Crimean operation, and should have done so for the desperate attack on Sweaborg. They did not because Graham never raised the matter. His reply was necessary 'to put on record an answer to a dispatch which placed us in a disadvantageous position'.[30] The object was to discredit Napier and save himself. Napier reported Sweaborg must be bombarded by mortars and rockets before the heavy ships attacked, and offered to resign. By 9 October the Board adopted a more conciliatory tone, in the wake of reliable intelligence from the Crimea. Napier was now at liberty to withdraw, keeping up the blockade with a light squadron. Parseval and Plumridge were recalled. Sweaborg was now impossible. The following day they returned to the attack, demanding to know why Jones had not been allowed to visit Cronstadt. Napier blamed the weather and the expense. He also announced the withdrawal of the squadron from the Gulf of Bothnia, the blockade of the Gulf of Finland by Watson's screw frigates, and his imminent departure for Ledsound. Replying to Napier's furious outburst of the 10th the Board accepted his view of Sweaborg, claiming their own had been based on the opinions of Jones, Niel, and his second inspection, and suggested more consideration should have been given to the opinions of the military officers before their departure.

Privately Graham blamed Napier for the early return of the French, claiming Baraguay, Jones and Niel were in agreement on the best method of attacking Sweaborg. Both opinions were without justification, and Graham knew it. His next letter to Napier was an outrageous provocation, suggesting twenty-five battleships with their 'means of vertical fire' might destroy Sweaborg. Graham knew there were only fifteen battleships in the Baltic, and such vessels had no 'means of vertical fire'. The object was to provoke Napier, and it was successful. Napier's next dispatch adopted an aggressive tone. His reply to Graham was even more candid, grasping the root of the Sweaborg debate, insofar as it related to attacking the fortress: 'Enough has not been done to satisfy an impatient public . . . All this stir has been caused by the opinion of two engineers, in addition to the reported capture of Sevastopol – not yet taken, though the fleet there is assisted by an army of 70,000 men.' Napier did not yet realise Graham meant to dismiss him. Graham never again wrote to him. His attempts to produce a face-saving forlorn hope having failed, he could only await his revenge when Napier returned. Even when the Board accepted Napier's view of Sweaborg they turned to criticise his reconnaissance methods, and warned him he must not accuse them of misreading his dispatches.[31]

The fleet left Nargen on 19 October, reaching Kiel on the 22nd. Watson's frigates remained at the entrance to the Gulf, with a discretion to retire when necessary. Napier had been in poor spirits at Nargen; the weather and the provoking correspondence told on his resolve. The move to Kiel, and a visit to Hamburg put him in better humour. He prepared an exhaustive defence of his conduct, stringing together largely unrelated elements from earlier dispatches. The Admiralty replied in kind, carping at his work, past and present. The discussion had no value, for although Napier was largely correct Graham had decided to supersede him. Watson only left the Gulf after a collision between *Imperieuse* and *Euryalus* in late November. No other ships moved in the area. Napier, unaware of the collision, recalled Watson on 27 November. The Board ordered him home on 1 December, leaving Chads to collect the cruisers. Napier had wanted to come home early to contest the by-election at Marylebone, but the Board guessed the nature of his 'urgent private affairs' and told him he must strike his flag. This he would not do, losing the chance to raise his case in the House before the end of the war. *Duke of Wellington* left Kiel on the 7th, anchoring at Spithead nine days later. On the 22nd Napier was ordered to strike his flag and go ashore.[32] It was the end of his seagoing career, although he had one last campaign to fight. For the rest of his life he conducted a bitter and ill-advised struggle to regain his reputation, both in print and on the floor of the House. This served to obscure the Baltic campaign of 1854 behind a screen of personal abuse. He died on 6 November 1860 without achieving his object. Like Dundas, Napier was made a scapegoat by an unscrupulous minister for the failure of his planning. The deliberate provocation of November was a device. However Napier's post-war complaints, as MP for Southwark from 1856, which included refusing the GCB, calling for a court martial and involving the Prince Consort and Palmerston, threw doubt on Graham's integrity. He never again held office.

Notes

1   Graham to Napier 27 Jun. rec.4 Jul. 1854: Add. 40,024 f347.

2   Graham to Clarendon 2, 11, 15, 16 Jul. 1854: Gr. B.120; Graham to Napier 2, rec. 10 Jul. 1854: Add. 40,025 f2; Berkeley to Napier 4, rec. 10 Jul. 1854: *ibid.* f26; Milne to Capt. Chads 22 Jul. 1854: Milne 169/6; Graham memo. 18 Jul. 1854: Add. 40,025 f86; Clarendon to Cowley 3 Jul. 1854: Cl. Dep. C129 f95.

3   Graham to Napier 2, 4 rec. 10 Jul. 1854: Add. 40,025 f2–20.

4   Clarendon to Graham 2 Jul. 1854: Gr. B.120; Graham to Clarendon 9 Jul. 1854: Cl. Dep. C14 f338; Napier to Berkeley 18 Jul. 1854: Add. 40,025 f86; Grey to Admiralty 7 rec. 14 Jul. 1854: ADM 1/5631; Milne to Berkeley 1 Jul. 1854: Milne 169/5.

5   Admiralty to Napier 11 Jul. 1854: PRO 30/16/1 f227; Graham to Burgoyne 11 Jul. 1854: WROTTESLEY, ii, p. 45; Graham to Napier 7, 18, 25 rec. 17, 24, 30 Jul. 1854: Add. 40,025 f32, 82, 106; Keppel to Capt. Stephenson 17 Jul. 1854: HTN/52A; Napier to Graham 24 Jul. 1854; PRO 30/16/13 f100.

6   Milne to Napier 11, 19 Jul., 7, 8 Aug. 1854: Add. 40,025 f58, 90, 161; Napier to Milne 9 Apr. 1854: Milne 166; Napier to Admiralty 1 Aug. 1854: PRO 30/16/7 f30.

7   Graham to Napier 1, 8 rec. 6, 15 Aug. 1854: Add. 40,025 f132, 165; H. Martin to T. Martin 9, 31 Jul. 1854: Add. 41,467 f205–13 and 220; Plumridge to Napier 20 Jul. 1854: Add. 40,025 f94; Chads to Napier 25, 30 Jul. 1854: *ibid.* f11, 121; Napier to Admiralty 25, 30 Jul. rec. 31 Jul., 7 Aug. 1854 no. 303, 310: ADM 1/5624; Log of *St Jean d'Acre*, 30 Jul. 1854: HTN/52A; EARP, p. 360.

8   Clarendon to Graham 4 Aug. 1854: Gr. B.120; Graham to Clarendon 15, 16 Jul. and 5 Aug. 1854: *ibid.*; Graham to Napier 1, 8 rec. 8, 15 Aug. 1854: Add 40,025 f132, 165; Berkeley to Napier undated, rec. 13 Aug. 1854: *ibid.* f194; Napier to Graham 3 Aug. 1854: WILLIAMS, p. 321; Napier to Admiralty 24, rec. 31 Jul. 1854 no. 296: NRS, p. 90; Admiralty to Napier 31 Jul. rec. 6 Aug. 1854: Add.40,025 f123; Plumridge to Napier 8 Aug. 1854: *ibid.* f159; Graham to Berkeley 1 Aug. 1854: Gr. CW19.
9   Napier to Caffin 10 Aug. 1854: PRO 30/16/7 f83; Caffin to Napier 11 Aug. 1854 in Napier to Admiralty no. 347: ADM 1/5625; Keppel, 'Capture of Bomarsund – August 1854' ed. Lambert in *The Naval Miscellany vol. V* (London, 1985), pp. 354–70; Lieutenant's log of HMS *Penelope* : GRIEVE MSS WRE/102; Admiralty order 20 Jan. 1855: ADM 2/1568; KING-HALL, L., *Sea Saga* (London, 1935), pp. 97, 210; Berkeley to Napier 14 May 1854: Add. 40,024 f175; OTWAY, p. 120.
10   Napier to Admiralty 21 rec. 28 Aug. 1854 no. 383: ADM 1/5625; Corres. of Admiral Gordon C-in-C Sheerness: ADM 1/5623; EARP, p. 406; H. Martin to T. Martin 26 Aug. 1854: Add. 41.467 f245.
11   Napier to Admiralty 27, 28 Aug. rec. 4 Sept. 1854 no. 410, 417: ADM 1/5625; OTWAY, p. 120.
12   Russell to Clarendon 3 Aug. 1854: GOOCH, G.P., *The Later Correspondence of Lord John Russell* (London, 1925, two vols.), vol. 11, p. 169; Graham to Napier 15, 22 rec. 21, 27 Aug. 1854: Add. 40.025 f210, 260; Graham to Clarendon 14 Aug. 1854: Gr. B.120; Aberdeen to Clarendon 16 Aug. 1854: Cl. Dep. C14 f71–2; Napier to Admiralty 18, 19 rec. 24, 28 Aug. 1854 no. 369, 380: ADM 1/5625; Newcastle to Graham 23 Aug. 1854: Gr. B.120; Palmerston to Clarendon 10, 22 Aug. 1854: Cl. Dep. C15 f146, 163.
13   Clarendon to Russell 26, 28 Aug. 1854: PRO 30/22/11B f201, 289; Newcastle to Graham 28 Aug. 1854: Gr. B.120; Clarendon to Graham 28 Aug. 1854: *ibid.*; Palmerston to Clarendon 27 Aug. 1854: Cl. Dep. C15 f170; Lansdowne to Clarendon 27 Aug. 1854: *ibid.* C14; Aberdeen to Clarendon 16 Aug. 1854: Add. 43,189 f124–5; Graham to Clarendon 27 Aug. 1854: Gr. B.120; Graham to Napier 25, 29 Aug. rec. 3 Sept. 1854: Add. 40.025 f266, 291; Foreign Office to Admiralty 27 Aug. 1854: PRO 30/16/3 f78.
14   Newcastle to H. D. Jones 29 Aug. 1854: NeC 10,795.
15   Magennis to Napier 30 Aug. 1854: Add. 40,025 f307.
16   Chads to Napier 5, 8 Sept. 1854: Add. 40,026 f25–30; Napier to Admiralty 5 Sept. 1854 no. 437: ADM 1/5625; H. Martin to T. Martin 15 Sept. 1854 Add. 41,467 f72–8; DOUGLAS, Sir H., *A Treatise on Naval Gunnery* (London, 1860) pp. 370–1.
17   Clarendon to Russell 25 Apr. 1854: PRO 30/22/11C f117; Russell memo. 20 May 1854: *ibid* 11D f56; Clarendon to Bloomfield 16 Mar., 9 May 1854: F.O. 64/364 f16 and /365 f116.
18   Clarendon to Aberdeen undated, July 1854: Add. 43,189 f108; Cowley to Clarendon 17 Aug. 1854: F.O. 519/3 f462; Clarendon to Russell enc. King of Prussia to Prince Albert 26 Aug. 1854: PRO 30/22/11D f284; Clarendon to Cowley 26 Aug. 1854: Cl. Dep. C129 f227; Clarendon to

Bloomfield 29 Aug. 1854: F.O. 64/366 f220; Clarendon to Graham 13 Sept. 1854: Cl. Dep. C14 f435–7; Clarendon to Russell 4 Sept. 1854: PRO 30/22/11E f5; Printed memo. by James Wilson, Financial Secretary to the Treasury, 23 Oct. 1854: Add. 43,355; Graham to Clarendon 1 Nov. 1854: Gr. B.115.

19 Graham to Napier 8, 15 rec. 15, 21 Aug. 1854: Add. 40,026 f163, 210; Berkeley to Napier 15, rec. 21 Aug. 1854: *ibid.* f20; Graham to Berkeley 31 Aug. 1854: Gr. CW19.

20 Berkeley to Graham 10 Jan., 6 Feb. 1854: Gr. CW19.

21 Graham to Berkeley 27 Jul., 31 Aug., 6 Oct. 1854: *ibid.*; Berkeley to Wood 22 Nov. 1855: HALIFAX A4/74.

22 Graham to Napier 22, rec. 27 Aug. 1854: Add. 40,026 f260; Berkeley to Napier 22, rec. 27 Aug. 1854: *ibid.* f257; Napier to Admiralty, enc. Scott and Otter to Napier 27 Aug. rec. 4 Sept. 1854 no. 410: ADM 1/5626; Napier to Admiralty 29 Aug. 1854 no. 428: *ibid.* H. Martin to T. Martin 28 Aug. 1854: Add. 41,467 f249.

23 Baraguay to Napier 31 Aug. 1854: Add. 40,025 f304; Graham to Napier 29 Aug. rec. 3 Sept.1854: *ibid.* f291; Berkeley to Napier 22, 29, 31 Aug. 5 Sept. 185: *ibid.* f257, 295 and 40,026 f17, 19; Admiralty to Napier 4, rec. 12 Sept. 1854: *ibid.* f13; Napier to Admiralty 29 Aug. rec. 3 Sept. 1854: ADM 1/5626; Graham to Clarendon 27 Aug. 1854: Gr. B.120.

24 Times 22 Jun., 8 Jul., 24, 30 Aug., 7, 13 Sept. 1854; Lord Sydney to Newcastle 24 Aug. enc. Paget to Lord Sydney (his brother in law), 10 Aug. 1854: NeC 10,623a, b; Newcastle to Graham 30 Aug., 1 Sept. 1854: Gr. B.120; Graham to Newcastle date burnt: NeC 10,244; Berkeley to Graham 7 Sept. 1854: Gr. CW19.

25 Napier to Admiralty 29 Aug. rec. 4 Sept. 1854 no. 428: ADM 1/5626; Graham to Berkeley 5 Sept. 1854: Gr. CW19; Graham to Newcastle 5 Sept. 1854: Gr. B.121; Jones' memo. in Admiralty to Napier rec. 8 Jun. 1854: Add. 40,024 f163; Aberdeen to Graham 9 Sept. 1854: Gr. B.121; Admiralty to Napier 9, rec. 16 Sept. 1854: Add. 40,026 f36; *Times* 7, 11 Sept. 1854; Admiralty to Napier 5 Sept. 1854: PRO 30/16/7 f284.

26 Niel to Baraguay and Baraguay to Napier 1, 2 Sept. 1854: Add. 40,026 f214; Napier to Admiralty 5 rec. 11 Sept. 1854 no. 444: NRS pp. 115–8; Napier to Admiralty 13, 16 rec. 18, 25 Sept. 1854: Add.40,026 f56, 71; Parseval to Napier 18, rec. 19 Sept. 1854: *ibid.* f78.

27 Admiralty to Napier 12. rec. 17 Sept. 1854: *ibid.* f47; Napier to Admiralty 18 rec. 25 Sept. 1854: *ibid.* f84.

28 Graham to Clarendon 25 Sept., 8 Oct. 1854: Cl. Dep. C14 f444–63; Clarendon to Palmerston 28 Sept. 1854: Bdlds. GC/CL f575; Graham to Clarendon 28 Sept. 1854: Gr. B.121; GREVILLE, vol. vii, p. 62, 64, 22 Sept., 2 Oct. 1854; Graham to Gladstone 6 Oct. 1854: Gr. B.122; Delane to Napier 4 Oct. 1854: WILLIAMS, pp. 360–1.

29 Berkeley to Napier 19, rec. 24 Sept. 1854: Add. 40,026 f102; Admiralty to Napier 23, 26 Sept., Graham to Napier 22 Sept. Berkeley to Napier 24, 25 Sept. rec. 2 Oct. 1854: *ibid.* f118–144; Graham to Clarendon 28 Sept. 1854: Gr. B.121.

30 Napier to Admiralty 25, 26 Sept. rec. 2 Oct. 1854; Add. 40,026 f138,

153, 162; Admiralty to Napier 2, 4 rec. 10 Oct. 1854: *ibid.* f167, 173; Berkeley to Napier 4, rec. 10 Oct. 1854: *ibid.* f171. ·
31 Napier to Admiralty 10, 17, 26 rec. 16, 24, 30 Oct. 1854: *ibid.* f191, 211, 218; Napier to Admiralty 17 rec. 24 Oct. 1854 no. 585: NRS p. 153; Admiralty to Napier 10, 17 Oct. 1854: *ibid.* pp. 152–5; Admiralty to Napier 9, 10, rec. 17, 18 Oct. 1854: Add. 40,026 f183, 257; Clarendon to Graham 6 Oct. 1854: Gr. B.122; Graham to Napier 17, 31 rec. 22 Oct., 2 Nov. 1854: Add. 40,026 f205, 225; Napier to Graham 6 Nov. 1854: WILLIAMS, pp. 378–9.
32 Napier to Admiralty 13, 27 rec. 17 Nov. 1 Dec. 1854 no. 642, 678: NRS pp. 168, 177; Napier to Admiralty 6 Nov. 1854: PRO 30/16/8 f75; H. Martin to T. Martin 15 Sept. 1854: Add. 41,467 f272; Codrington to Lady Bourchier 6 Nov. 1854: COD 113/1; Napier to Watson 27 Nov. 1854: NRS p. 177; Admiralty to Napier 22 Dec. 1854: *ibid.* pp. 187–8.

14

Politics and strategy

The Black Sea theatre

Graham's hopes for decisive blows in both theatres were only gradually disappointed. This was reflected in his reaction to the rumoured fall of Sevastopol: 'My hopes rise with respect to Sevastopol, I consider that it was captured on the 25th. We must not flag in the Baltic, if it be possible to follow up the blow in the Black Sea with a fair prospect of success.' The impact of this unhealthy mixture of wishful thinking and self-deception on the later stages of the Baltic campaign has already been observed. While the mood lasted Graham prepared the Anglo–French October Programme for 'a grand attack on the Russian fortresses in the Baltic next year'.[1] While the planning was more considered, including specialist craft, it still reflected the knock-out blow school of strategy. Eventually the hard lessons of war forced him to accept the limits of maritime power as an instrument of war. While this new wisdom was closely aligned with the opinions of Dundas and Napier, scapegoats for the failure of the 1854 campaigns, Graham linked his return to basics in strategy with a renewed attack on their reputations. He could shift his ground easily, having always been regarded as *the* naval expert in cabinet. Even the querulous Russell never doubted his fitness for the post, and when he had the temerity to express himself generally satisfied with the Black Sea fleet Graham was quick to point out Dundas's inaction on the day of the Alma, allowing the Russians to block the harbour, and weakening the battlefleet crews.[2] The attack was important, because Russell was Dundas's political leader and, as Prime Minister, had appointed him First Naval Lord and then Commander-in-Chief Mediterranean. To avoid a rift in the coalition it was essential to discredit Dundas. Graham did not trouble to pass on Dundas's refutation of these complaints. His cause was lost before they arrived.

Graham had other problems as winter approached. The demand for transport tonnage, initially seen as short term, increased once the armies were committed to winter in the Crimea. The French doubled the size of their army, although the British could not even keep theirs up to strength. This left the French desperate for shipping, even asking for the British Baltic fleet. Graham did not want to help, particularly as the French Baltic fleet lay idle at Cherbourg; Milne conveniently reported there were no more steam transports. On 10 November the cabinet discussed the French request. The majority, fearing a disaster in the Crimea, brushed aside Graham's objections. Raglan was instructed to send several large transports to Marseilles. Thereafter transport was a cabinet issue. Graham remained 'sore' on the subject until he left office.[3] In early December Palmerston floated the idea of a War Committee, similar to that of 1853. Graham had tolerated the earlier committee, but did not allow any naval officers to attend, or allow it to influence his policy. When Aberdeen pressed him for an opinion he found it necessary to claim the idea came from Herbert. Graham admitted the sense of the plan, but claimed no Board member could be spared. Graham's real objection was that the committee would necessarily consider naval policy; while he corresponded with senior soldiers he did not wish other politicians to consult his service chiefs. The only result of the initiative was a step to reform the Horse Guards and War Office.[4]

Despite these attempts to interfere in his department, Graham pressed ahead with his overhaul of strategic policy. After the cabinet of 17 October he expected a more effective blockade in 1855, although the vital roles in the Black Sea were Army support, blockading Sevastopol and ensuring the efficient administration of Balaklava. During the winter there would be no offensive opportunities worth considering. While the city appeared likely to fall he intended to recall Lyons to replace Napier, but the subject was later dropped. As the problems of the Black Sea increased he selected an efficient administrator, Rear-Admiral Houston Stewart from Malta, to be second in command. As Lyons did not want a Captain of the Fleet, Commodore Frederick Grey became Principal Agent of Transports. Boxer was sent to Balaklava, where Dacres had been relieved by Heath on 19 November. Only after the winter problems had been overcome could any realistic planning begin for a spring offensive. While certain the Sea of Azov would prove decisive, Graham did not consider providing steam gunboats. They were to be found in the theatre, those building at home were intended for the Baltic.[5]

The failure of the bombardment, followed by the Balaklava action, forced Newcastle to give up the over-sanguine view, encouraged by the knowledge that nothing less would give the allies security in winter or for re-embarkation, that the peninsula would be occupied before winter. Alarming accounts of the winter climate sent by Cattley, Raglan's interpreter, encouraged him to be satisfied with the capture of the city. He began to send out winter clothing, huts, food and fuel, while stressing the need to open the Sea of Azov and move Omer to Eupatoria. Unaware of Spratt's discovery, Newcastle still believed all routes could be cut at Perekop, and he proposed sending the Turkish army to attack the Russian field army in reverse. Despite the risk of 'great disasters' the cabinet agreed, although Russell preferred moving out from the allied camp. In view of Raglan's low opinion of the Turks, and the better claim of the Asian front for Omer and his troops, Newcastle's plan had little merit. Omer went to Eupatoria, but remained inactive, annoying the Russians only by his presence. Without strategic guidance, cavalry or allied support the Turks could only hold the town.[6] For Newcastle, Turkish troops would repair the greatest British weakness, lack of trained manpower. The 10,000 troops Palmerston had turned down eighteen months before were gravely missed. Militia regiments were embodied to relieve regulars on garrison duty and the depots reduced to a skeleton just to provide the five divisions originally dispatched. No more trained men could be had. 23,000 recruits taken up before 6 November 1854 were of no immediate value. Before the year ended plans were being prepared to raise the enlistment bounty, embody more militia units and create foreign legions. The last, a favourite of Palmerston, harked back to the last war. The offer of a 15,000-man Sardinian army, to be provisioned by Britain, but otherwise combat ready, was accepted on 26 January 1855. Hopes for troops from India were dashed by time, distance and more local dangers. The two infantry regiments brought home and not relieved had to be replaced, although two regiments of cavalry were spared. The policy formed by Newcastle, Herbert and Hardinge was to build up a reserve army of 16,000 men at Malta, ready for the spring. At the same cabinet, 1 December, Peto and Betts' offer to build a rail line from Balaklava to the camp was accepted.[7]

All this effort just to hold on to a few square miles of Crimean upland led Aberdeen to accept the destruction of Sevastopol and the fleet were now *sine qua non* for peace; hitherto he had not gone beyond the 'Four Points'. Cabinet consensus was already in advance of the Premier. Had this been a British war, without allies or attached neutrals, such a policy might have been adequate; however, France was unlikely to accept such simple, British, war aims. When Palmerston visited Paris in mid November he discussed the subject with Louis Napoleon and Drouyn. Both wanted large results, for political/dynastic reasons, allowing him to press his colleagues for a wider war. The only difference between Palmerston and Louis Napoleon lay in the location, not the extent, of their ambition. Palmerston was dominated by the desire to reduce the strategic threat of Russian power; Louis Napoleon was concerned with the Rhine and hoped to replace Russia as the dominant power in Germany. By accepting a premature end to the war he succeeded only in driving out Russian influence, leaving Prussia to take control. Palmerston considered the Habsburg regime lacked the energy and determination to conduct any decided policy, anticipating that Viennese diplomacy would attempt to end the war by long-drawn-out negotiations that did not satisfy the allies. Clarendon realised Austria occupied the middle ground, and that Buol's policies were essentially pro-western, although they avoided commitment. He tried to bring Austria into the allied camp by tempering Palmerston's harsh words.[8] He did not understand that Austrian policy was limited to weakening Russia where that would benefit Austria; the last thing Vienna wanted was permanent western interference. The 'Four Points' were Austrian rather than allied or Turkish aims, curbing Russia's ability and excuse to project power into lands east of the Habsburg empire.

The Baltic

Following the Sweaborg debate Graham accepted the need for specialist craft to attack the Russian Baltic arsenals. His October Programme included a variety of types, the most remarkable of which were the 'Floating Batteries', inspired by Louis Napoleon, armoured against shells and intended to fight at anchor. Because of the cost Graham was initially unenthusiastic, demanding full scale armour trials, preferring to concentrate on the Crimea. Up to the end of the hoax fall of Sevastopol he remained non-committal, but with disillusionment he ordered five batteries, five new blockships and a score each of gunboats and mortar vessels. The total cost, £600,000, led him to stress the value of these craft for harbour defence, against France. With an equal force of French craft they would be ready for the Baltic in April 1855.[9] This programme has been treated as a hasty, ill-considered response to the problems of the war with 'no unifying tactical idea', an opinion which overestimates of the power of gunboats. Contemporaries expressed a clear preference for a combination of arms in attacking sea forts; gunboats and mortars could bombard at long range, almost immune from their small size and mobility. The batteries would operate close in, and when the return fire began to weaken, the blockships could finish off the enemy works with concentrated broadsides. To attack with gunboats alone when several additional types were available, would limit the scope of operations. The fleet of 1854 had been equipped for an oceanic war with France, it did not have the resources to carry the war into coastal waters. Britain had abandoned the construction of flotilla craft after 1832. The most recent critique of the programme concludes:

It was not, however intended to send an army to the Baltic in 1855, and thus it appears that since the October plan was made with that sea in mind, it would have been far better to have concentrated all effort upon mortar vessels and gunboats. Sir Charles Wood certainly felt this, and complained of the waste of resources to R. S. Dundas in 1855.

The policy based on sending an army to the Baltic was only abandoned on 17 March 1855, by which time Graham was out of office. Furthermore, Wood's complaints later in the year related to problems with the French over the distribution of the batteries, not their combat value; after Kinburn no-one criticised them.[10] Having altered his policy, the sinister character of Graham's letters to Napier becomes apparent. Construction work was placed in private yards, leaving the Royal yards to fit out new vessels, convert the blockships and continue work on the battlefleet. Walker's policy was to prevent short term requirements interfering with the main element of his work, the battlefleet. From late 1854 the Thameside yards took an increasing share of the war effort, primarily building flotilla craft. This led to a rapid rise in wages, and bankruptcy for several yards as fixed price contracts took effect. The first flotilla craft, the *Arrow* class gunvessels, were not well received. True gunboats were only ordered in July, with the six *Gleaner* class; the following twenty *Dapper* class were part of the October Programme. No more were ordered during Graham's tenure.[11] Criticism of the continued construction of battleships was totally misguided, as the French would always be a greater danger at sea than the Russians. Sacrificing long term security for short term advantage would have been foolish, while the length of time required to build durable wooden battleships made continuity of effort vital. The initial reluctance to provide gunboats arose from their unpopularity, from Graham's reluctance to divert funds and his hopes of a Swedish alliance.

Graham directed the Baltic campaign of 1854 without interference from his cabinet colleagues; the Board proved to be a pliable instrument, as he had intended. Until the cabinet decision of 28 June the Baltic was not a secondary theatre; allied presence in both areas was essentially passive. Unable to bring Sweden into the war, Graham fell back on the Sevastopol plan. Conscious of his intellectual superiority, Graham would not allow any officers to thwart him, and used the secrecy of his planning to shift the blame onto Napier. The fleet available in 1854 could deny the open sea to Russia, but without a flotilla and, until August, troops, it could not project allied power ashore. Graham hoped the Swedes would provide those elements. Furthermore, he had no idea of the real potential of the theatre, or the distinction between limited and unlimited war. Cronstadt, key to St Petersburg, received little attention, while the illusory Swedish alliance led him to over-value Sweaborg. Cronstadt was largely ignored until late 1855, which explains the indecisive nature of the two Baltic campaigns. The real failure was that of the Government to prepare a coherent war aims programme. In the Euxine it was necessary to establish a large degree of allied co-operation. In the Baltic Graham had the freedom to act alone, yet his cabinet memorandum of 22 January, was a catalogue of problems, not a strategic programme.[12] Graham did not have a Baltic strategy until he ordered the October Programme. This explains the failures of the 1854 campaign, and where the responsibility lay. Without strategic guidance, theatre commanders are powerless; Napier did his best with a scratch manned fleet, with cautious, narrowly focused, instructions and the misleading Saumarez journals. Having drilled his fleet, set up a blockade and begun to investigate Sweaborg he was called away by the arrival of the French, and from that point was no longer free to conduct his own campaign. The delay off Bomarsund was not his fault, Graham commanded him to co-operate. The rumoured fall of Sevastopol encouraged Graham to apply pressure for an attack on Sweaborg: Napier refused, without the equipment he had long requested. His failings were in the area of professional relations; inability to delegate kept him bound with unnecessary labours, and the ill-feeling of his captains made him enemies in high places. Only Sulivan appreciated his talents. Despite his experience Napier allowed Graham to provoke him into a futile, self destructive argument with the Board; yet that never clouded his judgement.

The return of the Baltic fleet provided some relief from the problems of the campaign, but it also raised the need to prepare plans and ships for the following season, while attending to the Euxine. Throughout January and February the Sound remained open, obliging the Admiralty to send a battleship and some corvettes to to Scotland, where the Russians were expected. Graham and Berkeley interviewed Sulivan and, impressed by his opinions, directed him to prepare a memorandum on future operations in the light of the October Programme. He was to consider three heads:

1. What was possible with naval forces alone?
2. What if naval and military forces were to be employed?
3. What force of ships would be required for the Baltic if it were decided to confine the work there to a simple blockade?

Sulivan outlined the blockading stations and forces used by Napier in 1854; the major part of the paper concerned the most suitable method to attack Sweaborg, after an initial premise that nothing would justify attacking Sweaborg or Cronstadt with the large ships alone. At Sweaborg Sulivan favoured placing mortars on the outlying islets, but not Bakholmen. The large ships would carry a few heavy guns to support the flotilla craft operating close in; when the fire began to take effect, the battleships would close to complete the task. The similarities with Napier's plan of 25 September demonstrate both Sulivan's influence and the Admiral's good sense. If the weather proved hostile, or Russian guns more effective, a small scale attack with the flotilla craft could be substituted. Troops would be of little value, and Sulivan took the opportunity to criticise Jones' plan. They would be of even less use at Cronstadt, which was otherwise given little attention. Although Sulivan knew Cronstadt was more important, Graham's instructions had been specifically concerned with Sweaborg.[13] Graham remained in control of Baltic strategy throughout this period, referring specific questions to particular individuals from the returning fleet, including Chads and Watson. He kept faith in the blockade, blaming the failure of 1854 on the allies' 'excessive forbearance'.[14] Using Sulivan to outline the 1855 campaign was typical; he often used intelligent officers to put his ideas into shape, restrictive terms of reference ensuring they produced the desired result. The inclusion of a military force reflected the hope that Sevastopol would soon fall.

Political crisis

With the foundations of his new strategy in place, Graham's work was disturbed by the political crisis of January 1855. The cause was pressure in the Commons relating to the Crimea. Palmerston called for the dismissal of Raglan's staff, following attacks in *The Times*. Newcastle had written to Raglan in strong language in order to discover the truth of these allegations. When Raglan defended his staff Newcastle demonstrated he had learnt something from his attack on Dundas, he told Palmerston:

I am ready to advise the dismissal of anybody – nay everybody – on the staff or in any command if I can have the hope of saving the lives or health of the men, but what I am not prepared to do is to recall men against whom there is a Newspaper clamour and for whom I have no better substitutes; merely to save myself. No doubt two such tubs to the whales as Airey and Estcourt might save me from playing the part of Jonah. I am not anxious of being swallowed alive on the 23rd. inst. but I would sooner share that fate than escape it by a dodge.

This should be contrasted with Graham's conduct towards Dundas and Napier; Newcastle had a high conception of public duty, above politics and closely connected with personal honour. As the responsible minister he knew he would be made a scapegoat, but did not try to avoid his fate. Only Aberdeen shared his feelings; the rest were prepared to reform and try again. While Newcastle and Aberdeen were the political victims of the Crimean winter, Newcastle was also responsible for the measures which improved the position by spring, benefitting Palmerston. The railway, huts, sanitary officers and Land Transport Corps were his initiatives. It was unfortunate, both for Raglan and the progress of the war, that Newcastle was forced out of office just as he realised how the campaign was developing. His successor never achieved the same insight. The grim position of the British Army through December, January and February, under the dual afflictions of bad weather and poor organisation, has been considered many times and needs no restatement.[15] This debate reinforced the 'Crimeocentric' public awareness of the war, which has dominated all subsequent analysis. In early 1855 this did at least harmonise with Louis Napoleon's desire to capture the city.

The mounting torrent of criticism heaped on the Government by the press and the Commons culminated when, on 23 January, the radical MP James Roebuck tabled a motion of censure. Russell resigned that evening, his colleagues tendered their resignations the following day, but were sent away to try again. Without Russell the Government faced the Commons for the debate on Roebucks' motion on the 26th and 28th. Resoundingly defeated, 305 to 148 on the 29th, their resignations were accepted on the 30th. The break up of Aberdeen's ministry came at a very inopportune moment; Russian acceptance of the 'Four Points' as the basis for negotiations, and the problems in the Crimea, required decisions. The failure of Derby, Lansdowne and Russell forced the Palace to use its influence to reform the Aberdeen team behind Palmerston, the man of the hour, a process completed by 8 February. Lord Panmure replaced Newcastle, while the Secretary of State's office was combined with that of Secretary at War, pushing Sidney Herbert out to the Colonies. Panmure, 'the Bison' was a determined, capable administrator, but lacked the character and decision of his predecessor. Clarendon had serious reservations: 'Panmure is an honest, good fellow but by no means of the calibre for such an office at such a moment and I am sure he is and will be thought inferior to Newcastle.' Palmerston only doubted whether Panmure's gout would stand up to the work.[16] Combining the two offices, while making for commendable unity, replaced Newcastle and Herbert with Panmure, hardly the equal of either. However, Palmerston was determined to run the war his own way, and this included directing the service ministers; it was also necessary to appease the old Whig party, to prevent Russell causing trouble. Palmerston appreciated Panmure's limits, excluding him from most of the inner war cabinet meetings.

Graham, Gladstone and Herbert remained in the cabinet after understandings on two key issues. They opposed Palmerston's expanded war aims. To win them over he promised his aims were no wider than those of the Aberdeen cabinet, the 'Four Points', and entirely dependent on the fortunes of war. This satisfied Aberdeen, still the Peelite leader. The second issue was not treated so thoroughly; after the vote of censure on 30 January Roebuck moved for a Committee of Enquiry into the conduct of the war. The Peelites considered this an unjustified slur on their two colleagues, joining on a vague understanding that Palmerston would prevent the enquiry. Palmerston had always limited his hopes to deflecting it, and taking the sting out of any adverse findings; he did not anticipate it would be practical politics to prevent it. Certainly the temper of the Commons during the third week of February supported his analysis, and he had no intention of making it the subject of a vote of confidence. Nothing less would satisfy the Peelites, so he let them go, as the lesser of two evils. Their resignations, on 22 February, were badly received, Clarendon was adamant Graham had run away from Layard, who threatened to uncover the less satisfactory aspects of his administration.[17]

The temporary accession of the three Peelites allowed Palmerston to form a government; once established he courted popularity to keep himself in office, and could dispense with them. His other political problem, Russell, was more easily settled. After his desertion of Aberdeen few would serve with, and none under, Russell. He prudently declined the barbed offer of a post in Palmerston's ministry. Clarendon then proposed sending him to represent the Government at the Vienna Conference, to back up the Ambassador, Lord Westmorland, in whom no-one had much faith. Palmerston agreed, but had no intention of allowing the Conference to end in a moderate peace. Peace would only be made when the security of Turkey was assured by an Anglo–French interpretation of the third point, which, with Sevastopol still not taken, Russia was unlikely to concede. The same gesture would also complete the ruin of Russell. Russell left for Vienna convinced there was a chance for peace, and sensing a political advantage. He was encouraged by many in the lower echelons of government, reflecting their limited aims, the state of the war and opposition to Palmerston.[18] Attempting a diplomatic breakthrough, Russell exposed himself to further humiliation. After the Peelite secession he accepted the Colonial Office.

The Vienna conference

Throughout the war the majority in both British governments (the same people) supported war aims limited to the independence and integrity of Turkey. Ultimately this prevented the development of

Palmerston's wider aims, and the implementation of the related strategy. The majority considered Austrian support would force Russia to submit. They wanted a moderate, Austrian, war aims programme. Discussion of these aims reached a conclusion with an exchange of notes on 8 August 1854; Austria, Britain and France established the 'Four Points' as the basis for peace negotiations:

1. Russia must renounce any special rights in Serbia and the Danubian Principalities, which would be replaced by a collective guarantee of the powers with the Porte.
2. The navigation of the Danube to be unrestricted.
3. The Straits Convention of 1841 should be revised 'in the interests of the Balance of Power in Europe'.
4. Russia should renounce all claims to an official protectorate over the Orthodox Christians of the Ottoman Empire. This would be replaced by a collective guarantee of all Christians.

Point three was vague and open to conflicting interpretations, and while Austria accepted minor demands in the Baltic and Asia Minor, the 'Four Points' must remain the basis of any settlement.

While sufficiently concerned about Austrian intervention to evacuate the Principalities, Russia initially rejected the 'Four Points'. Under the terms of the agreement of 8 August Austria mobilised, but only on 22 October, having delayed to avoid the danger of a campaign before winter. Once again the diplomats, particularly Buol, hoped to piece together a settlement during the winter. Russia accepted the 'Four Points' as the basis for negotiations on 29 November. Further allied discussions with Austria produced the Tripartite Treaty of 2 December, Austria engaging to join the war if peace were not assured by the end of the year. Before committing himself Buol wanted to establish a binding definition of the Third Point, not satisfied by claims of Anglo–French moderation. This was wise, for while Aberdeen could report that the cabinet of 20 November did not favour demands for the Crimea, Finland or Poland, Argyll noted Palmerston's obvious contempt for the 'Four Points'. He wanted a definite understanding of allied war aims, the majority agreed. Clarendon proposed the end of Russian naval preponderance in the Euxine and the dismantling of the arsenals, since these were only useful for aggression. The cabinet accepted this on 1 December, although they felt such terms were too strong for Austria. It was agreed on the 13th to send a watered-down note to Vienna, while London and Paris exchanged a much tougher document. Austria would only be told of this when she had joined the allies in the field. The allies underestimated Russian statesmanship, expecting Russia to reject their interpretation and deliver Austria into their camp. Russia decided to negotiate, sending Prince A. M. Gorchakov to Vienna. On receipt of the allied terms he obtained fifteen days to refer to St Petersburg; the allies expected a rupture. When, after nine days, the Russians replied, they attempted to convince the German powers that the allied demands were too strong, before accepting in principle the end of Russian naval supremacy in the Euxine on 7 January. Unknown to the British, Louis Napoleon had known Russia would accept, although he expected the negotiations to fail. He saw the Conference as a device to keep open the chance of peace while he led a campaign in the Crimea. If that failed he could salvage something at Vienna; if not, Russia would accept allied terms.

The Bonapartist clique were alarmed by the idea of the Emperor's prolonged absence; Drouyn pressed for a compromise settlement, to avoid the danger. He was accompanied to Vienna by Russell, hamstrung by rigid instructions which permitted no modification of the allied interpretation of the Third Point. Arriving in Vienna on 4 March, Russell found the limitation of Russian naval power was the key to the process. By late March it was clear Austria would not make Russian rejection *casus belli*; Drouyn proposed alternative interpretations, including the neutralisation of the Euxine. During a visit to London, on 30 March, Drouyn agreed to accept either limitation or neutralisation. But in an effort to secure peace he worked out a compromise plan of 'counterpoise' with Buol and Russell. Russia would keep her existing force, while Britain, France and Austria were each permitted a pair of frigates at Constantinople. If Russia increased her strength, Britain and France would send in a combined force equal to that of Russia; if Russia rebuilt to the level of 1853, Austria would treat that as *casus belli*. Without authority Drouyn and Russell could only recommend. The idea appears to have held Louis Napoleon's attention for a few days. During his visit to Britain, Drouyn's plan arrived, and after waiting for his Foreign Minister to reach Paris he accepted a modified counterpoise plan. This lasted only four days, being rejected for two reasons – the repugnance felt by London and, more significantly, the opinion of Vaillant that the army would regard such a peace as dishonourable. Although the feared Crimean voyage had been given up, Drouyn felt obliged to resign, being replaced by Walewski. The conference broke up on 4 June. Russell had to resign on 16 July.

By sending Russell to Vienna Palmerston signalled to his critics a willingness to make peace that simply did not exist. Using the same gesture to complete the political destruction of his rival doubled its value. Similarly, vigour and determination had to be shown in the conduct of the war to deflect wider criticism. The success of his measures in this area would be measured by the level of control achieved over the Commons. Until then Roebuck's motion hung over the administration, endangering its cohesion and threatening to turn it out altogether. For this 'vigorous' conduct of the war Panmure had the requirements before him, and began with scarcely-veiled demands for the dismissal of Airey, Estcourt and Commissary General Filder. He sent out General Sir James Simpson to be Chief of Staff, and government spy, recalled Burgoyne, and demanded to know Raglan's intentions. Even the Queen accepted that his forthright language was justified.[19] After the Peelite secession, such vigour was even more necessary, if only on paper.

Baltic strategy under Palmerston

The impact of these difficulties and qualifications on Palmerston's strategy was surprisingly limited. He still favoured the wider war and enlarged aims denied in his correspondence with Gladstone. However, he had to overcome domestic political problems and wait for success in the Crimea before any new campaigns could be opened. This made the capture of Sevastopol the key to his policy. Only then could he switch resources to other areas. None of his colleagues shared his vision; Clarendon was prepared to go so far, but Lansdowne, the third member of the inner war cabinet, preferred to see the fall of Sevastopol as the end of the war. No-one else in the cabinet held higher aims. Lansdowne did consider Cronstadt, but believed it would be impossible. Graham, keeping his Baltic strategy secret, was replaced at the cabinet of 25 February by Sir Charles Wood (1809–1886).

Wood was a Whig of the old school, looking to Russell as his political leader. He had been Secretary to the Admiralty during Melbourne's government, and Russell's Chancellor. After surveying his period of office under Aberdeen, Conacher harshly characterised him as 'an uninspiring man of limited talents'. His colleagues held him in higher regard. Although not outstanding, Wood was a capable administrator. While the war lasted he consulted Graham on the details of Admiralty administration, being advised to rely on Walker, Milne and Berkeley, all familiar with Graham's methods. The real impact of Graham's departure was to reduce the political weight and independence of the Admiralty. This had a serious effect on the Baltic. Graham had prepared a fleet and a strategy; Wood replaced him just as Sulivan presented his report, but never understood what Graham had been attempting. Sulivan's plan, and the forces collected, were for an attempt on Sweaborg. Wood lacked the single-minded ruthlessness to conduct such a policy without cabinet sanction, but he did have certain gifts denied to Graham; being far better at handling men, he brought a degree of balance to the conduct of Admiralty. Significantly, he began by stating his opinon of the relative weight of public and private correspondence:

Private letters never can interfere with public orders, they never can bind your discretion, you can never be blameable for disregarding them if they clash with public orders or with the discretion which a full knowledge on the spot of how the service is most to be benefited enables you to exercise . . . But on the other hand they put you in possession more fully than public orders can do of the views entertained at home.[20]

Sulivan's memorandum arrived on the day Graham left office, providing a concise statement of what was possible, although Sulivan was not happy with the emphasis on Sweaborg. Unaware of this, the report formed the basis of Wood's Baltic strategy until the fall of Sevastopol. The problems of the 1855 season stemmed from the combination of misguided strategy and uninspired leadership in the Baltic. Even before the season opened Graham's Baltic plans were falling apart; without his governing hand the needs of the theatre were subordinated to the Crimea. Graham expected troops, Palmerston felt obliged to send every available man to the east. The influence of the French was also apparent; the Emperor did not appreciate the strategic value of the Baltic, complaining that Britain was wasting resources there. Although his own policy was influenced by the needs of the alliance, he was not above criticising his allies. His strategy of concentrating on the Crimea was dominated by the need to satisfy the army. The French elements of the October Programme were tardily completed, and largely dispatched to the Euxine, where the Emperor's only plan was to land 1,200,000 men, some from Sweden, on the Russian coast.

When the cabinet discussed the Baltic on 17 March, Clarendon reported that without French or Swedish troops nothing could be done, apart from the blockade. He thought it would be futile to capture fortresses, 'with an enormous force', only to treat them after the fashion of Bomarsund, although he did not state what it was intended to do at Sevastopol. Following Graham, he observed that Azov would be more useful. Cowley was instructed to allow Princess Lieven to hear that something major was planned for the Baltic in late summer. Palmerston suggested a lack of troops had forced his hand; the campaign would be limited to what could be accomplished by ships alone, which made Cronstadt or Sweaborg 'unwise'. Even so he held out some hope of a naval bombardment.[21] In part this reflected the demands of the Crimea, but Palmerston was really biding his time until success at Sevastopol, and the search for allies, allowed him to carry out his expanded war plans. An attack on St Petersburg might serve to end the war, forcing Russia to concede the loss of large areas of territory already captured.

Professor Vincent has pointed out the Parliamentary weakness of Palmerston's administration. His analysis of the Prime Minister's manoeuvres illustrate the problems that afflicted the government.[22] This weakness was critical. The cabinet could have dissolved at any moment; defeat in the Commons would would have pushed it to the limit. With so many cautious men, inherited from Aberdeen, Palmerston had to form an inner cabinet – Lansdowne, Clarendon and occasionally Panmure – to develop policy. Clarendon came closest to giving complete support, making the diplomacy of the expanded war far more effective than the operations. The failure to concert an effective Baltic strategy for 1855 reflected the position of the Government, the problems of the Crimea and French pressure.

Notes

1   Graham to Cowley 26 Sept. 2, 8 Oct. 1854: F.O. 519/208 f65–70, 97–101,.105–10.
2   Graham to Clarendon 1 Nov. 1854: Cl. Dep. C14 f480–2; Russell to Clarendon 27 Sept. 1854: *ibid.* C15 f646–8; Russell to Graham 7 Nov. 1854: Gr. B.123; Graham to Russell 7 Nov. 1854: PRO 30/22/11F f15–18.
3   Cowley to Graham 11 Nov. 1854: F.O. 519/212 f192; Graham to Clarendon 9 Nov. 1854: Cl. Dep. C14 f499–505; Milne to Graham 9 Nov. 1854: enc. in above; Newcastle to Clarendon 9 Nov. 1854: *ibid.* C15 f869; Aberdeen to the Queen 10, 17 Nov. 1854: Add. 43.050 f3, 14; Clarendon to Palmerston 19 Feb. 1855: Bdlds. GC/CL f591/2.
4   Palmerston to Newcastle 4 Dec. 1854: NeC 10,044; Graham to

Aberdeen 27 Dec. 1854: Add. 43,191 f281; STANMORE, *Herbert*, i, p. 244.

5   Graham to Clarendon 1 Nov. 1854: Cl. Dep. C14 f480–2; Graham to Lyons 18 Dec. 1854: Gr. B.123; Graham to Gladstone 6 Oct. 1854: Add. 44,163 f153–6; Lyons to Berkeley 16 Jan. 1855: LYONS 9KD4.

6   Newcastle to Raglan 9, 23, 28 Nov. 1854: RAGLAN 6807–283; Newcastle to Clarendon 2 Dec. 1854: Cl. Dep. C15 f877; Russell to Clarendon 3 Dec. 1854: *ibid.* f738–40; Clarendon to Stratford 30 Oct. 1854: F.O. 352/38.

7   Palmerston to Clarendon 15 Nov. 1854: PRO 30/22/11F f50–1; BAYLEY, D., *Mercenaries for the Crimea* (London, 1977); Aberdeen to the Queen 1, 16 Dec. 1854, 26 Jan. 1855; Add. 43,050 f35, 55, 119; Clarendon to Stratford 3 Nov. 1854: F.O. 352/38; Wood minute, 22 Dec., Graham 24 Dec. Granville 28 Dec. Russell, Herbert and Clarendon 30 Dec.1854, Palmertston 6 Jan. 1855: WOOD F78/20.

8   Aberdeen to Clarendon 10 Dec. 1854: Cl. Dep. C14 f115–6; Clarendon to Stratford 25 Dec. 1854: F.O. 352/38; Palmerston to Clarendon 2, 19, 21 Nov. 1854: Cl. Dep. C15 f225–46 Russell to Clarendon 4 Nov. 1854: *ibid.* f700–1;

9   BAXTER, J.P., *The Introduction of the Ironclad Warship* (Cambridge, Mass. 1933); OSBON, G.A., 'The First Ironclads', *Mariner's Mirror*, vol. 50, 1964, p. 189; Graham to Cowley 5, 28 Sept. 1854: F.O. 519/208 f49, 81–7; Walker to Cowley 7 Sept. 1854: *ibid.* f53–7; Graham to Clarendon 5 Aug., 28 Sept. 1854: Gr. B.120, 121; Surveyor's Estimate, Sept. 1854: ADM 1/5632; Graham to Gladstone 6 Oct. 1854: Add. 44,163 f153.

10   HAMILTON, pp. 109–10; Admiralty to Sheerness Dockyard 3 Oct. 1854: ADM 87/49; Palmerston to the Queen 18 Mar., 9 Apr., 1855: R.A. G26.

11   OSBON, G.A., 'The Crimean Gunboats', *Mariner's Mirror*, vol. 51, 1965; BANBURY, P., *Shipbuilders of the Thames and Medway* (Newton Abbot, 1971); Memo. on the Wages of Thames Shipwrights: WALKER WWL/10; Berkeley to Napier 24 Sept. 1854: Add. 40,024 f134; Dundas to Admiralty 2 Dec. 1854: ADM 87/50 f1105.

12   Graham to Aberdeen 27 Dec. 1854: Gr. B.123; RICHMOND, pp. 231–55.

13   Graham to Berkeley 15 Jan. 1855: Gr. B.124; Remarks on the different Methods that may be adopted in conducting the Operations in the Baltic during the ensuing season: NRS Baltic 1855, pp. 382–98; SULIVAN, pp. 272–3.

14   Chads to Wood 9 Mar. 1855: Add. 49,554 f128; Chads to Graham 31 Dec. 1854: M.C.M. GD 51/2 1008/2 f208; Graham to Clarendon 25 Jan. 1855: Gr. B.124.

15   Palmerston to Newcastle 4 Jan. 1855: Bdlds. GC/NE f97; Newcastle to Palmerston 9 Jan. 1855: *ibid.* f74; HIBBERT, pp. 232–313; Newcastle to Raglan Dec.–Jan. 1854–5: RAGLAN 6807–283.

16   Clarendon to Palmerston 4 Feb. 1855: Bdlds. GC/CL f585; Palmerston to Lawrence Sulivan 4 Feb. 1855: *The Letters of the Third Viscount Palmerston to Lawrence and Elizabeth Sulivan, 1804 – 1863*, ed. K.

BOURNE (Camden Society, 1979), pp. 184–6; Graham to Clarendon 22 Feb. 1855: Cl. Dep. C30 f86–9; Clarendon to Russell 24 Feb. 1855: PRO 30/22/12A f85–6.

18 Palmerston to Clarendon 8, 10 Feb., 23 Mar. 1855: Cl. Dep. C31 f19–20, 21–2, 69–70; GOOCH, G.P., i, pp. 184–218; CONACHER, J.B., *Britain and the Crimea, 1855–56* (London, 1987), is unreliable on the the conference, attributing more independence to Russell.

19 *The Panmure Papers*, ed. DOUGLAS and RAMSAY (London, 1908, two vols.), i pp. 56–60: hereafter PANMURE.

20 MOORE R. J., *Sir Charles Wood's Indian Policy 1853–66* (Manchester, 1966), is the only scholarly work dealing with Wood's career; Lansdowne to Palmerston, early Feb. 1855: Bdlds. GC/LA f82; Wood to Graham 25 Feb. 1855: Gr. B.125; CONACHER, *Aberdeen Coalition*, p. 41; Clarendon to Russell 24 Feb. 1855: PRO 30/22/12A f134–5; Palmerston to Russell 24 Feb. 1855: *ibid.* f145; Correspondence with Graham: HALIFAX A4/70; BRIGGS, p. 117; Wood to Lyons 12 Mar. 1855: Add. 49,562 f14.

21 Palmerston to the Queen 18 Mar., 9 Apr. 1855: R.A. G26, 28; Clarendon to Cowley 4, 16, 17 Apr. 1855: F.O. 519/171 f294–301, 218–20, 221; Cowley to Clarendon 15 Mar. 1855: F.O. 519/4 f347;

22 VINCENT, J.R., 'The Parliamentary dimension of the Crimean War', in *Transactions of the Royal Historical Society* (1982, 5th series), vol. 31, pp. 37–48.

15

The Black Sea theatre, January–April 1855

Command of the sea remained vital to the allied position in the Crimea, never more so than during the winter of 1854–55. After the departure of Dundas and Hamelin the structure of the allied fleets changed. Sailing battleships were replaced by steamers of every class. The British ships went home, their crews being required for the enlarged 1855 Baltic fleet, the French used their spare ships as transports. A small number were kept as depots, *Rodney* in Kazatch Bay and *Leander* at Eupatoria. *Queen, Albion* and *London* at Beicos sent men to the Naval Brigade. At the end of January *Princess Royal* and *St Jean d'Acre* arrived, giving Lyons six steam battleships, although *Algiers* was a very inferior specimen. The cruisers were also reinforced; *Retribution* and *Sampson* went home, being replaced by *Leopard, Odin, Valorous* and *Dauntless*. Six *Arrow* class gunvessels, and the ex Prussian iron gunvessels *Weser* and *Recruit* arrived for the Sea of Azov; in June six gunboats and six mortar vessels completed the force. The French fleet, under Bruat, was reduced to six active battleships, seven frigates and eleven cruisers. The French concentrated on logistics support.

Left in local command Lyons shifted the steam squadron from the Katscha to the Chersonese, closer to Raglan. He was less concerned by the remaining Russian ships and ridiculed Hamelin's fear of another sortie, keeping one steam frigate off the harbour a fortnight at a time.[1] *Terrible, Dauntless, Highflyer* and *Sidon* filled this role during January and February. Well aware of the First Lord's policy Lyons wanted to instil a more aggressive spirit into the fleet. The period from 31 December to 22 February was the only time when Graham's mature policy was conducted by an enthusiastic commander; it would be easy, although inaccurate, to credit the institution of the blockade, improvements at Balaklava and Constantinople and preparations for the offensive to Lyons. Lyons, although active and forceful, lacked the intellectual stature to control a large theatre, as he demonstrated by failing to divide the fleet. His elevation emphasised Graham's centralised control. Lyons did bring some qualities to the command, notably a willingness to take responsibility.[2] He had earned the loyalty of his officers by his conduct on 17 October, and this revitalised the fleet. Diplomatic experience and easy command of French earned him a powerful voice in the all too frequent councils of war. Bruat relied on him to urge the Generals to more active measures.

With ten or eleven steam battleships off the harbour there was no possibility of an effective Russian sortie, or of the allies being driven off by the weather, allowing Lyons to spread his cruisers for the blockade. In addition he knew the armies were stuck on the plateau until the weather improved, making a maritime campaign a valuable part of the battle of attrition. These were crucial advantages. Lyons also had more cruisers, and Graham finally provided flotilla craft. Lyons attended to Admiralty demands that he re-embark the marines as there were more troops coming out and there was no chance of an assault. Men with the Naval Brigade from ships ordered home went aboard *Vengeance* on 22 January, she completed the crews and guns of the ships at Beicos; *Sans Pareil* followed her home on 4 February. The storm of 14 November revealed some of the problems of a winter blockade, damaging the rudder heads of several sailing ships; *Royal Albert*'s rudder broke during a storm on 22 December, those of *Algiers* and *Agamemnon* were damaged.[3]

Graham's most immediate concern was the administration of Balaklava and Constantinople. He followed the public in blaming Boxer and Christie, ordering Lyons to send either, or both, home. These two worthy officers had performed to the best of their abilities. Boxer had succeeded in creating order at Constantinople before he was removed; if he had been as inefficient as was suggested, sending him to Balaklava was an act of criminal stupidity. In truth he was an able officer, placed in charge of something beyond the talent of any man to organise quickly. Lyons, concerned by complaints about Balaklava which partly related to the period when he had been senior officer, was happy to leave the work to Heath.[4] Constantinople was turned over to Grey, too well connected to be made a scapegoat. Boxer and Christie were shuffled about until cholera ended their humiliation. After the war the administration salved their collective conscience by awarding both posthumous decorations. The second major issue was the blockade. Dundas had prepared for a declaration on 1 February, and Graham was anxious to have news before the opening of Parliament. Lyons obliged. The Euxine blockade was a simple affair compared with the Baltic, Sevastopol was necessarily covered, and the Danube had long been blockaded, along with Odessa and Kinburn. The one area left open had been the Straits of Kertch. *Leopard*, *Snake* and *Fulton* were sent on 17 January, while instructions went to all detached cruisers to notify neutral Consuls of the imminent blockade. Unfortunately the French continued to provide passes for Austrian vessels leaving the Danube with provisions for their army, making the whole exercise of doubtful legality.[5] Few neutral captures were made in 1855; most Russian craft were destroyed.

Rumours were circulating in London that the barrier across the harbour could be forced; Graham was unenthusiastic, although he requested more information. Lyons reported two booms inside the barrier intended to foul paddles or propellers, and mines. He was convinced there was no passage for heavy ships.[6] More realistic harassing operations were also considered. Shelling Odessa and the works in the Danube were suggested, but Graham left the decision with Lyons. There was also a possibility the Russians might reoccupy the Circassian forts. However all these would be pinpricks compared to opening the Sea of Azov; the Straits of Kertch being iced up, nothing could be done until mid February. The key document was a report by Cattley, for many years resident at Kertch, on the extent of Russian dependence on the Don basin. Irrelevant to the original grand raid, the Azov had become vital to the battle of attrition. The major obstacles were a barrier of sunken ships and batteries; Cattley anticipated the ships would be moved by the ice, but the batteries could not be passed without troops. Lyons called for more small steamers, particularly gunboats. Graham knew the operation would be decisive, but still relied on makeshift craft to reinforce the eight gunvessels and two cruisers drawing under fourteen feet.[7]

The Commanders-in-Chief assembled at Raglan's headquarters on 28 December, the Generals requesting transport for Omer and 35–40,000 Turkish troops from Varna to Eupatoria. Lyons and Bruat agreed because the Turks, arriving at Varna in small groups, could be carried aboard three transports and two French steam frigates. Graham wanted a British force at Eupatoria. In the event the

Russians sealed off the town and the Czar ordered Menshikov to attack. He moved on 17 February, but Omer already had 31,000 men. After driving in the Turkish pickets a column of infantry assaulted undamaged earthworks, supported on the flanks by allied warships. The Russians were driven off losing 700 men, the Turks 350. Nicholas replaced the despondent Menshikov with Gorchakov, but died within days.[8] thereafter Eupatoria was masked so effectively that Omer could do nothing. His army became a pawn in the strategic debate between Britain and France. The Sardinians, with 15,000 men, 2,000 horses, thirty-six guns and 264 vehicles added to Heath's problems at Balaklava.[9] Constant demands for transport prevented the development of a more effective maritime campaign. Large warships were used to provide the manpower to embark troops. The departure of Graham increased the difficulty, Wood being initially more susceptible to cabinet demands, which reflected a desire to preserve allied unity.

While French weakness at sea was annoying, limiting their contribution in both theatres, their most significant input was the Crimean strategy. From the beginning of the war the Emperor had looked for no more than the capture of Sevastopol, a triumph to bolster his regime at home and abroad. Increasing disparity in size between the two armies gave the French the lead in decision making. Economic difficulties, a poor harvest and the Crimean impasse meant the French people were becoming ill disposed toward the war. The Emperor wanted peace, but only if the British alliance could be preserved, while Vaillant never stopped reminding him that the future of his regime was bound up with the capture of Sevastopol. Canrobert had hoped to assault in early December, but the 7 November conference put this off until spring. Louis Napoleon, believing the commanders in the Crimea were weighed down by responsibility, thought this would be relieved if he took overall command. He also favoured a new strategy based on field operations. General Niel, reporting on the campaign, favoured an assault, but discussions with Burgoyne on 29 January convinced him this would lead to a huge loss of life. Field operations then became central to French strategy; an army would march toward Simpheropol and Batschi Serai, defeating the Russians and completing the investment of the city. The new plan, adopted on 1 February, and in particular the Emperor's role, caused consternation in London. Alarmed by opposition to the war in France the government could not reject the plan. Their alarm was shared by the Bonapartist clique, who feared for their positions. To aggravate Palmerston's problem the Emperor was the only Frenchman who could be relied on to continue the war; if he were overthrown France might become revolutionary. The new strategy was approved, but only if separated from the Imperial voyage. Such issues could not be debated in full cabinet. Clarendon went to Boulogne to persuade him not to go, with some success, although the plan was not finally abandoned for another month.[10]

In the Crimea the gradual recovery of the armies, improved weather and preparations to renew the bombardment allowed the commanders to consider the future. This had become a political imperative for the British government; nothing was to interfere with the campaign, particularly the Vienna Conference. Once the new strategy had been adopted Louis Napoleon sent Niel back to Canrobert's headquarters, arriving for the second time on 23 February. Niel now urged delay and opposed an assault, reinforcing Canrobert's timidity. The Emperor's plan envisaged three armies; Britain and France had built up reserves, with the Sardinians and a substantial force of Turks these troops would suffice. One army, French and Turkish, would continue the siege; a second, English and Turkish, under Raglan would move against Batschi Serai; the third, French, Turkish and Sardinian would land at Aloushta on the south coast of the Crimea to march on Simpheropol. If the Russians concentrated around the depots the two field armies would link up; if they fell back on Sevastopol the allies would drive them into the city, establish a complete blockade and starve them out. The British Government considered the plan, although it was hardly original. Burgoyne pointed out the dangers of marching inland with the siege unresolved; communication and supply problems must weaken the allies. He preferred pushing out to the head of the harbour and continuing the bombardment. Canrobert was equally unenthusiastic, eventually blaming Raglan for his unwillingness to make the attempt. Raglan, following Newcastle, favoured striking at Russian communications from Eupatoria and the Sea of Azov, as did the Government. Louis Napoleon persisted, ordering Canrobert to carry out the plan when he gave up the Crimean voyage.[11]

With Canrobert under the influence of Niel allied co-operation was strained by divergent views on strategy. Omer's army was an early problem. Without adequate cavalry they could not push back the Cossack screen at Eupatoria; while Raglan looked to send them into the field, Canrobert wanted them at Sevastopol, for the Emperor's plan. Panmure, agreeing with Raglan, reflected British strategy. Omer declared he could not take the field and would be better employed with 20–25,000 men at Sevastopol. This was accepted at the 12 March conference, 12–15,000 would hold Eupatoria. Lyons, unimpressed by the new strategy, caustically observed Canrobert was 'bent on having on these heights as many troops or what not as can find standing room'.[12] This was galling when he needed only a small force to open the Azov. Another cause of friction was the cavalier manner in which the British-financed Sardinians had been attached to the French force in the Emperor's plan. Raglan was instructed to prevent the French giving orders to General de la Marmora, and to avoid treating him as a mercenary.[13]

Opening the Azov, a fundamental of British strategy once the grand raid failed, required light draft steamers for the shallow sea and troops to clear the batteries at Kertch. Wood followed Graham, suggesting makeshift gunboats could be found at Constantinople, or in the Greek islands. Only six mortar vessels were intended to reinforce Lyons' flotilla. Lyons wanted proper gunboats, reporting that the local craft Walker could remember had disappeared since the advent of steam, while the Turks had no spare dockyard capacity to build or modify such vessels. Although disappointed, Wood gave way, adding six steam gunboats.[14] The blockading squadron, under Captain Giffard, *Leopard*, reported the Kertch Straits open when the ice cleared in mid February, but the batteries occupied commanding positions. Wood hoped to make do with a naval operation, but Berkeley and Panmure were less sanguine. Raglan was instructed to prepare a force; Lyons admitted troops were necessary, but hoped the Straits could be kept open by naval forces. Bruat agreed, but Canrobert refused to send any men, and Raglan did not have enough to act alone. At the Conference of 12 March Canrobert 'hoped' to provide 12,000 men in early April. His subsequent refusal disgusted the Admirals, they could only speculate on the external pressures holding him back. To make matters worse the Russians were throwing up more earthworks.[15]

The theatre was dominated by Sevastopol. While nothing could be done to assist an assault, the Russian ships had to be masked. Thereafter Azov was the first priority, and Wood believed operations in Circassia would produce significant impact on the Asiatic Kingdoms and Persia. Lyons decided that once the weather improved he could cover the Russian fleet with the sailing battleships, leaving the steam fleet free to take the offensive. The number of sailing ships needed was significantly reduced on 24 and 25 February, when the Russians scuttled another four heavy ships to form a second line across the harbour. While Wood and Lyons were puzzled, it is possible the Russians had heard rumours of schemes to charge the outer barrier. The Russian fleet was reduced to six battleships, two frigates and eight steamers.[16] These ships became important when Buol pressed the allies to accept Russian strength at the present level; once Wood provided figures the idea was rejected. Lyons also reported a three-decker at Nicolaiev, waiting for her embargoed British machinery, two two-deckers on the stocks, four steamers in the Azov, and a flotilla on the Danube. The covering squadron, *Queen* and *London*, arrived on 27 April, under Captain Michell, *Queen*.[17]

In March the railway and roads were completed, fresh guns, gunners and ammunition were brought up. At the conference of 2 April the commanders decided to resume firing on the 9th. The squadrons would leave the Chersonese anchorage and take threatening positions just out of range of the sea defences. *Leopard* and *Sidon* were dispatched to Corfu for two British regiments. Transports brought the first 10,000 Turkish soldiers down from Eupatoria, and the remainder would be sent when their Eygptian replacements arrived. The French showed no sign of bringing up their reserve army from Constantinople. After a week of sustained firing at up to 100 rounds per gun per day, little effect had been produced, Russian counter-battery fire remained heavy. The conference on the 14th reduced the rate of fire to thirty rounds a day. Lyons was furious. As Canrobert would do nothing about Kertch he pressed for orders to be sent from Paris.[18] The failure of the bombardment, and of Canrobert, paralysed the campaign; to break the impasse Lyons, Raglan, Wood and Panmure favoured attacking Russian logistics. The Emperor looked for a dramatic victory. His directions to prepare for the three armies strategy hamstrung Canrobert, explaining why he admitted the sense of Kertch, but would not provide the men. The telegraph from Varna to Balaklava, open from 13 April, completed Canrobert's misery. He lacked the mental resilience to take responsibility, and knew that even if the allies could batter their way into Sevastopol it would avail them little while the Russians held the commanding northern shore of the harbour. This view was expressed with surprising vehemence by Simpson, who also defended the staff, despite his scarcely-veiled orders that they were to be dismissed. Palmerston would be denied his Crimean scapegoats. The same political necessity led him to consider more radical plans, including Dundonald's gas attack. Informing Wood that the Government would not be discredited if the plan failed was not particularly reassuring. The Premier supported field operations which, if successful, would drive the enemy out of the entire peninsula. By late April anything appeared decidedly superior to the existing situation. Palmerston began to doubt the Kertch operation.[19]

This uncharacteristic pessimism arose from the actions of Louis Napoleon; cognizant of his political weakness Palmerston knew he could not survive a rupture with his ally. Hoping to dissuade the Emperor from his projected voyage, he sent Granville to Paris to continue the work begun by Clarendon and Cowley, but did not think it appropriate to press a British maritime strategy on the French, particularly as they would have to provide the troops. The Emperor's brief visit to Britain in mid April produced the desired result, reducing the chances of the Crimean voyage, modifying the three armies strategy and giving a larger role to Raglan. Raglan considered the original scheme required too many men and munitions and would take too long; the return of his *eminence grise*, Burgoyne, encouraged Panmure to support field operations. The whole was agreed at a Council of War at Windsor on the 18th. Palmerston, Louis Napoleon, Prince Albert, Clarendon, Panmure, Cowley, Vaillant, Burgoyne and Walewski were present; significantly, Wood was not. Burgoyne had been directed to set out the government's objections to the Emperor's plan. He wanted to avoid any division of force, moving out from the heights, and possibly Eupatoria. With 113,000 French, 60,000 Turks, 25,000 British and 15,000 Sardinian troops available, the Council settled on a four army strategy. Raglan, with 60,000 men, would move out from the camp, with a similar number of French troops in support, to cut off Sevastopol from the interior. While they considered Louis Napoleon's Aloushta scheme 'visionary', Panmure and Vaillant signed it on the 21st.[20] The details revealed the atmosphere of bargain in which they were cobbled together. The real object was secured soon afterwards when the Crimean voyage was given up.[21] The Emperor now found fault with Raglan's plan to use the new field army from Eupatoria, rather than Aloushta; he considered this would expose the flank of the force. His own plan differed only in having no secure base, and exposing both flanks. However, the plan was abandoned, Panmure sharing the Emperor's real objection, not wanting to trust anything to the Turks.[22]

During this expedient policy making the claims of Kertch were ignored. The loss of Graham was largely responsible for the lack of any direct Admiralty protest. Wood sent three copies of Blakesly's memorandum on the Russian use of Azov to Palmerston, claiming the capture of Kertch would be worth 50,000 men to the allies. One reached Louis Napoleon, who was 'much struck'. Within the suspiciously short time of four days Canrobert had been ordered to release the necessary troops. Canrobert and Niel had already put off an assault for twenty to thirty days. When the telegraph ordered up the French reserve army, Lyons believed his wait was over. He would be disappointed. Palmerston, committed to the modified field operations, wanted to order Raglan to act; suitable instructions were sent to the Emperor on the last day of April.[23] They dashed Lyons' hopes, for the army he had to bring from the Bosphorus was intended for field operations, not Kertch.

Notes

1 Lyons to Graham 13 Dec. 1854: Gr. CW8.
2 Stewart to Panmure 26 Mar. 1855: PANMURE, i, pp. 126–9.
3 Admiralty to Dundas 25 Dec. 1854 no. 888: NRS p. 413; Admiralty to Lyons 6 Jan. 1855 no. 16: NRS (1855), p. 48; Lyons to Raglan 3, 31 Jan. 1855: RAGLAN 6807–299; Graham to Lyons 18 Dec. 1854 1, 12 Jan. 1855: Gr. B.123 4, LYONS L286–7; Lyons Journal 22 Jan. 1855: ADM 50/264; Lyons to Berkeley 1 Jan. 1855: LYONS B66.
4 Graham, to Lyons 18 Dec. 1854: Gr. B.123; Admiralty to Lyons 4, 29 Jan. 1855 no. 6, 111: NRS pp. 44, 60; SLADE, pp. 346–9; Lyons to Admiralty 13 Jan. 1855 no. 31: NRS p. 65.
5 Lyons to Raglan 15 Jan. 1855: RAGLAN 6807–299; Lyons to Admiralty 13 Feb. 1855 no. 122: NRS p. 76; Admiralty to Lyons 12 Jan. 1855: *ibid.* pp. 50–2.
6 W. Denman to Walker 25 Dec. 1854: WALKER Bc526; Graham to Lyons 5 Jan., 1 Mar. 1854: Gr. B.124, LYONS L286–7; Lyons to Graham 9 Jan., 6 Feb. 1855: Gr. CW8.
7 Graham to Lyons 12 Jan., 1 Mar. 1855: LYONS L286–7; Lyons to Graham 27 Jan., 6, 17 Feb. 1854: *ibid.*, Gr. CW7; Raglan to Lyons 23 Jan. 1855: RAGLAN 6807–299; Newcastle to Raglan 23 Nov. 1854: *ibid.* 283; Captain Giffard to Lyons 13 Feb. 1855: NRS pp. 78–9; Lyons to Admiralty

20 Feb. 1855 no. 135: (enc. above); Admiralty to Lyons 19 Feb. 1855 conf.: NRS pp. 72–4.
    8 Newcastle to Raglan 28 Nov. 1854: RAGLAN 6807–283; Lyons to Raglan, Raglan to Lyons 31 Jan. 1855: *ibid.* 299; Lyons to Admiralty 2 rec. 15 Jan., 20 Feb. rec. 8 Mar. 1855 no. 8, 140: NRS pp. 53–5, 82–5; Graham to Lyons 19 Jan. 1855: LYONS L286–7; CURTISS, pp. 365–6.
    9 Admiralty to Lyons 5 Feb. 1855 no. 152: NRS p. 71; Lyons to Admiralty 10 rec. 28 Mar. 1855 no. 191: *ibid.* p. 93.
    10 WROTTESLEY, ii, pp. 149–61, 202–7; Cowley to Clarendon 4, 14, 15 Feb. 1855: F.O. 519/215 f110, 130–4; Palmerston to Clarendon 18, 28 Feb. 1855: Cl. Dep. C31 f30–9; Clarendon to Palmerston 28 Feb. 2 Mar. 1855: Bdlds. GC/CL f592–4; The Queen to Clarendon 1 Mar. 1855: BENSON and ESHER, iii, p. 111; Panmure to Raglan 9 Mar. 1855: PANMURE, i, pp. 99–101.
    11 Panmure to Raglan 15 Feb. 1855: *ibid.* pp. 64–5; Cowley to Clarendon 26 Mar. 3 Apr. 1855: F.O. 519/215 f245, 270, blaming Westmorland for Raglan's supposed timidity; Lyons to Wood 17 Apr. 1855: Add. 49,535 f40, re. Canrobert; Louis Napoleon to Canrobert 28 Apr. 1855: GOOCH, B. p. 185; Palmerston to Panmure 28 Feb. 1855: PANMURE, i, p .87; WROTTESLEY, G., *The Military Opinions of General Sir John Burgoyne* (London, 1859), pp. 210–20; WROTTESLEY, *Life*, ii, pp. 134–5, 202–7.
    12 Raglan to Panmure 24 Feb. 1855: PANMURE, i, pp. 77–8; Panmure to Raglan 7 Mar. 1855: *ibid.* pp. 99–101; Lyons to Admiralty 13 rec. 28 Mar. 1855 no. 199: NRS pp. 98–9; Lyons to Wood 31 Mar. 1855: Add. 49,535 f22–7; Lyons to Berkeley 10 Mar. 1855: LYONS L507; Lyons to Raglan 27 Mar. 1855: RAGLAN 6807–299.
    13 Palmerston to Panmure 28 Feb. 1855: PANMURE, i, p. 87; Clarendon to Panmure 26 Mar. 1855: *ibid.* pp. 124–5; Panmure to Raglan 30 Mar. 1855: *ibid.* pp. 134–5.
    14 Raglan to Lyons 23 Jan. 1855: RAGLAN 6807–299; Wood to Lyons 9, 12 Mar., 2, 6 Apr. 1855: Add.49,562 f5–18, 39–41; Wood to Grey 6, 13 Apr. 1855: *ibid.* f33, 52; Lyons to Admiralty 20 Feb. rec. 8 Mar. 1855 no. 135: NRS p. 77; Lyons to Wood 24 Apr. 1855: Add. 49,535 f45–7.
    15 Wood to Lyons 9 Mar. 1855: Add. 49,562 f5–8; Panmure to Raglan 26 Feb., 9, 19 Mar. 1855: PANMURE i, pp. 79, 99, 112; Stewart to Panmure 24 Mar. 1855: *ibid.* pp. 120–4; Lyons to Wood 24, 27 Mar. 1855: Add. 49,535 f8–15; Lyons to Admiralty 13, rec. 28 Mar. 1855 no. 199: NRS p. 98; Lyons to Raglan 27 Mar. 1855: RAGLAN 6807–299.
    16 Panmure to Raglan 26 Feb. 1855: PANMURE, i, pp. 79–80; Wood to Lyons 12, 19 Mar. 1855: Add. 49,562 f14–18, 24; Lyons to Wood 27 Mar. 1855: Add. 49,535 f12–5; Lyons to Admiralty 27 Feb., 17 Mar. rec. 21, 28 Mar. 1855 no. 161, 211: NRS pp. 89–90, 104–6; WROTTESLEY, ii, pp. 134–5, 202–7.
    17 Palmerston to Clarendon 25 Mar. 1855: Cl. Dep. C31 f75–6; Wood to Clarendon 27 Mar. 1855: Cl. Dep. C29 f384; Russell to Lyons 21 Mar., Lyons to Russell 28 Mar. enc.in Lyons to Admiralty 31 Mar. rec. 14 Apr. 1855 no. 252: NRS p. 107; Lyons Journal 27 Apr. 1855: ADM 50/264.
    18 Lyons to Admiralty 3, 7, 17 rec. 17, 20, 25 Apr. 1855 no. 261, 269,

304: NRS pp. 11–2, 113, 118; Lyons to Wood 3, 17 Apr. 1855: Add. 49,535 f28–30, 40; Raglan to Panmure 7 Apr. 1855: PANMURE, i, pp. 143–4; Stewart to Panmure 21 Apr. 1855: *ibid.* pp. 160–4; PASLEY, L., *Life of Admiral Sir T. S. Pasley*, (London, 1900), p. 192.

19 Lyons Journal 13 Apr. 1855: ADM 50/264; Stewart to Panmure 21 Apr. 1855: Panmure, i, pp. 160–4; Simpson to Panmure 16 Apr. 1855: *ibid.* pp. 150–3; Palmerston to Panmure 15, 30 Apr. 1855: *ibid.* i, p. 150, 174; Palmerston to Wood 10 Apr. 1855: HALIFAX A4/63 f24; Palmerston to Clarendon 26 Apr. 1855: Cl. Dep. C31 f153–4; Panmure to Palmerston 12 Aug. 1855: Bdlds. GC/PA f114.

20 Raglan to Panmure 3 Apr. 1855: PANMURE, i, pp. 174–5; Panmure to Raglan 16, 20 Apr. 1855: *ibid.* pp. 141, 154–5; WROTTESLEY, ii, pp. 287–9; copy of accord in Cowley MSS: F.O. 519/298.

21 Cowley to Clarendon 26 Apr. 1855: F.O. 519/216 f48–50; Clarendon to Palmerston 26 Apr. 1855: Bdlds. GC/CL f619.

22 Cowley to Clarendon 25 Apr. 1855: F.O. 519/216 f45; Panmure to Raglan 27 Apr. 1855: PANMURE, i, pp. 168–9.

23 Wood to Lyons 20, 27 Apr. 1855: Add. 49,562 f60, 67; Wood to Palmerston 23 Apr. 1855: Bdlds. GC/WO f36; Lyons to Berkeley 1 May 1855: LYONS L509 9KD4; Lyons to Admiralty 28 Apr., rec. 9 May 1855 no. 333: NRS pp. 126–7; Admiralty to Lyons 30 Apr. 1855 Telegraph: *ibid.* p. 115; Palmerston to Clarendon 30 Apr. 1855: Cl. Dep. C31 f158–61.

16

Kertch

The Straits of Kertch were dominated by a sand spit projecting from the eastern shore into the middle of the channel, forcing vessels close to the western shore. The channel was over one mile wide, and fifteen feet deep close to the spit, with four fathoms reported in mid channel. The Straits were blockaded by Captain Giffard's squadron from mid January. To report on the state of the ice, the barrier and batteries, Giffard pushed up within two miles of Kertch. On his first approach, 2 February, the Russians fired red-hot shot, but accurate return fire persuaded them not to try again four days later. On the 22nd *Leopard* drove a large body of troops out of a position on the Kouban Lake, returning on the 24th to destroy ten heavy guns, boats, barracks and provisions. Giffard reported troops were passing into the Crimea almost daily; new batteries were thrown up to cover their passage. Reinforced by *Highflyer*, *Swallow* and *Viper*, Giffard drove the Russians out of Soujak Kaleh on 13 March and on the 8th *Viper* demolished another martello tower on the Anapa–Kertch road.[1] Rejoining the fleet in early April Giffard left Captain Moore, *Highflyer*, in command, while Lyons sent Spratt to join the squadron. On 24 April Moore captured a coaster carrying a nobleman's coach and sent *Viper* inshore under a flag of truce, offering to return it. Aboard the gunvessel were Major Gordon, RE and Commandant de Sain, sent to inspect the Straits at Paget's suggestion. The offer being accepted, the coach was landed on a beach near Kamisch Point, which proved ideal for amphibious operation. Although Russian defensive preparations were advancing, Lyons was satisfied with the report and, on 1 May, Canrobert agreed to provide the troops.[2]

Canrobert had given provisional assent on 29 April, but on returning to his Headquarters, conveniently discovered a report crediting the Russians with an enormous force around the Straits.

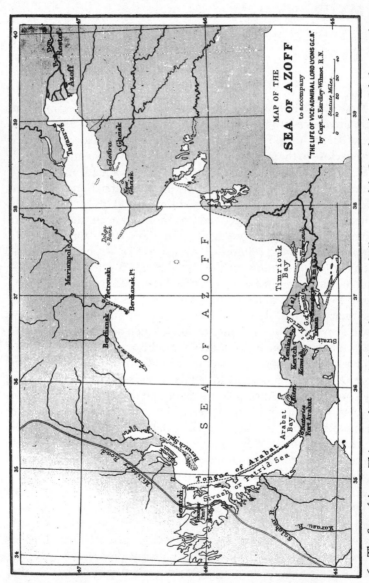

6   The Sea of Azov. This map does not indicate the extreme shallowness of the Sea, less than 4 fathoms at best. From the *Life of Lord Lyons*

Kertch and Kaffa had garrisons of 15,000 men, another 12,000 were at Theodosia and all the smaller villages were strongly held. He did not pause to consider why the Russians would hold so many men out of the combat zone. Canrobert had opposed the operation, giving way only under pressure from Raglan and the Admirals; Niel then made him regret his weakness. Sir George Brown, selected to command the expedition, found him dominated by Sevastopol, dismissing Kertch as peripheral, and unimpressed by the vital argument that control of the Azov would destroy the Russian logistics support, claiming the campaign would be settled in fifteen days. Realising that detaching troops was his major objection Raglan compromised on a suprise raid, to avoid the phantom armies and return for the decision at Sevastopol. Canrobert pledged 8,500 men and three batteries of field artillery, to be back at Kamiesch in fifteen days, Brown would have 2,500 and one battery; Lyons, while satisfied, would have preferred a permanent occupation.[3]

The expedition began embarking at Kamiesch and Balaklava on the afternoon of 3 May. Many of the French troops went aboard British warships, for lack of French transport; *Hannibal* took 620 men, *Terrible* over 600 and a complete field artillery battery. Four sailing battleships and four steamers under Captain Michell, *Queen*, were left to blockade the harbour. At 18.40 fifty-six ships weighed from the Chersonese anchorage proceeding north, as if for Odessa, burning lights. At 21.00 the formation extinguished lights and reversed course. This was intended to mislead the Russians, although it is unlikely they even noticed. The lack of lights caused a transport to back into *Princess Royal*, more significantly the ruse added over four hours to the brief passage. Lyons would have cause to regret the delay, for during the night of 3–4 May the telegraph bore out Canrobert's worst fears. Just after 22.00 he arrived at Raglan's Headquarters, reporting orders to bring up his reserves immediately, to land at Aloushta and march inland to attack Simpheropol and Batschi Serai. For this he would require half of Omer's army and the Kertch force. By 01.00 Raglan had persuaded him not to recall the expedition, and in return had promised steam transport for the French reserves. At 02.15 an aide woke Raglan to inform him that after another imperative telegraph, which he forwarded, Canrobert had recalled the French element of the force. The critical third sentence read, 'As soon as the Corps of Reserve joins you, assemble all your forces and do not lose a day'.[4] The opening clause qualified the second, leaving Canrobert a discretion to assemble his forces *when* the Corps of Reserve joined. This interpretation would have saved the expedition, explaining his reluctance to discuss the message with Raglan. Taken aback by Canrobert's unilateral action Raglan sent Lyons and Brown discretion to carry on alone, hoping the recall would arrive after the landing had commenced.

Canrobert's irresolution became evident at the first meeting of the commanders aboard *Royal Albert* on the evening of the 4th. The French were 1,500 men and one battery short, fortunately Brown had four extra companies of the Rifle Brigade. After planning the disembarkation for the following day the meeting broke up. Later Bruat went back to Lyons with the recall, stating that he must return. With so many French troops aboard British ships Canrobert expected the British to follow suit. Lyons persuaded Bruat to go on to the rendezvous the next morning, as much because thick fog made it dangerous to reverse course as from any force of logic. *Royal Albert* met *Spitfire* off the Straits at day-break (04.00), Spratt had a full survey, and was confident of success. Soon after Bruat and General D'Autemarre came aboard: Lyons, Brown and later Stewart failed to dissuade them. Although 10,000 troops lay scarcely two hours from the beach, arguing with Bruat was useless. His orders were imperative, to disobey would be mutiny. Lyons and Stewart could only contest the mistaken interpretation they thought Canrobert had placed on an unseen telegraph, they could not act alone. After some time Lyons followed, meeting Raglan's dispatch boat at sea. By the end of the day the British warships were once more off Sevastopol.[5]

The British commanders were disgusted; Panmure agreed Canrobert was 'utterly incapable of High Command' and feared the newspapers would have a field day when details of the fiasco leaked out, causing problems with France. Wood condemned the 'hesitation and indecision' of the French commander; the British Admirals were understandably worried, for their campaign was controlled by a man whose 'dread of responsibility and indecision of conduct' was damaging the moral ascendancy of the Royal Navy. While politicians and officers were united in condemning Canrobert they differed on the future of the operation. The politicians believed the recall was the end of Kertch, anticipating a decision at Sevastopol; Wood felt helpless: 'All that can be done now is to aid and assist in the greater operations which I suppose they will conduct with their concentrated force', the irony was deliberate. 'I cannot help wishing that we had a distinct operation in which we (the English I mean) could take our own part and responsibility.'[6] This theme came to dominate his planning later in the year. For the present he could only reinforce the batteries at Sevastopol with guns from *Albion*. The Admirals were more optimistic; believing the operation was vital Lyons continued to press, keeping Raglan up to the mark with the less-than-honest assertion that the Government hoped the plan was not given up. Returning some letters from Wood and Graham, Stewart was more direct: 'If they won't press their views of the importance of the Sea of Azov upon the French Govt. and so obtain *orders* to Canrobert to carry it out – what can we possibly do?' Echoing these sentiments to Wood Lyons stressed he would attack somewhere.[7] A more reflective officer would have made better use of the argument; Kertch was *the* maritime operation.

Central to any hope of renewing the operation was the Emperor's strategy. Palmerston wanted it adopted, for political reasons, Panmure condemned it as 'visionary' in part. If the three-pronged attack were launched the navies would be reduced to transport duty, as the Admirals were fully aware. The sheer scale of the plan made it inevitable warships would be used, even the blockade might have to be given up. Fortunately the Headquarters conference of 12 May rejected the Emperor's plan. Raglan refused to divide his army and Canrobert would not replace the British in their trenches if they took the field. Canrobert's resignation was equally welcome; with the failure of the Emperor's strategy he saw no reason to continue. Since mid January his independence had been a sham, Niel and the telegraph bound him to the Emperor's dictation. On 16 May he telegraphed Louis Napoleon, suggesting the senior corps commander, Pelissier, should take over. Niel recommended acceptance, and while the Emperor preferred Niel, Vaillant persuaded him Pelissier was the better man. The appointment was confirmed on the 19th. Unlike his refined and courteous predecessor Pelissier was blunt, aggressive and determined; he did not fear responsibility or his Emperor, and believed Sevastopol could be captured by a series of limited assaults, dismissing field operations, ignoring orders from Paris, and directing Niel to communicate with the Emperor only through himself. Within days the French were preparing to clear Russian rifle pits in front of their earthworks. There were enough troops for this, and to attack Kertch. Maritime operations had a low priority in Paris and Vaillant anticipated Kertch would not be resumed. Pelissier disagreed, he

Table 5: Allied troops in the Black Sea Theatre, May 1855

French	120,000
British	32,000
Sardinian	17,000
Turkish	55,000
TOTAL	224,000

knew it was vital to restore allied harmony.[8]

Lyons was more interested in the strategy needed to end the campaign. He anticipated the Vienna process would fail, and Austria would remain aloof:

If Russia should have nothing to fear from Austria she will naturally pour into the Crimea as many troops as she can feed, and there will scarcely be any limit to that if she should retain command of the Sea of Azov. The plan of campaign should therefore be, in my very humble opinion, to have as many troops in our present position before Sevastopol as are necessary for maintaining it. Then to secure free ingress and egress to and from the Sea of Azov, and to send any disposable men to Eupatoria to operate from thence toward Simpheropol or Perekop. In that way we may probably become masters of the whole Crimea this campaign, certainly the next, but I fear we shall see another siege of Troy if we adopt any other plan, always taking it for granted that we do not mean to retreat from the Black Sea without gaining our point, even if we should be twice ten years in siege.

Stewart concurred.[9] There was nothing original in Lyons' plan, he had distilled the views of Graham and Newcastle, outlining a grand attack on Russian communications. The determined execution of both Azov and Perekop plans would have forced the Russians to pull out of the southern Crimea. Although only half of the plan was carried out it forced the Russians to take an impossible chance to preserve their position. Lyons' plan was not carried out in full because Louis Napoleon was dominated by the need to take the city, and Pelissier, who shared this object, preferred to do so by direct methods. While Palmerston was beginning to plan for a war after the fall of Sevastopol, this was the Emperor's only military object.

Pelissier agreed to renew the operation, and make the occupation of Kertch permanent. The details were settled at the Council of War on 20 May. Omer wanted to command an all-Turkish force, but his allies knew London and Paris would not tolerate that; the Turks would form the garrison. A total of 15,000 men, 3,000 British with one battery, 5,000 Turks with another and 7,000 French with three batteries would be used. The extra force would counter recent

Russian preparations, including new blocking ships, piles and elec-
tric mines, or 'infernals'. The troops began embarkation on the
morning of the 22nd. That evening the squadrons weighed and
steamed direct for Kertch in thick fog. Captain Michell remained in
command off Sevastopol, with *Queen, London, Rodney, Inflexible,
Spiteful* and *Jean Bart.* On the morning of the 23rd the allies demonstrated off Kaffa, to persuade the Russians they were about to land.
During the night they shifted to appear off Kamisch Borru, the new
beach selected by Spratt five miles south of Kertch, early on the 24th.
The troops went ashore under covering fire from the steamers while
the flotilla craft pushed up to Kertch and Yenikale. The Russians
retired, blowing up their earthworks on both sides of the Straits and
destroying three steamers and other armed vessels. Both towns were
abandoned during the day, leaving 17,000 tons of coal. At 14.00
Captain Lyons led the flotilla into the Azov, his father's flag flying in
Miranda.[10]
    While the destruction of the batteries was completed, elements of
the three armies, with some of the local Tartar population, sacked
both towns. Although this was destructive of discipline, it did encourage the other towns on the Azov to surrender their ships and
magazines. Once the land defences had been strengthened the Turks
would be left to hold Yenikale, with a regiment each of British and
French, totalling 7,500 men. The offensive would be left to the
flotilla. The remaining troops were available to attack Soujak Kaleh
and Anapa, the last Russian strongholds on the Circassian coast. On
the 26th Moore carried news of Kertch to the natives and examined
the forts. Soujak had been abandoned on 28 April, the troops concentrating at Anapa. Spratt outlined a combined attack, while
Raglan and Pelissier sent reinforcements to replace the troops at
Kertch. Louis Napoleon, far from pleased by the renewed Kertch
operation and alarmed by Anapa, ordered a recall. Wood and Panmure countered with specific permission to continue with British
forces, if that would not cause delay. Although happy to ignore the
Emperor, Pelissier believed the evacuation of Soujak indicated a
determination to hold Anapa. Like Raglan he did not want troops
tied up in another siege when the assaults began, and he allowed only
three or four extra days.[11] Clarendon also feared a prolonged operation. Wood, reflecting his time at the Board of Control took a wider
view:

I do not know of any position in which, according to my notions, more injury may be done to Russia than in this quarter. We ought not to shut our eyes to the future interest of England in Persian and Asian politics, nor do I think it of little consequence to the maintenance of the independence of Turkey that her Asiatic frontier should have the protection of independent tribes between Russia and herself.

Clarendon accepted that if Britain did not liberate Georgia and Circassia a 'moral effect' would be produced in India, yet Sevastopol must take priority. Palmerston accepted the Emperor's view that Asian operations were a diversion, political necessities temporarily overrode his interest.[12]

Political discussions were rendered irrelevant by the Russian evacuation of Anapa on 5 May. It was assumed the garrison retired across the Kouban Lake. Lyons and Bruat detached *Hannibal*, *Napoleon*, *Highflyer*, *Primauget* and *Lynx* under Stewart and Rear-Admiral Charner on the 11th. The fort and over 200 guns and barracks for 7,000 men were ruined. Stewart believed the position had never been capable of resisting a powerful squadron; *Highflyer* and *Primauget* remained on the coast. The French troops left Kertch on the 13th. Lyons considered stopping at Kaffa, although Raglan left him at discretion. Pelissier did not even want to hear about such operations, and he doubted it was worth a few hours' delay. When Michell reported movement in the harbour Lyons took his squadron to Anapa on the 14th, reaching Sevastopol the following day. Wood telegraphed orders for an attack on Taman, if the Anapa garrison were there, but they had gone north to the Don.[13]

The campaign in the Sea of Azov

Once Kertch and Yenikale were in allied hands the flotilla under Captains Lyons and Sedaiges, initially seventeen vessels, could attack Russian logistics. The Admiral's son, with the only post ship able to operate in the shallow water, was already held in high regard. After buoying the channel and clearing Russian works on the Chetna Spit, the flotilla entered the Azov early on the 25th. On the 26th they arrived off Berdiansk, the ships covered the harbour and shipping while the boats destroyed the ships and a store house. At daylight on the 27th they moved up to cover the town, where Rear-Admiral Wolff had scuttled four small steamers that escaped from Kertch. Landing parties destroyed shipping and government stores. Without opposition at sea Lyons divided his force. Arriving off Fort Arabat on the 28th elements of the squadron cleared the fort, but could not land. The ships then joined *Swallow* and *Wrangler* off Genitchi. As the town refused to deliver up its shipping and stores, Lyons bombarded the works before sending the boats to fire seventy-three vessels and huge stacks of corn and hay. One man was slightly wounded. All told, Lyons could claim the destruction of four war steamers, 246 vessels, and grain and fodder estimated as equal to two months' rations for 100,000 men. At Kertch over 4,000,000 pounds of grain and 500,000 of flour destroyed by the Russians doubled the effect as Kertch had been sending flour to the field army daily. After these rapid attacks Lyons moved into the Gulf of Azov with twenty launches from the fleet, to attack Taganrog, which was too shallow even for his gunboats. On 3 June they destroyed the storehouses and government buildings, and the same force attacked Marianpol and Geisk on the 5th and 6th, to similar effect. The launches left on the 9th, with Lyons handing over to Commander Osborn, *Vesuvius*. The whole coastline was in a state of terror; no boats could be seen, and the natives were happy to provide fresh provisions. The damage done to the Russian army was incalculable; in addition, all future supplies drawn from the Don basin would have to carried overland. This wrecked Russian hopes of holding Sevastopol. It proved impossible to provide fodder for the supply wagons, and this destroyed the cavalry. The Russians were forced to fortify all routes into the central Crimea, because without cavalry they could offer little resistance. Their response to the belated movement from Eupatoria demonstrated how effective the Azov campaign had been.[14]

Spratt's report on the Tchongar bridge in late 1854 added another task for Osborn's force. Captain Lyons proposed pulling a boat over the Arabat spit into the Putrid Sea, leaving the execution to Osborn. The attempt failed. After struggling through waist-deep mud, the exhausted crew had to give up just three miles short of the target. Reports on the Don estuary suggested the Russians were holding a large number of vessels there, while the towns of Rostov and Lugar were the major munitions depots for the Crimean army. However, they were too far inland for a naval operation. Lyons sent the six *Pelter* class gunboats in early July, with instructions to clear the Azov of fisheries, stores and mills in excess of local requirements,. Osborn also destroyed any vessel over one ton. The Russians had taken precautions to preserve scuttled ships, particularly Wolff's steamers.

Osborn brought up the diver and explosives sent to clear Sevastopol harbour and demolished their machinery. He also sent boats far inland, at one point capturing 200 wagons. The only Russian success came on 23 July when the gunboat *Jasper* ran aground on the Crooked Spit, and was hastily abandoned. In early August Osborn closed the mouth of the Don, finding the water very shallow, and extensive Russian defences, including a steam launch, oared gunboats and 2,000 troops, he could do nothing. For most of August the weather prevented active operations, but on the 27th a huge store of forage on the Sevastopol road north of Genitchi was fired. In late September the squadron supported an attack on Taman and Fangoria by the garrison of Kertch. Operations were hampered by the removal of the flotilla for Kinburn. After their return Osborn went round the coast repeating his work. Everywhere the destruction was immense; Russian batteries effected little, the squadron could always bring up more guns. The only chance of stopping Osborn was to close the Straits, for while he had control of the sea they could do nothing. One succesful ruse was to hoist Austrian colours over the rebuilt granaries at Marianpol; however, Osborn knew he was being deceived and the grain never left the area. By mid November the Gulf of Azov began to ice up. Osborn sent his ships back to Kazatch, leaving *Snake* off Kertch until 1 December. When the campaign ended Osborn went home to discuss requirements for 1856.[15]

As the flotilla began to sweep the Azov the value of the Kertch operation was obvious; Wood and Graham agreed it must be decisive. Palmerston demonstrated an appreciation of the benefits flowing from a maritime strategy:

The capture of Kertch and the occupation of the Sea of Azov will greatly cripple the operations of the Russians, and as the steppe begins immediately to the north of Simpheropol if they are driven out of that place they would be very much distressed; and they would be unable to feed and supply with ammunition any large force – we have the sea open to us and we can send an infinite amount of supplies of all kinds to our armies – with us it is merely a question of expense, with the Russians it is a question as to the limits of physical possibility.

He also anticipated Kertch would end any French inclination to accept Buol's counterpoise scheme. Only Prince Albert raised the idea of sending 2,500 British troops to assist the squadron, which Stewart wanted, but it was rendered impossible by the alliance. British satisfaction was not echoed in Paris; Cowley found the

Emperor 'out of spirits', frightened this success would encourage the Generals to start more peripheral campaigns. He still believed Simpheropol to be the key. Pelissier used Kertch to increase his own standing.[16] Kertch achieved in large measure the object of the Emperor's field strategy; had it been followed by an effort against the Perekop route, success might have been achieved at the least cost. The Russians claimed the campaign was not particularly effective as the coast was not held; however, such opinions do not accord with their strenuous efforts to defend the entrance to the Don, preserve scuttled ships and keep open the routes into the Crimea. Nor does it appear to be a very objective response to the tremendous destruction. If the Azov littoral was of so little value, why did the Russians build so many earthworks, employ so many troops and put pressure on the garrison at Kertch? Among allied commentators only Slade supported their analysis.[17]

As military operations, the capture of Kertch and the subsequent control of the Sea of Azov rank among the finest achievements of the war. The combination of considered planning, irresistible force and initiative completely destroyed a position the Russians knew to be vital, and which they had eight months to defend. It was the decisive blow of 1855, leading to the battle of Tchernaya and the fall of Sevastopol, with more initiative among the Generals it offered the chance of a great strategic victory. The Russian army was the first concern of their high command. After the Alma, the city and fleet were sacrificed to keep it in the field. The destruction of the army was the greatest blow that could be inflicted in the Crimea. The allies failure to do this kept Russia in the war. The problem lay in the uncertainty of allied war aims. If the object was only to secure a European Congress for Louis Napoleon's benefit such an effort was not relevant. In the field the Russians had a tremendous respect for allied infantry firepower which, in part, made the Emperor's strategy appear sound. At Sevastopol the allied armies were playing into Russian hands, they would have achieved far more in open country. Although the statesmen and Admirals could see the advantages, the Generals were happier in the steady grind of Pelissier's trench warfare. They were taking no risks; caution and safety were the watchwords of the Crimean campaign. They had never suited the grand raid of 1854, and did not make the best use of allied advantages in 1855. Raglan's caution was characteristic; he understood what was wanted, but allowed himself to be persuaded into other methods by less able men. Simpson was prematurely aged, and dominated by Pelissier – the most determined advocate of simple, direct methods.

Notes

1 Giffard to Lyons 13, 25, 26 Feb. 1855: NRS pp. 78–9, 87–9; Armytage to Giffard 8 Mar. 1855: *ibid*. pp. 102–3.
2 OTWAY, p. 169; Moore to Lyons 26 Apr.in Lyons to Admiralty 28 Apr. 1855 no. 333: NRS pp. 126–131.
3 Canrobert to Raglan 30 Apr., 1 May 1855, Brown memo. 30 Apr., Raglan to Canrobert 1 May 1855: NRS, p. 140; Lyons to Wood 1 May 1855: Add. 49,535 f58–60.
4 OTWAY, p. 170; HIBBERT, p. 320.
5 Raglan to Lyons 4 May 1855 (03.15): NRS pp. 145–7; Raglan to Panmure 4 May 1855: PANMURE, i, pp. 182–3; Lyons to Admiralty 6 rec. 21 May 1855 no. 353 confidential: NRS pp. 133–48; Stewart to Panmure 7 May 1855: PANMURE, i, pp. 184–9; Lyons Journal 8 May 1855: ADM 50/264; PASLEY, p. 193.
6 Raglan to Panmure 8 May 1855: PANMURE, i, p. 189; Panmure to Raglan 7 May 1855: *ibid*. pp. 183–4; Wood to Lyons 7, 11 May, 28 Mar. 1855: Add. 49,49,562 f81, 85, 32; Stewart to Panmure 7 May 1855: PANMURE, i, pp. 184–9; Lyons to Wood 12 May 1855: Add. 49,535 f68–71; Wood to Grey 7 May 1855: Add. 49,562 f83.
7 Stewart to Panmure 7 May 1855: PANMURE, i, pp. 184–9; Lyons to Wood 8, 12 May 1855: Add. 49,535 f61–4, 68–71; Lyons to Raglan 11, 13 May 1855: RAGLAN 6807–299; Stewart to Lyons 11 May 1855: LYONS L288.
8 GOOCH, B., pp. 199–207.
9 Lyons to Wood 15 May 1855: Add. 49,535 f75–6; Stewart to Wood 19 May 1855: Add. 49,541 f12–18; Lyons to Admiralty 19 May rec. 6 Jun. 1855 no. 383 Confidential: NRS pp. 152–3.
10 Lyons to Raglan, Raglan to Lyons (2) 19 May 1855: RAGLAN 6807–299; Stewart to Panmure 7 May 1855: PANMURE, i, pp. 184–9; Raglan to Panmure 21 May 1855: *ibid*. pp. 202–3; Lyons to Admiralty 26 May rec. 13 Jun. 1855 no. 398: NRS p. 164; PASLEY, p. 193.
11 *Russell's Despatches from the Crimea*, ed. Bentley, N. (London, 1966), pp. 195–206; Lyons Journal 26 May 1855: ADM 50/264; Lyons to Admiralty 2 Jun. 1855 telegraph: NRS p. 176; Lyons to Raglan 2 Jun. 1855: RAGLAN 6807–299; Cowley to Clarendon 3 Jun. 1855: F.O. 519/216 f138; Wood & Panmure to Lyons 4 Jun. 1855 telegraph: NRS p. 176; Raglan to Lyons 4 Jun. 1855: RAGLAN 6807–299; Lyons to Wood 6 Jun. 1855: Add. 49,535 f97–100.
12 Clarendon to Wood 5 Jun. 1855: HALIFAX A4/57ii; Clarendon to Palmerston 5 Jun. 1855: Bdlds. GC/CL f648; Palmerston to Clarendon 7 Jun. 1855: Cl. Dep. C31 f262–3; Palmerston to Panmure 26 May 1855: PANMURE, i. pp. 211–12.

13 Lyons to Admiralty 10, 15 Jun. 1855 telegraphs: NRS pp. 185, 195; Stewart to Lyons 11 Jun. enc. in Lyons to Admiralty 11 rec. 28 Jun. 1855 no. 441: *ibid.* pp. 186–9; Lyons to Raglan 10 Jun, Raglan to Lyons 11 Jun. 1855: RAGLAN 6807–299; Lyons Journal 13, 14, 15 Jun. 1855: ADM 50/264; Wood to Lyons 12 Jun. 1855 telegraph: NRS p. 190; Wood to Clarendon 19 Jun. 1855: Cl. Dep. C29 f431.

14 For clarity the campaign in the Azov will be treated in full here rather than following a strictly chronological approach. Captain Lyons to Lyons 25 May, 3 Jun. enc. Lyons to Admiralty 2, 6 rec. 25 Jun. 1855 no. 419, 429: NRS pp. 170–6; Lyons to Admiralty 2 rec. 25 Jun. 1855 no. 420: *ibid.* p. 175; Lyons to Admiralty 7 Jun. 1855 telegraph: *ibid.* p. 185; Osborn to Lyons 15 Jun. enc. Lyons to Admiralty 23 Jun. rec. 4 Jul. 1855 no. 483: *ibid.* pp. 205–6; Van Crefeld, M., *Supplying War* (London, 1977), pp. 34, 111; Wood to Raglan 1 Jun. 1855 telegraph: NRS p. 168; Lyons to Admiralty 19 Jun. rec. 4 Jul. 1855 no. 464: NRS pp. 200–1; Wood to Lyons 4 Jun. 1855: Add. 49,562 f116.

15 Admiralty to Lyons 4 Jul. 1855 no. 428: NRS pp. 207–8; Lyons to Admiralty 7 Jul. 1855 no. 528: *ibid.* pp. 208–11, EARDLEY-WILMOT, pp. 333–5; Osborn to Lyons enc. Lyons to Admiralty 18 rec. 29 Aug: 8 rec. 26 Sep: 9 Oct. rec. 7 Nov: 1 rec. 18 Dec. 1855, no. 686, 746, 843, 962: NRS pp. 262–8, 281–90, 331–6, 418–22; Graham to Wood 1 Jun. 1855: HALIFAX A4/70.

16 Wood to Cowley 30 May 1855; F.O.519/208 f257–9; Clarendon to Palmerston 3 Jun. 1855: Bdlds. GC/CL f647; Palmerston to Clarendon 28, 30 May 1855: Cl. Dep. C31 f237, 243; Prince Albert to Panmure 28 May 1855: PANMURE, i, pp. 213–14; Cowley to Clarendon 28 May, 6 Jun. 1855: F.O. 519/216 f120, 148.

17 HAMLEY, p. 242; CURTISS, pp. 431–2; SLADE, pp. 393–5.

17

The turning point

As the campaign season opened in the Black Sea theatre political problems on two levels prevented the unfolding of Palmerston's strategy. Domestic opposition threatened to overthrow his ministry, if it could unite on any single issue, while British military weakness ensured that progress in the Crimea depended on, and had to reflect, French policies. French co-operation was also vital to the Government, forcing Palmerston to accept the Emperor's plans, despite his own, more ambitious, strategy. The Emperor's visit in April produced a paper on Crimean strategy. Palmerston was determined to move the armies into the field, if only to keep Louis Napoleon in Paris. He had to be cautious, demanding the Army had a safe line of retreat for the political consequences of defeat were unthinkable. As safety was hardly possible Panmure called for a war cabinet, including Wood. There was no cabinet, and Palmerston continued to urge an unreceptive Panmure throughout April, although far from arguing on military merit, he stressed the political imperative.[1]

The theme of political requirement was a commonplace during the Parliamentary session. Until mid April the Vienna Conference provided a smokescreen for hasty attempts to solve the Crimean impasse. Once those hopes had been disappointed, Russell returned to the House on the 30th and Palmerston knew he would have to fight. He knew the most dangerous line of attack was that of Roebuck, concentrating on incapacity and inertia, so he urged Panmure to recall Raglan's staff. Panmure was not certain this was proper, although he put pressure on Raglan. Lord Ellenborough, the Tory spokesman, adopted this line, but spoiled his attack by trying to win over the radical and peace movements, and was decisively defeated in the Lords on 14 May. Palmerston deliberately remained vague on the subject of peace, as much to hold his cabinet together as to avoid external problems. Only Clarendon, and possibly Lansdowne, knew his real war aims. Disraeli's speech on 24 May, committing the Tories to the war, ended the danger that peace could be used to attack the Government. Palmerston had a majority of 319 to 219 to continue, but that was not a mandate to act as he pleased. Professor Vincent contends Palmerston lured the Tories into a commitment by appearing weak.[2] It would perhaps be more accurate to conclude that he was weak. Disraeli's motion provided only temporary relief from pressures in cabinet, Parliament and on strategic planning. When Earl Grey's motion for peace was debated on the 28th, the Tory leaders supported the war.

In the political struggle Palmerston made use of any military success; Kertch and the Sea of Azov were a godsend. The resulting confidence led him to essay another 'decisive' Crimean strategy; with an army of 40,000 French and 30,000 Turks at Eupatoria, 60,000 could advance on Simpheropol to complete the destruction of Russian logistics. Parallels with Lyons' views are obvious; both looked for a pincer movement against the Russian supply line to clear the peninsula. The French, whose troops Palmerston was moving, had a very different idea; Louis Napoleon always treated Simpheropol as the centre of the campaign, but considered Kertch an inferior alternative. He wanted a decisive battle, the British preferred to do without. The Generals rejected both plans. Clarendon remained nervous, blaming the French for the delay before Sevastopol. Turkish weakness in cavalry precluded significant operations from Eupatoria. By early June Palmerston shared Louis Napoleon's distaste for the proceedings at Sevastopol, calling for the attack on Simpheropol from Eupatoria. The Emperor condemned Eupatoria, and without men the British were in no position to argue; they looked rather foolish, 40,000 men short of the voted establishment. Pelissier and Raglan had the last word, refusing to consider Eupatoria for lack of transport. Increasingly out of touch with his Premier, Panmure supported Raglan on most issues. Louis Napoleon wanted to recall Pelissier, but was dissuaded by Vaillant. Success at the Mamelon and Quarries did not improve his view. Palmerston, resigned to the siege, wanted to move across the head of the harbour, as suggested by Burgoyne. Panmure, alarmed at the prospect of Pelissier being recalled, tried to link his strategy with that of the Emperor, moving onto the Mackenzie Heights. Failure at the Malakhoff and Redan ended Louis Napoleon's interest, although Palmerston still hoped for field operations. Clarendon preferred waiting for the results of the Azov campaign, and keeping Pelissier. Palmerston shared the Emperor's low regard for the insubordinate General.[3]

Lacking the political and military power to carry out his strategy Palmerston had to compromise, so his Georgian plans were necessarily subordinated to the capture of Sevastopol. He still wanted to sacrifice Raglan's staff and take the field, to deflect the political pressures which had already resulted in a breakdown of relations with Panmure and applications to Wood for the use of Admiralty patronage. This also prevented him recalling Stratford, who had become even more obnoxious to the French – the Ambassador was too knowledgeable and powerful an opponent to bring home.[4]

The end of June marked a turning point. Russell's resignation removed his only serious rival for the liberal leadership, and ended the succession of crises which had interfered with the conduct of government since February. Palmerston's wider Black Sea strategy was brought back into play with the capture of Kertch and Russian pressure on Kars; he wanted to clear Georgia and Circassia, but admitted that handing the areas to the Turks would only disgust the natives. Kars was a serious problem, with nearby Ezeroum it would provide Russia with an easy *quid pro quo* for Sevastopol. He agreed with Clarendon that Omer should be sent, his troops being replaced by the British-funded Turkish units, 20,000 infantry under Vivian at Eupatoria and 3,000 horse under Beatson at Sevastopol. The French opposed this, seeing Asia Minor as a British interest linked with India. In a letter intended for French eyes, Wood stressed the importance of Asia Minor as the heartland of Ottoman rule, dismissing the Indian connection. After applying fruitless pressure at Paris Palmerston ordered Beatson's force to Eupatoria, ready for the fall of Sevastopol. Wood read letters from Lyons and Stewart to the cabinet of 8 August, with alarming descriptions of military inertia. The British commanders were ordered to assist Omer to Asia, but Louis Napoleon and Pelissier, for once in agreement, prevented his departure.[5]

Under these constraints the formation of a more ambitious grand strategy had to be subordinated to political survival and the maintenance of the French alliance. Only after success in the field could Palmerston press the war aims outlined back in March 1854. Although designed around British forces, British money and British-funded allies his plans still depended, as they always had, on the French. This had been the dangerous variable from the opening of the crisis, forcing the demands of allied solidarity to the front. Palmerston and Prince Albert shared Wood's desire for British campaigns and British interests.[6] In consequence the new strategy for the Baltic took shape before any overview of the Black Sea theatre was politically possible.

With the squadrons at Kertch Pelissier prepared his campaign, reorganising the French army and directing General Bosquet, Second Corps, to prepare for an assault. The Malakhoff was the key to the city, and the Russians could be forced out by pressure from the camp. Field operations would be considered once the city fell. Louis Napoleon had long decided Sevastopol was the only worthwhile object in the Crimea; once captured it should be destroyed, or left for the Turks. His letter to Pelissier of 30 May, containing these views, only reinforced the General's refusal to move inland. Ultimately Pelissier could always hide behind the need to preserve allied unity, and rely on Vaillant to handle the Emperor. The new round of operations began with a Russian sortie on the night of 21 May. The captured rifle pits were retaken the following night, to impress all concerned with Pelissier's resolve. On the 25th the Corps of Observation moved off the heights, crossed the Tchernaya and destroyed the Russian camp at Tchorgun, without pressing the earthworks on the Mackenzie Heights.

The Emperor bluntly ordered Pelissier to invest the city before continuing the siege; Pelissier ignored this for two days. After a heavy bombardment on 6 June, the Mamelon and Quarries were captured on the night of the 7th. These works were essential for an assault on the Malakhoff and Redan, the latter a supporting operation, to keep the British involved. Louis Napoleon was unimpressed, renewing his order on the 14th. The decisive assault was to follow quickly, too quickly for Bosquet, whose protest led to his replacement only two days before the assault. Raglan wanted a general attack, taking in several works, but Pelissier preferred a limited, specific operation, and unilaterally altered the timing of the assault at a late stage. During the 17th, allied artillery smashed down the Russian defences, ceasing at nightfall. The plan was for a two-hour resumption of fire at dawn, with an assault at 06.00; Pelissier brought the attack forward to 03.00, cutting out the bombardment. One of the French columns started too soon and the rest blundered on after them, meeting a shattering storm of grape and musketry. One column did penetrate the Malakhoff, but were driven out by

Russian infantry. Seeing his allies in trouble, Raglan launched his own column at the Redan, despite misgivings. The result was futile; the French lost 3,500, the British 1,500.

Chastened by the repulse Pelissier recalled Bosquet and accepted Raglan's view; he also promised the Emperor he would move on Simpheropol, after taking the city. As another attempt was being prepared Raglan joined the growing list of summer cholera victims, dying on 28 July. While all admitted his wisdom, Stewart saw the flaw; Raglan never insisted, never declared his views, allowing other men to dominate.[7] This had been the great defect of alliance warfare, ruining the grand raid. Raglan's good sense and tact had made up for the lack of British bayonets, held the alliance together and supported Lyons; he would be impossible to replace.

Pelissier's problems with his Emperor reached a crisis after the failure. By 3 July Louis Napoleon had decided to order him to hand over to Niel, unless he took the field immediately. However, Vaillant held up the telegraph until his master's temper had cooled; thereafter Pelissier's plans had his grudging acceptance, a shift that became more apparent as the year progressed. Anglo–French discussions on strategy produced something like consensus by 20 July, Clarendon reporting that Pelissier's plan must be followed through. On the same day Louis Napoleon sent another 15,000 men and 200 mortars, and by 2 August he joined his General in opposing Omer's request to leave for the relief of Kars.[8]

The allied squadrons returned on 15 July, only *Miranda* had seen any action. Lyons considered it essential for morale that they aid the land attack, although as nothing worthwhile could be achieved he fell back on a night bombardment plan devised by Paget and perfected by Spratt. By placing two coloured lights in Streletska Bay the ships could fire into the town when the lights coincided. They would also be under the guns of Fort Constantine, 1,200 yards away. *Valorous* tried the scheme in mid April, producing genuine surprise in Sevastopol, but once the Russians knew what to expect an accurate response could be guaranteed. Several steamers went in, and on the 23rd the two flagships were to have followed, but *Montebello*'s engines broke down. Returning from Kertch Lyons and Bruat discovered a major assault was intended for 18 July, so the Generals requested more night attacks. Ten vessels, with rocket launches, went in on the night of the 16th, Paget's battleship joining them the following night. This time the return fire took effect – three were killed and Captain Lyons badly wounded, along with thirteen others. Reporting the reverse, the Admiral noted the desire of the fleet to go under fire, a desire which led him to send in too many ships. The idea was to divert and annoy, rather than cause damage, which could be achieved by one or two ships. Sending larger forces on consecutive nights only offered the Russians a target; remaining under fire for thirty minutes was equally futile. During and after the assaults of the 18th the squadrons demonstrated off the harbour. *Miranda* was ordered down to Therapia, where Captain Lyons died on the 23rd. On the night of the 19th *Leopard* went in alone. The fleets would have been better employed elsewhere, but French attitudes and lack of troops made this impossible. Six gunboats and six mortar vessels arrived, the former went to the Azov, the latter were used at Sevastopol.[9]

Lyons was deeply affected by the death of his son, and the death of Raglan, to whom he had become greatly attached. From 26 June to the end of the war his private correspondence bore the black edges of mourning. Although he had largely recovered his spirits by September, the intervening months hampered the campaign. Bruat, with whom he was on good terms, was controlled by Pelissier and could do nothing for a maritime campaign. Outside the Azov the squadrons were still bound hand and foot to the armies, constant demands for transport and supplies left few vessels to spare. Some relief came from opening Circassia as a source of bullocks and vegetables, in place of Sinope. The detached cruisers were rotated, apart from *Highflyer*, which was kept on the Circassian coast to exploit Moore's expertise. Balaklava was turned over to Rear-Admiral Charles Fremantle, the youngest unemployed flag officer. Initially Lyons was hostile, and Fremantle disgusted at being misled as to the nature of his post. Heath resigned, having been passed over twice. Fortunately Fremantle proved resourceful and diligent, establishing good relations with Lyons. Lushington, Senior Officer of the Naval Brigade, received his flag and turned over to Keppel. Fleet manpower was becoming critical, forty stokers had to be sent out for the gunboats. While naval recruiting was going well the Board had other plans for those men, wanting the Naval Brigade afloat once the city fell, if not before.[10]

While the siege continued the naval role was limited. Heavy guns were sent out in *Powerful* to replace those worn out by constant firing, but only the mortar vessels could fire on the city, and their weapons would have been better employed ashore. Pelissier had become very enthusiastic for bombarding the city, as distinct from the defences. At the Headquarters conference of 4 August he over-ruled Jones and Niel's call for an early assault in favour of bringing up more mortars. By destroying the city he hoped to reduce the number of troops that could be held in reserve south of the harbour. Lyons had been calling for the city to be attacked from the start of the siege, as opposed to the grand raid. The failure of 18 June persuaded Pelissier of the need, and two steam frigates were sent for mortars, *Gladiator* went to Corfu between 4 and 18 July, collecting eight, *Terrible* left for Gibralter on the 6th, only returning on 7 September. At the conference on 11 August Pelissier insisted on waiting for mortars, rejecting Lyons' call for an attack into the heart of the peninsula. After the battle of the Tchernaya the Russians built a bridge of boats 15–20 feet wide across the harbour, completed on the 25th. The pessimists ashore saw it as a method of speeding up the reinforcement of the city; Lyons realised it was a preparation for retreat.[11]

The apparent inactivity of the fleets up to the fall of Sevastopol reflected several difficulties. While the majority reflected the primacy of military operations, others demonstrated the weakness of available forces. Lyons had enough cruisers to keep up the blockade, enough flotilla craft to control the Azov, and nine battleships, six of them steamers. While the Russians had a small force at Sevastopol a covering squadron was needed, but not one of such power; four British battleships, with one or two French and four cruisers would have been perfectly adequate. However, the fleets were short of flotilla craft, battleships were of little use for coast attack. With his flotilla in the Azov, and no troops, Lyons could not act; when he did undertake a major operation, significantly after the fall of Sevastopol, he had to recall the gunboats from the Azov and withdraw several cruisers. Even then the operation only had value because troops were available to follow up the naval attack. There were no suitable targets that did not require troops. The need was recognised, but a large proportion of the marines were still at Balaklava.

The French reinforced their Euxine flotilla, but this did not please Wood. He had come to favour Baltic operations, but the October programme was an allied effort. By mid May it was clear the French would send their vessels to the Euxine. When Wood protested Hamelin, now Minister of Marine, claimed the Emperor had no desire for a serious Baltic campaign; Walewski blamed Clarendon, who had told him back in February there would be no major operations. Wood pointed out that the floating batteries were not wanted for the Bug or the Danube, but Cowley reported they were being sent at Bruat's request for those operations. Wood was annoyed; drawn to attempt the Graham/Sulivan Baltic strategy he lacked the resources. Cowley obtained six gunboats, and pressed for batteries and mortar vessels. Only the latter were sent, on the pretext that Penaud did not want batteries. Wood wished the British batteries had never been built, but the mood passed.[12] The lesson was clear; the Baltic had become a British theatre, but the Baltic fleet was, relatively, weaker than that in the Black Sea. Nothing could be done about this before Sevastopol fell; until then Wood had to make the best use of available forces.[13]

In the Black Sea theatre Kertch had been the vital operation, but there were other important targets, including Odessa. Hamilton Seymour believed Nicolaiev was open, while Stratford obtained a map of the Bug as far inland as the arsenal. Circassia was clear, but Russian communications were second only to Sevastopol. Wood wanted a more active campaign, and hoped to prevent the Russian army leaving the Crimea, and to this end even the Putrid Sea should be occupied. He knew Pelissier would ensure there were no more 'external' operations in the immediate future, calling on Lyons to reduce the number of steam transports held in the theatre for strategic lift. After the failure of 18 June he pressed for more active naval operations. Lyons and Raglan hoped to exploit allied strategic mobility, but later French demands were used to keep the transports in place.[14] With Lyons in low spirits Stewart temporarily became the First Lord's correspondent, noting the benefits arising from the end of the Vienna conference. However, Stewart remained Panmure's confidant, stressing the essential nature of the Azov and Don. The munitions factory at Lugar, and stores collected at Rostov, were the most important targets; with 1,500 British troops they could be destroyed. He did not want to trouble Odessa, unless it could be occupied, and shared the maritime strategist's desire to close the Isthmus of Perekop.[15] Underlying his good sense was an anxiety to command, but Lyons hardly allowed him out of sight all year.

As Lyons' spirits revived his discussions with Wood became more direct. He persuaded Bruat to consider Odessa, once the French mortar vessels arrived, while Wood urged attacks on the Perekop

road, which he observed the Russians were trying to macadamize.
When the Emperor finally accepted Pelissier's strategy Clarendon
urged Palmerston to press Wood and Panmure to provide transport
for 200 mortars and 15,000 troops, but the service ministers were
more interested in bombarding the city. By late July Lyons was
complaining of Pelissier's secrecy and, like Canrobert before him, of
packing the heights with troops. Lyons calculated there were already
80,000 men spare and wanted to land some on the southern coast to
march on Batschi Serai, in a manner reminiscent of the Emperor's
Aloushta scheme. Pelissier refused.[16] Both Wood and Lyons were
hamstrung by the same factors that constrained the development of
Palmerston's grand strategy. The French prevented the redistri-
bution of forces to the Baltic, and stopped any 'external' operations
in the Euxine. This tied the squadrons to the armies, and ignored the
interests of Turkey and Britain in Asia Minor. All this was in spite of
the demands of the Emperor, of many in the French army, of the
British Government and armed forces, and the Turks and Sardinians.
The lessons were obvious, but unfortunately they were old lessons
which pointed up old difficulties and had no simple solutions, particularly in a war with so many political tensions. The British response, led by Wood, was a gradual shift toward single nation operations, and even this was not ideal as it would deprive the British of
any influence over the French. After the death of Raglan this was no
longer important.

The failure of 18 June and the death of Raglan placed the British
Government under renewed pressure. Pelissier's policy, having won
grudging approval, was thrown into doubt, while the command of
the British Army became a major issue. Palmerston still saw moving
onto the Mackenzie Heights as the 'intelligent' alternative to
attrition, but Panmure preferred to combine it with an assault. He
had reports that the Russians had only 130,000 men in the Crimea,
and 50,000 of them were in hospital, as a result of the Azov campaign.[17] The command posed problems. Brown, Raglan's second,
had been invalided home, leaving Simpson to take over. Panmure,
with the Duke of Cambridge, wanted to keep him, anticipating he
would be more pliable than Raglan, but Palmerston and Clarendon
wanted more proof of his ability. Palmerston favoured Campbell,
but Raglan's opinion that he was too excitable helped Panmure
secure Simpson, although he then felt obliged to call on the new
commander to justify his appointment. Those on the spot knew

Simpson was inadequate; Simpson himself complained of poor health and lack of faith in the task in hand. He wanted to be superseded by 'some general of distinction'. Lyons and Stewart went straight to Headquarters on learning of Raglan's death to stiffen his resolve, but they realised he would be no match for Pelissier; within a week they noted he had grown older than his years. The alternatives, Campbell apart, were hardly inspiring; Sir Richard England was the ranking second, but only Simpson favoured him. The Admirals preferred Sir William Codrington, elder brother of the Baltic Captain, or Harry Jones.[18] The Queen favoured Codrington, having been lobbied by his sisters. On 14 July the cabinet called for a report on Codrington's health, but four days later Panmure secured Simpson, with Codrington as his second. The Queen insisted that Campbell be placated with the promise of India; the inconvenient England was ordered to Malta. Stewart called on both service ministers to replace the feeble Simpson immediately. Under the dominance of Pelissier Simpson became increasingly despondent, calling for the evacuation of the Crimea. Panmure urged him to accept the task or resign.[19] Simpson did neither. Despite the protests of the Admirals Simpson never held out against Pelissier, but the real problem was Panmure. His stolid temperament defied all efforts to introduce a sense of urgency into the proceedings, yet Palmerston's political position was not strong enough to stand the dismissal of a leading orthodox Whig, even when Panmure gave him a perfect excuse. On 29 June he made an unauthorised statement in the Lords, doubling army field pay. Palmerston's initial 'incivil' letter was withdrawn the following day, despite a strong feeling against Panmure in the cabinet. The compromise extra 6d. a day only increased drunkenness. Panmure's defiance was a major problem for Palmerston.[20] No amount of prodding could achieve results, for Panmure was as cautious as the Generals, and supported them against the Government. A Secretary for War either more pliable, or more intelligent, would have been invaluable; a Prime Minister unable to change his team must be content to be ruled by them. This encouraged a concentration on diplomatic activity, for Clarendon could be relied on. Even there the cabinet proved troublesome, restricting Palmerston's freedom of action.

The siege resumed, pressing closer to the Malakhoff and Redan. While the latter was only a supporting gesture, Simpson continued the work, and accepted Pelissier's shift back to partial attacks. A major Russian sortie on the night of 16–17 July was beaten back. The mortars began to flatten the city, firing night and day, wearing down the defenders, just as many in the allied camps began to think of another winter outside the city. Pelissier meant to drive the Russians out by bombardment and limited assaults. Inside the city the deaths of Admirals Nakhimov and Istomine and a serious wound to Totleben, left the garrison short of resolute leadership. Gorchakov realised the position was hopeless back in March, but continued to feed in reinforcements. Finally Alexander II ordered him to attack the allied positions. Reinforced by over 20,000 men in two fresh divisions he elected to attack across the Traktir bridge on the Tchernaya, with a possible sortie by the garrison. He did not anticipate success. With the field army weakened by the Azov campaign he could not mount any sustained pressure on the heavily defended allied flank. His only credible gesture was an assault, but outnumbered at least three to two that would be expensive and futile. The allies were aware of the new troops. Anticipating an attack on the Tchernaya, and a sortie, Simpson put off a planned rest aboard *Royal Albert* on 13 August. This was no display of military genius as the options were limited. However, nothing was done to exploit the inevitable repulse.

At 04.00 on the 16th two formations of infantry and artillery under Generals Read and Liprandi moved up to the Franco–Sardinian positions. Read, misunderstanding his orders, crossed the Traktir bridge and launched an impossible assault uphill against well-prepared artillery and rifle positions on the Feduikhine Heights. A leak in the Russian Embassy at Berlin provided several hours' warning, and by 08.00 the Russians were in full retreat, with up to 10,000 casualties. There was no sortie, the allied preparations were too imposing for Gorchakov to order another futile gesture. His generalship had been as faulty as Menshikov's, making no attempt to control the battle. After the battle Gorchakov decided to evacuate the city, realising that by holding out he was only delaying the inevitable, at tremendous cost. The first sign of this was the pontoon bridge across the harbour. A convalescent Totleben was directed to plan the evacuation.[21]

Pelissier's determination to press on with the siege precluded any attempt to follow up the defeated enemy, although suitable forces were available. The dominant French General had achieved a victory in the field, creating a tenuous link between his strategy and that of the Emperor. The morale effect of the battle on both sides was considerable. While the Russian field army could press the allied flank some relief could be brought to the city. This linkage, established by Menshikov, broke down when the army could no longer maintain a credible threat. Although not entirely free from concern, Pelissier could press on with the final assault, and three weeks after the battle the city fell. The effect of this flank pressure on Canrobert and Pelissier can be quantified. Both felt obliged to crowd every available man onto the heights, fearing another Inkerman. This stopped any wider operations from Eupatoria, or elsewhere, and led directly to the fall of Kars. Louis Napoleon could not overrule his General and the British did not have the military strength to press their own strategy.

Having prepared to evacuate the city, Gorchakov had a change of heart, resolving to stand one more assault. After the Tchernaya the allied bombardment resumed on an unprecedented scale, over 400 guns and mortars rained projectiles down without cease between 17 and 27 August. Russian casualties were in excess of 1,000 a day. The following week was taken up restocking the magazines, and advancing the saps and parallels. When firing recommenced on 5 September, it was concentrated on the Malakhoff, Redan, Little Redan and Bastion du Mat; against the Malakhoff it was quite irresistible – guns, carriages and embrasures were smashed, gunners and reinforcements killed and the gabions and fascines set alight. Hardly a gun in the key Russian bastion remained serviceable, and there was little point bringing up more as the embrasures had collapsed. On 6 and 7 September the allies fired some 52,000 rounds; the Russians replied with 20,000 and another 2,500 Russian casualties were incurred.

On the 8th heavy firing continued from day-break until 09.00, and it then fell away until 11.20 when it resumed with a new level of intensity, ceasing suddenly at noon. French troops then rushed across the last twenty-five yards separating them from the Malakhoff, and within ten minutes their colours had been established. Pelissier had selected the time to coincide with the changing of the guard, the relieved men actually had to leave the works before their reliefs could enter. This was the centre-piece of the assault, but three more works were attempted, although only after the Malakhoff had been captured. They were a diversion, and after initial success powerful columns of Russian infantry drove out the allies. However these efforts delayed attempts to recapture the Malakhoff, a failure of Russian command. By 16.00 Gorchakov gave up hope of re-entering the position. Sevastopol was lost. Casualties were high, 13,000 Russian and 10,000 allied. Galvanised by defeat, he decided to evacuate while the French were still expecting another counter-attack. Leaving a rearguard screen he ordered the army out at 17.00, by 19.00 the task was well in hand. Fuses were laid to all magazines, to explode the following day, and where possible guns and stores were thrown into the harbour. By 08.00 on the 9th the last elements were across the bridge, which was dismantled and towed to the north shore. The last six battleships were burnt.

The squadrons played a very minor role, although it had been intended that they would move in at noon to attack the Quarantine Fort, which enfiladed the left French attack. Even the sailing ships would be used, *Queen* lashed alongside *Leopard*. On the day a north-westerly gale blew up, causing a heavy swell to run close inshore, at 10.30 Stewart advised against using the heavy ships; their role was limited and he had no desire to manoeuvre in 'close company with our allies'. The only naval force to join were the six British mortar vessels and four French mortar brigs, moored in Streletska Bay, which kept up a steady fire on the Quarantine Fort from 08.00 to 19.30. On the following day fires and explosions made the town unsafe, but the allied fleet, noting the five steamers were still afloat, formed a cordon from the Belbec to Streletska. These precautions were kept up until the 12th when the Russian steamers, collected under Fort Constantine, were set alight, burning from 03.30 to 07.00. The last elements of the Russian Black Sea fleet had been destroyed. With nothing left in the harbour but wreckage, Lyons was anxious to begin work elsewhere, sending four steamers to Eupatoria in case the Russians attacked on their way out of the Crimea. Other cruisers carried the news around the coast. The strategic problem was how the Navy could exploit absolute command of the sea, and its release from subservience to the Army. The latter point was symbolised by re-embarking the Naval Brigade, although the marines were still ashore. Without troops the fleets could do little.[22]

Notes

1 Palmerston to Clarendon 30 Apr. 1855: Cl. Dep. C31 f158–61; Panmure to Palmerston 1 May 1855: Bdlds. GC/CL f101; Palmerston to

Panmure 16 May 1855: PANMURE, i, p. 201.
2   Panmure to Raglan 15, 23 Apr. 1855: *ibid.* pp. 149–50, 164–6;
Palmerston to Panmure 1, 8 May 1855: *ibid.* pp. 180, 190–2; VINCENT,
pp. 42–3.
3   Palmerston to Clarendon 30 May, 2, 22, 25, 27 Jun. 1855: Cl. Dep.
C31 f243–4, 251–2, 278–89, 294–9; Cowley to Clarendon 25, 28 May, 3,
15, 22 Jun. 1855: F.O. 519/216 f114–16, 120–5, 128, 133, 172, 188–9;
Clarendon to Palmerston 28, 29 May, 4, 22 Jun. 1855: Bdlds. GC/CL
f640–3, PANMURE, i, p. 225, Bdlds. GC/Cl f655; Panmure to Raglan 8, 18
Jun. 1855: PANMURE, i, pp. 226–7, 242–4; Palmerston to Panmure 10, 21
Jun. 1855: *ibid.* pp. 231–7, 247.
4   Palmerston to Wood 5 Jun. 1855: HALIFAX A4/63 f29; Palmerston
to Clarendon 2 Jun. 1855: Cl. Dep. C31 f251.
5   Wood to Stewart 14 Jul. 1855: Add. 49,563 f59; Clarendon to Palmerston 29 Jun. 16 Jul. 8 Aug. 1855: Bdlds. GC/CL f650, 669, 677;
Palmerston to Clarendon 12, 19 Jul. 2, 3, 30 Aug. 1855: Cl. Dep. C31
f322–3, 349, 373, 381–6, 421–3; Palmerston to Panmure 23 Jul. 16 Aug.
1855: PANMURE, i p. 311, Add. 48,579 f43–4; Panmure to Palmerston 3
Aug. 1855: Bdlds. GC/PA f113; Panmure to the Queen 31 Jul. 1855:
PANMURE, i pp. 324–5; Wood to Cowley 5 Aug. 1855: F.O. 519/208
f333–40; Cowley to Clrendon 29 Aug. 1855: F.O. 519/217 f16.
6   Palmerston to Clarendon 20 Jul. 1855: Cl. Dep. C31 f345.
7   GOOCH, B., pp. 202–30; HIBBERT, pp. 338–42; Stewart to Panmure 30 Jun. 1855: PANMURE, i, pp. 258–64.
8   Cowley to Clarendon 5 Jul. 1855: F.O. 519/216 f216–21; Clarendon
to Palmerston 20 Jul. 1855: Bdlds. GC/CL f345; GOOCH, B., p. 234.
9   OTWAY, pp. 162–9; EARDLEY-WILMOT, pp. 307–10, 314–17;
SPRATT, SPR1/3; Lyons to Admiralty 17, 21 Apr. 19 Jun. rec. 2, 4 May 4
Jul. 1855 no. 304, 312, 462: NRS pp. 118–20, 123–4, 199–200; Lyons
Journal 19, 25 Jul. 1855: ADM 50/264; Wood to Lyons 23 Jun. 1855: Add.
49,563 f22.
10   Lyons to Wood 19 Jun. 1855: Add. 49,535 f112–8; PARRY, A., *The
Admirals' Fremantle* (London, 1971), pp. 176–95; Stewart to Wood 4 Sept.
1855 Add. 49,541 f67–72; Admiralty to Lyons 22 Jul. 6 Aug. 1855 no. 745,
856: Journal entry ADM 50/264 and NRS pp. 251–4.
11   Lyons to Admiralty 31 Jul. 25 Aug. rec. 13 Aug. 5 Sep. 1855 no. 624,
717: *ibid.* pp. 239–41, 270–1; Lyons to Wood 4, 11, 25 Aug. 1855: Add.
49,536 f1–4, 17, 73–93; Lyons Journal 16, 25 Aug. 1855: ADM 50/264.
12   Wood to Cowley 14 May, 9, 19, 23 Jun. 3 Jul. 1855: Add. 49,562
f88, 49,563 f13–14, F.O. 519/208 f293–300, 305–11, 321–3; Cowley to
Wood 15 May 15 Jun. 1855: F.O. 519/216 f92, 173–4; Cowley to Clarendon 18 May 1855: *ibid.* f96–100.
13   Wood to Cowley 25 May 1855: Add. 49,562 f103; Wood to Lyons
25 May 1855: *ibid.* f103.
14   Wood to Lyons 1, 4, 15, 23 Jun. 1855: *ibid.* f112, 116, 49,563 f10,
22; Lyons to Admiralty 23 Jun. rec. 11 Jul. 1855 no. 479: NRS pp. 203–4;
Lyons to Wood 24 Jul. 1855: Add. 49,535 f188–93.
15   Stewart to Wood 26 Jun. 7, 24 Jul. 1855: Add. 49,541 f28–50;

Wood to Stewart 14 Jul. 1855: Add. 49,563 f59; Stewart to Panmure 17 Jul. 1855: PANMURE, i, pp. 296–303.
    16   Lyons to Wood 7, 17, 21, 28 Jul. 1855: Add. 49,535 f160, 182–5, 188–93, 198–202; Wood to Lyons 14, 23 , 30 Jul. 1855: Add. 49,563 f59, 71, 79; Clarendon to Palmerston 22 Jul. 1855: Bdlds. GC/CL f671; Clarendon to Wood 22 Jul. 1855: HALIFAX A4/57ii f79; Panmure to Simpson 23 Jul. 1855: PANMURE, i, pp. 310–11.
    17   Panmure to Palmerston 21 Jun. 1855: *ibid.* pp. 247–8; Panmure to Raglan 23 Jun. 1855: *ibid.* pp. 249–50.
    18   Cambridge to Panmure 30 Jun. 1855: *ibid.* pp. 255–6; Panmure to Palmerston 30 Jun. 1855: Bdlds. GC/PA f107; Clarendon to Palmerston 30 Jun. 1855: *ibid.* GC/CL f660; ARGYLL, Duke of, *Autobiography and Memoirs* (London, 1906, two vols.), i, pp. 385–7; Panmure to Simpson 2 Jul. 1855: PANMURE, i, pp. 271–2; Simpson to Panmure 30 Jun. 1855: *ibid.* pp. 256–7; Stewart to Panmure 30 Jun. 1855: *ibid.* pp. 258–64; Stewart to Wood 7 Jul. 1855: Add. 49,541 f35–41; Lyons to Wood 10 Jul. 1855: Add. 49,535 f180–1.
    19   The Queen to Panmure 12, 19 Jul. 1855: PANMURE, i, pp. 286, 304; Stewart to Panmure 17 Jul. 1855: *ibid.* pp. 296–303; Stewart to Wood 28 Jul. 1855: Add. 49,541 f51–8; Panmure to Simpson 28 Jul. 1855: PANMURE, i, pp. 316–17.
    20   FITZMAURICE, Lord E., *The Life of Granville George Leveson Gower; Second Earl Granville, 1815–1891* (London, 1905, two vols.), i, pp. 137, 114–15; ARGYLL, i, pp. 533–4; Palmerston to Panmure 14 Aug.1855; Bdlds GC/PA f108
    21   Simpson to Panmure 14 Aug. 1855: PANMURE, i, pp. 347–8; Lord Augustus Loftus (Ambassador in Berlin) to Clarendon 15 Aug. 1855: *ibid.* p. 348; pp. 440–4.
    22   CURTISS, pp. 444–57; GIFFARD, p. 159; MENDS, p. 295; Stewart to Lyons 8 Sept. 1855: LYONS B39/2; Lyons to Admiralty 10, 18 Sept. rec. 26 Sept. 8 Oct. 1855 no. 753, 785: NRS pp. 291–4, 306; Lyons to Admiralty 12 rec. 13 Sept. and Lyons to Wood 14 rec. 15 Sept. 1855 Telegraphs: *ibid.* p. 279; Lyons to Wood 10 Sept. 1855: Add. 49,535 f145–7.

18

After Sevastopol

British politicians and Admirals agreed that further operations were vital after the fall of Sevastopol, without loss of time. Marshal Pelissier and Simpson were quite happy to rest, and there were good reasons for temporary inaction. Disorganised by the year-long siege the armies required a period to reform and prepare for the winter, and neither the Army nor the Government could afford another logistics disaster. This tended to cancel out the political pressure for movement. Finally, the Russians held a powerful position, the north side of the harbour was unassailable, the heights stretching from the head of the harbour to the sea east of Balaklava were covered with field works, apparently containing a significant army. Pelissier had no idea where the main Russian army was; he expected them to retire, and would pursue them. Simpson concurred, having no plan of his own. Both rejected the risky strategy of dividing the army for amphibious operations, or a new line of attack from Eupatoria.[1]

The consensus in the British cabinet favoured driving the Russians out of the Crimea, although Wood's plan to cut them off at Perekop was not raised. It was assumed the 29,000-strong Turco–Egyptian garrison at Eupatoria would be reinforced and take the field. No definite plan was ordered, although suggestions were made, and pressure applied. Relying on Pelissier's reports Vaillant opposed an attempt on the Mackenzie Heights, preferring Eupatoria. The Emperor disagreed, although Palmerston considered his objections were based on 'pique'. Despite his low opinion of Pelissier and Simpson, Palmerston left the decision to them: 'if they think it good and practicable they will adopt it; and if they do not think it so, we should not take on ourselves the responsibility of overruling them'. Burgoyne opposed any flank move from Eupatoria, convinced the Russians must retreat, and once past Simpheropol their supply line would collapse. His only fear was that they might attempt to gild the disaster with a battle. In this he agreed with Pelissier. Both failed to see that Russia valued her army more than the Crimea, and would be harder hit by defeat in battle than any loss of territory.[2] However Burgoyne was no longer in favour with Palmerston or Panmure. His simple approach ignored the political imperatives that forced Palmerston to call for a rapid campaign.

Pelissier refused to move against the Russian positions, claiming he had intelligence of a withdrawal. The Emperor was already in favour of shifting the scene of operations to Bessarabia. Once again Palmerston's strategy, which depended on the movement of allied forces, had to bend to the will of Louis Napoleon and accept Pelissier's policy. Wood realised that nothing short of exhaustion would force Russia to submit, sharing the cabinet view that clearing the Crimea and Georgia were British aims, the former to complete the destruction of Russian seapower, the latter to form the buffer state between Russia, Persia and Turkey. More immediately, the cabinet wanted to send Omer to relieve Kars.[3] Plans to operate in separate theatres and inaction in the Crimea reflected the increasing divergence between Paris and London after mid-September. On the 17th Panmure tried bluff cajolery to stir Simpson, pointing to the Plain of Baidar as the route to turn the Mackenzie Heights and move on Simpheropol. In the light of Pelissier's promotion he accepted Prince Albert's view that the armies should be separated. Palmerston became resigned to inaction, turning his attention to such petty details as trophies, policing the city and collecting old guns. Following Stewart, Albert called for a force to be put aboard the fleet, to destroy Nicolaiev or Kherson, or bombard Odessa. Palmerston agreed, claiming these options were covered by the latest instructions to Simpson, which was not true. However, the imperative for action remained. Private letters from Lyons and Newcastle produced a powerful effect on the cabinet, leading to strong calls for action, both to Paris and to Simpson. This danger, political rather than strategic, led Panmure to demand action:

The dispatches of the 15th disappoint us. They give no details or information as to the enemy and no guide as to their designs – The subsequent telegraphic communications are equally silent.
  The public are getting impatient to know what the Russians are about – The government desire immediately to be informed whether either you or Pelissier have taken any steps whatever to ascertain this, and further to observe that nearly 3 weeks have elapsed in absolute idleness, this cannot go on and in justice to yourself and your army you must prevent it. Answer this on its

receipt.[4]

Simpson resigned. Palmerston, considering this 'fortunate', wanted to appoint Campbell, but had no support in cabinet. Codrington was selected, even though he was implicated in the second failure before the Redan. Eventually the Government settled on the worst possible situation – Simpson remained in command until early November.[5]

The only active measures of September were carried out by the French. They extended their right flank on to the Plain of Baidar, but encountered formidable defences in the hills. Then 2,000 cavalry under General D'Allonville went up to Eupatoria for strategic reconnaissance. At Pelissier's request Lyons took the entire fleet to Balaklava, pretended to embark an army and then joined Bruat on an excursion to Eupatoria on the 22nd to 24th. The cabinet were unimpressed by the sham, but had nothing better to offer. On the 29th D'Allonville led his three regiments south to the village of Sak and, supported by allied steamers, attacked and drove off eighteen squadrons of Russian regular cavalry, with Cossacks, and captured six guns, 200 horses and camels, fourteen wagons and 100 prisoners. However, this did not provide much information; instead *Terrible* cruised along the coast from Sevastopol to the Bosphorus. Furthermore, D'Allonville's action did nothing to alleviate the chronic shortage of water at Eupatoria. Further sorties on 22–25 and 27–29 October found the Russians strongly dug in behind the village, unwilling to risk combat in the open. Both sorties were hampered by lack of water for the horses. When the allies moved again the Russians had decamped inland.[6] The Russian forces were well handled in the skirmishes around Sak; their object was almost certainly to cover a well, vital to the allied advance, and destroyed before the withdrawal. D'Allonville considered shortage of water prevented any wider movement against Russian communications; Simpson only reinforced the British cavalry in time to withdraw.

Lyons wanted to reinforce his hold on the Azov by clearing the eastern end of the Crimea. After a fruitless conference he telegraphed home calling for 16,000 men to be landed at Kaffa, to capture Fort Arabat. Pelissier refused to divide his army on the 13th, saw no benefit at Kaffa and would not discuss Odessa without reference to Paris. Bruat suggested Kinburn, but Lyons was unimpressed, unless it was held over the winter. He was ready to open Sevastopol harbour, where a passage had been found, if the Russians retreated, although he began to doubt they would as the Star Fort would still command the waterway.[7] The harbour would solve allied supply problems, explaining his desire to clear the northern cliffs. While the Russians remained, the harbour was no more than a wide ditch separating two armies.

Operations in the Azov continued. Wood, convinced the Russians had a flotilla hidden on the Don ready to throw supplies into the Crimea, wanted Osborn to hold on until the ice formed. Lyons was more concerned for Kertch, after Simpson tried to remove the Anglo–French units. Fortunately he secured Pelissier's support, but even so anxiety for the vital choke-point was a major factor in allied preparations for the winter. Wood, already making plans for the next Baltic campaign, believed Kherson and Nicolaiev were the best targets, dismissing Kaffa before he received Lyons' views. He wanted the allies to operate in separate sectors, the British east of the Crimea, the French to the west. The priority was to drive the Russians out of Asia Minor; Lyons was to find a suitable base, and consider attacking Rostov.[8] The needs of the Baltic led him to request the return of any spare flotilla craft. Lyons insisted he would require those he had, and those building at Malta, just to keep control of the Azov. Other units were withdrawn. *London, Rodney, Albion, Wasp* and *Niger* went to Malta, to demonstrate off Naples; *Queen* replaced *Albion* in the Bosphorus. If the mortar vessels and anticipated floating batteries were not required they were also to be sent home. *Sans Pareil*, with spare mortars from the Baltic, was recalled.[9]

The Russians had serious problems. The hospitals at Batschi Serai and Simpheropol were overcrowded, the invalids being sent overland to southern Russia, an eight-day journey by cart to Kherson. Epidemics of typhus and cholera were only checked in April 1856. The impact on this sick and demoralised army of a significant attack anywhere between Eupatoria and Odessa would be difficult to calculate; at the very least it would have caused further heavy losses in manpower. Alexander II refused to admit defeat, even at Sevastopol, ordering Gorchakov to hold his new positions, prepare for a possible attack by Austria and look for gaps in the allied flank. The Council of War in mid-September approved these policies. He then visited the war zone, including the Crimea, Odessa and Nicolaiev. Another Council at Nicolaiev resolved to stay in the Crimea until defeated in battle.[10]

British pressure on the Emperor to achieve a more active policy in the Crimea eventually bore fruit. Louis Napoleon had long considered Sevastopol would be enough for the campaign in the Crimea, while Pelissier's report on the lack of water at Eupatoria ended any discussion of field operations from that base. Instead he sent the Marshal a résumé of the options: force the Mackenzie Heights, land at Eupatoria and Kaffa for attacks on Perekop and Arabat respectively, clear the Caucasus, attack Kherson or land 100,000 men in Bessarabia. Finally a telegraph of 26th September ordered the least of all the proposed operations, the capture of Fort Kinburn. Pelissier called a conference for the 29th. Cowley, only informed on the 28th, was pressed for British support. The French argued that as Kinburn commanded the confluence of the Bug and the Dnieper its occupation would interrupt communications between Odessa, Nicolaiev and Kherson, and might even force the Russians out of the Crimea. Palmerston, informed by Persigny on the 27th, did not 'see the very great advantage of occupying the point in question, but at all events it commands the entrance to Nicolaiev'. He would recommend it to the commanders, 'leaving it to them, to decide as to undertaking it or not'.[11] On the 28th Palmerston, Panmure, Wood and Clarendon approved the plan, to the satisfaction of the Emperor. Wood was not happy. Although Kinburn was the key to Nicolaiev, it was a French object, intended to open the way for their 1856 campaign in Bessarabia. He advised Lyons to ensure they garrisoned the place, linking the operation with a bombardment of Odessa. While Lyons reported the allied commanders accepted the plan, and hoped to bombard Odessa later, he favoured Kaffa, though both were inadequate in the existing situation. Less than two months before he had condemned the idea of attacking Kinburn without taking enough troops to reach Nicolaiev, for to act otherwise would warn the Russians. Only a desire to end the 'lamentable inaction' of Pelissier and Simpson could explain his change of heart; he realised they saw it as a final sop to their governments before the season ended. With 8,000 troops the Fort could be taken, but no thought was given to ascending the Bug or Dnieper. The decision was French, both at a strategic and theatre level, adopted by the British for the want of anything else. Captain Loring, *Furious*, had been off Kinburn for some time, claiming it was almost as strong as Sevastopol, which was nonsense.[12] The Fort was a moderate sand and stone work, at sea level, on a sand spit that masked Dnieper Bay; it was not a commanding casemate work, it lacked the artillery power of Sevastopol, and housed only a fraction of its garrison.

Had Kinburn been a British initiative the object would have been the destruction of Nicolaiev; Kherson, without a major dockyard, was of less interest. The position was valuable to the Russians; before the construction of railways in the 1860s the two rivers were the major means of transport in southern Russia. Kinburn and Fort Ochakov on the opposite shore had been built to shelter coastal and riverine shipping from allied cruisers. With no consideration of how to exploit the success of the plan, Kinburn was almost unequalled in strategic futility; Panmure saw its only value was to give the Navy some work.[13] By contrast it was the best handled operation of the war, a model of maritime power projection.

Before the operation could begin Lyons recalled the flotilla, which reached Kazatch on 4th October, leaving Osborn only five vessels in the Azov. The military force was fixed at 8,000, half from each army with a 950-man brigade of marines under Colonel Hurdle. General Bazaine was in overall command, with General Spencer leading the British troops; the 17th, 20th, 31st, 57th and 63rd regiments. The marines embarked aboard *St Jean d'Acre* at Balaklava on the evening of the 3rd, the other units at Kazatch. As ever, the first step was a survey. Both Admirals sent their officers. Spratt left Kazatch on the 5th with orders to rendezvous off Odessa on the 9th. The allied fleets, each thirty-five strong, departed at 11.00 on the 7th, leaving the Captain of the *Megeara* as the senior officer afloat, the reserve squadron having departed. In Lyons' absence command devolved on to Fremantle, who had pressing reasons to stay at Balaklava. The fleets anchored off Odessa during the afternoon of the 8th, where they would remain until the 14th. Spratt reached Kinburn at 23.15 on the 5th, spending the next four days and nights surveying before rejoining the fleet at midnight on the 9th, with a detailed plan of attack. With thirty-five feet of water within 1,200 yards of the spit, the battleships could come into action. The French surveyors, backed by existing Russian charts, claimed the water was too shallow. Anxious for a grand attack with all arms, Lyons accepted Spratt's offer to return. Spratt confirmed his findings at Kinburn on the 11th. The details of the operation were finalised; Bazaine's troops would occupy the neck of the spit and Stewart would lead a force into Kinburn Bay, isolating the fort. Gunboats and mortar vessels would then bombard the forts before the battleships closed in.

Lying off Odessa the weather had been far from ideal and a heavy swell and westerly gales made landing operations impossible. Bruat was pleased. He was waiting for the three floating batteries, then under repair at Kazatch; the first reached the Crimea on 12th September, the others on the 29th. The fleets eventually weighed on the 14th, anchoring off Kinburn soon after 14.00. Spratt, his lieutenant and sailing master spent the next two days laying buoys and piloting vessels into the bay. During the first night eight gunboats went in. At 09.00 on the 15th the troops and marines landed two miles south of the fort under the direction of Giffard, *Leopard*. Once ashore they dug a double line of trenches to cut off the garrison, and oppose any attempt at relief. In the evening the mortar vessels and cruisers tried the range, but the following day a heavy swell prevented all but an occasional shell being thrown in. Spratt then discovered the French had moved his buoys for the battleship attack; Stewart was furious, but thought it best not to raise the issue with Bruat.[14]

The significance of 17 October was not lost on Mends. He anticipated a more successful day's work than the previous year. During the early morning Spratt rebuoyed the battleship approaches for the second time as the French had twice moved his marks further out. As Bruat had only four of the line it was considered polite to send one of the British ships down to the end of the spit, leaving nine positions a cable and a quarter (250 yards) apart, 1,200 yards from the main fort. To turn and anchor in such a tight position the ships ran in their bowsprits. At 08.00 the boats were sent to the storeship *Industry*. The light wind from the north was almost perfect for the attack.

The action opened at 09.00 with the French floating batteries and the mortar vessels moving into position. The fort kept up a steady fire on the ironclads as they anchored, 900 to 1,200 yards from the fort. All three were hit more than sixty times. Once anchored they returned over 3,000 shot and shell. By 10.30 the fort was on fire and the parapets began to crumble. In marked contrast the crew of *Princess Royal* were piped to dinner at 11.10. Ten minutes later *Hannibal*, with the paddle frigates under Stewart and Rear-Admiral Pellion, *Valorous* and *Asmodee* weighed. *Hannibal* took up a raking position across the end of the spit 600 yards offshore. Opening fire at 12.50 she forced the Russians to abandon the spit battery, covering the passage of Stewart and Pellion into the bay, piloted by Spratt's

PLAN OF THE ATTACK
UPON KINBURN.

From a drawing by a French Officer.

7   The bombardment of Kinburn, 17 October 1854, from the *Life of Sir W. Mends*

sailing master in *Cracker*. When this force anchored at 13.30, the action was almost over. As Stewart moved toward the bay Lyons and Bruat weighed and steamed toward the fort. *Princess Royal* anchored at 12.30, coming to in twenty-eight feet of water, 650 yards from the centre battery. She was the most heavily engaged of the battleships; being hit three times, the last shot struck the gangway and sent a shower of splinters across the main deck. At 13.15 *Royal Albert, Agamemnon, Montebello, Wagram, Ulm* and *Jean Bart* moored, then *St Jean d'Acre* joined at 13.20 and *Algiers* ten minutes later. Once anchored the battleships worked up a heavy fire, *Agamemnon* expending 500 rounds in little more than forty-five minutes, the supporting frigates 200–300 rounds each. At 14.10 Mends convinced Lyons that the shattered, blazing fort was beaten; all return fire had stopped fifteen minutes before. The cease-fire was hoisted, with a flag of truce. The fort could not reply, the flagstaff having been shot away early in the action. By 15.00 Major General Kokonovitch had accepted the allied terms. The 1,400-man garrison marched out with the honours of war, piled arms on the glacis and surrendered; some officers had wanted to blow up the fort, but the men were in no mood for such a gesture. Shortly after 15.00 the heavy ships shifted to the deep water anchorage, the cruisers and gunboats remaining in the bay.

The bombardment of Kinburn was almost entirely one-sided: the defences were overwhelmed. Going ashore the British found the main fort and the two batteries reduced to shapeless heaps with large breaches in their sides. The embrasures had been knocked down on to the guns by shot striking the wooden supports and shaking down the sand ramparts. Inside the mortars had penetrated into supposedly bomb-proof dug-outs, causing heavy casualties. Afloat, the allies lost two killed aboard the floating battery *Devastation*, with wounded aboard all three; *Princess Royal* alone of the other ships had two wounded. The garrison lost forty-five killed and 130 wounded.[15]

Initially Lyons had shared the widespread dislike of the batteries, which was hardly surprising when he was willing to take a wooden battleship within 500 yards of Fort Constantine. After the 17th he was more favourably disposed:

It is amusing to see how delighted Bruat is to send a favourable account of the Emperor's pet batteries. He attributes the fall of the place to them, whereas they had but little to do with it. The mortars ploughed the whole fort up and rendered it impossible for anyone to live in it and then the tremendous fire of the ships gave them the *coup de grâce* tho' it is true that in a few hours more the floating batteries would have brought the whole sea face down . . . still you may take it for granted that floating batteries have become elements in amphibious warfare, so the sooner you set about having as many good ones as the French the better it will be.

Stewart agreed: 'They will be admirable for assisting the ascent of the Bug to Nicolaiev – and in every conceivable case of "Assault & Battery" they must be formidable and valuable.' The role of the floating batteries at Kinburn has been much exaggerated by later commentators, who have not understood that much of the favourable comment was unjustified, intended to please Louis Napoleon. The British Admirals realised they would be criticised for taking such a large force against a small enemy, stressing the need to 'insure' success and reduce casualties. Stewart considered Lyons' handling of Bruat was the vital element, and pressed for his chief to have higher local rank, as Bruat was to be replaced by Vice-Admiral Trehouart in 1856.[16]

With the fort captured the essential flaw in the operation was revealed; Mends wondered why the gunboats were not immediately sent up the rivers to threaten Kherson and Nicolaiev, blaming the allied command structure. The allies lacked the troops and back-up for any sustained operation away from the coast. On the morning of the 18th the Russians blew up Fort Ochakov, removing the last limitation on exploitation of the Bay. On the 19th Bruat sent some gunboats into the Dnieper without consulting Lyons. Having restored allied harmony Stewart, aboard *Stromboli*, joined Rear-Admiral Pellion to make a complete examination of the Bay, provoking much Russian activity. After midday *Spitfire* joined, Spratt piloting *Stromboli*, *Cracker* and *Grinder* almost five miles up the Bug. At Volbjsk point they encountered the first significant barrier. Two sand spits reduced the river to a channel only 2,000 yards wide, where they skirmished for an hour with six or eight Russian guns before withdrawing. Spratt spent the next two days sounding the Bay before pushing up the Dnieper on the 24th. The troops, apart from the engineers and sappers, left Kinburn on the 20th for a reconnaissance towards Kherson. Penetrating as far inland as Petrovskoi the force met no coherent resistance. Returning on the 23rd one or two stragglers fell to Cossacks, but there were no regular Russian units.[17]

The garrison was embarked on *Vulcan* on the 20th and sent down to Constantinople. The wounded were placed in *Colombo* and dispatched to Odessa to be exchanged. On the 24th the allied commanders met aboard *Montebello* and unanimously decided the repaired fort could be held through the winter. The ice in the bay would not be thick enough to support troops. The floating batteries would remain with 1,700 French troops, the rest would return to Kazatch on 1 November. The option of bombarding Odessa had been specifically prohibited by the Emperor; Lyons understood Louis Napoleon wanted to lead the 1856 campaign in person with his base in an undamaged city. Lyons sent his gunboats back to the Azov immediately after the conference. The two British batteries arrived on the 25th, but went to Kazatch for repairs. *Agamemnon*, *Highflyer* and *Gladiator* left for Circassia on the 27th, the other ships followed on the 30th, 31st and 1 November; *Sidon*, *Curacao*, *Tribune* and *Dauntless* and four gunboats remained to deny the bay to the enemy.[18]

British opinion of the operation had never been very favourable. The French persuaded themselves the loss of Kinburn would stop the Russians sending more troops into the Crimea, but Lyons doubted they could feed any more and regretted the warning given for Nicolaiev. Like Stewart he realised an opportunity had been lost. Wood had preferred sending men to Eupatoria. The first telegraph from Lyons persuaded him Kinburn had been a worthwhile target, while public reaction was favourable. On reflection Stewart believed that in late September 15,000 men could have taken Nicolaiev as the operation had been a complete surprise; Lyons was less certain. Spratt, the best informed man on the scene, reported a naval attack could not move thirty miles up the Bug to Nicolaiev; the banks, up to 120 feet high, commanded the river and would have to be cleared by troops. Lyons accepted, adding Nicolaiev to the 1856 operations. The occupation and destruction of the yard would require more than 15,000 men. While a naval attack was improbable the Russians were alarmed. A captured British straggler reported fortifications at Nicolaiev adequate to deal with a raid, making the operation too grand for the British. The French had little enthusiasm for burning Russian dockyards.[19]

The significance of Kinburn lay outside the small strategic advantage, or the lost opportunity to attempt Nicolaiev. The essential point was the demonstration of allied amphibious power, the combination of strategic mobility and advanced weapons that gave the allies a decisive edge over the Russians, an edge they had abandoned by laying siege to Sevastopol. The arrival of an allied force was the signal for the Russians to abandon their coastal works, Hango, Anapa, Kertch and Ochakov being the best examples; they only fought when unable to retreat, at Bomarsund and Kinburn. Through the experience of Bomarsund, Sevastopol, Kertch and Sweaborg, new tactics for attacking coast forts had been developed; Kinburn was a small scale demonstration. Mortars and gunboats opened the action, avoiding damage by keeping underway, or anchoring out of gun range. Once their fire took effect the batteries moved in, leaving the battleships to finish the task. Wood and the progressive officers saw these methods as the key to Cronstadt; Mends was convinced they would succeed.[20]

When the French decided not to bombard Odessa, Lyons was anxious to return to Kazatch and press for more operations. Wood had taken up his idea for Kaffa and Arabat, the one area where naval forces would find a role, although Lyons agreed with the cabinet that Eupatoria offered the only chance of clearing the peninsula before winter. Success there would make Kaffa unnecessary, otherwise it should be undertaken as an 'English' operation. Lyons did not press Kaffa, fearing the Generals would see it as an excuse to ignore Eupatoria. To ensure an early start he kept the Kinburn force, still 6–7,000 strong, afloat and sent Simpson a lecture: 'the government at home are in hopes that you and Marshal Pelissier will undertake some serious operations from Eupatoria, I hope so too, and I need hardly say that all the resources of the fleet, to which indeed there is scarcely any limit, shall be at your disposal.' This minatory letter, like Panmure's earlier efforts, was entirely counter-productive. Simpson had decided to wait for the Admirals before discussing Kaffa, and Lyons did nothing to predispose him to their case.[21] Arriving at Kazatch late on 2 November Lyons called for a conference on the following day. For once the British Admirals were denied the support of Bruat, soon to leave for home. Simpson appeared to favour Kaffa before the meeting, but then gave his 'entire confidence' to Pelissier's objections. Disgusted, Stewart did not reserve all his contempt for Simpson: 'I can hardly anticipate the English government incurring the responsibility of ordering it to go forward.' Both Admirals still hoped to demolish Arabat by naval means, to increase the deep cordon round Kertch, provide food and forage for the garrison and flotilla and relieve the transport service of a burden. It would also open up the Putrid Sea, commanded by the Arabat spit, allowing the destruction of the Tchongar bridge. While Wood and Panmure could not understand the French objections they fulfilled Stewart's prophecy. Lyons kept the troops afloat, the appointment of Codrington bolstering his hopes until they were landed on 11 November. Without them the fleet was powerless. Lyons was particularly unhappy at abandoning the operation because General Wrangel's forces at Arabat were forcing in the cavalry pickets from Kertch. He considered sending the batteries, *Glatton* and *Meteor*, but the glacis at Arabat had been covered with sand. Codrington concluded that the operation would require two-thirds of the British force at Sevastopol and could not be justified.[22]

With the campaign over Lyons looked round for a scapegoat, selecting Niel, the 'wet blanket upon the expedition'. Wood took comfort from the fact that the Navy had always been pressing for action, but admitted 'more might have been done'. To make matters worse the demolition of the docks, only sanctioned by the cabinet in late October, proved particularly difficult. The task was only completed on 6 February; continued flooding, enemy fire and good masonry caused innumerable delays. The real end of the campaign was signalled, as in the Baltic, by the departure of the fleet surveyor; Spratt left Kazatch on 20 November to survey the Egyptian coast for a Suez canal harbour. Offensive measures continued in the Azov until ice formed. As the Euxine promised little for the Navy in 1856 Spratt reported Lyons was anxious to command the Baltic fleet.[23] The French were certain the campaign was at an end; Bruat, now a full Admiral, left Kamiesch on 7 November with six battleships and six steam frigates. Significantly, the Imperial Guard were aboard the battleships. Rear-Admiral Pellion was in temporary command, with *Napoleon* and *Wagram* at Kamiesch, the batteries at Kinburn and a handful of cruisers. Bruat cleared the Bosphorus for Toulon on the 15th, but died on passage through the Aegean. Lyons regretted he had not lived to tell his Emperor of the need for more active measures.[24]

Wood had long anticipated sending elements of the fleet out of the Euxine, partly to recuperate, partly to show the flag in the Mediterranean. *Algiers*, *Agamemnon* and *Diamond* left Kazatch on the 12th, Stewart took *Hannibal*, *Princess Royal*, *St Jean d'Acre* and *Sphinx* on the 15th. Lyons wanted the floating batteries at Kinburn and Kertch, but was ordered to have them ready to withdraw, leaving him aboard his flagship with two batteries, a large, scattered, force of cruisers and the flotilla then leaving the Azov. Stewart suggested that Wood recall him for rest and consultation.[25] The rest was long overdue; Lyons was infuriated to hear that Berkeley was telling all who would listen that he had given the Times correspondent information about Kinburn, which led to him receiving special praise in the newspaper. He sent a copy of his denial to Wood. Berkeley was provoked by Lyons' success, his easy relations with the politicians and his popularity. The final straw came when, at Stewart's suggestion, he was given temporary local rank as Admiral of the Blue while Commander-in-Chief, Mediterranean. Berkeley lamented: 'Lyons is an ambitious man and a diplomatist and knows how to make others work for him'. He was convinced the extra rank was Lyons' idea and, allowing for Lyons' inordinate vanity, he may well have been correct. The Senior Naval Lord was a jealous and vindictive man, as his attacks on Napier had demonstrated. This time his malice misfired, Lyons was too well established. As for *The Times*, Delane was not impressed: 'I am sorry you have let Reeve praise Lyons and the Black Sea Fleet. I think they have been sadly inactive – worse even than under Dundas.' Delane, like the public at large, had no conception of seapower.[26] He did not realise how far the fleet had been tied to the Army, and by ignoring its work fostered a distorted image of the war.

The fall of Kars

The Turkish army in Asia had been defeated and ruined by corruption in 1854; by early 1855 it was causing concern, then in June it was blockaded inside the fortress of Kars by General Mouraviev. Kars, the last major fortress on the Russo–Turkish frontier, was vital to Turkey. Colonel Fenwick Williams, with a party of British and Hungarian officers, had been sent in late 1854, but after the landing in the Crimea no significant assistance could be obtained from the allied armies, or the Turkish government. Palmerston's plan to send General Vivian's Turkish contingent could not be carried out. Concern for Kars among British strategists was universal; Lyons wanted to reinforce, Palmerston suggested pulling back, Clarendon believed Stratford's jealousy of Williams was responsible. Omer presented a memorandum to the allied commanders in the Crimea on 11 July calling for his forces to be released to relieve Kars; three days later he requested transport for 25,000 infantry and 3,000 cavalry. Pelissier refused, wanting to keep up allied force levels to extend his right flank; Simpson, nervous for Balaklava, supported him. Omer could only move if his troops were replaced, he left for Constantinople in disgust.[27] Asia Minor was vital for the Turks, and while Palmerston proposed bringing all the British funded Turkish units to the Crimea to release Omer, he would not act without the concurrence of the French. Panmure wanted to ignore Paris, but was persuaded to hold back. Louis Napoleon supported Pelissier, delaying Omer's troops until after the fall of Sevastopol; once released, Lyons and Fremantle spared no effort, moving a substantial force to Batoum. Two cruisers were on station to assist the sluggish Turkish advance, but Omer arrived too late and moved too slowly. On 29 September Mouraviev, aware of the fall of Sevastopol, and of Omer, assaulted Kars. Although beaten off with over 7,000 casualties, he kept up the blockade. Without food or ammunition the garrison were forced to surrender, on very easy terms, on 23 November. To his credit Mouraviev immediately threw in a convoy of supplies.[28] The British blamed the French for holding up Omer, but Clarendon admitted they could hardly make that public. French indifference is evident in their historiography; Gooch declares Kars was relieved. Divergence of aims and objects prevented any effective measures being taken to aid the city. The British Government could not afford to offend the French by acting alone, and had to accept the consequences. Palmerston's reaction was to urge the dispatch of a Turco–Eygptian force from Eupatoria to Trebizond. He feared negotiations might open during the winter, leaving Kars as a counterweight for Sevastopol, but he would not commit British troops.[29] The Asian theatre never reopened after the winter.

Notes

1 Lyons to Admiralty 15 Sept. rec. 3 Oct. 1855: no. 775: NRS p. 306; Lyons to Wood 15 Sept. 1855: Add. 49,535 f151–7.
2 Panmure to Simpson 10 Sept. 1855: PANMURE, i, pp. 377–8; Palmerston to Panmure 11 Sept. 1855: *ibid.* p. 378; Palmerston to Clarendon 11, 14 Sept. 1855: Cl. Dep. C31 f470–8; Lansdowne to Palmerston 11 Sept. 1855: Bdlds. GC/LA f87; Panmure to the Queen 12, 14 Sept. 1855: PANMURE, i, pp. 382–4; Cowley to Clarendon 12 Sept. 1855: F.O. 519/217 f38–41; Burgoyne to Panmure 17 Sept. 1855: WROTTESLEY, ii, pp. 305–7.
3 Cowley to Clarendon 15 Sept. 1855: F.O. 519/217 f45–52;

Palmerston to Clarendon 16 Sept. 1855: Cl. Dep. C31 f487–9; Clarendon to Palmerston 16 Sept. 1855: Bdlds. GC/CL f693; Wood to Grey 8 Sept. 1855: Add. 49,564 f35; Panmure to Simpson 22 Sept. 1855: PANMURE, i, pp. 396–7; Wood to Lyons, Wood to Stewart 24 Sept. 1855: Add. 49,564 f51–6.

4   Panmure to Simpson 17 Sept. 1855: PANMURE, i, pp. 389–90; Prince Albert to Clarendon 17 Sept. 1855: ibid. pp. 390–4; Palmerston to Panmure 22, 24 Sept. 1855: ibid. pp. 397, 402–3; Prince Albert to Panmure 23 Sept. 1855: ibid. p. 401; Palmerston to Clarendon 24 Sept. 1855: Cl. Dep. C31 f515–6; Palmerston to Wood 26 Sept. 1855: HALIFAX A4/63 f46; Panmure to Palmerston 26 Sept. 1855 enc. Panmure to Simpson, telegraph 26 Sep. 1855: Bdlds. GC/PA f120.

5   Panmure to Simpson 29 Sept. 1855: PANMURE, i, pp. 407–9; Palmerston to Clarendon 1 Oct. 1855: CL. Dep. C31 f543–4; Panmure to Wood 3 Oct. 1855: HALIFAX A4/65; Palmerston to Panmure 30 Sept. 1855: PANMURE, i, p. 411; Panmure to the Queen 30 Sept. 1855: ibid. p. 411.

6   Simpson to Panmure 25 Sept. 1855: ibid. pp. 404–5; Lyons to Admiralty 18, 22 Sept. 1855 no. 785, 801: NRS pp. 306, 315; Lyons to Wood 18, 22 Sept. 1855: Add. 49,535 f159–62, 168–71; CURTISS, p. 459; MENDS, p. 297; Simpson to Panmure 2 Oct. 1855: Further Correspondence Relating to the Military Expedition to the East (hereafter F.C.) (eight vols.), vol. VII pp. 1459–60; Geo. Paget to Simpson 25, 30 Oct. 1855: ibid. pp. 1608, 1664; Captain Hamilton to Freemantle 24, 29 Oct. enc. in Lyons to Admiralty 31 Oct. rec. 20 Nov. 1855 no. 885: NRS pp. 365–6.

7   Lyons to Wood 15, rec. 17 Sept. 1855 telegraph: NRS pp. 304–5; Lyons to Wood 15, 18, 25 Sept. 1855: Add. 49,535 f151–62, 177–80; Lyons to Stopford (Malta) 28 Sept. 1855: ADM 50/264;

8   Wood to Lyons 2, 8, 14, 17, 24 Sept. 1855: Add. 49,564 f18–51; Lyons to Wood 22 Sept. 1855: Add. 49,535 f168–71; Wood to Cowley 5 Sept. 1855: F.O. 519/208 f349–52.

9   Lyons to Wood 18 Sept. 1855: Add. 49,535 f159–62; Wood to Lyons 17 Sept. 1855 telegraph: NRS p. 306; Wood to Panmure 13 Sept. 1855: Add. 49,564 f35; Wood to Lyons 22 Sept. 1855: ibid. f50–1.

10   CURTISS, pp. 465–8, 472–3; Palmerston to Russell 20 Sept. 1855: GOOCH, G., i pp. 214–15; Palmerston to Panmure 17 Oct. 1855: PANMURE, i, p. 449.

11   Cowley to Clarendon 22 Sept. 1855: WELLESLEY and SENCOURT, Conversations with Napoleon III (London, 1934), pp. 91–2; GOOCH, B., p. 253: The Emperor's telegraph is in NRS p. 328; Cowley to Clarendon 28 Sept. 1855: F.O. 519/217 f80–3; Palmerston to Wood 27 Sept. 1855: HALIFAX A4/63 f48.

12   Palmerston Diary 28 Sept. 1855: Bdlds. D16; Cowley to Clarendon 30 Sept. 1855: F.O. 519/217 f86–70; Wood to Lyons 29 Sept. 1855: Add. 49,564 f63–4; Wood to Lyons 28 Sept. 1855 telegraph: NRS p. 319; Lyons to Wood 1 Oct. 1855 telegraph: ibid. p. 324; Lyons to Wood 7 Aug. 29 Sept. 2, 6 Oct. 1855: Add. 49,535 f5–15, 181–2, 49,537 f1–4, 14–17; Lyons to Grey 29 Sept. 1855: LYONS L507; Loring to Lyons enc. in Add. 49,566

f98–9.
13   Wood to Lyons 4 Aug. 1855: Add. 49,563 f91; Panmure to Simpson 19 Oct. 1855: PANMURE, i, pp. 451–2.
14   Lyons to Wood 13 Oct. 1855: Add. 49,537 f22–5; SPR1/3; GIFFARD, pp. 160–1: MENDS, pp. 297–300; CHEVALIER, E., *Histoire de la Marine Français* (Paris, 1905), p. 284 Stewart to Lyons 15 Oct. 1855: LYONS L288; Lyons Journal: ADM 50/264; Log of *Spitfire*: ADM 53/4860.
15   MENDS, pp. 302–3; GIFFARD, pp. 160–1; EARDLEY-WILMOT, pp. 360–72; Logs of all major British Warships: ADM 53/ ; Lyons to Admiralty 20 Oct. 1855 no. 860: NRS p. 353.
16   Lyons to Grey 29 Sept. 1855: LYONS L507; Lyons to Wood 20 Oct. 1855: Add. 49,537 f27–32; Lyons to Berkeley 20 Oct. 1855: LYONS L507; Stewart to Wood 22 Oct. 1855: Add. 49,541 f86–92.
17   MENDS, p. 303; SPR 1/3; Log of *Spitfire*; Lyons to Bruat 19 Oct. 1855: LYONS L507; Stewart to Lyons 22 Oct. Hurdle to Lyons 24 Oct. enc. Lyons to Admiralty 23, 25 Oct. rec. 8, 15 Nov. 1855 no. 863, 871: NRS pp. 354–60.
18   Lyons to Admiralty 24, 28 Oct. and Lyons to Wood 22 Oct. 1855 telegraph: NRS pp. 357–8, 364, 354; Lyons to Wood 27 Oct., 19 Nov. 1855: Add. 49,537 f58, 102.
19   Lyons to Wood 20 Oct. 12 Nov. 1855: *ibid*. f27–32, 94–7; Stewart to Wood 22 Oct. 6 Nov. 1855: Add. 49,541 f86–97; Wood to Stewart 20 Oct. 1855: Add. 49,564 f96–7; Wood to Palmerston 20 Oct. 1855: Bdlds. GC/WO f59; Wood to Lyons 22 Oct. 5, 12 Nov. 1855: Add. 49,564 f102, 120, 128–31; Lyons to Admiralty 6 rec. 23 Nov. 1855 no. 896: NRS pp. 372–5; SPR1/3 and EARDLEY-WILMOT, pp. 370–2.
20   MENDS, p. 302.
21   Wood to Lyons 22, 27 Oct. 1855: Add. 49,564 f102–3, 109–111; Wood to Lyons 24, 26 Oct. 1855 telegraph: NRS pp. 357, 363; Lyons to Wood 30 Oct. 1855: Add. 49,537 f69–71; Lyons to Simpson 29 Oct. 1855 enc. in above; Simpson to Panmure 30 Oct. 1855: PANMURE, i, pp. 467–70.
22   Stewart to Wood 6 Nov. 1855: Add. 49,541 f93–7; Lyons to Wood 3, 10 Nov. 1855: Add. 49,537 f77–8, 88; Lyons to Wood 4, 11 Nov. 1855 telegraph: NRS pp. 370, 392; Wood to Lyons 5 Nov. 1855: Add. 49,564 f120; Panmure to Simpson 5 Nov. 1855: PANMURE, i, p. 477; Codrington to Panmure 13 Nov. 1855: *ibid*. p. 487.
23   Spratt to Lyons 10 Nov. 1855: Add. 49,537 f109–114; Lyons Journal 20 Nov. 1855: ADM 50/264; Lyons to Wood 10 Nov. 1855: Add. 49,537 f88; Spratt to Captain Washington (Hydrographer of the Navy) 17 Nov. 1855: H SL41a f124.
24   CHEVALIER, p. 289; EARDLEY-WILMOT, p. 374; Lyons to Wood 8 Dec. 1855: Add. 49,537 f182.
25   Wood to Lyons 24 Oct. 1855 telegraph: NRS p. 357; Lyons Journal 12, 15 Nov. 1855: ADM 50/264; Lyons to Admiralty 12 Nov. 1855 telegraph: NRS p. 392; Admiralty to Lyons 13 Nov. 1855 telegraph: *ibid*. p. 393; Stewart to Wood 6 Nov. 1855: Add. 49,541 f93–7.

26   Lyons to Wood; Lyons to Berkeley 30 Nov. 1855: Add. 49,537 f161–8; Lyons Journal 11, 12 Dec. 1855: ADM 50/264; Berkeley to Wood 8, 12 Nov. 1855: HALIFAX A4/74; Delane to Dasent 1 Oct. 1855: DASENT, i, pp. 209–11.

27   Admiralty to Lyons 14 Apr. 1855 no. 415: NRS pp. 108–110; Palmerston to Panmure 26 May 1855: PANMURE,i, pp. 211–2; Lyons to Wood 10 Jul. 1855: Add. 49,535 f164–7; Palmerston to Clarendon 12 Jul. 1855: Cl. Dep. C31; Clarendon to Herbert 26 Jul. 1855: HERBERT F/53 f2057.

28   Palmerston to Panmure 2 Aug. 1855: PANMURE,i, p. 332; Panmure to Palmerston 2 Aug. 1855: *ibid.* p. 333; Clarendon to Panmure 2 Aug. 1855: *ibid.* p. 333; For details of Omer's advance see NRS pp. 371–2 and 388–92; SLADE provides a hostile account; CURTISS, pp. 408–10.

29   Clarendon to Palmerston 16 Dec. 1855: Bdlds. GC/CL f758; · FITZMAURICE, i, p. 132; GOOCH, B., p. 235; Palmerston to Panmure 26 Dec. 1855: Add. 48,579 f94–5; Palmerston to Wood 26 Dec. 1855: *ibid.* f96; Codrington to Panmure 18 Dec. 1855: PANMURE, ii, pp. 22–3.

19

Return to the Baltic

During the Russian War the Royal Navy built two fleets; one, of coastal craft, for the conflict in hand, and an ocean-going steam battlefleet for the war to follow. During 1854 the steam battlefleet was expanded by the conversion of five 80-gun ships, which Walker believed would provide battleships at a fraction the cost of rush building new ships. As he did not want the return of the Baltic fleet to hamper work on new ships the dockyards were put on notice in September. Ordering the October Programme vessels in private yards assisted this policy, allowing the Royal yards to concentrate on battleships. All repair work on the Baltic ships would be carried out by the ships' artificers, alterations were forbidden; the crank *Royal George* and the undermasted *Amphion* were taken into the yards, but the other ships had to fend for themselves. Some Baltic units were used for trooping runs to Malta, the sailing battleships were paid off, with those returning from the Black Sea, to man the new ships. *Monarch* went to the Pacific station, but Captain Erskine took the new 91 *Orion*. To emphasise Walker and Graham's long term view four new battleships were ordered at the turn of the year, although they would take five years to build. Pressure on British yards led Graham to consider reopening the expensive building facilities in India.[1]

For 1855 the Baltic fleet was joined by *Orion, Exmouth*, 91s, *Colossus*, 80 the corvettes *Centaur, Esk, Falcon, Harrier, Pylades* and the impounded Russian vessels *Cossack* and *Tartar. Retribution* was refitted for the flag of the Rear-Admiral third-in-command while Sulivan and Otter were given larger vessels, *Merlin* and *Firefly*. All large boats were fitted to fire rockets, the gunboats would be attached to the battleships as tenders.[2] Graham also planned a reserve fleet in the Channel, to demonstrate British reserve strength to the United States and France. *Neptune, St George, Powerful* and

Calcutta would be based at Portsmouth under the Port Admiral, Sir Thomas Cochrane. The Baltic fleet for 1855 would comprise:

Battleships	11
Blockships	9
Cruisers, screw	15
Cruisers, paddle	15
Floating batteries	5
Gunboats	26
Mortar vessels	22
Dispatch gunboats	2
TOTAL	105

The October Programme vessels would form a separate division for coastal attacks. *The Times* criticised the Admiralty for continuing work on battleships when only gunboats were required, confusing short term needs with long term security. By contrast Graham stressed the need to match French battleship construction: 'These cannot be directed against *Russia* . . . if we can but man our fleets we may still defy the world'. On the manning question Berkeley ignored the lessons of the *Cumberland* incident, sending men just returned from four years in the Mediterranean straight out to the Baltic, only taking care to split up the crews.[3] The French force was initially reported as five battleships, two frigates six corvettes, five batteries, five mortar vessels and ten to twelve gunboats. Cowley warned they would not all be sent.[4] The French would be supplied with coal, at a commercial rate.[5]

In place of Napier, Graham decided to appoint the safe, if uninspiring, Rear-Admiral Sir Richard Saunders Dundas, second son of the second Lord Melville. Through his political patronage Dundas was the first post-1815 entrant to gain his flag, in July 1853. While Lewis observed 'he was not a great man', Dundas was a capable administrator, fluent in French and an excellent seaman. His failings were less evident, although Graham would have been aware of them; he was indecisive and lacked resolve. Graham intended to use these flaws to control the campaign. The junior Admirals would be Seymour, a reliable informant with Baltic experience, and Robert Lambert Baynes, about to hoist his flag as third. The appointments were made official on 14 February, Henry Eden taking over from Dundas as Second Naval Lord.[6] This was Graham's last contribution to the 1855 campaign. His successor had to deal with the ill-feeling arising out of the 1854 campaign; Chads felt slighted by serving less than a year with his flag up, but had to wait two years for another post, and Plumridge replaced Seymour as Port Admiral at Devonport, having been promised the Western Squadron, but one was never formed. Other senior officers viewed the Baltic as a poisoned chalice. Cochrane, at Portsmouth, had offered his services in 1854, and been the subject of a rumoured exchange with Napier. In 1855 he pointedly did not offer because the Baltic command would only ruin his reputation; Government, public and newspapers had all abused the senior officers and he had no desire to join the scapegoats.[7]

However these issues were of little importance alongside the Government's failure to provide politico/strategic guidance for the theatre commander. Without any positive cabinet policy Wood was left to give the new commander instructions based on Sulivan's memorandum. He was to co-operate with his allies, keep up a strict blockade, carry out minor attacks to tie down Russian troops, examine the major arsenals and report on Bomarsund. Wood sent Sulivan's report on Sweaborg with a private letter making it clear he would be satisfied by a blockade.[8] As the campaign progressed Wood became more optimistic, reflecting a growing independence of cabinet control, a better appreciation of the theatre and the improved position in the Crimea.

Graham intended the flying squadron, Captain Watson, *Imperieuse*, should leave the Downs in early March, to set up the blockade before the battlefleet, due to follow at the end of the month, arrived; the third division would leave in May. After a mild December and January the Baltic experienced an exceptionally severe winter, which delayed the fleet. *Imperieuse*, *Euryalus*, *Arrogant*, *Amphion*, *Esk*, *Tartar* and *Archer* finally cleared the Downs on 28 March, making a quick passage to the Skaw, but were detained for a week at Landscrona, virtually prisoners in the ice. All lost anchors and cables and, in attempting to leave, *Arrogant*, *Amphion* and *Imperieuse* went aground.[9] The battlefleet arrived at Elsinore on 13 April, almost catching the flying squadron. This was surprising as Dundas delayed his departure, and then suffered an accident. Although directed to sail on 7 April, it had been intended that the fleet leave on the 3rd.[10] The fleet finally left Spithead late on the 4th in hazy weather, and during the night the flagship collided with a large American merchant ship ten miles WSW of Beachy Head. *Duke of Wellington* was ordered back to Portsmouth and artificers put to work night and day. Dundas transferred his flag to *Nile* in the Downs before proceeding. Wood found the delay inexplicable. Dundas, considering the Board had shown no confidence in him, wanted to resign. Wood sent off a soothing reply, arguing that his candid tone reflected confidence, stressing the need to create a 'good effect', even if only in matters of no consequence.[11] This incident had a happy outcome; Wood and Dundas now understood each other, and were able to use their private correspondence in its proper role. By late 1855 Wood was prepared to support Dundas against complaints in cabinet.

Napier had left the fleet in good order. With no further need for emergency drill, the captains were soon at home under the new regime. Codrington observed: 'Things are going on in our squadron in the quiet gentlemanlike way in which I have always, *before last year*, seen the service carried on since I have been in the Navy. We now feel at ease.' It is open to question how far a fleet on war service should 'feel at ease' or go along quietly. Dundas, like his captains, had no experience of a major war and did not appreciate the need for a vigorous, belligerent, spirit to pervade the fleet. Cooper-Key shared the general view.[12] Only Sulivan, the one officer in the fleet with an appreciation of the campaign anticipated problems: 'I like all I see of our chief – cautious and careful, but with much judgement and, I should think, firmness; but I wish I could instill a little more activity into his disposition – I mean activity of mind.' *The Times* also looked for more activity: 'Admiral Dundas has before him the services of Admiral Napier, and whatever his instructions, if any, no doubt he knows he has to do more than Admiral Napier. If he does not accomplish more, he will certainly find himself next November under orders to lower his flag, with small prospect of hoisting it again.'[13] There was much to be done in the Baltic before offensive measures, and the October Programme would not be ready for many weeks.

The main body left the Downs on 9 April, and after being delayed in the Skaw by strong winds, arrived at Kiel on the 18th. Sulivan had been delayed, forcing Dundas to rely on Danish pilots. Once *Merlin* joined she went ahead to buoy the shoals. Wood pressed for economy with coals, Dundas was more concerned to ensure Watson's notification of blockade would satisfy the Queen's Advocate, as he saw no purpose in leaving Kiel before the Gulf of Finland began to clear, taking the opportunity to visit Copenhagen for discussions with the King and Buchanan. When Watson's first report arrived, on the 22nd, Dundas was worried by the prominent part given to the French, who were no closer than Cherbourg. Watson declared Libau blockaded on the 17th, the Gulf of Riga on the 19th. Anticipating a move into the Gulf of Finland, Dundas sent *Basilisk* and *Vulture* to reinforce the flying squadron. The state of the ice ensured Watson went no further than Port Baltic and Hango, where he issued another notice of blockade on the 28th, which was invalid as he had not entered the Gulf. Dundas tried to correct the error, but Watson's notice reached Copenhagen and Stockholm and was published before the retraction arrived. To compound his problems Watson had to detach *Arrogant*, with an outbreak of smallpox to the hospital on Faro.[14] Further cases were landed, thirty-eight from *Duke of Wellington*.

Wood began to develop a Baltic policy; encouraged by rumours of poor quality troops in the Crimea he believed the diversionary effect of the fleet might be increased, without major operations. If so, the Baltic could be used to train up more seamen as the heavy ships were unlikely to see any service. He also revived the Scandinavian seamen idea, influenced by Berkeley, or Graham. With considerable prompting the French prepared three screw battleships and two corvettes under Rear-Admiral Penaud, second-in-command in 1854. They left Cherbourg on 1 May and made very slow progress. Realising the batteries and flotilla were destined for the Euxine, Wood pressed the French, and sent the reserve fleet to sea.[15]

Dundas, worried by the lack of news from Watson, returned to Copenhagen for more meetings and a chance to inspect Danish gunboats. The battlefleet finally left Kiel on 3 May, placing *Bulldog* off Travemunde. *Conflict* brought news of Watson as the fleet passed the Fermen Belt. At Faro he found further news: the squadron, seven strong, was cruising between Hango Head and Dager Ort without sighting any merchant ships. Seven gunboats had already reached Faro, 'Nemesis' Hall, *Blenheim*, was left in charge. The fleet arrived at Nargen on the 10th. Nargen had been an important anchorage during 1854, but it became the central point of Dundas's strategy. He sortied out aboard *Merlin* to inspect Reval on the 11th, and Sweaborg the following day; Reval had a few extra turf batteries, and reinforcements at Sweaborg, Sulivan estimated, added sixty guns. There were five battleships in harbour, one hulked and another housed over. Intelligence reports suggested six sail and four frigates had left for Cronstadt in the early spring. On the 13th *Imperieuse* and *Tartar* collided. Both had to return home and they were replaced by *Caesar*, delayed by a late trooping run. Dundas reserved his view of Sweaborg for the private correspondence, noting that only Sulivan would position the ships in the roadstead – even if the navigational problems could be overcome there was no secure base for the operation. However, he hoped to attempt something in the following month, enquiring how many mortars would be available. Wood was then trying to complete the batteries, *Aetna* had been burnt, but Walker was certain they would meet their design purpose. Wood began to appreciate that Cronstadt was the real target and would justify greater risks than Sweaborg, pressing for the French batteries to go north.[16]

Cooper-Key inspected Bomarsund, finding the ruins had only been disturbed by the locals, although Russian officials had collected the taxes in February and taken away Islanders accused of collaborating with the allies. Dundas wanted to blockade the Gulf of Bothnia, but already short of cruisers and believing the Gulf would need another eight, elected to wait. The gunboats did not impress; he thought they would be useless for anything but bombardment, throughout the war he displayed no enthusiasm for new weapons. After delays for fog the fleet finally entered the Gulf of Finland on 25 May. Two days later *Merlin* and *Magicienne* were detached to examine the Straits of Biorko 'with a view to intercept the traffic which appears to be carried on along the coast between Sweaborg and Cronstadt'. Biorko, the one place where this traffic could be intercepted behind the rocky outcrops of the Finnish shore, was given added significance by rumours of Russian steam gunboats. Operating from Sweaborg, they could impose considerable restrictions on Dundas.[17] Soon after detaching Sulivan the fleet gave chase to a few coasters, mistaking them for warships. In the evening *Orion* went to examine Cronstadt. In hazy weather Captain Erskine entirely mistook the positions of the Russian ships, reporting they lay outside the harbour, between Forts Alexander and Risbank. There was a considerable coincidence with the rumoured position of the Russian ships before Sweaborg in early 1854. The following day *Magicienne* reported the capture of two galliots laden with dressed granite blocks six feet square, intended for the defences of Cronstadt. *Cossack* and *Esk*, detached to Hango to intercept coastal traffic, captured six vessels and destroyed an abandoned fort on the 26th and 27th. Dundas lamented his shortage of cruisers, and privately complained about the late arrival of the battering squadron, although he believed the batteries would only be a nuisance if they did come out, preferring mortar vessels, the conventional coast attack type. The captains shared his concern at the late arrival of the battering squadron. Graham tacitly admitted the October Programme had been ordered too late for the opening of the campaign. Even so, the vessels were ready long before Baynes brought them out, but they were delayed by shortage of men. The blockships were ordered to fit for 600 men as early as 2 February, but were still short-handed on 21 May. The batteries were to fit for 200 men, and on the 24th, *Powerful* and *Calcutta* were detached from the reserve fleet to land their lower decks guns to embark the guns and stores of *Meteor* and *Glatton*. Wood hoped to complete the crews, reported the excellent performance of the ironclads on trial, and suggested fitting the gunboats with smaller guns for blockade service. He also retailed rumours of sixty-five steam and 100 oared gunboats at Cronstadt, with seventy-five oared gunboats at Sweaborg.[18] These alarming figures were inaccurate, particularly the first.

Dundas and Sulivan landed on Tolboukin Island, 3,000 yards from the outer defences of Cronstadt on 31 May. From the lighthouse Dundas observed the Russian fleet, which was secure between Fort Menshikov and the island. Only five battleships were rigged for sea. Four more, with seven smaller vessels, were moored to cover the north channel barrier – a series of wooden frames filled with stones stretching from Cronstadt to the Finnish shore. Influenced by Sulivan he believed this was the only effective line of attack, but had too few flotilla craft. Privately he sent details of what might be attempted; mortars and rockets could reach the island from beyond the barrier, but only if supported by a powerful force of gunboats. Just as he began to plan his campaign Dundas was joined by Penaud on 1 June, and his freedom was at an end.[19] Wood accepted little could be done. Baynes left without the batteries; he had planned to send two for Dundas to examine, but as the French were not sending theirs, nothing but a blockade could be expected. Penaud informed Dundas that the Emperor expected little more. Seeing how few Russian battleships were fitted out, Dundas reorganised his force, strengthening the detached squadrons with the old blockships. *Hogue*, with the gunboats *Gleaner* and *Badger*, joined *Cossack* and *Esk* off Hango. *Amphion*, equally ill-suited to fleet duties, went to cover Sweaborg on 6 June. Three days later Captain Warden, *Ajax*, took command of *Firefly*, *Driver*, *Harrier*, *Porcupine* and *Cuckoo* to blockade the southern half of the Gulf of Bothnia (the Aland Islands were not included). *Edinburgh* remained as guardship at Nargen, while *Arrogant* and *Ruby* went to Biorko.

On 5 June a boat from *Cossack*, commanded by Lieutenant Geneste, landed near Hango under a flag of truce to return some Finnish seamen. As they walked along the jetty, still under the flag, they were fired on by Russian troops. Five men, two of them Finns, were killed, one wounded seaman escaped reporting his comrades were all dead. News of this affair caused outrage in Britain; although most of the boat party survived, as prisoners, that was not known for several weeks. The conduct of Captain Fanshawe could only be described as incompetent. Like many British officers he had a very partial attitude to flags of truce, and as that flown from *Cossack* had not been acknowledged from the shore he was not justified in sending the boat. Furthermore it was highly improper to send arms, even if unloaded, in the boat. Allowing for that the conduct of the Russians was unjustifiable. It was open to them to reject the flag when flown aboard *Cossack*, or when the boat approached the shore, but there was no need to shoot unarmed men, who could as easily have been taken prisoner. Dundas had already warned Captain Heathcote, *Archer*, to be more careful before *Cossack* arrived off Tolboukin on 11 June. During 1854 there had been several examples of British ships stretching the legitimate use of flags of truce, notably when Sulivan steamed into Sweaborg after Gamla Careleby. The Russian Minister of War, alleging British violations, limited such intercourse in future to Cronstadt, Sweaborg and Reval.[20]

On 9 June *Merlin*, *Dragon*, *Firefly* and *D'Assas* took Penaud and several British captains to examine Cronstadt. While still two miles out the two surveying ships were struck by 'infernals'. The only damage was to *Merlin's* copper and the crockery of both ships. Dundas reported such weapons might have a serious effect on more lightly built vessels, forgetting *Merlin* was the flimsiest ship in the fleet. The boats of the fleet did not find any more infernals. *Magicienne*, finding two more granite galliots, continued to harass the troops near Biorko. This constant employment of force on the shores of the Gulf of Finland distinguished the 1855 campaign from that of 1854. Encouraged by Dundas's letter of the 4th, Wood pressed him to consider Cronstadt, a target that would justify 'risks of some magnitude'. The shortage of flotilla craft could be covered by the fleets' boats, but he left the final decision to Dundas, adding that, in view of their small force, he would not give too much attention to the French. After his second inspection Dundas urged him not to send the batteries. Nothing could be done without an adequate flotilla and the existing flotilla would be better employed at Sweaborg. Wood retained the batteries, loading *Calcutta* with heavy ammunition. Sweaborg would be worthwhile, if it could be attempted without much loss; if not, the lack of French assistance would justify confining the season to a blockade.[21]

Dundas left Tolboukin on the 14th, taking the fleet down to Seskar, where the men went ashore. *Majestic*, Captain Hope, and *Euryalus* remained off Cronstadt. On the 16th Dundas visited Biorko, an excellent anchorage, although too vulnerable to the shore for a fleet base. Seymour, *Exmouth*, took *Blenheim* and the gunboats *Pincher* and *Snap* to the mouth of the River Narva on the 17th for an ineffective engagement with the batteries. In the Gulf of Bothnia Warden set up a blockade as far north as Nystad. The Gulf of Finland squadron, under Ramsay, startled by the *Cossack* incident, worked off their anger on the semaphore system. Lying at Seskar Dundas considered a long range bombardment of Sweaborg: 'Nobody will suffer more than myself by *doing* nothing, but I must keep my judgement as clear as I can, and nobody will thank me for folly or a failure.' The fate of Napier must have been ever in his thoughts, seated in the cabin that his predecessor had occupied scant months before. The same problems, particularly the weather, led him to doubt the possibility of an attack. The fleet left Seskar on the 20th. As the ships anchored off Tolboukin, *Vulture*, almost the last to arrive, was struck by an infernal. The following day the boats fished up several of the primitive mines and both Dundas and Seymour inspected them aboard their flagships. Dundas extracted nine or ten pounds of powder before setting off the prussic acid and detonating powder fuse in his face. Seymour fired the complete charge, leaving him blind in one eye and seriously wounding some of his crew. Dundas admitted to 'a complete insight having been obtained . . . to the method of explosion'. The infernal was a zinc cone two feet deep and fifteen inches wide at the base. Fortunately for the British, who hauled up fifty of them, one had been set off by a Russian boat crew, ensuring many more were put down with their safety devices in place. Dundas was little the worse for his experience, inspecting the northern barrier on the 23rd aboard *Merlin.* While noting a Russian battleship with a funnel he was more concerned by twenty steam gunboats that came out and opened fire at a range in excess of 3,000 yards. This reinforced his decision not to attempt Cronstadt.[22]

Arrogant and *Magicienne* continued to harass Biorko, blowing up two abandoned forts and sinking another pair of granite galliots in Werolax Bay. On 30 June *Magicienne* and *Ruby* returned to the quarry, destroying thirty galliots. *James Watt* was detached to the northern shore to prevent Russian troops interrupting the assault on the coastal trade, reflecting the opinion of Dundas and Penaud that the only value of the allied battleships lay in discouraging the Russians from fitting out their own.[23] The French government, prompted by Penaud, objected to Dundas leaving the Alands outside the blockade. Clarendon accepted their argument that the islands might become a general depot for Russian trade, to be forwarded when the ice formed. Dundas was ordered to adopt the French policy on 3 July, although he had anticipated this, presumably to satisfy Penaud. As Dundas reasoned, there was no point blockading Aland; there were no military forces on the islands, and they depended on trade with Sweden to avoid starvation. Wood was forced to agree within the month.[24]

Notes

1   LAMBERT, pp. 41–5; Graham to Wood 12 Jan. 1855: HALIFAX A4/70.

2   Admiralty Orders 28 Dec. 1854, 25 Jan. 15 Feb. and 16 Mar. 1855 no. 191, 370, 539, no. 226–7: ADM 2/1568 and 2/1569; Admiralty to Surveyor 26 Feb. 1855: ADM 87/52 f1209.

3   Chads to Wood 9 Mar. 1855: Add. 49,558 f128; Wood to Dundas 16 Apr. 1855: Add. 49,558 f57; The Queen to Wood 24 Mar. 1855: HALIFAX A4/73; The Queen to Palmerston 19 Mar. 1855: Bdlds. RC/F f573; Statement by Graham 16 Feb. 1855: HANSARD CXXXVI; Times, Editorial 3 Apr. 1855; Graham to Wood 6 Apr. 1855: HALIFAX A4/70; Berkeley to Wood 1 Apr. 1855: *ibid.* A4/74.

4   Foreign Office to Admiralty 15 Mar. 1855: ADM 1/5662.

5   Dundas to Viscount Melville 1 May 1855: MCM GD/51/8/7/62 f22.

6   LEWIS, pp. 30, 79, 124–5; Statement of Services: BAYNES BAY/1; Graham to the Queen 14 Feb. 1855: Gr. B.125; The Queen to Graham 15 Feb. 1855: *ibid.*

7   Admiralty Order 19 Feb.1855: ADM 2/169 no. 2; Graham to

Plumridge Feb. 1855: Gr. CW19; T. Martin to H. Martin 22 Aug. 1854: Add. 41,467 f237–9; Cochrane memo. 7 Feb. 1855: Add. 49,554 f121.
8   Admiralty to Dundas 7 Apr. 1855: Add. 49,533 f9–13; Wood to Dundas 24 Apr. 1855: Add. 49,565 f64.
9   Admiralty to Foreign Office 12 Feb. 1855: ADM 1/5661; Admiralty to Dundas 14, 15 Mar. 1855: ADM 2/1703 f1–5; COLOMB, pp. 252–6.
10   Admiralty to Dundas 7 Apr. 1855: Add. 49,533 f9–12; Clarendon to Cowley 2 Apr. 1855: F.O. 519/171 f282.
11   *Times*, 5, 7, 10 Apr. 1855; Admiralty to Surveyor 5 Apr. 1855: ADM 87/53 f2087; Wood to Dundas 7, 10 Apr. 1855: Add. 49,558 f42, 48–50; Dundas to Wood 8 Apr. 1855: Add. 49,533 f15–17.
12   Codrington to Lady Bourchier 28 Apr., 2 May 1855: COD 113/1; COLOMB, Admiral P. H., *Memoirs of Sir Astley Cooper-Key* (London 1898), p. 256 (letter of 13 May).
13   SULIVAN, p. 281 (letter of 13 May); Times 3 Apr. 1855.
14   Dundas to Admiralty 19, 24 Apr. 3, rec. 8 May 1855 no. 28, 47, 72: ADM 1/5647 and NRS pp. 28, 30; Wood to Dundas 16, 17 Apr. 1855: Add. 49,562 f57; Dundas to Wood 20, 22 Apr. 1855: Add. 49,533 f19–24.
15   Wood to Dundas 24, 30 Apr. 1855: Add. 49,562 f64, 72; Cowley to Clarendon 5 Apr. 1855: F.O. 519/4 f384; BAXTER, p. 82.
16   Dundas to Wood 2, 15 May 1855: Add. 49,,533 f28–33, 42–5; Dundas to Admiralty 3, 8, 13 rec. 8, 15, 21 May 1855 no. 72, 77, 85: NRS pp. 30–45; SULIVAN, p. 282; Magennis to Clarendon 22 Jan. 1855: F.O. 73/270 f6; Wood to Dundas 7, 22 May 1855: Add. 49,533 f83, 95; Wood to Cowley 15 May 1855: *ibid.* f89.
17   Dundas to Admiralty 21, 22, 28 rec. 28 May, 4 Jun. 1855 no. 103, 104: ADM 1/5647; Dundas to Wood 22 May 1855: Add. 49,533 f52–7; Clarendon to Wood 11 May 1855: Cl. Dep. C29 f413.
18   Dundas to Admiralty 2 rec. 18 Jun. 1855 no. 130: NRS pp. 56–8; Dundas to Wood 28 May 1855: Add. 49,533 f59–61; SULIVAN, p. 286; Codrington to Lady Bourchier 23 May 1855: BOURCHIER, p. 423; Wood to Dundas 29 May 1855: Add. 49,562 f106; Admiralty Orders 2 Feb. 21, 22, 24, 25 May 1855: ADM 2/1568 no. 434–8, 2/1570 no. 57–81, 91, 103, 106.
19   SULIVAN, p. 287; Dundas to Admiralty 4 rec. 18 Jun. 1855 no. 142: NRS pp. 59–61; Dundas to Wood 4 rec. 11 Jun. 1855: Add. 49,533 f63–7.
20   Wood to Grey 1 Jun. 1855: Add. 49,562 f111; Wood to Dundas 5 Jun. 1855: *ibid.* f124; Dundas to Admiralty 7, 11, 18 Jun., 2 Jul. 1855: ADM 1/5647; SULIVAN, pp. 199–202.
21   Dundas to Admiralty 11 Jun. 1855 no. 168, 173: ADM 1/5647; Wood to Stewart 8 Jun. 1855: Add. 49,49,562 f132; Wood to Dundas 12, 26 Jun. 1855: Add. 49,563 f4, 31; Wood to Cowley 19 Jun. 1855: *ibid.* f12; Wood to Palmerston 22 Jun. 1855: *ibid.* f18; Dundas to Wood 18 Jun. 1855: Add. 49,533 f78–81.
22   Dundas to Admiralty 18, 21, 25 Jun. rec. 25 Jun. 2 Jul. 1855: ADM 1/5647; Dundas to Wood 18 Jun. 1855: Add. 49,533 f79–81; Admiralty Orders 26, 27 Jun. 1855 no. 233–4: ADM 2/1570; SULIVAN, pp. 301–3.
23   Dundas to Admiralty 25 Jun. 2 Jul. rec. 2, 9 Jul. 1855 no. 203, 224:

ADM 1/5647; Dundas to Wood 4 Jun. 1855: Add. 49,533 f63–7.

24   Cowley to Clarendon 27 Jun. 1855: F.O. 519/5 f2–3; Clarendon to Wood 2 Jun. 1855: HALIFAX A4/70ii; Admiralty to Dundas 3 Jul. 1855, no. 353: ADM 2/1703 p. 309; Dundas to Admiralty 9, 16 Jul. 1855, no. 232, 247; ADM 1/5647; Wood to Dundas 24 Jul. 1855: Add. 49, 563 f73.

20

Sweaborg

Rear-Admiral Baynes, *Retribution*, reached Nargen on 27 June with the blockships, mortar vessels, the remaining gunboats and the corvette *Falcon*. The blockships appeared well manned but required final fitting out, and the other vessels were equally ill-finished. The blockading cruisers were proving effective. From the Gulf of Riga Heathcote reported only a few boats attempted to move. *Arrogant* went into Lovisia Bay on 5 and 6 July, destroying a fort and government buildings. Yet Dundas anticipated the Russians would attempt to drive off his ships with steam gunboats before the season ended. As he did not want the batteries Wood wished they had never been built; Berkeley held them in low regard and Panmure was having to defend them in the Lords. He was resigned to the blockade, reporting no-one expected more.[1]

With his forces finally assembled Dundas returned to Sweaborg, leaving Baynes off Cronstadt in place of the injured Seymour and the battleships spread around the Gulf. In private he reported that having seen Russian guns range out to 4,000 yards at Cronstadt he feared the mortar vessels would go into action under fire. When the mortar expert attached to the flagship, Captain Nugent, RE referred to an eight-day bombardment, Dundas feared a counter attack. While there appeared to be little purpose in attacking, apart from the hope of some glory, Dundas decided the heavy ships should not take part. Wood believed Sweaborg was the only target for the mortar vessels, they could then be sent home. Although anxious to annoy the enemy, pointing to the southern shore of the Gulf, he considered the blockade the most effective measure. With Palmerston he was looking at new methods of attack.[2]

Dundas and Penaud arrived at Nargen on the 16th. The allied forces were still incomplete, there were no mortar shells and a French floating battery crew found their vessel was on passage to the

Crimea. Dundas realised the fleet was desperate for action, but found little encouragement when he inspected the arsenal on the 18th. Several commanding new works had been built: 'In short it seems impossible to take up positions anywhere in which mortars would be out of range of heavy guns, but still here are the mortars & here will be the shells when *Calcutta* and *Aeolus* arrive & they may be here this week.' The two Admirals saw little prospect of doing any real damage; 'the wish to do something must be the principal inducement'. While the blockships worked up the rest of the fleet remained active. Baynes reported no change at Cronstadt, although *Arrogant*, *Cossack* and *Magicienne* attacked troops near Frederickshamn, and renewed activity in the Gulf of Riga led Penaud to send *Austerlitz* and a corvette without consultation, which alarmed Dundas. In the Gulf of Bothnia Captain Warden conducted the operations with more sense than those of 1854. Yelverton's squadron, with five gunboats and four mortar vessels, captured the island of Kotka near Hogland on 26 July, destroying government buildings.[3]

By the end of July the allied forces at Nargen comprised four blockships, one French and fourteen British gunboats, fifteen British and five French mortar vessels. The ammunition had arrived, and the French were expecting more flotilla craft. The two Admirals agreed a 'serious attack' was impossible. Dundas was alarmed by the weather and the conduct of Penaud. At home no-one appreciated quite how cautious Dundas had become; the Queen shared Wood's view that Cronstadt was the place to take risks, not realising Dundas had no intention of taking any risks. Sulivan blamed this lack of resolve on the Captain of the Fleet, Frederick Pelham. Arriving off Sweaborg on 6 August Dundas spread his cruisers on the coast, and although the weather was far from ideal, he now anticipated causing significant damage to parts of the island of Vargon, the closest of the Sweaborg group. With the approaches still imperfectly charted Sulivan had to place all the ships and mortar vessels. Wood became alarmed when he realised Dundas was only attacking 'because' he had the mortars, being more concerned to plan a grand attack across the northern barrier at Cronstadt for 1856. The unwanted batteries had already left for the Euxine. Waiting for news from Sweaborg he did not anticipate any worthwhile result, although he sent out more ammunition.[4]

As Dundas was going to bombard Sweaborg using Sulivan's plan

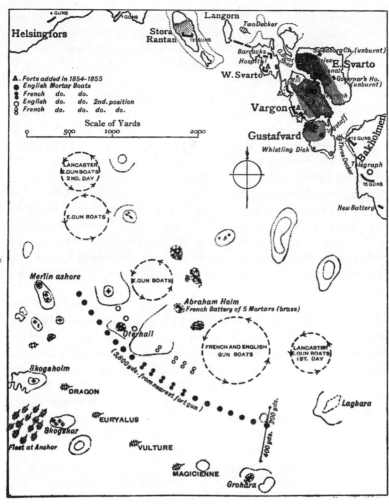

8 The bombardment of Sweaborg, 8–10 August 1854, from the *Life of Admiral Sir Bartholomew James Sulivan*

most presumed Sulivan would direct the operation, but Dundas allowed the Captain of the Fleet to take charge, restricting Sulivan to a subordinate role. The final forces were sixteen gunboats and sixteen mortar vessels from Britain, with five of each from France. As the French had fewer craft Dundas agreed to them landing four 10-inch mortars on Oterhall. The only battleships present were the two British flagships, three new blockships, all three French battleships and *Edinburgh*; with so few heavy ships it was obvious to the Russians that there would be no serious attack. Sulivan's plan called for the mortars to be 3,000 yards from the nearest batteries, but Dundas insisted they be a further 300 yards back. After consulting Captain Wemyss, RM, Sulivan reluctantly concurred; they agreed that the increased range would hamper attempts to reach the more distant parts of the arsenal. The mortar vessels were supported by the frigates *Magicienne*, *Euryalus*, *Vulture* and *Dragon*, 400 yards further back. Pelham wanted the craft even further back, but when given orders to this effect Sulivan merely swung them on their cables.

Going aboard the mortar vessels late on the 7th Sulivan found they were anchored on too short a cable to haul up into range. He then postponed the attack for a day on his own authority. On the night of the 8th Sulivan found several mortar vessels stationary when they should have been hauling up into range, but after waiting for the French vessels the attack finally commenced at 07.00 on the 9th, several hours after dawn. Wemyss had decided to throw as many shells as possible in a short time, to build up a body of flames. During the first hour *Growler*'s mortar, cast in 1813, fired over thirty rounds, an unprecedented feat which the new barrels could not match. The gunboats engaged the batteries, keeping underway to draw off counter-battery fire; *Stork* and *Snapper*, armed with Lancaster guns, forced the three-decker *Rossiya* to withdraw from an enfilading position between Bakholmen and Gustafsvard.

In addition to Sulivan's plan Dundas ordered diversionary attacks on either side of the arsenal, although without troops these were hardly convincing. *Cornwallis*, *Hastings* and *Amphion* engaged the batteries at Sandhamn, six miles to the east. During the three-and-a-half hour firefight several gunboats joined the defences. The British suffered fourteen wounded and some damage to their ships, the Russians had one gun overturned. Sulivan criticised the attack, which he believed exposed ships to damage for no purpose. The ships went into action at 800 yards, as a diversion; had they been serious and opened at 500 yards they would had more effect. To the west *Arrogant*, *Cossack* and *Cruiser* shelled a body of troops out of the woods on the island of Drumsio.[5]

The main bombardment aroused a powerful response from the Russians, although the flotilla suffered no casualties. After initially using every gun, the Russians settled for a few long range pieces and mortars. After 10.00 fires took hold of buildings on Vargon, where two large explosions were observed. At noon a far larger explosion occurred on Gustafsvard, thereafter Russian fire slackened. The British had little cause to celebrate, their mortars were defective and the rate of fire had to be reduced to preserve them. Dundas recalled the gunboats before dark as they risked running aground. They were replaced by the boats of the fleet armed with rockets, which kept up a heavy fire for three hours, adding to the conflagration. Fourteen men were injured by a premature detonation. As much of Vargon and Svarto were already burnt to the ground the mortar vessels warped closer and resumed firing early the next morning, but defective barrels prevented them reaching the more distant parts of the arsenal. One mortar burst, although no one was injured. The Inspector of Machinery, Mr Ward, worked from the factory ship *Volcano* repairing the damaged barrels with molten zinc. *Beacon*'s weapon was repaired six times, each allowing a further burst of up to thirty rounds. It would have been preferable to replace the damaged barrels, but Wood had decided against sending any spares. Two more barrels burst as the mortars kept up a steady fire during the night of the 10th supported by the rocket boats, and another premature detonation injured one man belonging to *Vulture*.

During the night Dundas spent several hours searching for Penaud, to discuss ending the bombardment, before a midshipman aboard his flagship revealed that the Admiral had taken his gunboats to attack the two-decker lying between Langhorn and West Svarto. This wild project came to a sudden end when the gunboats ran aground. In the glare from the burning arsenal they made excellent targets. Penaud considered abandoning them, but they floated off before dawn. Dundas wanted to cease fire at dawn, from lack of targets in range and the dangerous condition of his remaining mortars, and a shaken Penaud was happy to agree. By this time the Russian fire had almost ceased, and although the batteries were not badly damaged the arsenal was ruined. In public Dundas was sparing of praise, although he did tell Sulivan: 'everyone in the fleet knows our success is due to you'. This was correct; Sulivan was responsible for everything of value in the 1855 campaign, Dundas's contribution was caution.[6]

The failure of the mortars created considerable interest, particularly as the French barrels remained serviceable after the action. The British had been unsafe from the afternoon of the 9th. Some observers blamed the unprecedented rate of fire, but the 1813 weapon in *Growler* fired faster and longer than any of the new barrels. It was necessary to provide some explanation, so Wemyss was sent home with a detailed action history; Dundas suspected they had been cast of inferior metal. In fact the Admiralty had already been warned some were incapable of prolonged firing; on 7 May Captain Julius Roberts, RMA, reported holes in the bores of the six barrels supplied for the vessels fitted with his swinging suspension gear. This was a matter for the Board of Ordnance, but with more pressing matters in hand the enquiry was long winded. The barrels were traced to Grissell and Co. of the Regent's Canal Ironworks. The holes were caused by the lathe used to bore the barrels, and had in some cases been covered by a plug of soft iron. When tried at Shoeburyness one weapon failed, although Brunel and John Fowler, superintendent at Woolwich, considered Grissells had carried out the work satisfactorily. On enquiry Grissells stated that the contract price for a 13-inch sea service mortar was £24, but they cost £28 to produce. Substandard pieces were being submitted, and improper methods employed. Panmure eventually declared the holes were a weakness of which the Ordnance should have been informed. Eight barrels burst at Sweaborg exactly where Grissell's had placed their iron plug. The bombardments of Sweaborg and Kinburn were the last use of mortars by the Royal Navy; with the development of rifled artillery they fell out of favour, despite considerable success during the American Civil War of 1861–65. At Sweaborg the mortar performed well as an engine of destruction; 3,141 shells were fired, using 100 tons of powder, the French fired 2,828 shells. *Havoc's* weapon was used only ninety-four times, *Growler's* 355. Nine of the sixteen barrels fired less than 200 rounds, only two managed more than 300. Eleven barrels were repaired, some more than once. *Growler's* was not repaired, indicating the approximate service life of a well made mortar. The failure of the others reflected poor casting and boring. Captain Roberts' suspension gear, which allowed the barrel to train, rather than being fixed to the base, was given a combat trial; *Growler* used the system to achieve the highest rate of fire, the equipment in *Surly* and *Drake* broke during the first day, while *Havoc*'s barrel failed after ninety-four rounds. While Roberts's system was an advance, Wemyss observed that it would make changing barrels more difficult. Several of the vessels built for the 1856 campaign were fitted on Roberts's plan. Sulivan and Wemyss decided mortars should be expendable stores, to be replaced from stock.[7]

The attack exceeded the expectations of all, except perhaps Sulivan, both in the damage inflicted (fully three-quarters of the arsenal was ruined), and the absence of fatal casualties. Before publishing Dundas's dispatch the Board removed all references to the failure of the mortars. Penaud, once he had recovered his nerve, alarmed Dundas by proposing all manner of wild schemes, including a direct attack on the man-of-war harbour, and bombarding Helsingfors. The lessons of the attack were clear to both British and Russians; the flotilla had demonstrated the tactics required to assault sea forts, the way to Cronstadt was open. Up at Seskar Codrington complained that the fleet should have been present, in case the arsenal had been laid open to a real attack. Cooper-Key was more concerned about the public reaction to what he saw as exaggerated claims.[8]

The essential differences between Sweaborg and Cronstadt lay in the object and scale of the attack; at Sweaborg the intention was to destroy the arsenal, workshops and support facilities, it was not necessary to deal with the batteries. The 1855 attack ruined Sweaborg as a base for ships and gunboats. However, as Sulivan had always known, and Dundas, Wood, Palmerston and even the Queen had come to accept, Sweaborg was not vital to Russia. Helsingfors was open to attack and Finland could be more easily invaded anywhere else; closing with the batteries would have been as futile and costly in 1855 as in 1854. By contrast the batteries at Cronstadt covered the deep water passage to St Petersburg. They would have to be silenced to open the Russian capital and fleet to attack. The destruction of Cronstadt would require the fleet to destroy the granite casemates with concentrated close range broadsides, which could only be done after prolonged bombardment. The fall of Cronstadt would open the Russian capital to any insult the allies cared to inflict, a tremendous blow to the Russian state. The forces available in 1855, even with the floating batteries and the full French complement, were not adequate to attempt Cronstadt. Anything less than a decisive attack would be worse than useless, pointing out weaknesses and giving the Russians a winter to remedy them. Sweaborg made the best use of the available light forces, achieving a useful result at very small cost.

Dundas announced the success of the attack in a telegraph of the 11th. News of the mortar failure did not reach London for another nine days. Returning to Nargen soon after the attack Dundas prepared the mortar vessels to return to Britain. They left on the 17th and 18th, escorted by three cruisers; once clear of the Gulf they proceeded independently to Elsinore where a cruiser and a transport would assist them past the Skaw. Unaware of this the Board ordered *Sans Pareil* to load eight new barrels, two steamers would carry the ammunition. The following day the battleship was ordered to land her lower deck guns and embark sixteen mortars. Wood was determined Dundas would not lose an opportunity for lack of material. Like Graham, he was not satisfied with one success; where he had looked for no more than a blockade, he now wanted another bombardment. On the 24th Dundas was telegraphed to keep his mortar vessels and await *Sans Pareil*; Dundas reported their departure, claiming that even with new barrels they would only be a nuisance, and protested at the dispatch of new barrels. He also claimed the mortar beds were defective, when they were still quite sound, but Wood was more concerned to prepare for Cronstadt than pick a quarrel.[9]

While Dundas attacked Sweaborg Baynes found little to report off Cronstadt. *Hogue* demolished some semaphores on 7 August, and a sortie by six Russian steam gunboats on the 16th was driven back by *Imperieuse*, *Centaur* and *Bulldog*. This was the first time the Russians had been so far out of the harbour in full view of the blockading ships. Their failure to adopt a more aggressive policy left the British an easy task, although Dundas feared they would prove more enterprising once fully equipped with steam. Seymour went up to Cronstadt on the 16th to relieve Baynes for service in the Gulf of Bothnia. Dundas shared Napier's view that mid August was the end of the season for major operations, dismissing Penaud's desire to bombard Reval and Helsingfors. The one area that did appeal was the Bay of Viborg. *Arrogant* and *Magicienne* remained active and he still had the gunboats and blockships. Seymour was instructed to avoid Viborg until Sulivan arrived, but Yelverton and Vansittart reported new batteries and barriers, which discouraged Dundas. He proposed sending home the gunboats and blockships by the end of September. Until then he would keep the battlesquadrons at Seskar and off Cronstadt, distributing the remaining forces along the coast. *Hawke*, Captain Ommaney, went to the Gulf off Riga, where he engaged the batteries and row gunboats at the mouth of the river Dwina on the 10th, and the forts at Domeness on the 14th. The Vice-Consul at Memel reported that an attack on the fortified camp at Dwinamunde would produce unrest in the Baltic provinces, but Dundas left Ommaney to attack anything he pleased, while ridiculing his exaggerated reports. *Edinburgh* and *Amphion* were detailed to watch the coast to the east and west of Sweaborg. Local newspapers indicated the Russians were attempting to play down the significance of the bombardment, the Finns tended to the other extreme. The squadron in the Gulf of Bothnia continued to be active ashore.[10]

By remaining at Nargen Dundas kept Penaud away from Cronstadt, as the French Admiral considered his place was alongside his colleague. This left Seymour in command with an all-British force. Ater 27 August most of his ships were at Seskar, the weather being too unsettled at Tolboukin. His decision was influenced by the Russian battleships housing their topmasts, with a small detachment off Cronstadt he would now have ample warning of a sortie. *Nile* and *Colossus* were left off Cronstadt, while *Arrogant* went to report on the anchorages near Viborg Bay. Even at Seskar the weather was boisterous, *Cressy* pitching her bowsprit under water, and breaking her rudder, forcing Seymour to keep *Nile*, which he had planned to send down to Nargen. No sooner had Dundas persuaded Wood to recall the mortars than Penaud produced long range rockets to attack Reval. Fortunately specific orders arrived, restricting their use to Cronstadt. For the winter Berkeley, encouraged by Codrington, anticipated problems keeping the men afloat and hoped to leave some ships in the Baltic. Dundas and Wood believed there would be more trouble if they were marooned in Sweden. Dundas accepted the rest of the campaign would involve blockading an enemy who had no intention of fighting, work that would necessarily fall to those who missed the action at Sweaborg. Wood merely hoped the Russian battleships would be iced in before Dundas left. In the long term Dundas was frightened by Russian steam gunboats, calling for more of his own, long range guns and mortars, and twelve first class steam battleships. Palmerston observed his pessimism, but supported the call for improved artillery, although he had more faith in the batteries.[11]

On 31 August Seymour detached *Nile*, Captain Munday, *Pylades* and two gunboats to occupy the Straits of Biorko, to interrupt the inshore traffic. Dundas was determined to keep steam gunboats away from Sweaborg and Hango; he did not appreciate that while the British fleet lay at Seskar the Russians were unlikely to spare resources to attack him elsewhere. The proper method of keeping the Russians on the defensive was to threaten their central position. The blockade was tested on 2 September. The steam battleship *Viborg*, a screw frigate and several gunboats sortied out at 14.00. *Colossus*, Captain Robinson and *Imperieuse*, lying at anchor ten to twelve miles beyond Tolboukin, slipped and gave chase. The Russians turned for home, although Robinson reckoned he came within two miles of them before they reached the safety of the forts. Seymour added a paddlesteamer to the force, stationing repeating ships between Cronstadt and Seskar. At Biorko Munday was forced into action by Russian preparations to occupy Biorko Island. Once established there they would make the anchorage untenable. Munday cut out the vessels prepared for this; Seymour gave an open permission to withdraw, but *Nile* remained. There was hardly an officer in the fleet who would abandon a station that promised some action. Although he wanted to keep up the occupation of Biorko as late as possible, Dundas privately feared this would only encourage the Russians to build batteries before the following campaign: Biorko had been selected as the base for the Cronstadt operation. The Board approved keeping strong forces at the head of the Gulf, Wood complained about the anticipated removal of *Nile* while she was still in place. Munday was joined by *Arrogant* and *Centaur* for another attack on 13 September, fourteen vessels and several boats were taken.[12]

At Nargen *Tourville* broke loose and ran into *Duke of Wellington*. The British spent much of their time ashore, playing cricket. Dundas prepared to send the new blockships home. Once again the Admiralty had prepared a list of home ports for every ship. Munday continued his operation at Biorko with the destruction of six vessels in Schmelska Bay on 18 September, only a battery and a pontoon remained that were of any interest. Dundas went up to Seskar on the

27th, leaving Codrington in command, for one last look at Cronstadt, and to discuss the timing of a withdrawal with Seymour. The ice was expected in mid November, so he left Seymour at liberty to withdraw from late October. The occupation of Biorko would have to end before that. *Nile*, a poor steamer, would have to leave before more efficient ships.[13] In the Gulf of Bothnia Baynes found only a petty boat trade, carried on in atrocious weather.

Believing poor metal caused the mortar failure Palmerston called for the old Russian guns at Bomarsund to be recovered and recast. More logical enquiries were made for supplies of Swedish ore and mortars. After initial problems the export of pig iron was allowed from 1 January, 1856, although the normal tariff was charged. Wood passed Palmerston's request to Dundas, the work was then delegated through Baynes to Warden. All told, eighty-two guns were found. Dundas did not conceal his activities from Penaud, who was entitled to half, but the French had no need for the old barrels. 'Nemesis' Hall found more guns off Hango Head, where he had been sent on 25 September. After firing a salute for the fall of Sevastopol he knocked down several telegraphs and attacked the batteries at Eckness. He discovered nine large guns and two 10-inch mortars, thrown into the sea when the Russians evacuated Hango in late 1854. However, as Dundas observed, Hall 'never fails to mix up some absurdities with all his good deeds', landing at Hango to conduct a funeral for *Cossack*'s men.[14]

The end of the 1855 campaign proved timely. The activities of British recruiting agents in the USA provoked a strong official complaint and the arrest of one agent. Palmerston ordered two battalions of infantry to Canada, and called for naval reinforcement. Wood offered *Powerful* and *Calcutta* from the Channel squadron, *Sans Pareil*, two blockships and a steamer. While the demonstration that Britain did have reserves was useful, relations improved and part of the force was never sent. Some believed this was a coincidence, although Palmerston preferred to credit the ships. Realising he might need a fleet at short notice Wood invited Dundas to send home some ships for refit. During October the British forces began to withdraw from both Gulfs. Dundas examined Cronstadt on the 2nd, returning to Nargen on the 4th to co-ordinate the move to Kiel. *Nile* and the gunboats were withdrawn from Biorko, leaving *Arrogant* and *Pylades* in occupation. The British gunboats were disarmed and sent home; their ubiquity demonstrated why little was achieved in 1854.

The cruisers in the Gulf of Riga continued to harass the Russians; Heathcote, *Archer* led the squadron in a brush with Fort Comet at Riga and other local batteries. He noted numerous new earthworks, although they could do nothing to stop the ships capturing every vessel that put to sea. Toward the end of the month the old blockships were ordered home and the ships in St Petersburg Bay were forced to run down to Seskar by the weather. Seymour then cleared the anchorage of auxiliaries, leaving *Orion* off Tolboukin to cover the frigate squadron. The main force left Seskar on the 26th. On passage *Caesar* and *Arrogant* broke their propeller shafts and were sent home. *Nile, Royal George* and *Cressy*, being poor steamers, went to Kiel. Dundas went up to Fogle Fiord on the 20th to confer with Baynes. The Gulf of Bothnia would be left to the powerful corvettes *Tartar* and *Harrier*. Baynes would then take command in the Gulf of Finland, while Dundas went to Kiel with the battlefleet. Although Dundas had hoped to prolong his stay at Nargen he knew that while he stayed Penaud would also remain. Wood encouraged an early return to spread the load on the dockyards and brief Dundas for the Council of War.[15]

Sulivan, with little to do after Sweaborg, left the Baltic in late October depressed by petty attacks on defenceless targets. Back in Britain his enthusiasm was rekindled by discussions of the 1856 campaign, and these took on a new urgency with reports from Kinburn. On 6 November Wood and Sulivan agreed that floating batteries would be an important element for the Cronstadt attack. Palmerston initially believed they had done all the work at Kinburn; while it was polite to tell Louis Napoleon as much, Wood was careful to give him a more accurate account.[16]

Baynes reached Nargen on 3 November to meet Dundas. *Magicienne* returned from Sweaborg the same day, reporting new batteries and some rebuilding. Sending Seymour on to Kiel with three battleships on the 5th, Dundas prepared to follow. Wood wanted Seymour home early to recuperate. Dundas finally left Nargen on the 11th with *Majestic*; Penaud followed the next day. *Orion* remained to support Baynes for another week. Leaving Watson with the end-of-season blockade, Baynes remained near Hango until the break up of the first ice indicated pack and sheet ice would soon form. *Falcon* went to Stockholm to cover an American merchant ship suspected of carrying arms. Dundas arrived at Kiel on the 14th after a rough passage, and *Orion* joined on the 29th. *Nile, Royal*

George and *Colossus* cleared for Britain on the 28th, to avoid the worst of the weather. Although he had hoped to visit Stockholm Dundas never found the time, which was unfortunate in view of the negotiations then in progress. Meeting Canrobert at Kiel on the 30th Dundas realised the French wanted to land a large army in the Baltic during 1856, but remained convinced the Russians could hold Cronstadt. He left Kiel on 6 December, reaching Spithead on the 19th, the day Baynes lifted the blockade.[17]

While British activity in the Baltic during 1855 produced no decisive results it fulfilled several important roles. Primarily it created strategic problems for the Russians, forcing them to keep a large army, estimated at over 200,000, spread along the coast. Second, the minor operations provided a regular display of British moral ascendancy which could only discourage the enemy. Finally, the way to Cronstadt was examined and new lessons learned at Sweaborg; the defects revealed could be rectified before the next season. The attack also convinced the Russians that Cronstadt was vulnerable; Dundas did not believe it could be taken, but Sulivan was certain. These new tactics dovetailed with the diplomatic and strategic developments of late 1855. All pointed to the Baltic becoming the decisive theatre in 1856. The new strategy only became irrelevant when diplomatic pressure brought Russia to accept the allied terms.

Dundas demonstrated a much better grasp of the principles of theatre command than the other wartime Admirals, controlling the campaign in a more distant fashion and entrusting important tasks to Seymour and Baynes. His caution, which was hardly justified by the performance of the Russians, hampered Sulivan. In both campaigns the ability of the fleet to attack Russia was reduced by a shortage of light forces and troops. Despite that, the fleet forced Russia to build major defences, or abandon exposed positions. For a campaign of which so little was expected in March, the results were significant. 1856 promised much more.

Notes

1 Dundas to Admiralty 27 Jun. 9 Jul. rec. 9, 16 Jul. 1855 no. 242, 247: ADM 1/5647; Baynes to Dundas 30 Jun. 1855: MCM GD51/2/1008 f219; Dundas to Wood 2 Jul. 1855: Add. 49,533 f86–90; Wood to Dundas 3 Jul. 1855: Add. 49,563 f40; Codrington to Lady Bourchier 18 Jun. 1855: BOURCHIER, p. 429; Panmure statement 3 Jul. 1855: HANSARD

CXXXVII, col. 2037.
2 Dundas to Wood 9 Jul. 1855: Add. 49,533 f97–104; Wood to Dundas 10, 17, 24 Jul. 1855: Add. 49.563 f53, 64, 73; COLOMB, p. 259; Palmerston to Wood 16 Jul. 1855: HALIFAX A4/63 f37; Wood to Palmerston 16 Jul. 1855: Bdlds. GC/WO f31.
3 Dundas to Wood 17, 24 Jul. 1855: Add. 49,533 f106–20; BAXTER, p. 82; Dundas to Admiralty 21, 23, 24 Jul. 1855 no. 283, 302, 307: ADM 1/5647.
4 Dundas to Admiralty 30, 31 Jul., 6 Aug. 1855 no. 335, 337, 357: *ibid.*; Dundas to Wood 31 Jul., 6 Aug. 1855: Add. 49,533 f122–3, 129; Dundas to Viscount Melville 31 Jul. 1855: MCM GD51/8/7/63 f17x; The Queen to Wood 4 Aug. 1855: HALIFAX A4/73; SULIVAN, pp. 274–5, 320; Wood to Dundas 7, 14 Aug. 1855: Add. 49,563 f100, 114.
5 Dundas to Admiralty 13 Aug. 1855 no. 367: ADM 1/5647; COLOMB, p. 261: SULIVAN, p. 334.
6 Wood to Dundas 17 Jul. 1855: Add. 49,563 f64–7; Dundas to Wood 21 Aug. 1855: Add. 49,533 f137–40.
7 Dundas to Admiralty 21 Aug. 1855 no. 416: ADM 1/5647; Captain Roberts to Admiralty 7 May 1855: ADM 2/1570 pp. 4–5; Parliamentary Papers 1856 vol. XL p. 391 and SULIVAN, p. 342.
8 Codrington to Lady Bourchier 22 Aug. 1855: COD 113/1; COLOMB, p. 262.
9 Admiralty to Sheerness 20 Aug. 1855: ADM 2/1570; Admiralty to Ordnance 20, 21 Aug. 1855: ADM 2/2681; Wood to Dundas 21, 28 Aug. 1855: Add. 49,564 f2, 11; Admiralty to Consuls at Kiel, Elsinore and Dantzig 21, 24, 27 Aug. 1855: NRS pp. 240–1; Dundas to Admiralty 27 Aug. 1855 no. 421: ADM 1/5647; Dundas to Wood 28, 29 Aug. 1855: Add. 49,533 f142–8; Deptford Dockyard to Surveyor 8 Oct. 1855: ADM 87/55 f5430.
10 Dundas to Admiralty 16, 20 rec. 27 Aug. 1855 no. 378, 392: ADM 1/5647; Seymour to Dundas 18 Aug. 1855: MCM GD51/1008/2 f15; COLOMB, p. 260; Dundas to Admiralty 21, 31 Aug., 4, 21, 27 Sep. 1855 no. 404, 405, 431, 448, 476: ADM 1/5648.
11 Seymour to Dundas 23, 27, 29, 30 Aug. 1855: MCM GD51/1008/2 f4–14; Dundas to Wood 21, 28, 29 Aug., 11 Sept. 1855: Add. 49,533 f137–54; SULIVAN, p. 344; Berkeley to Wood 4 Sept. 1855: HALIFAX A4/74; Codrington to Berkeley 18 Jun. 1855: COD 109/1; Wood to Dundas 18, 28 Aug. 1855: Add. 49,564 f11, 46; Palmerston to Wood 18 Sept. 1855: Add. 48,579 f61.
12 Dundas to Admiralty 4, 10, 11, 17 Sept. 1855 no. 447, 494, 505, 515: ADM 1/5648; Foreign Office to Admiralty 14 May 1855: ADM 1/5663; Seymour to Dundas 3 Sept. 1855: MCM GD51/1008/2 f19; Admiralty to Dundas 4, 17 Sept. 1855: NRS pp. 263, 287; Wood to Dundas 18 Sept. 1855: Add. 49,564 f46.
13 Dundas to Wood 18 Sept. 1 Oct. 1855: Add. 49,533 f159, 165–7; Times 19 Sept. 1855 and SULIVAN, p. 361; Dundas to Admiralty 18 Sept., 1 Oct.1855 no. 520–4, 570: ADM 1/5648; Seymour to Dundas 28 Sept., 5 Oct. 1855: MCM GD51/1008/2 f37–9; Admiralty to Dundas 19 Sept. 1855

no. 589: NRS p. 295; Wood to Dundas 25 Sept. 1855: Add, 49,564 f58.
14 Baynes to Dundas 18 Sept., 6 Oct. 1855: MCM GD51/1008/2 f55, 60; Wood to Palmerston 21 Sept. 1855: Bdlds. GC/WO f58; Magennis to Clarendon 17 Oct. 24 Dec. 1855, 19 Jan. 1856: F.O. 73/271 f75, 114 and 73/278 f7; Dundas to Wood 25 Sept., 14, 23 Oct. 1855: Add. 49,533 f162, 171–4; Dundas to Baynes 26 Sept. 1855: BAYNES BAY/2; Dundas to Admiralty 3, 8 rec. 15 Oct. 1855 no. 573, 582: ADM 1/5648.
15 Palmerston to Clarendon 24 Sept. 1855: Add. 48,579 f73–4; Wood to Clarendon 27 Sept. 1855: Cl. Dep. C29 f477; Clarendon to Palmerston 15 Nov. 1855: Bdlds. GC/CL f724; ARGYLL, i, p. 591; Wood to Dundas 30 Oct. 1855: Add. 49,564 f114; Dundas to Admiralty 9, 20, 23, 30 Oct. 1855 no. 498, 552, 598, 635, 662: ADM 1/5648–9; Dundas to Wood 23, 30 Oct. 1855: Add. 49,533 f174–9.
16 SULIVAN, pp. 353–4; Wood to Dundas 6 Nov. 1855: Add, 49,564 f122; Wood to Palmerston 16 Jan. 1856: Add. 49,565 f59; Clarendon to Cowley 23 Nov. 1855: F.O. 519/172 f530.
17 Wood to Dundas 13, 26 Nov. 1855: Add. 49,565 f2, 17; Dundas to Admiralty 6, 15, 20 Nov., 10 Dec. 1855 no. 676, 686, 697, 759: ADM 1/5649; Dundas to Wood 15, 28 Nov. 1855: Add. 49,534 f4, 9–12, 14–16; Baynes to Admiralty 10 rec. 12 Dec. 1855: NRS p. 378.

21

The limits of power

After the fall of Sevastopol the German states, principally Austria and Prussia, but also Saxony and Bavaria, wanted to end a war which threatened to involve them. The Turkish government was satisfied no further benefit could accrue from continuing, while Walewski was among the majority in France calling for an early settlement. Russia was exhausted, and most accepted only further defeats awaited, but the regime was too proud to treat for terms. Neutral Austria had the freedom to lead the peace process, and did not lack pressing reasons of her own for acting. Despite Louis Napoleon's public rejection of peace Walewski allowed Borqueney to open secret discussions with Buol in early September. While the basis of any settlement remained the 'Four Points', Buol had to secure terms acceptable to both sides. He considered that if he issued an ultimatum to Russia he could then moderate western demands. However, his position as 'honest broker' was compromised by the addition of blatantly Austrian aims: the return of the strategic Russian-held sector of Bessarabia to the Principalities, and the complete exclusion of Russia from the navigable waters of the Danube and its tributaries in order to reduce Russian influence in the Balkans and ensure the Danube remained an artery of German trade.

The French Emperor opened unofficial links with Russia, through his half brother Count Morny, and the Saxon diplomat Seebach, Nesselrode's son in law. He also floated wider schemes to overthrow the 1815 settlement in favour of nationalities and natural frontiers, to be settled at a European conference. These designs were discussed with the British. Palmerston did not favour such far reaching changes, and Walewski used this to press for some moderation of British war aims, although Louis Napoleon's position appears to have been genuine.[1] The Emperor's grandiose objects emphasised the difference between his policy and that of Palmerston. Baumgart, incorrectly, considers Palmerston the more revolutionary. While both wanted large alterations in the map, Palmerston only looked to reduce the power of Russia. Louis Napoleon had more fundamental aims, which did not coincide with those of Palmerston. This was most apparent when Louis Napoleon wanted to raise the Polish question. Unwilling to alienate the German powers, Palmerston would only do so if the Poles rebelled. The Prince Consort agreed, considering the liberation of Germany from Russian dominance had been the major result of the conflict.[2] Palmerston would only enlarge the conflict into Germany if he could destroy the strategic threat posed by Russia for a generation. Schroeder suggests Palmerston encouraged Austria, to compromise her with Russia, and hoped then to play off France and Austria, introduce new terms and prolong the war to secure the Crimea, Georgia and Circassia. With further success the 'Four Points' could be expanded to cover his aims.

Walewski persuaded Louis Napoleon to accept the Buol-Borqueney sketch at the Council meeting of 17 October. The British demand to include Palmerston's three favoured areas was pressed by Cowley, but being short of an outright rejection it was ignored. Walewski informed the Austrian envoy on the 22nd, offering French support for the Austrian aims in return for a fifth point – the ability to raise any issue of European interest – which he hoped would cover British objections. On this basis Buol persuaded Franz Joseph to adopt the plan. It was initialled on 14 November, and specifically avoided committing Austria to enter the war. This was an admission of weakness; the Austrian army was then being demobilised to save money.[3] The threat of Austrian military action did not force Russia to make peace. Reliable details reached London on the 18th; Clarendon believed Russia could not accept, the Queen hoped she would. Palmerston emphasised the additions necessary to make the project match his conception of British aims; the neutralisation of the Euxine should be part of a five-power treaty, not a Russo–Turkish agreement, and it should include the Azov, Bug and Dnieper rivers. Nicolaiev was to be demilitarised, as were the Aland Islands. All Russian Black Sea ports were to have British Consuls, to oversee the implementation of the treaty. The status of the eastern shore of the Euxine must be open for discussion. After a six-hour cabinet debate on 20 November Palmerston agreed the project should not be rejected, but added his terms, hoping they would cause Russia to reject.[4]

After negotiations with Walewski neutralisation of the Azov was dropped and the Consuls clause left in abeyance until the final treaty. The issue of warships would be settled between Russia and Turkey, while Asia must depend on the military situation. Walewski did not pass on the new conditions to Buol, and Buol later refused to convey them to St Petersburg. The final text of the Austrian Ultimatum was drawn up on 16 December, and presented to Russia on the 28th. Palmerston and Clarendon believed the fifth point gave them the option to present new conditions unacceptable to Russia; they did not realise that Austria and France had assured the Russians this point would not cover any cession of territory, or financial indemnity. When Palmerston demanded prior acceptance of his terms before signing any armistice Buol ignored him, leaving Walewski to cobble up a compromise, unofficial, communication of the terms to Russia, linked to a promise of support at the peace conference. On 1 February 1856 the belligerent powers and Austria signed the protocol of the preliminaries for peace, after Buol categorically rejected a Russian attempt to modify Point One and delete Point Five.[5]

The Russian Crown Council discussed the Austrian Ultimatum, agreeing on the need to avoid the open Fifth Point; but they accepted that Russia, defeated and exhausted, could not resist the existing coalition, let alone one reinforced by Austria and Sweden. Only an exaggerated sense of honour and patriotism could support carrying on a hopeless war. When Buol refused to drop the Fifth Point the Council reconvened on 15 January; Austria offered some flexibility on the Bessarabian cession and the Fifth Point. In accepting, the Council justified their action by reference to the diplomatic and economic difficulties. Both Austria and Sweden were moving toward outright hostility, although the Austrian army could not take the field before the middle of 1856. The Czar anticipated the loss of the areas Palmerston had been aiming at for the past two years. The irresolute King of Prussia, under pressure from the allies, urged his nephew to make peace. He believed 1856 would see the French across the Rhine, Austrian troops in Silesia and a crippling British blockade. Russia was effectively isolated. At the economic level Miljutin argued that the serf economy could not support a long war; peace, reform and reconstruction would place Russian power on secure foundations. His argument carried real weight; exports were down four-fifths on 1853 figures, primarily due to the efficiency of the blockade in preventing the export of bulk produce. By contrast, imports were only down one-third, and this, with the interruption of trade, created massive inflation. In addition the sharp reduction in customs revenue left the Government able to meet only one-quarter of its wartime expenditure.[6] The most humiliating aspect of the process was the realisation that Britain was prepared to insult the Russian capital in 1856. The plans were on too large a scale not to be known to the Russians, while Sweaborg and Kinburn were too recent for there to be any doubt of success. This element has never been given proper weight in explaining the Russian decision for peace, although it was the immediate military threat, far more direct than campaigns in the Crimea, Asia Minor or even Galicia.

Another major omission from the historiography of the war has been the failure to appreciate the direct link between Palmerston's diplomacy and strategic planning. To view either in isolation underestimates the coherence of British policy, and ignores the real reasons why Russia made peace. Many commentators dismiss Palmerston as a poor war Premier, unable to develop or execute war-winning strategies. Rich states: 'there was never any chance that his plans would be successful'.[7] This is misleading; Palmerston adopted a grand strategy that took full account of French war weariness and the need for rapid success. In response the Russian Government accepted the Austrian Ultimatum. After the fall of Sevastopol many of the restrictions on Palmerston disappeared. His Parliamentary problems were over, the reports of the Committees and Boards of Enquiry became establishment whitewashes. Public opinion was firmly pro-Palmerston. In this atmosphere strategy developed to meet a new imperative. With Sevastopol taken he could adopt wider plans for Asia Minor and the Crimea, leading to the neutralisation of the Euxine. However, he could not rely on the luxury of another campaign. The French were tired of the war, and their Army felt satisfied by the capture of the Malakhoff. The first indication of this new urgency came with the pressure on Simpson to clear the Crimea before winter. From the lateness of the fall of Sevastopol nothing significant could be done elsewhere in the Black Sea theatre. With his hopes for 1855 disappointed Palmerston had to depend on Russia remaining in the war for another year. If they did he hoped to clear them out of Georgia and Circassia, settling the potentially difficult triple frontier between Russia, Turkey and Persia. This, like any other reduction of Russian territory, would be preferable to a financial indemnity. However, he realised these terms could not be achieved without inflicting further serious defeats, and these would require another twelve months. He did not favour attacking St Petersburg.

In October Persigny proposed switching allied resources north in 1856 to liberate Finland. Palmerston expressed a clear preference for Asia Minor. Despite his work to secure the Swedish Treaty and Wood's efforts to prepare a flotilla for Cronstadt, the Baltic remained secondary in Palmerston's thinking – a strategic diversion – into November. He was even prepared to give the French the chief command in the north, in exchange for that in Asia Minor. The fall of Kars and the threat to Ezeroum reinforced the need to operate in Asia, but by late November Palmerston was coming to accept the idea of a strategic attack on Cronstadt.[8] After discussions in December he favoured moving Lyons, his only successful commander, to the north. The apparent expansion of British strategy contained in Palmerston's planning has encouraged some historians to treat the post-Sevastopol phase as profoundly altering the character of the 'Crimean War'.[9] The war *never* had such a character. The concept of a Crimean War was developed by later commentators, ignoring all that occurred outside the peninsula and the chancelleries. In truth Palmerston, fearing an early and inadequate peace, changed the method by which he hoped to secure his aims from long term peripheral campaigns to a knock-out blow. Although convinced the Austrian ultimatum had been developed in concert with Russia, he was still ready to make peace, but only on terms which the state of the war in late 1855 could not justify. His war aims remained those of March 1854, to push back all of Russia's frontiers, or at the very least prevent future expansion. This should involve loss of territory and the neutralisation of the Euxine, the latter would enable Turkey to hold the Crimea and Asia Minor. To make this effective he wanted to demilitarise Nicolaiev, the major rivers and the Sea of Azov; Nicolaiev would otherwise be an inland, and less vulnerable, Sevastopol. This was a major issue for Palmerston, but remained subordinate to Asia Minor. The most obvious demonstration of his priorities came with the distribution of forces: wherever British interests were paramount British troops and British commanders were to be used; Nicolaiev and Kherson were left to the French.[10]

New opportunities were opening in the Baltic; Sweaborg and Kinburn demonstrated that sea forts could be overcome, with adequate resources. Cronstadt was, for the first time, a real possibility, although it would be necessary to enlarge the fleet, and determine the position of Sweden. A well equipped dockyard, and a diversionary attack in Finland offered worthwhile benefits. The Admiralty prepared the naval forces, but Sweden was a matter for the Government. Palmerston's shaky cabinet, and the Crimean impasse, had prevented the adoption of any wider plans, yet when the need arose he began to side-step and wear down the resistance of his more pacific colleagues, continuing to hope for a Swedish alliance. Before the war Sweden and Russia had been in dispute over the Finnmark, particularly the Warranger Fjord. In September 1853 Russia had closed the frontier. A defensive treaty, guaranteeing this area, would prevent Russia building a naval base on the Northern Ocean and tie Sweden to the allies, forcing Russia to prepare for an attack in the Baltic. Palmerston opened by considering the Finnmark. King Oscar wanted to cover Norway as well, while the French wanted to include the Danes. As the Danes were believed to be in Russia's power, and the Straits were a recognised British interest, Palmerston rejected the initiative. Schroeder argues that France paved the way for the November Treaty, but Knaplund demonstrated the policy was British.[11]

Clarendon confronted the cabinet with a Swedish treaty on 13 August. Argyll objected, with support from Lewis and Sir George Grey. Staying in the background, Palmerston did not press the issue. Unaware of the inner cabinet, Argyll was alarmed by Lansdowne's support for the policy, arguing that a defensive treaty meant taking up a burden for no benefit. At the cabinet of 20 August Argyll continued his protest, with little support, and when the matter was not raised again he concluded he had won. In fact Palmerston merely abandoned the attempt to gain cabinet sanction. By early September Clarendon had a draft treaty, offering to defend Sweden and Norway against Russian demands. The French were dilatory, objecting to the defensive cast of the terms, as Louis Napoleon wanted to bring Sweden into the treaty signed with Austria. Palmerston responded with a concise statement of his war policy. The Swedish treaty would be 'the attainment by anticipation of part of the objects of the war'. It would check Russian expansion in the north, and prevent Sweden acting against the interests of the allies. 'The Treaty we propose would be a *part of a long line of circumvallation* to confine the future expansion of Russia even if the events of the war should not enable us to drive her outposts in at any part of her present circumference.'[12]

Palmerston had always been making war on Russia, rather than defending Turkey. British strategic and economic interests required Russia to be kept away from the Turkish Straits, and they would also benefit from keeping her away from the Finnmark and Gotland. Supporting the states on the Russian periphery and allying them to Britain and France would create a *cordon sanitaire*. Clarendon forwarded the note to Cowley, and the Ambassador won over Louis Napoleon, although it is unlikely the full extent of British aims were revealed. French attempts to enlarge the Baltic theatre were more direct, leading Austria to credit her for the Swedish treaty.[13] This suited Palmerston, disguising his interest from the cabinet.

General Canrobert went to the Scandinavian courts in November, ostensibly for an exchange of decorations. The Swedish envoy sent to Paris at the same time, Admiral Virgin, admitted that if the allies were serious in the Baltic, Sweden would have to join them. Throughout October and November the Swedes tinkered with the terms of the treaty – a sign of reluctance, as the points raised were petty. Clarendon made it clear that the object of the treaty was Cronstadt. When Cowley suggested a Council of War to determine future strategy Palmerston thought this would be waste of time: 'the outline is clear. We must send fleets and troops to the Baltic to take Cronstadt and Helsingfors, and Finland and threaten St Petersburg. In the Black Sea we must hold the southern part of the Crimea and send a British and Turkish army to sweep the Russians out of Georgia and Circassia.' Louis Napoleon insisted, informing the Duke of Cambridge that as neither the British Government nor the Generals in the Crimea had proposed anything, it was necessary to act elsewhere. He took up the Council of War, adding the Baltic to Cowley's original Black Sea theatre discussion. Obliged to accept, Palmerston complained that if the plans were not kept secret they would be useless. The Swedish treaty was signed on 21 November, and ratified one month later. With this final hurdle cleared, Palmerston adopted a Baltic strategy culminating with the destruction of Cronstadt. The treaty, with Canrobert's successful mission to inspect the Swedish army, encouraged the British to believe Sweden was at last in earnest.[14]

Palmerston and Louis Napoleon wanted Prussia to abandon her dubious neutrality before the 1856 campaign opened. The Emperor had already warned Prussia of the dangers; Palmerston agreed the pressure must be increased in 1856 'when we have a real campaign in the Baltic'. The message was passed through Paris and Vienna to Berlin.[15] Behind the diplomacy lay Canrobert's northern army. Despite his failure in the Crimea, Canrobert was widely regarded as the inevitable choice to command the allied land forces in the Baltic in 1856. His mission was seen as a step toward a major campaign. In Stockholm between 7 and 19 November he met the King, inspected the army and discussed his plans with Magennis; he hoped to land 150,000 troops, French, British, Swedish and Danish in the Baltic provinces or Finland. The visit to Copenhagen on 24 to 29 November followed a similar pattern, estimating the Danes could provide 15,000 troops, with transport for almost 8,000. If Sweden joined he was certain Denmark would follow. He looked to combine a naval attack on Cronstadt with a land attack on St Petersburg. Despite this it was clear the French were not enthusiastic, leading the British to give more weight to the Swedish treaty as a method of intimidating Russia. Canrobert's meeting with Dundas and Penaud on 30 November was inconclusive; Dundas remained pessimistic about Cronstadt. Louis Napoleon considered it could be taken with 60–80,000 men, and promised to enlarge on this at the Council of War.[16] The size of this army raised the perennial problem of transport.

The plans of Louis Napoleon and Canrobert reflected how little they had learnt at Sevastopol, and how far they ignored Sweaborg and Kinburn. Cronstadt was open to naval attack, but there was hardly room on the island for the troops Louis Napoleon suggested. Sulivan's plan offered a more logical method. Suggesting an offensive in Finland demonstrated how little the French knew of the terrain. The only justification lay in the Swedish alliance, but to invade Finland for the benefit of Sweden would add another burden to the alliance, one which would not be counterbalanced by Sweden. To land anywhere on the Russian Baltic coast committed the army to overthrowing the Russian state, or being destroyed. The Russians had more men available than Canrobert could even hope for, and once ashore his forces would be tied down in another Crimean campaign. The British remained unimpressed. Dundas considered 20,000 British troops would be useful, but experience at Sweaborg made him aware that allied forces created more problems than they solved. Wood, preparing a naval force to carry out the attack, was unimpressed by French designs, and made no effort to find the transport in the hope that Louis Napoleon would abandon the plan.

He wanted 5,000 British troops and, like Dundas, saw good reason to prefer divided commands.[17]

Wood developed a more rational strategic view of the war than any of his colleagues. Even before the fall of Sevastopol he was preparing the flotilla for a naval attack on Cronstadt and St Petersburg through the north channel. His rationale for the attempt to 'strike a home blow at the heart of Russia' was simple: 'I do not in truth expect that even the total fall of the place [Sevastopol] would tend much to bring the war to an end.' To prepare for this shift of objective he consulted Graham, Walker and Berkeley, with others. Graham was still convinced that Swedish co-operation was essential. His increasing disenchantment with the war reflected the political benefits flowing to Palmerston, rather than a loss of faith in the Navy. Nothing concrete remains of Walker's opinion, almost certainly because the Surveyor's Office had moved into Whitehall from Somerset House during the year, but it is clear he supported the plan, and was present when Wood and Berkeley interviewed Sulivan. From Berkeley's language when outlining the forces needed for 1856 it can be inferred he reached his figures after consulting the Surveyor:

Table 6. The proposed British fleet for Baltic operations in 1856

Steam battleships	18
Large screw frigates	4
Corvettes	12
Paddle steamers	20
Gunboats	100
Mortar vessels	46
Mortar frigates	3
Despatch vessels	20
Floating batteries	2
Total number of warships	225

This fleet was intended to attack Cronstadt, without French assistance. To man it Berkeley needed another 9,000 men, paying off the Channel Squadron and draining all other sources of manpower. He kept his faith in arbitrary measures. Despite the belated success of recruiting and the break up of the Naval Brigade, he would not release men with five years' service. Wood preferred recalling the sailing two-deckers from the Black Sea.[18] The return of Sulivan added a new realism to Admiralty planning. He proposed attacking from the north channel in June, before the Russians anticipated. To deal with the forts, which were too far apart for mutual support, he suggested a creeping bombardment by the flotilla. The barrier across the north channel, which he described as resembling a breakwater, would be breached by underwater explosives, placed by divers; Sulivan and his brother volunteered for this task. Once the barrier had been forced and the Russian flotilla driven off, mortars would cause the real destruction. Sulivan believed no fort could resist the floating batteries, and after the success at Kinburn he also assigned them the task of holding off the Russian gunboats, once the barrier had been breached. The only obstacle to a successful bombardment, and the capture of the island, was the Russian flotilla. Berkeley was confidant it could be dealt with, with more gunboats and batteries as an insurance. He also advised that Chads blow up something similar to the barrier before the season opened. To ensure all this effort was not wasted he wanted more control: 'Two years we have left operations in the Baltic to the judgement and decision of the Admirals in command. I think we should now come to a decision as to what is to be done and I am willing to take my share in the responsibility.'[19] This sudden, uncharacteristic willingness to take responsibility reflected unanimity at the Board; he would not have advanced such an opinion against opposition. Sulivan added a practical note to the planning process. With grand tactics decided and construction in hand, Wood turned to fit the Baltic into Government policy.

The decisive moment came in mid November, when the details of the Austrian Ultimatum reached London. At the cabinet of 20 November Palmerston accepted the majority view that the initiative should be pursued, provided certain points were clarified. Realising he could not rely on the luxury of another campaign the Premier had to find a strategy that would force Russia to concede his terms quickly. The only possibility was that offered by Wood. Within two days the Cronstadt attack had become central to Palmerston's strategy; Clarendon declared, 'a real campaign in the Baltic next year will double up Russia'. Palmerston looked for a knock-out blow at Cronstadt/St Petersburg to secure the concessions he required early in the next campaign. It had the added benefit of not drawing troops away from Asia Minor. By the time Dundas arrived in London he was anxious to adopt any idea that promised to assist the destruction of Cronstadt, including a submarine and Dundonald's gas attack. At the War Committee meeting of 19 December Wood allowed his enthusiasm to cloud his judgement, claiming that if Cronstadt had been properly examined by Napier it would already have been taken. The opinion, and the sentiments behind it, were Berkeley's. At least the Admiralty plans, hesitantly presented by Dundas, did not provoke opposition in cabinet. The previous Baltic discussion on the 13th concerned joint operations, and proved indecisive. The shift to an all-British attack reflected the growing divergence of allied policy; Palmerston, Clarendon and Wood considered Russia would reject the allied ultimatum, only Wood did not view this with satisfaction.[20]

Palmerston's adoption of the Cronstadt plan marked a shift from limited peripheral territorial seizures to an unlimited thrust at the centre of gravity of the Russian state, St Petersburg and the army that defended the city. The purpose was obvious. The original strategy of rolling back Russian frontiers in limited campaigns where distance, seapower and small armies would suffice, was no longer valid. After the crucial cabinet of 20 November it was clear that time, allies and cabinet support were all running out. Palmerston wanted to continue limited campaigns, and if Russia had rejected the Austrian Ultimatum he would have done so, at the expense of Cronstadt. That would be kept as a final blow to secure the new frontiers created by the limited campaigns. However, with peace more likely, Cronstadt became essential, for diplomatic rather than strategic reasons. It was the only measure which offered the chance of securing adequate terms before Palmerston ran out of support. If he could save the 1856 season he could win a great victory. If not, the latent power of the Great Armament would reinforce British diplomacy. Clarendon agreed: 'It seems to me impossible that Russia should accept the ultimatum but whether she does or not I am sure we should proceed (ostentatiously if possible & with reference to Parliamentary Questioning, vigorously) with the preparations for next year's campaign.'[21] The two most important elements in those preparations were the Great Armament for the Baltic and the Paris Council of War.

Notes

1 SCHROEDER, pp. 311–12; RICH, N., *Why the Crimean War?* (London 1985), pp. 162–3, 168, 172; SAAB, KNAPP and KNAPP, 'A reassessment of French foreign policy during the Crimean War, based on the papers of Adolphe de Borqueney', *French Historical Studies*, 1986, pp. 466–96; Cowley to Clarendon 13, 24 Oct. 1855: F.O. 519/217 f135;

ECHARD, W. E., *Napoleon III and the Concert of Europe* (Baton Rouge 1983), pp. 50–1; WELLESLEY and SENCOURT, pp. 94–6.

2 BAUMGART, W, *The Peace of Paris, 1856* (Santa Barbara, 1981), p. 16; Palmerston to Clarendon 16 Sept. 1855: Bdlds. GC/CL f487–8; Clarendon to Palmerston 16 Sept. 1855: *ibid.* f674; ARGYLL, i, pp. 583–4;

3 SCHROEDER, pp. 322–6; RICH, p. 165; Palmerston to Clarendon 16 Oct. 1855: Bdlds. GC/CL f577–80.

4 Clarendon to Palmerston 18 Nov. 1855: *ibid.* p. 324; The Queen to Clarendon 19 Nov. 1855: *The Letters of Queen Victoria, 1837 – 1861* (London 1907, three vols.). ed. BENSON and ESHER, iii, p. 193; Palmerston to Clarendon 20 Nov. 1855: Cl. Dep. C31 f81; RICH. pp. 170–2; SCHROEDER, pp. 324–6.

5 RICH, pp. 174–81.

6 SETON-WATSON, H., *The Russian Empire 1801–1917* (Oxford, 1967), p. 329; MOSSE, W. E., *The Rise and Fall of the Crimean System, 1855–1871* (London, 1963), pp. 24–31; BAUMGART, pp. 68–80; CURTISS, p. 484; HAMILTON, C. I., 'The Royal Navy, Seapower, and the Screw Ship of the Line, 1845–1860' (Unpub. Ph.D. Thesis, Cambridge 1973), p. 95.

7 VINCENT; RICH, p. 159.

8 Palmerston to Clarendon 18 Oct. 8 Nov. 1855: Cl. Dep. C31 f588–9, 627–8; Palmerston to Clarendon 9, 16 Oct. 1855: Add. 48,579 f77–80; Palmerston to Clarendon 26 Oct., 4, 22 Nov. 1855: Bdlds. GC/CL f606–9, 620–1, 669–71.

9 BAUMGART, p. 14.

10 Palmerston to Clarendon 28 Oct., 23 Nov. 1855: Cl. Dep. C31 f610–13: Add. 48,579 f82–4.

11 Palmerston to Clarendon 3 Jun. 1855: Bdlds. GC/CL f64; SCHROEDER, pp. 197, 333; KNAPLUND, pp. 496–7; Magennis to Clarendon 11 Jun. 1855: F.O. 73/270 f52; Cowley to Clarendon 12, 26 Jun. 1855: F.O. 519/4 f1, 54; Clarendon to Cowley 21 Jul. 1855: F.O. 519/172 f75–83.

12 ARGYLL, i, pp. 563, 570; Argyll to Clarendon 13 Aug. 1855: Cl. Dep. C29 f552; Clarendon to Cowley 8, 19 Sept. 1855: F.O. 519/172 f200, 265; Cowley to Clarendon 24 Sept. 1855: F.O. 519/5 f180; Palmerston to Clarendon 25 Sept. 1855 (copy): Add. 48,579 f73–4. There is no original of this letter in the Cl. Dep.

13 Clarendon to Cowley 26 Sept. 1855: F.O. 519/5 f270–1; Clarendon to Palmerston 3 Oct. 1855: Bdlds. GC/CL f702; SCHROEDER, p. 330.

14 Cowley to Clarendon 23, 30 Oct. 1855: F.O. 519/5 f223, 235; Magennis to Clarendon 1, 7, 19, 20, 21 Nov. 1855: F.O. 73/271 f86, 93, 97, 100, 111; Clarendon to Cowley 16 Nov. 1855: F.O. 519/172 f491–500; Clarendon to Palmerston 7 Nov., 17 Dec. 1855: Bdlds. GC/CL f724, 746; Cowley to Clarendon 16, 18 Nov. 1855: F.O. 519/217 f189–206; Palmerston to Clarendon 8, 18, 22 Nov. 1855: Cl. Dep. C31 f627–8, 664–5, 669.

15 BAUMGART, pp. 26, 55; Palmerston to Clarendon 17 Dec. 1855: Cl. Dep. C31 f756; Clarendon to Cowley 26 Dec. 1855: F.O. 519/172 f661–2; SCHROEDER, p. 331 quoting a letter from Buol to the Austrian minister at Berlin, Esterhazy of 14 Jan. 1856; Bloomfield to Clarendon 26,

31 Dec. 1855: F.O. 64/388 f278, 287; CRAIG, G., *The Politics of the Prussian Army* (Oxford, 1955), p. 134.
16 Cowley to Clarendon 30 Oct., 24 Nov. 1855: F.O. 519/5 f235, 286; Magennis to Clarendon 19 Nov. 1855: Cl. Dep. C31 f88; Buchanan to Clarendon 20 Nov. 1855: F.O. 22/123; BAPST, C.G., *Le Maréchal Canrobert* (Paris, 1904), vol.III, p. 44; Clarendon to Cowley 28 Nov. 1855: F.O. 519/172 f667–70; NRS Baltic 1855, pp. 12–13 and WELLESLEY and SENCOURT, pp. 99–101.
17 Wood to Lyons 8 Jan. 1856: Add. 49,565 f44–5.
18 Wood to Lyons 2 Sept. 1855: *ibid.* f18; Wood to Grey 8 Sept. 1855: *ibid.* f35; Graham to Wood 12 Oct. 1855: HALIFAX A4/70; Graham to Newcastle 23 Nov. 1856: MARTINEAU; SULIVAN, p. 365; Berkeley to Wood 18, 22 Oct. 22 Nov. 1855: HALIFAX A4/74; Wood to Graham 18 Nov. 1855: Add. 49,565 f8; Wood to Berkeley 21 Nov. 1855: *ibid.* f8; Palmerston to the Queen 19 Nov. 1855: R.A. G39 f55.
19 SULIVAN, pp. 356, 367, 406, 408, 429; Berkeley to Wood 9, 24, 27 Nov. 1855: HALIFAX A4/74; Wood to Lyons 12 Nov. 1855: Add. 49,564 f128–31.
20 ARGYLL, i, pp. 596–7, 602; FITZMAURICE,i, pp. 132–3; Clarendon to Wood 15 Nov., 16 Dec. 1855: HALIFAX A4/63ii; Palmerston to Wood 17 Dec. 1855: *ibid.* A4/63 f54; Wood to Grey 17 Dec. 1855: Add. 49,565 f36.
21 Clarendon to Wood 16 Dec. 1855: HALIFAX A4/63ii.

22

The Great Armament

Before Sweaborg the construction of flotilla craft had not been attended with any great urgency; the only order placed after October 1854, that of 18 April, was for ten gunboats and six gunvessels. After Sweaborg Dundas declared he could not have too many gunboats for Baltic operations, particularly if they could carry double the present armament. He also favoured enlarged mortar vessels. Wood then ordered thirty more gunboats and gunvessels; enlarged gunboats were considered impractical but Wood was alarmed by Dundas's pessimism.[1] The issue of mortar failure was settled by ordering 200 for 1856, and the Surveyor's Department also considered iron rafts and floats to carry them. Dundas suggested building long-barrelled mortars, or cutting down 10-inch guns. Palmerston supported the idea of long range weapons with an enquiry into the best metal for casting new mortars, having already ordered two of Mallet's 36-inch mortars. The Committee was directed to consider rifled mortars, among other new proposals. Confidence in existing weapons was not improved when another barrel burst during the trials of an iron float at Shoeburyness. The danger increased when the weapons were fired at extreme range – the object of both Dundas and Palmerston. At Sweaborg, Russian guns and Dundas's caution had forced them to the outer limit of performance.[2] Palmerston was an enthusiast for new weapons, sending all manner of schemes to the Admiralty and the War Office and accusing Berkeley of preconceived objections to Brunel's shot-proof gunboat. Even Dundonald's gas and smoke screen plan was given another airing, Wood was unenthusiastic but allowed the Earl to discuss it with Dundas. The submarine built to Palmerston's order by Scott-Russell and Sir Charles Fox was delayed by the defection of the German inventor, Wilhelm Bauer, to Russia. Palmerston hoped this simple oar-driven craft could be used with divers to breach the

Cronstadt barrier. Wood sent Sulivan, Cooper-Key and James Hope down to Poole harbour for the trials; they went underwater, but were not impressed. Wood refused to pay the £10,000 Palmerston had promised out of Admiralty funds, or to sanction an improved version.[3]

Work on more regular vessels continued. A new floating battery was ordered to replace the burnt-out *Aetna* in November, as well as three iron-hulled versions in December after Wood and Walker consulted Sulivan. Gunboats were ordered as quickly as the private builders on the Thames could fulfil the existing contracts. Shipwright wages increased by 50 per cent in the period June–October 1855, remaining at this level until peace, which caused severe problems for builders on fixed price contracts. After Sulivan's report twenty more were ordered in late November, before a general enquiry to Pembroke Dockyard and the private builders, to determine how many could be built by 1 March 1856, led to orders for another sixty-eight. The machinery contract for this armada was divided between the leading engine building firms, John Penn and Sons and Maudslay, Field and Sons. Rush built hulls of green timber were not expected to last; the 1854 gunboats required up to £100 worth of repairs after one season.[4]

Walker kept the majority of this work in private yards because the progress of the French steam battlefleet made any slackening of work on battleships and frigates unthinkable. Although this work bore no relation to the Russian War, it dominated construction policy throughout the conflict. Walker, Wood and Graham accepted that the end of the war would signal an early return to Anglo–French hostility. The newspapers continued to criticise the construction of battleships when only gunboats were required. The launch of the 120-gun *Marlborough*, on 1 August 1855, provoked more hostile comment. While the war made few demands on the British battlefleet that did not mean the battleship was obsolete or unnecessary. Prince Albert suggested that the number in commission might be reduced; Palmerston agreed, hoping to save money. After Albert's memorandum had been read to the cabinet Wood consulted Graham, who provided a clear restatement of the guiding principles of British naval policy:

Unless France, Russia and America cease to build Line of Battle Ships of the largest size adapted to the screw we must keep pace with them, and even go ahead of them, unless our maritime superiority be renounced. If it is to be upheld, we must have the ships provided and ready to meet these Great Naval Powers at any moment on equal terms. Concert with France is good, while it lasts; but the hope that this friendship will be eternal is a vain delusion.

The Prince Consort's memorandum called for battleships to be used as transports, and the construction of more gunboats. Wood provided a comprehensive reply, pointing to problems with the United States; the value of battleships for amphibious operations; the diplomatic requirement for a powerful Mediterranean fleet, and plans to reinforce the flotilla to avoid having to depend on the French in 1856. His reservations proved well founded, although the French did not reveal the limited nature of their Baltic fleet until after the Council of War; twelve gunboats, five mortar vessels and two batteries, with sixty oared gunboats, were not the forces for a decisive strategy in the north. Louis Napoleon's plans had either been rejected, or never seriously considered.[5] French strategy remained Crimeocentric to the end.

The organisation of the flotilla craft was modified. The 1855 system of treating them as tenders to the heavy ships had not been successful. The great increase in numbers for 1856 led to the creation of divisions, each of which would have a part-armed steam battleship as tender, magazine and workshop. Three divisions, each with six gunvessels and forty gunboats were formed under Codrington, *Algiers*, Keppel, *Colossus*, and Yelverton, *Brunswick*. Another division of two gunvessels and twenty gunboats was formed under Cooper-Key, *Sans Pareil*. As senior Captain, Codrington was rumoured to have his pendant, and to be third in command. Another dozen small gunboats were ordered on 19 January as a reserve. The mortar vessels and floats were similarly organised. The depots *London* and *Rodney* would retain their lower masts to hoist out the mortars, but would otherwise be rigged on the reduced scale of fifth rates and disarmed to save manpower. Beside powder and shell they would carry spare mortars, mortar beds and stores to effect repairs. There would be fifty mortar vessels, and the same number of floats.[6]

It was planned to have the Great Armament completed by 1 March. 1856. However, the ambitious nature of the project, involving a large measure of co-operation with the new War Department for the supply of artillery, caused some delay. Deep-rooted fear of France ensured that Walker only stopped work on ships not required for the Baltic on 19 February; the same day the Board pressed for delivery of the mortars. The only element of the 1856 fleet to reach the Baltic was the flying squadron, again under Watson, reinforced by *Caesar* and *Majestic* to counter the Russian steam battleship.[7] Before the remainder of the fleet and the bombarding squadrons were completed, diplomatic developments made their departure irrelevant. Walker's control of the nation's shipbuilding resources developed to meet the increasing demands placed on his Department by the shift in strategy. By late 1855 he had brought much of Britain's economic and technical strength to bear on the war effort, as represented by the Great Armament.

As Wood, and later Palmerston, developed plans for the Baltic they did not ignore the Euxine. The policy outlines were clear. Active operations should concentrate in Asia Minor, leaving a defensive force in the Crimea while the French moved into Bessarabia. The details were left to Wood and Lyons, who agreed that Georgia and Circassia would be the main theatre, but were uncertain how the Navy could assist. Lyons selected Soukham Kaleh as the main base for the Army, with operations in the Azov, on the Don and even the River Rion in support of Omer. Nicolaiev could be attempted by a combined force using the floating batteries and light draft steamers. Even the Danube was still possible. Wood favoured Nicolaiev, but could not spare the batteries after interviewing Sulivan; the Black Sea had become the second theatre. Lyons was urged to send home any spare vessels, to increase or man the Baltic fleet. Unfortunately Osborn reported the Russians had up to 400 40–50-ton decked boats on the Don, which could be used as gunboats, and were rebuilding their depots and magazines just far enough inland to avoid the guns of his flotilla. He suggested 400 marines were needed to strike inland.[8]

The Council of War provided Wood with a welcome excuse to recall Lyons, who was directed to discuss the theatre with Codrington before leaving and bring de la Marmora. As Stewart had already taken the two-deckers into the Mediterranean, Lyons had to turn over to Fremantle, who commanded less than twenty vessels. His duties were restricted to supporting the Army and keeping watch on the Danube. Everything else was frozen solid, although Kertch caused some concern.[9] Lyons left Kazatch on 20 December, transferring from *Royal Albert* to *Caradoc* at Beicos on the 23rd. He arrived at Marseilles on the 30th, calling on the Emperor in Paris and reaching London in time for the War Committee of 4 January.

During December Clarendon developed a policy for the Council of War: Palmerston's cynicism was countered by the idea of binding the French to act. This required the Government to decide policies for Asia Minor and the Baltic. The idea that the French would accept the decision of the Council, and carry it out, was naïve and unworthy of a man in such high office; the French had no intention of staying in the war to suit their allies. The cabinet debated the instructions for the delegates on 3 January: a memorandum from Prince Albert called for the evacuation of the Crimea, but that was considered impossible; 30,000 men in British pay must be left, the rest would go to Asia Minor, with a small force proceeding immediately to Trebizond. Argyll felt that too narrow a view was being taken and, unaware of the tacit division of the theatres for 1856, proposed a campaign in Bessarabia and objected to the involvement of India. The following day Clarendon, Lyons and Hardinge attended, the Duke of Cambridge and General Airey joining on the 5th. The military plenipotentiaries had no specific instructions, although the Government believed it would be a disgrace to evacuate the Crimea, useful to separate the armies, and important to clear Georgia. Granville and Airey wanted an immediate move to support Ezeroum, but were out-voted.[10]

The councillors left London on 8 January, led by the Duke of Cambridge, a frequent visitor to Paris during 1855, with Lyons, Dundas, Airey and Jones. Spratt accompanied Lyons, having private discussions with the Emperor. High policy was entrusted to Cowley. The French members were the Emperor as chairman, Prince Jerome, Prince Napoleon, Walewski, Hamelin, Bosquet, Canrobert, Martimprey, Penaud and Rear-Admiral Jurien de la Graviere (Bruat's Chief of Staff). De la Marmora represented Sardinia. The Council assembled at the Tuileries on 10 January, with an opening address by the Emperor at 09.30. He set the tone by urging the members to concern themselves only with military matters; final decisions rested with the allied governments and would reflect political issues. Demonstrating his conception of a war in two distinct theatres, he divided the officers into two sub-committees. After that the Council adjourned for two days.[11]

The Baltic sub-committee comprised Canrobert as President, Niel, Dundas and Penaud. Dundas had been briefed on British policy by Wood, and discussed the subject with Lyons and Cambridge en route. He was to secure the adoption of Wood's strategy for 1856.

Wood wanted an entirely British operation at Cronstadt, with a small military force. More troops, even British, would be of doubtful value, for once a large army entered the Baltic it would paralyse the fleet. The simple answer to the French plan for a large army remained lack of transport, which proved adequate. Even before the councillors reconvened Louis Napoleon accepted there would be no large land campaign in the Baltic during 1856, but kept open the question of sending a smaller force to bring Sweden into the war. At the meeting of the 12th, from 14.00 to 17.00 the Council heard from the Black Sea sub-committee, but the Baltic report was incomplete and had to be held over for a further two days. The questions under discussion were:

1. How to burn Cronstadt.
2. How to take St Petersburg.
3. The time necessary and the number of vessels required to transport to Finland 60,000 men from France and Britain.
4. Can Riga be taken?
5. Can Reval be taken?
6. Can Sweaborg be taken?

The first question provoked little discussion, everything depended on the Russian preparations. Canrobert suggested landing 150,000 men at Biorko to march along the coast and attack St Petersburg; transport problems, and the uncertainty of the operation, led to the effective withdrawal of the proposal. Riga was too strong for all but regular siege operations, while Reval could be bombarded, but not taken. Sweaborg also required a large army.[12]

Cambridge considered the Baltic sub-committee weak, fearing Dundas would not press the need to attack Cronstadt with sufficient vigour when another fruitless season in the Baltic would ruin British naval prestige. Palmerston shared his low opinion of Dundas. Already pessimistic, Dundas arrived home to find himself outmanoeuvred by Sulivan, complaining that the surveying Captain encouraged the Admiralty and Government to hold over-optimistic opinions. His performance at the cabinet War Committee did not improve his standing; while he outlined the attack on Cronstadt it was clear he was not convinced. On 14 January Palmerston declared he was 'little better suited for the Baltic than his namesake was for the Black Sea', wanting to move Lyons to the north and leave Stewart to control the reduced demands of the Euxine, because Dundas would only 'keep his ships safe, and maintain a blockade'. Graham had intended to make the change when Sevastopol fell, and *The Times* heard rumours. In the event Dundas retained the command; Wood admitted he was not 'an enterprising officer', but trusted him to carry out the operation.[13]

When Dundas attempted to sum up his impressions of the sub-committee his natural pessimism came to the fore. The attack on Cronstadt could develop into a long drawn out bombardment which might not overcome the defences before the end of the season. This would have a serious effect on the rest of the theatre, drawing off the gunboats needed to blockade the Gulf of Riga and the northern parts of the Gulf of Bothnia. However he was careful not to reject the possibility of attacking. Airey wanted 60,000 troops in the Baltic, to tie down Russian forces away from the Black Sea; Penaud, like Dundas, considered blockade the first task, admitting the possibility of attempting Cronstadt and Reval. After the meetings at the Ministry of Marine on 17, 18 and 19 January the Baltic committee reported that the Cronstadt attack was possible, if the Russians were not too strong. They included Canrobert's scheme for St Petersburg, but with so many reservations that it was effectively dismissed. The Emperor followed the report, accepting that there were neither the troops nor the transports required. He favoured a naval attack on Cronstadt, requiring twelve battleships to cover the Russian fleet, 100 gunboats to deal with the flotilla, floating batteries and sixty gunboats for the bombardment. He envisaged a long range attack with new guns and rockets reaching beyond 5,000 metres, avoiding the need to penetrate the barrier, or occupy the island.[14]

The British Councillors returned to London on the 22nd, with copies of the papers. When they assembled at the War Office nothing was said about the Baltic. Wood eventually sent his response to Clarendon, on 2 February.

SECRET AND CONFIDENTIAL MEMORANDUM.
Her Majesty's Government concur in the opinion expressed by the Emperor of the French, that it is not advisable to send a large military force to the Baltic next summer.
They think however, that it may be desirable to send more than the usual number of marines in the ships employed there. If it should be found necessary to establish a depot or a hospital on shore, either at Nargen or elsewhere, these men might be landed to occupy the place during the

absence of the ships of war.

Her Majesty's Government also concur in the opinion of the Emperor, that an attack upon Cronstadt ought to be considered as the principal object to be aimed at in the Baltic next summer; but they are not disposed to limit that attempt merely to burning, and then at once abandoning the place.

The possibility of further operations can only be decided on the spot, after the first success; but the orders to be given to the Admirals should be to push any advantage to the utmost extent which may be in their power, if an entrance into the inner waters of Cronstadt can be effected. The Emperor's Memorandum contemplates the following force:

I Twelve ships of the line to meet the Russian fleet, if it should come out.

II A flotilla of 100 steam gunboats to engage the Russian gun-boats.

III Sixty mortar-boats to bombard and burn Cronstadt.

Her Majesty's fleet, as was stated in the paper sent to the Council of War at Paris, will consist of many more ships and vessels than the number mentioned by the Emperor.

It is intended by Her Majesty's Government to send the following ships and vessels to the Baltic:

Ships of the line	80 to 130 guns, screw	10	
	60 guns, blockships, screw	9	
	Divisional ships for gun boats, screw, without lower deck guns	4	
	Divisional ships, with powder and shells for mortar vessels, without lower deck guns	2	
		—	
			25
Frigates	34 to 50 guns, screw	4	
Corvettes	8 to 21 guns, screw	12	
Paddle steam vessels	4 to 22 guns		20
Floating batteries	14 to 16 guns		8
Gun boats	1st class	6	
	2nd class	14	
	3rd class	118	
	4th class	20	
	Paddle gun vessels	6	
		—	
			164
Mortar frigates			4
Mortar vessles and floats			100
			—
Total			337

Factories, Tenders and Store Ships, &c.

To which might be added, if it was thought necessary, a large number of boats carrying one gun, and rowed by seamen, as it is supposed that those boats will be which the French Government propose to send.

It is understood that the French force for the Baltic will consist of the

following ships and vessels:
    2 Vaisseaux mixtes
    2 Grands vapeurs, pour remorquer les batteries flottantes.
    2 Batteries flottantes armées de 16 canons de 30 rayes.
    4 Cannonières mixtes de première class armées, chacune, de 4 canons de
        30 rayes et d'un obusier.
    8 Cannières mixtes de deuxième classe armées chacune, de 2 canons de
        30 rayes.
    5 Bombardes à voile armées de 2 mortiers de 32 cm.
    60 Chalans armées d'un canon de 24 rayes.
Nota. – Chaque canon raye de 24 ou de 30 sera approvisioné pour 500
coups.

Some of the frigates and smaller vessels will be required for the blockade
of other ports; but after making full allowance for this service, there can be
no doubt of the superiority of the naval force of the Allies at Cronstadt.

No opinion, however, can be formed of the defences which the Russians
may have been able to construct during the winter until the fleets arrive off
Cronstadt.

Her Majesty's Government entertain some doubt as to the supposed
advantages of the bombardment from the outside of the barrier, as proposed
by the Emperor. They are inclined to believe that no serious impression can
be produced upon the place without forcing entrances through the barrier;
and they would regret any delay in commencing the effective attack, which
would only give to the enemy further opportunity for strengthening his
defences, and would curtail the time for operations, which is necessarily so
short in that sea.

This paper combined a statement of the forces to be employed with
the policy of the British Government, that Cronstadt be taken and
destroyed. The critique of Louis Napoleon's proposals was firm,
because he realised the French would do nothing. Clarendon urged
that continuing preparations offered the best hope of securing peace,
and while the French agreed they did nothing.[15]

Early in the new year the Swedish Government began to press for
an offensive alliance to supplement the November treaty. They
considered their involvement inevitable, which would explain their
prevarication before signing the original treaty; the delay prevented
them becoming involved in 1855. Magennis reported King Oscar
wanted an offensive alliance, with or without Austria, to increase the
pressure for peace. Realistically Oscar could see the war was coming
to an end, and unless he made a commitment Sweden would gain
nothing in the peace settlement. Russian sources contend a 'secret'
clause of the November treaty covered operations around Cronstadt
and St Petersburg; had such a clause existed there would have been

no requirement for a new treaty. Another document, Oscar's 'secret memorandum', stated that an army of 165,000 Swedes, Norwegians, Danes, French and British would drive the Russians out of Finland and destroy Cronstadt. Such a plan suited Swedish requirements, but nothing of the sort had been considered by the allies at the Council of War. While there were no 'secret' clauses or agreements, Sweden moving into the allied camp, with the implication of a major land campaign, played a part in bringing Russia to accept terms. The real object of Oscar's policy was illustrated by the demands he sent to the peace conference: the surrender or demilitarisation of Finland west of Helsingfors, and some check on Russian naval power.[16] The careful timing of his move, and the use of blatant propaganda, suggest the Swedish King looked for the maximum benefit, without fighting. He delayed too long: the war was over before he could earn the allies' gratitude, unlike Sardinia. Oscar's diplomacy did not win any great prize for Sweden, but it served the allies well.

The Black Sea sub-committee comprised Lyons as President, with Bosquet, Jones, Airey, General Martimprey and Jurien de la Graviere. The meetings at the War Ministry, discussed the options:

1. Whether to evacuate the Crimea.
2. How many men would be required to hold the Chersonese?
3. How many men were presently in the Crimea?
4. How many men could be moved with the available transport?
5. Whether 30,000 men at Arabat and 60,000 at Perekop could completely invest the Crimea.
6. Whether it was possible to attack the Mackenzie Heights.
7. The value of Eupatoria as a base for large operations.
8. Whether Kaffa would be a suitable base.
9. Was it possible to land 100,000 men in Bessarabia?
10. Could Kherson and Nicolaiev be attacked?
11. What should be done in the Azov?
12. What should be done in Asia Minor?
13. Should operations be continued during the winter?

Evacuation was dismissed as impossible and dishonourable; 66–70,000 men could hold the Chersonese, and with up to 250,000 available that left at least 150,000 for wider operations. No final figure was placed on the transport capacity, but at least 60,000, possibly 100,000 could be moved. Kaffa was rejected as too wide of the main theatre, while Spratt's evidence condemned Perekop, although Lyons favoured Arabat, for a dash at the Tchongar bridge.

Any attempt on the Mackenzie Heights was rejected, and Eupatoria considered only fit for a diversion. Lyons suggested landing at the Alma. Bessarabia was rejected, for lack of a suitable base. The Danube, Kherson and Nicolaiev were considered too difficult, the latter pair being of little value, while Kinburn was retained. Continuing operations in the Sea of Azov was agreed, with action in Asia Minor to support Omer. Winter operations were impossible. The French opposed operations in Asia, although they were prepared to consider separating the armies after the Russians had been cleared out of the Crimea; Lyons and Cambridge were pleased no-one seriously suggested evacuation. Lyons, depressed by the negative tone of the meetings, pointed out to the Emperor that it was extraordinary that even with 150,000 disposable men and a mighty steam fleet, nothing could be done. The source of the negative spirit was only too obvious, Prince Napoleon and his supporters were blatantly in favour of peace, and had increasing public support. While the British condemned the French attitude the French had every reason to be negative; unlike the British, they knew peace was inevitable. As the meetings ended Lyons realised the Council of War was only a noisy charade. Even Palmerston was resigned to peace, only hoping to keep up the pressure on Russia.[17]

While the French knew they would only be of academic interest the development of strategic plans for 1856 continued, and continued to create inter-allied tension. Lyons' proposal for 4,000 men to operate against the Tchongar bridge from Arabat was rejected. Martimprey, Pelissier's Chief of Staff, developed an elaborate strategy for a double operation to clear the Crimea, landing 100,000 men at Eupatoria and pushing south to catch the Russians between two forces. Four British divisions would make a feint at Kaffa, land at Old Fort and form the allied right for the advance on Simpheropol; de la Marmora would be in command at Sevastopol. Continually optimistic, Lyons mocked the difficulties raised by the French over transport and opposed landings. His military opinions, advanced by Jones and Airey, ridiculed French alarm about lack of water at Eupatoria. He echoed Martimprey's plan, but saved 60,000 men for immediate use in Asia Minor. Once the Russians had been driven out he shared the general desire to evacuate the Crimea. The French began to air objects guaranteed to annoy the British; Niel advised occupying Constantinople, and made scarcely veiled hints about operating in Germany. The Prince Consort rose to the bait, but

Palmerston had long anticipated a French attempt to secure Constantinople.[18]

When Louis Napoleon delivered his summary on the 20th he adopted Martimprey's plan to take the Russians in the flank and rear with 100,000 men from Eupatoria, starting on 15 May, or earlier if possible. He insisted the British councillors remain in Paris after the meetings, ostensibly to await his summary. Lyons knew that although this was a response to Russia accepting the Austrian Ultimatum, it was necessary to keep up the allied facade just a little longer. Cambridge, understanding French difficulties, urged them to keep up their preparations until the allied terms were accepted. While Vaillant and the Emperor concurred, such pretence proved impossible; the French people were already celebrating peace. Before returning to London Lyons secured copies of the papers, including the Emperor's summary, which as Prince Albert observed was clever, but hardly a plan of campaign.[19]

When the cabinet War Committee met on 25 January, Granville realised how far French opposition to the Asian theatre had been carried. A brief survey of the papers made it appear British views had not been emphasised, but the meeting resolved that an army of 40,000 ought to be sent to Asia concurrently with operations to clear the Crimea. The cabinet of 2 February agreed and sent an outline of British policy on the areas of disagreement:

1. Sevastopol should not be evacuated until a definitive Peace had been signed.
2. The allied armies should be divided
3. Operations in the Crimea should commence in April, not on 15 May.
4. 40 – 50,000 men should be sent by Britain to Asia Minor to operate on Tiflis, helping the Turks to reconquer their territory.

Panmure explained the rationale to the Queen:

if no operations were undertaken in Asia, the Campaign would turn out certainly a disappointment to Your Majesty's people, and any credit gained would be more likely to accrue to the Army commanded by the French General than to that under the English.

Lord Panmure does not expect a candid co-operation in the plan now sent over on the part of the Emperor, nevertheless he thinks that a general assent will be afforded to it, partly in the hope that peace may override any operations at all, and partly because, if His Majesty's calculations of the number of his troops be correct, it is in reality the only rational method of employing the force.

It was clear Louis Napoleon had exaggerated his disposable force, for as with everything else in Paris, the object was peace. He admitted this in his reply and, along with the inevitable casualties and disease, advanced it as a reason to postpone operations in Asia. British disappointment was doubled by the decison to leave Pelissier in command at Eupatoria, objections that were upheld at the Cabinet War Committee of 7 February, Lyons and Airey attending.[20] The British memorandum of this meeting envisaged 200,000 allied troops taking only one month to clear the Crimea.

SECRET AND CONFIDENTIAL MEMORANDUM 7 FEBRUARY.

Her Majesty's Government having received through Lord Cowley the observations of His Majesty the Emperor of the French upon the Memorandum forwarded to Paris on the 2nd instant, and having considered His Majesty's arguments with that respectful attention which they will at all times command, have resolved to forego their proposal for a descent in Asia by an English force contemporaneously with the operations about to be undertaken from Eupatoria.

Her Majesty's Government observe with satisfaction that the Emperor concurs with them in the vast importance of immediate action in the beginning of April, as also on other points relating to the duration of the armistice, and the immediate orders to be given for moving troops before the armistice is agreed to; but they are especially induced to give up their own views by the confidence which they feel in the Emperor's opinion that this forward movement from Eupatoria, if conducted with due vigour and activity, should not require above one month, at the farthest, for its complete success.

The plan of campaign, therefore, now definitively settled, consists in the occupation and maintenance of the position on the Tchernaya, with a mixed army of English and French, under an English Commander; and the assumption of active operations from a new base at Eupatoria, by another mixed army of French, English and Sardinians, under a French Commander.

To carry out these two distinct military operations, His Majesty the Emperor now reckons that there will be 200,000 allied troops, of all arms, in the Crimea by the end of March. Of these Her Majesty's Government reckon that the following will be found ready to act under, or in connection with, the British Standard:—

British Cavalry	5,000
British Artillery	9,000
British Sappers	1,000
British Infantry (inclusive of Malta reserve)	46,000
British Foreign Legion	10,000
British Turkish Contingent	15,000
British Osmanli Cavalry	3,000
	89,000
Sardinians	15,000
	104,000
Leaving for the French to bring into the Field	96,000
	200,000

It appears to Her Majesty's Government that at Eupatoria, where the troops are by common consent to be under a French Commander, the bulk of the army should consist of French troops, and that at Sevastopol, on the other hand, where the English General is to command, the bulk of the British Forces should be concentrated.

Bearing this consideration in view, the first point to be decided is the strength of the respective armies.

It appears to Her Majesty's Government that 65,000 effective men will be amply sufficient for the army of Sevastopol, leaving 135,000 for that of Eupatoria and other stations. It appears, further, to Her Majesty's Government that the Turkish Contingent, viz. 15,000 of all arms, should continue to occupy Kertch and Yenikale, this would leave 120,000 disposable for Eupatoria. Proceeding first to form this army, Her Majesty's Government propose to assign for that service the following force from the British ranks:—

2 Divisions British Infantry	12,000
3 Troops Horse Artillery	
6 Battalions Foot Artillery and 54 guns	2,000
Sapper and Miners	500
British Cavalry	3,000
Foreign Legion	5,000
Osmanli Horse	3,000
	25,500
Sardinians	15,000
	40,500
Leaving French to complete	79,500

120,000

This army being formed, there would remain for the Sevastopol army:—

British Infantry	34,000
British Artillery	7,000
British Cavalry	2,000
British Foreign Legion	5,000
British Sappers	500
	48,500
French troops	16,500
	65,000
Turkish Contingent, to remain at Kertch	15,000
	80,000
Add, as above, the Army of Eupatoria	120,000
Total	200,000

This appears to Her Majesty's Government a fair division of the respective forces of the allies, and one which is likely to accomplish the object of driving the enemy from his strong posts opposite Sevastopol and on the Mackenzie heights, and of finally expelling him from the Crimea. Her Majesty's Government are of opinion that it will be sufficient for each Government to indicate to the Commander of its army the general plan of campaign and the force which each country is to contribute to the two armies to be formed at Eupatoria and Sevastopol respectively; leaving to the Generals in command on the spot those arrangements which appear to them most calculated to carry out the great objects which are to be accomplished.

The Emperor will doubtless instruct the Commander in chief of the French army in the objects which the two Governments seek to attain by the movement from Eupatoria, and as to the contingencies which may arise in these operations; and Her Majesty's Government will, in like manner, instruct Sir William Codrington as to the course to be followed at Sevastopol, and as to the contingencies which may possibly arise there. It will be advisable that the two Governments should communicate these instructions to each other.

This new strategy, which placed Codrington in command of 80,000 on the Chersonese plateau, was adopted and communicated to the Commander-in-Chief. He was also instructed to prepare for the subsequent campaign in Asia. Codrington, who had never favoured dividing the armies, was unimpressed, believing this strategy would exclude the British from any glory that might be gained.[21] Long before his objections arrived in London it had become clear that there would be no campaign, and no glory. The British Government had been obliged to accept Louis Napoleon's plans for the Black Sea, in the same way they had forced their Baltic design on the French. As he provided the largest part of the allied land forces the Emperor had the power to command, it would have been both futile and counter-productive to argue. Palmerston had already turned his attention to securing the best terms of peace. Strategy and military preparations were once more subordinated to diplomacy.

After the winter of 1854–55 concern over the administration of military supply and welfare became paramount for public and Government, as Simpson's original orders emphasised. As Prime Minister Palmerston's concern with the army was dominated by the political consequences of another debacle, his correspondence with Panmure contained far more on improvements to the supply, health and comfort of the troops than strategy. After the death of Raglan, Simpson, still no more than chief-of-staff, was dominated by logis-tics and the need to prepare for the winter. After the fall of Sevasto-pol he would not take the field in case the camp and the Balaklava road were not ready for the first storms. His letters to Panmure were full of fears on these heads. His intransigence, allied to the Govern-ment's inability to decide on a successor, left Codrington with no time to act. However, Codrington soon confirmed the wisdom of Simpson's policy. The leading critic of military inertia, Lyons, was inconsistent, complaining of the refusal to move against the enemy and inadequate winter preparations.

The events of the second Crimean winter proved Simpson correct. While the British Army remained healthy, the French collapsed. By February 1856 scurvy, typhus, tuberculosis and other diseases were killing 250 French soldiers every day; the smaller British force, 40,000 strong against 150,000 French, lost only three. This disaster had a powerful influence on the Emperor but, fortunately for the allied diplomats, was unknown to the Russians. Palmerston attributed the disaster to the collapse of sanitary arrangements in the French camp, something he had referred to several times during the year. Once peace had been secured he allowed himself the luxury of sneering at his erstwhile allies. Even before the treaty was signed Panmure admitted the grand strategy prepared in January would have been ruined by the French losses. Despite recruiting 45,403 men in the first nine months of 1855 the British Army was never going to be large enough to operate alone.[22] The collapse of the French Army in the Crimea emphasised the significance of the Great Armament. No-one was prepared to rely on the French after the two Baltic campaigns and the Kertch fiasco. The Great Armament was the only major stroke the British could bring off unaided. It should be no suprise that the Baltic fleet was chosen to celebrate British power when the war ended.

Notes

1 Admiralty to Surveyor 18 Apr. 29 Jun., 10 Sept. 1855: ADM 87/53 f2357, /54 f3785, /55 f4870; OSBON, G.A., 'Crimean Gunboats' in *Mariner's Mirror*, vol. 51, pp. 103–15, 211–20 is not reliable on this issue; Dundas to Wood 4 Sept. 1855: Add. 49,533 f150–2; Wood to Palmerston 19 Sept. 1855: Bdlds. GC/WO f50.

2 Admiralty to Ordnance 13, 29 Sept., 11, 18 Oct. 1855 to War Dept. 31 Oct., 3 Nov., 22 Dec.1855: ADM 2/1681 p. 313, 390, 406, 453, 2/1682 p. 2–3, 15, 189; Admiralty to Surveyor 18, 19 Oct. 1855: ADM 87/55 f5646, 5705; Dundas to Wood 18 Sept. 1855: Add. 49,534 f134–7; Palmerston to Wood 18 Sept. 1855: Add. 48,579 f61; Palmerston to Sir Hugh Ross 1 May 1855: *ibid.* f11.

3 Palmerston to Wood 5 Aug., 16,17 Dec.1855: HALIFAX A4/63 f41, 53; Wood to Palmerston 22 Nov., 16 Dec. 1855, 18 Mar.1856: Bdlds. GC/WO f62/2, 64/1, 68; Wood to Dundonald 7, 9 Jan. 1856: Add. 49,558 f9–10; Dundonald to Wood 8 Jan. 1856: Add. 49,565 f54; LLOYD, C., 'Dundonald's Crimean War Plans' in *Mariner's Mirror*, 1946, pp. 147–54; Scott-Russell to Palmerston 23, 28 Jan. 1856: Bdlds. GC/RU ; SULIVAN, pp. 372–4; Wood to Prince Albert 31 Jan. 1856: Add. 49,565 f67.

4 Admiralty to Surveyor 12, 16, 22, 28 Nov. 1855: ADM 87/56 f6148, 6384, 6572, 6784; Walker memo. undated: Walker WWL/10; SULIVAN, p. 366; PRESTON and MAJOR, *Send a Gunboat* (London, 1967); Admiralty Order 31 Oct. 1855: ADM 2/1571 p. 191.

5 LAMBERT, pp. 53–4; Palmerston to Clarendon 1 Oct. 1855: Cl. Dep. C31 f543–4; Graham to Wood 12 Oct. 1855: HALIFAX A4/70; Palmerston to the Queen 19 Oct. 1855: R.A. G39 f55; Hamelin to Lyons 21 Jan. 1856: LYONS B63.

6 Wood to Keppel 30 Nov. 1855: Add. 49,565 f18; Admiralty to Medical Director 24 Jan. 1856: ADM 2/1682 p. 332; *Times* 21 Feb. 1856; Admiralty to War Department 19 Jan. 1856: ADM 2/1682 p. 307; Admiralty to Portsmouth Dockyard 2 Feb. 1856: ADM 87/57 f7771; Admiralty to Surveyor 7 Jan. 1856: *ibid.* f8205; Wood to Lyons 9 Nov. 1855: Add. 49,565 f126–7.

7 Admiralty to Surveyor 19 Feb. 1856: ADM 2/1682 p. 434; Admiralty to War Department 19 Feb. 1856: *ibid.* p. 432; Dundas Journals for 1856: ADM 50/338.

8 Lyons to Wood 10, 24, 30 Nov. 1855 enc. Osbon to Lyons 26 Nov.: Add. 49,537 f88, 140–3, 146–57; Wood to Lyons 12 Nov. 1855: Add. 49,564 f128–32.

9 Wood to Lyons 6 Dec. 1855 telegraph: NRS p. 423; Wood to Freemantle 21 Dec. 1855: Add. 49,565 f39.

10　Clarendon to Panmure 15 Dec. 1855: PANMURE, ii, p. 20; Clarendon to Wood 16 Dec. 1855: HALIFAX A4/63ii; FITZMAURICE,i, pp. 136–8; Argyll to Clarendon 4 Jan. 1856: Cl. Dep. C48 f1–6.

11　Clarendon to Palmerston 7 Jan. 1856: Bdlds. GC/CL f778; SPRATT SPR1/3; Lyons to Wood 10 Jan. 1856: Add. 49,538 f4–6.

12　Wood to Lyons 8, 11, 14 Jan. 1856: Add. 49,565 f44–9; Summary of Baltic Commission, Dundas 14 Jan.1856; F.C. vol. viii, pp. 1882–3.

13　Cambridge to Clarendon 14 Jan. 1856: Cl. Dep. C135 f76; SULIVAN, p. 365; FITZMAURICE, i, p. 128; *Times* 2 Jan. 1856; Berkeley to Wood 9 Nov. 1855: HALIFAX A4/74; Palmerston to Wood 9 Nov. 1855: Add. 48,579 f61; Palmerston to Wood 14 Jan. 1856: HALIFAX A4/63 f55; Graham to Lyons 6 Jan. 1856: LYONS L286–7; Wood to Palmerston 16 Jan. 1856: Add. 49,565 f59.

14　Memoranda by Dundas, Airey, Penaud 17 Jan. 1856; Report of Baltic Commission 19 Jan. Opinion of the Emperor 20 Jan.1856; F.C. vol. viii, pp. 1891, 1895–6, 1908, 1912–17.

15　Memo. by Panmure 29 Jan. 1856: DAL. GD45/8/349/5 (in full); The Queen to Panmure 3 Feb. 1856: PANMURE, ii, p. 91; Memo. by Wood 2 Feb. 1856: Cl. Dep. C48 f471–8; Palmerston to Clarendon 2 Feb. 1856: Cl. Dep. C49 f104; Wood to Lyons 18 Jan. 1856: Add. 49,565 f49–50; Clarendon to Cowley 28 Jan. 1856: F.O. 519/173 f91–4.

16　SCHROEDER, p. 330; CURTISS, pp. 479–80; KNAPLUND, p. 501; SCOTT, pp. 320–2; Magennis to Clarendon 12 Jan. 1856: Cl. Dep. C59 f3; ANDERSSON, I., *A History of Sweden* (London, 1956), p. 334; BARROS, J., *The Aland Islands Question*, (New Haven, 1968), p. 7.

17　Memo. by de la Gravière 14 Jan. 1856: F.C. viii, pp. 1874–82; Lyons to Wood 12, 13 Jan. 1856: Add. 49,538 f12–17; Cambridge to Panmure 12 Jan. 1856: PANMURE, ii, pp. 60–2; Prince Albert to Panmure 17 Jan. 1856: *ibid.* p. 70; Wood to Lyons 18 Jan. 1856: Add. 49,565 f49–50; Palmerston to the Queen 17 Jan. 1856: BENSON and ESHER, iii, p. 165.

18　Memoranda by Cambridge, Lyons, Airey, Niel 17 Jan. 1856: F.C. viii, pp. 1886–91, 1904–7; Lyons to Wood 17 Jan. 1856: Add. 49,538 f37–8; Prince Albert to Panmure 21 Jan. 1856: PANMURE,ii, p. 79; Palmerston to Clarendon 9 Jan. 1856: Cl. Dep. C49 f15–16.

19　Memo. by Cambridge and opinion of the Emperor 20 Jan. 1856: F.C. viii, pp. 1911–12, 1919–20; Lyons to Wood 17, 18 Jan. 1856: Add. 49,538 f37–8, 42; Cambridge to Panmure 20 Jan. 1856: PANMURE, ii, pp. 73–4; Prince Albert to Panmure 21, 23 Jan. 1856: *ibid.* pp. 79–80.

20　FITZMAURICE, i, pp. 147, 162; Memoranda by Panmure undated and 22 Jan. 1856: DAL. GD45/8/349/5, GD45/8/350/1/3; Panmure to the Queen 2, 8 Feb. 1856: PANMURE, ii, pp. 87–8, 97–8; The Queen to Panmure 3 Feb. 1856: *ibid.* p. 91; Louis Napoleon to Cowley 4 Feb. and Cowley to Clarendon 5 Feb. 1856: DAL. GD45/8/350/3/1; Palmerston to Clarendon 2 Feb. 1856: Cl. Dep. C49 f114–15.

21　Memo. by Panmure 7 Feb.1856: DAL. GD45/8/350/3/2 (in full); Panmure to Codrington (Secret and Confidential) 11 Feb. 1856: F.C. viii, pp. 2007–9; Codrington to Panmure 28 Feb. rec. 18 Mar. 1856: *ibid.* pp. 2130–1.

22   Palmerston to Panmure 16 Aug. 1855: Add. 48,579 f42 is typical; Panmure to Clarendon 28 Mar. 1856: Cl. Dep. C49 f312–14; Hardinge to Panmure 3 Nov. 1855: F.C. vol. vii, p. 1562.

23

A limited peace

Once Russian acceptance of the Austrian Ultimatum became known in Britain late on 16 January, interest in practical strategy evaporated. The Baltic and Black Sea campaigns were drawn up in outline to support the diplomacy of peace. Cabinet acceptance of Louis Napoleon's plans indicated the reduced significance of strategy. Allied diplomatic co-operation was now the key to success. However, neither Palmerston nor the court were pleased by this turn of events. Public opinion, at least as voiced by the newspapers, was firmly opposed to peace. All anticipated success in 1856, recompense for the disappointments of the Redan and Kars. Palmerston observed:

if peace *can* now be concluded on conditions honourable and secure, it would, as Your Majesty justly observes, not be right to continue the war for the mere purpose of prospective victories. It will, however, be obviously necessary to continue active preparations up to the moment when a definitive Treaty of Peace is signed, in order that the Russians may not find it for their interest to break off negotiations when the season for operations shall approach.

These preparations were primarily for Cronstadt, although the reinforcement of the Crimea continued.[1] Yet all this was little more than an insurance of Russian good faith. The real issues were diplomatic. Diplomacy had replaced strategy as the process to secure war aims. The object remained the same: to prevent Russian expansion on her northern and southern frontiers.

Before the conference the Government had to decide on the plenipotentiaries, and the terms they could accept. It was revealing that Palmerston's first thoughts were for the eastern shore of the Euxine; he wanted no reconstruction of the forts on the Circassian shore, free commercial relations and a Russo–Circassian treaty. The last would be difficult in the absence of any coherent Circassian authority. To secure these strong, and largely unjustified, terms he wanted Lyons to lead the delegation:

He is a practised diplomatist as well as an able naval commander . . . learned in international law as well as in cannon law, moreover not only is he well acquainted with the Black Sea and the Baltic, but he is also a man of clear head, firm and determined mind, not likely to be cajoled or swayed by sinister influences.

Palmerston had several reasons for favouring Lyons: Louis Napoleon valued his opinion, and his wartime prestige would help to offset any disappointment with the terms. Furthermore, Palmerston realised the major areas of contention involved naval issues on which Lyons could command the respect of any audience. Clarendon rejected him, existing accounts suggest because of his poor French. In truth Clarendon had other objections: 'he has no knowledge whatever of the main questions that will come under discussion & tho' he has some ability & considerable firmness I think him singularly deficient in judgement, he is moreover irritable & one of the vainest men I ever knew.' While Lyons' command of French was perfect there was much truth in Clarendon's appreciation of his character; his knowledge of the issues lay somewhere between the views of the two statesmen. At root Clarendon opposed Palmerston's basic object, trying to browbeat the conference with an armed ambassador. In the event Clarendon reluctantly accepted the commission himself.[2]

Clarendon was aware that the terms of peace, like the details of allied strategy, would be determined by France. Louis Napoleon explained to Walewski that his object was peace, but only at a high price that would maintain the British alliance. Therefore while the main themes of the settlement had been decided before the conference assembled the secondary issues were left open. The selection of Paris was another sign of the Emperor's influence, although arrived at after a process of elimination in which the British categorically rejected Vienna. It was confirmed in the protocol, signed in Vienna on 1 February, for the conference to open on the 25th. British policy was now limited to securing the best settlement on points of detail. Neutralisation of the Euxine had been conceded, but the number and size of the police vessels was still undecided. Palmerston wanted to extend neutralisation to cover Nicolaiev and the Azov. Circassia and Austria's demand for Bessarabia posed major problems. Only the demilitarisation of the Aland Islands reflected the

Baltic campaigns, but this was an issue on which Britain was not prepared to compromise. On the first point Clarendon consulted Lyons, who proved hopelessly out of tune, comparing Russia's needs in the Euxine to those of the British Isles. Consequently the number and size of the proposed vessels exceeded Palmerston's expectations. The Azov and Nicolaiev were obsessions with the Premier, but nowhere near as significant as he imagined. Circassia proved insuperable; in practical politics the territory could neither be made independent, nor given back to Turkey.[3] Austria's Bessarabian cession had a major interest for Britain, despite the weight of historical opinion to the contrary.[4] When Buol offered to modify the demand, to secure Britain's Baltic *sine qua non* Palmerston was unimpressed:

We never considered the cession of part of Bessarabia as a concession to Austrian interests; it is a concession to Turkish interests by giving a better and stronger frontier to Turkey on the borders of Moldavia.

It is an Austrian interest only so far as it is an additional security to Turkey. But we are not prepared to give up an acquired security for Turkey in order to barter it for a security to Sweden. We insist on having both, and have them we must.

Aside from creating a long term rift between Austria and Russia the purpose of the original demand had been to establish a defensible mountain frontier, excluding Russia from the Danube, and its navigable tributary, the Pruth.[5]

On the Aland question Sweden came forward in January calling for a limitation of the Russian Baltic and White Sea fleets and the restoration, or demilitarisation of the Alands. Meeting a lukewarm response Baron Manderstrom only pressed the final point, the one condition the allies could justly claim. Before the conference the French demonstrated little interest in the Baltic, and were willing to return the Islands unconditionally. Clarendon considered this would be a disgrace. Demilitarisation, Palmerston believed, would secure Sweden against surprise attacks. In an uncharacteristic letter he also expressed reservations about Cronstadt. Schroeder misunderstood this, claiming the British Government anticipated failure in 1856.[6] In truth Palmerston's reservations were intended to sweeten the idea of peace. He had hoped to limit Russian naval power in the north, but as the ships and arsenals remained in Russian hands this was not possible. In the event political and technical changes brought about by the war ensured Russian power in the Baltic did not recover for ninety years.

The Russian decision for peace left the Great Armament shorn of its design function, but it could be turned to effect as a potent propaganda weapon symbolising British willingness to continue the war. Wood was convinced it played the decisive role in bringing Russia to accept peace, and when the Austrians requested access to British military establishments Clarendon sent them Spithead, in time to have some influence at Paris. The impact on the Russians was more direct. Before the conference opened Brunnow, one of the Russian delegates, claimed the British population were tired of the war. Clarendon silenced him, observing that they really wanted to see their 'grand preparations' put to use, and the most popular thing Russia could do was to break off negotiations. Wood supported this style of diplomacy, referring to a statement in the House that 350 gunboats would be sent to the Baltic and 100 to the Euxine as powder and shot' for the conference table.[7] At the first meeting, on 25 February, the delegates agreed to an armistice for a month, effective from the 29th; the belligerents would avoid all hostilities on and against the land, excluding the blockade. Wood had hoped to exclude the naval campaign as well. The French took this to be the end of the war, stopping what little work was in hand on flotilla craft.[8] Louis Napoleon was more concerned with the diplomatic possibilities of the peace process and the impending birth of his first child. The Russians attempted to exploit these developments.

On 24 February the Flying Squadron, Captain Watson, was ordered to the Baltic. Wood felt obliged to cover the remote possibility of the Russians going to sea. The public instructions treated coal as not being contraband, although in private Watson was ordered to stop it reaching Russia at all costs. Dundas, reappointed on the 19th and unaware that the 1856 campaign would have seen Sweden in the allied camp, considered this would be counter-productive. During the winter a small force of paddle steamers had attempted to keep station in the Kattegatt, retiring to Hull for the worst of the weather. This only demonstrated the folly of exposing inefficient vessels to the full fury of a North Sea winter. During the afternoon of 29 January *Polyphemus*, Captain Warren, was driven ashore and destroyed near the Hansholm light on the coast of Jutland; the master and twenty-seven men were drowned.[9] *Polyphemus* was the only British warship lost during the Baltic campaigns, although she never entered the Baltic and was lost in year when there was no campaign. Dundas and Baynes were reappointed, Seymour went to the troubled East Indies station.

The Aland Islands question was settled at the third meeting of the conference. Orlov, leading the Russian delegation, agreed to demilitarisation, hoping Russian concession here would be recalled when other issues were debated. The surrender of Aland as a military position ended Russia's forward policy in the Baltic under the Czars. With the revolution in naval architecture it sharply reduced Russian influence in the western basin. The inclusion of the Aland provisions in the Treaty gave them greater durability than the terms would otherwise have justified. Part of the *quid pro quo* was permission for Russia to complete two battleships building at Nicolaiev and send them to the Baltic. The Aland clause was completed on 26 March and approved by Palmerston the following day.[10]

Despite Russian acceptance of the Austrian Ultimatum the details of the Four Points remained to be settled at Paris. The most important were those relating to the neutralisation of the Black Sea. Palmerston's desire for a complete demilitarisation was impractical. The Russians had a genuine need for police vessels, while Nicolaiev and the Azov, being inland, could not be included. This did not prevent him raising difficulties. Realising there was no chance of French support, he accepted Orlov's declaration that Nicolaiev would not be used to construct warships beyond the permitted level, which was inserted in the protocol of the treaty.[11] The number and size of the vessels permitted was to be included in a Russo–Turkish Convention, while Britain had the right to be consulted during the drafting. The Russians tried every method to improve their position. Orlov started by asking for six frigates, which were easily rejected, frigates were clearly warships. Palmerston argued for craft modelled on British revenue cutters. Orlov then asked for hulks to serve as barracks, but the British knew these were only battleships in reserve. To emphasise British determination Clarendon warned Orlov that the Mediterranean fleet, the one element of power not dependent upon the French, would remain in the Black Sea until the concessions were made. Orlov then requested armed transports, which were also rejected. Whenever Clarendon threatened to break off negotiations Orlov retracted, excusing his demands on the flimsy pretext of his being ignorant of naval matters. Clarendon must have wondered if his rejection of Lyons had been altogether wise. Eventually the compromise was for six 800-ton steamers similar to French *avisos* (dispatch boats) and four 200-ton vessels. This force posed no threat to Turkey which, although prohibited from operating a larger force in the Euxine, had a battlefleet in the Bosphorus. This achieved the major British aim in the Black Sea – removing the possibility of a Russian amphibious assault on the Straits. Palmerston also secured British Consuls at the Russian ports to oversee the implementation of the terms.[12]

In other areas the negotiations were less successful. With the aid of Louis Napoleon Russia secured the strategic fortress of Chotin and the mountain ridges on the Bessarabian frontier. Palmerston wanted to exchange this concession for the demilitarisation of Nicolaiev. In the event only the Danube could be secured, and on that Buol had to rest his claims of Austrian success. French support also enabled the Russians to avoid the British claim for the neutralisation of the Asian coast, although the Emperor did not renege on his agreement that the return of Kars should be *sine qua non*. Orlov was allowed to use it as a bargain for the improvement of the Bessarabian frontier. The Treaty was signed on 30 March, the armistice being extended to the sea until ratification. On 12 April the Orders in Council prohibiting British ships from clearing for Russian ports were revoked. The Treaty was ratified and published on 28 April.[13]

While the representatives of the powers were assembled at Paris the issue of war at sea came under review, specifically the two most controversial areas, blockade and privateering. Initially the delegates intended to sign a resolution against privateering, but extended their discussions to bring in the blockade. Clarendon, who had played a major role in forming British maritime warfare policy, decided Britain could earn much international goodwill by renouncing the old arbitrary system. His action was provoked by an American circular to the maritime powers, urging them to accept that the neutral flag should cover the goods carried, which was clearly anti-British. Convinced the Americans would not renounce privateering, Clarendon outmanoeuvred them. Palmerston was pleased, stressing that if America did not sign Britain would be free to use the old rules against her in the event of war. Wood was cautious, but considered the bargain a good one.[14] The Declaration of Paris was signed on 16 April by representatives of Britain, France, Prussia, Sardinia and Turkey. As expected the United States refused to sign any declaration against privateering. The terms of the document were a codification of allied practice during the war, both an admission of their value in preserving good relations with neutrals, and a reflection of the efficiency of the steam blockade:

1. Privateering is, and remains abolished.
2. The neutral flag covers the enemy's goods, except contraband of war.
3. Neutral goods, with the exception of contraband of war, are not liable to capture under the enemy's flag.
4. Blockades, in order to be binding must be effective, that is to say maintained by a force sufficient really to prevent access to the coast of the enemy.

Opinion in Britain, both contemporary and historical, was predominantly hostile. Most considered the Declaration removed the most formidable element of seapower from Britain's arsenal. This was wrong; in the French wars privateers made the greatest number of merchant ship captures and with steam they would become even more effective, as the *Alabama* demonstrated ten years later. The essential point was that under the 1856 Declaration any use of privateers would allow Britain to return to the old methods, something that was done in 1914 and 1939. Without mercantile auxiliaries France, Russia and the United States could not wage an effective maritime war against Britain in the nineteenth century; once they were used Britain was free to act as she wished, and she could do so from the start against the United States. Palmerston saw the Declaration as a diplomatic triumph which did not reduce British power. Finally the document was incomplete without a binding, agreed definition of contraband which, as Clarendon reasoned, could be stretched very wide.[15] Steam made the blockade simpler and more effective.

The Treaty was signed at 12.30 on Sunday 30 March, allowing British statesmen to reflect on the war. Wood summarised the view of the cabinet majority: 'I think we have got an excellent peace. Another years war might have enabled us to obtain still better terms, but we have attained all the objects for which we went to war, and everything considered we have good reason to be well pleased with the result of our two years operations.' Palmerston was not concerned by the original objects of British involvement, which had always been subordinate to the real purpose of his policy: weakening Russia as 'security against future aggression'. The peace was only satisfactory for him because the French were unwilling to play their part any longer. Typically, Clarendon's thoughts turned to a hostile coalition, including France and the United States. The Queen accepted the inevitable. Stratford was disgusted, expecting more trouble from Russia in the immediate future. Public reaction was generally favourable, although one newspaper came out in mourning. This left the political opposition disorganised and bitter; Graham continued to blame the naval commanders.[16]

The peace confirmed the results of the war; the allies could attack Russia where they pleased, but had not carried out any decisive operations. Russian influence in Europe, particularly in Germany and the Baltic, was much reduced. The corollary to this was a marked increase in French prestige which, far from improving Britain's strategic position, merely shifted the focus of defence policy back to France. The intervening years had robbed the Army of its Waterloo prestige and dimmed the glories of the Navy. Fortunately the battlefleet remained superior to that of France.

The transfer of naval resources from war to peace was rapid. On 27 March the Flying Squadron was telegraphed to keep up the blockade and the War Department pressed to send every available mortar. Three days later Watson was ordered home. The combination of a powerful fleet in the Home Ports and peace made a general review inevitable. Dundas, already quarrelling with the Commander-in-Chief at Portsmouth, Sir George Seymour, over seniority, considered this would only result in accidents and condemned the idea of a vain spectacle.[17] Although the fleet continued to assemble the War Department was requested to take back the mortar shells and unload them. At the first steam review, in August 1853, Captain Eden described the steamers as 'Wolverhampton moving down on them'. The Board ordered all ships to load with Welsh steam coal to prevent the Queen's view being obscured and, almost as an afterthought, to avoid accidents. This was in stark contrast to the Baltic campaigns, when an immense pall of North Country smoke followed the fleet everywhere. The mortar depots *London* and *Rodney* would anchor as the pivots around which the steamers would proceed in two columns, led by Dundas and Sir George Seymour. Sulivan protested that the lead belonged to the surveyors, and this was accepted.[18] The force collected at Spithead, manned by 31,527 men, was remarkable:

Battleships	24
Cruisers	37
Floating batteries	4
Gunboats	120
Mortar vessels	50
Auxiliaries	5
Total no. vessels	240

This was not even the complete 1856 Baltic force, and had no units from the Mediterranean fleet. It was a demonstration of Britain's industrial, economic and naval power, and of her determination to bring the war to a satisfactory conclusion. The Review passed off without incident on St George's Day, 23 April. The Queen sent her congratulations to the Surveyor's Department, two months later Walker was created a baronet. In the intervening months the fleet was run down to a peace establishment as all eyes turned to the French battlefleet.[19]

This first all-steam review has been dismissed as merely a triumphal celebration, a victory parade for the 'Crimean' War; this reflects the failure of historians to appreciate how the war was conducted, and how it ended. The real impact of the review was not intended for the Queen, the assembled parliamentarians or the taxpayers. It was directed at a foreign audience; France, the real naval rival, the truculent Americans and the bitter Russians. The fleet at Spithead was a restatement of overwhelming naval power, with the addition of a fully prepared coastal flotilla, purpose-built to carry the war into the shallowest waters and destroy the most powerful forts. America and Russia were wide open to such an attack, while Cherbourg, Brest and Toulon were hardly safe. The lessons of the Russian War, as demonstrated at Spithead, were soon forgotten, and throughout the second half of the nineteenth century naval power continued to be measured in battleships. The Baltic campaign of 1854 demonstrated that battlefleets can do little against an unwilling enemy without the flotilla.

The alliance between Britain and France was a wartime expedient with no lasting foundation, constantly threatened by rivalry in the Mediterranean and the naval race. Graham had been well aware of this even before the war. Both in and out of office his policy was dominated by the maintenance of British naval supremacy. By late

1855 many had come to share his view, finding the French even more troublesome as allies than they had been as rivals. Graham's answer was to keep up the fleet; Wood, Palmerston and the Queen agreed. The key to Anglo–French relations was, as Graham pointed out, French construction policy. The naval race that began in 1851 with the Second Empire and the wooden steam battleship had been codified by the French Naval Laws of 1855.[20] This was a direct challenge, leading to fears for the security of the British coast and overseas possessions, particularly in the Mediterranean.

Throughout the war there had been a long running struggle for dominant influence at Constantinople between Stratford and his French 'colleagues'. Slade observed the steady growth of French influence. The war forced Britain to treat France as an equal partner. The French then built up their reserve army just outside the city, alarming many. Stratford's fear that the French intended to occupy the city was treated seriously, and given credence by Niel's proposal at the Council of War. British policy makers were alarmed, seeing the city as the key to the Eastern Mediterranean and the Straits. De Lesseps' Suez canal project had long been viewed by Palmerston as a French device aimed at British naval and mercantile interests. When the new Pasha of Egypt accepted the plan in late 1854 every effort was expended to defeat the scheme. Linked to the French activity at Constantinople Palmerston considered this was too great a coincidence to be as innocent as de Lesseps maintained.[21] Sending Spratt to check the hydrographic details indicated serious Government interest. Once peace became inevitable, and before it had been signed, Anglo–French friction at Paris turned all attention to the post-war situation. Writing from the conference table Clarendon urged Panmure to reinforce Malta and Gibraltar with the guns being brought home from the Crimea. Panmure had anticipated the need, reinforcing the garrisons and landing guns from the Mediterranean fleet. Palmerston wanted to keep secret many wartime plans, including his submarine and Dundonald's gas attack. Plans against naval arsenals might be needed in the near future, at Cherbourg.[22] When Wood reduced the Navy for peace he paid off the specialist craft, floating batteries, blockships, gunboats and mortar vessels as 'no longer of any use'. He was also anxious to reduce the establishment to 56,000, 20,000 down on the number voted, but only 12,000 down on the number actually in service. This high figure, just above that for 1854, was justified by problems with the United States and

the need to relieve ships overdue on distant stations. At the height of
the Napoleonic Wars the Royal Navy used up to 140,000 men; that
it went through the Russian War with less than half that number
demonstrated how far this had been a limited/maritime effort,
conditioned by fear of France and a desire not to let spending get out
of control. The rapid casting away of the Great Armament reflected
the prejudices of the service, and ignored the lessons of the war. The
Queen wanted to keep up the fleet, to avoid having to vote sudden
increases, against France or the United States. In the immediate
aftermath of peace Wood was more concerned with the Americans.
Only under pressure from the Queen did he agree to send the Baltic
fleet to embark the Crimean army. Having created the most powerful
fleet yet seen and given it a very public review he was unwilling to
dissipate the attendant prestige. Continued Anglo–American tension
led to the dispatch of four 1,000-man regiments direct from the
Crimea to Canada.[23]

With peace certain Palmerston had no qualms about allowing the
French alliance to cool. He had no desire to follow Louis Napoleon's
policy, which he realised was at least partly anti-British. He could
not hope to make the Emperor follow his plans. France had outlived
her usefulness by ending the war too soon. Her support had been
necessary to take the war to Russia, but: 'when we realise the
different interests of England and France, the different characters
and habits of the two countries, we ought rather to be thankful at
having got so much out of the alliance, and to have maintained it so
long, than to be surprised or disappointed at its approaching end.'
Increasingly concerned by the growth of French power Palmerston
called for defensive works around the British dockyards. Wood was
initially more interested in the expansion of Cherbourg.[24] Later
Palmerston would court French support against Prussia during the
Danish Duchies crisis, and against the Federal Government during
the American Civil War. In both cases the object was the same as it
had been during the Russian War: employing French power for
British strategic objects, which were otherwise impossible. Louis
Napoleon realised this, and his reluctance to serve Palmerston's
purpose was as significant as his continued efforts to achieve naval
parity. Both leaders hoped to use the other to achieve their own ends,
however well these were disguised.

Notes

1   Palmerston to the Queen 17 Jan. 1856: BENSON and ESHER, iii, pp. 165–6; Palmerston to Clarendon 19 Feb. 1856: Cl. Dep. C49 f123.

2   Palmerston to Clarendon 17 Jan. 1856: Add. 48,580 f100; MAXWELL, H., *the Life and Letters of the Fourth Earl Clarendon* (London, 1913, two vols.), ii, p. 114; Clarendon to Palmerston 17 Jan. 1856: Bdlds. GC/CL f783; Clarendon to Henry Reeve 26 Jan. 1856: MAXWELL, ii, pp. 114–15.

3   ECHARD, p. 55; BAUMGART, pp. 104–5; Lyons to Clarendon 9 Feb. 1856: Add. 49,538 f64; Palmerston to Clarendon 31 Jan., 10 Feb. 1856: Cl. Dep. C49 f87, 116; Wood to Russell 15 Jan. 1856: Add. 49,565 f59–60; Wood to Clarendon 19 Jan. 1856: *ibid.* f63–6.

4   RICH, p. 185 provides a summary.

5   Palmerston to Hamilton Seymour (Ambassador at Vienna) 24 Jan. 1856: Add. 48,579 f101–3; Palmerston to Clarendon 25 Feb. 1856: Add. 48.580 f1–5.

6   BAUMGART, pp. 112–13; BARROS; pp. 7–9; WELLESLEY, p. 95; SCHROEDER, p. 400; Clarendon to Palmerston 17 Jan. 1856: Bdlds. GC/CL f738/2; Palmerston to Clarendon 25 Feb. 1856: Add. 48,580 f1–5.

7   Wood to Stewart 21, 26 Jan. 1856: Add. 49,565 f52–4; Clarendon to Palmerston 11 Feb. Palmerston to Clarendon 12 Feb. 1856: Add. 48,580 f118–19; Clarendon to Wood 8 Mar. 1856: HALIFAX A4/57 ii; Wood to Clarendon 10 Mar. 1856: Add. 49,565 f75; Clarendon to Palmerston 20 Feb. 1856: Bdlds. GC/CL f798/2; Wood to Clarendon 18, 23 Feb. 1856: Cl. Dep. C48 f481, 488.

8   Admiralty to Foreign Office 28 Feb. 1856: ADM 1/5674; Panmure to Clarendon 28 Feb. 1856: Cl. Dep. C48 f304; Wood to Clarendon 26 Feb. 1856: Add. 49,565 f85; Palmerston to Clarendon 30 Jan. 1856: Cl. Dep. C49 f83–6; Clarendon to Palmerston 28 Feb. 1856: Bdlds. GC/CL f810.

9   Admiralty Order 24 Feb. 1856: ADM 1/5674; Admiralty to Captain Watson 18 Feb. 1856: ADM 2/1704 p. 230; Wood to Watson 19, 22 Feb. 1856: Add. 49,565 f79, 80; Dundas to Wood 23 Feb. 1856: Add. 49,534 f22; Foreign Office to Admiralty 4 Feb. 1856: ADM 1/5678; GOSSET, W., *The Lost Ships of the Royal Navy; 1793–1900* (London, 1986), p. 114; Wood to Seymour 5 Mar. 1856: Add. 49,565 f85–6.

10   Clarendon to Palmerston 1, 26 Mar. 1856: Bdlds. GC/CL f812, 840; BARROSS p. 11; LAMBERT, p. 113; Palmerston to Clarendon 28 Feb., 27 Mar. 1856: Add. 48,580 f9, 50.

11   For a more detailed study of the peace process see BAUMGART, but this work is subject to reservations, see RICH, p. 243; Palmerston to Clarendon 1, 2, 5 Mar. 1856: Add. 48,580 f12–14, Cl. Dep. C49 f148–9, 153–4.

12   Wood to Palmerston 11 Mar. 1856: Bdlds. GC/WO f66; Palmerston to Clarendon 11, 15, 22, 26 Mar. 1856: Cl. Dep. C49 f166–71, 182–5, 203–5, Add. 48,580 f49–50; RICH, pp. 191–2.

13   BAUMGART, pp. 109–13; Clarendon to Palmerston 30 Mar. 1856 telegraph: Bdlds. GC/CL f846.

14   Orders in Council 12, 20 Apr. 1856: ADM 1/5680; Clarendon to Palmerston 3, 6 Apr. 1856: Bdlds. GC/CL f853–6; Palmerston to Clarendon 5, 8, 10, 12 Apr. 1856: Add. 48,580 f67–80; Wood to Clarendon 7 Apr. 1856: Add. 49,565 f90–1.

15   Foreign Office to Admiralty 16 Apr. 1856: ADM 1/5675; RICHMOND, Adm. H., *Statesmen and Seapower* (Oxford, 1946), p. 266; SEMMEL, B., *Liberalism and Naval Strategy* (London, 1986), pp. 53–9; RANFT, B. in HOWARD, M., ed. *Restraints on War* (London, 1967), p. 43; ANDERSON, O., pp. 272–3; PIGGOTT, Sir F. T., *The Declaration of Paris, 1856* (London, 1919).

16   Wood to Stewart 31 Mar. 1856: Add. 49,565 f96–7; Palmerston to the Queen 30 Mar. 1856: BENSON and ESHER, iii, p. 183; Clarendon to the Queen 30 Mar. 1856: *ibid*. p. 184; The Queen to Clarendon 31 Mar. 1856: *ibid*. pp. 184–5; Stratford to Clarendon 15 Apr. 1856: LANE-POOLE, ii, p. 438; Graham to Newcastle 23 Nov. 1856: MARTINEAU.

17   Wood to Palmerston 27 Mar. 1856: Bdlds. GC/WO f70; Admiralty to War Department 27 Mar. 1856: ADM 2/1683 p. 2; Admiralty to Watson 31 Mar. 1856 telegraph: ADM 2/1704; Dundas to Philip Dundas 4 Apr. 1856: MCM GD 1008/2 f99; Dundas to Seymour 27 Mar. 1856: *ibid*. f239.

18   Admiralty to Dundas 5 Apr. 1856: ADM 2/1683 p. 25; Wood to Palmerston 27 Apr. 1856: Add. 49,565 f101–2; Admiralty Order 9 Apr. 1856: ADM 1/5675; SULIVAN, p. 365.

19   List of vessels 23 Apr. 1856: ADM 87/60 f11391; Admiralty to Surveyor 25 Apr. 1856: *ibid*. f10645; Palmerston to Walker 17 Jun. 1856: Add. 48,580 f97; Admiralty Order 9 May 1856: ADM 1/5676; Surveyor to Portsmouth Dockyard 11 Jun. 1856: ADM 87/60 f11848.

20   Graham to Milne 14 Nov. 1853: MILNE MLN/165/5; Graham to Wood 6 Apr., 12 Oct. 1855: HALIFAX A4/70; The Queen to Wood 16 Nov. 1855: *ibid*. A4/73; Palmerston to Wood 5 Dec. 1855: Add. 48,579 f87; LAMBERT, pp. 97–111, and generally for the naval race.

21   Slade to Stratford 1 Sept. 1854: F.O. 352/38/2; Raglan to Burgoyne 26 Mar. 1855: WROTTESLEY, ii, p. 282; Palmerston to Clarendon 9 Jan. 1856: Cl. Dep. C49 f15–16; HOSKINS, H.L., *British Routes to India* (London, 1928), pp. 291–342.

22   Clarendon to Panmure 27 Mar. 1856: PANMURE, ii, pp. 166–7; Panmure to Clarendon 28 Mar. 1856: Cl. Dep. C48 f312–14; Palmerston to Wood 19 Mar. 1856: HALIFAX A4/63; Palmerston to Dundonald 5 Apr. 1856: Add. 48,580 f67.

23   Wood to the Queen 17, 27 May 1856: R.A. E49, G47 f85; The Queen to Wood 18 May 1856: BENSON and ESHER, iii, p. 191; Palmerston to Panmure 30 Mar. 1856: PANMURE, ii, p. 172.

24   Palmerston to Clarendon 10 Dec. 1856: PURYEAR, p. 431; Palmerston to Wood 1 Sept. 1856: Add. 48,580 f133–4; Wood to Milne 5 Aug. 1856: MILNE MLN 165/13.

24

British strategy and the war

Any assessment of British strategic planning in the period 1853–56 should emphasise that success in war is relative. The basic question must be how far British strategy achieved the war aims set out by the politicians. War aims, like strategic plans, do not long survive the first contact of armies; they are modified by the passage of time, the level of commitment and an acceptance of what is possible. British war aims were never fixed, beyond the 'Four Points', and always subject to powerful external influences and the limitations inherent in the British position. These can be summarised in descending order.

1. The French Alliance, which as a partnership of approximate equals had to act by co-operation. This was not always achieved, because of the weakness of the British Crimean army. After January 1855 Britain had to accept French direction of the war, and this was most evident in the concentration of forces in the Crimea. France and Britain had different aims in making war on Russia, and in times of stress these became evident in strategic decision making.

2. The lack of trained manpower: throughout the war the British Army was far short of the voted war establishment. The first impact of this could be seen in the planned operations in Turkey and the grand raid on Sevastopol. The need was for an operation where limited forces could achieve the greatest impact. After the *coup de main* against Sevastopol turned into a battle of attrition, this weakness gave the French the dominant voice. It also led to attempts to raise mercenary forces, which alienated the United States and some German states. Without some form of conscription this was inevitable, given the small peacetime force.

Reluctance to use coercion also affected naval recruitment. There were never more than 56,000 men afloat, against 140–150,000 at the height of the war against Napoleon. Allied to the shortage of steam warships for the principal theatres, this prevented the execution of a more rigorous maritime strategy. It also indicated the limited British commitment; impressment and the bounty were both available and relatively inexpensive, but neither was raised in cabinet, let alone in the House.

3. Austrian neutrality. The central position of Austria, as a Balkan power and the effective leader of the German states allowed her to limit the conflict to Russia's maritime flanks. While the allies wanted her support they were careful not to alienate her by pressing Turkish claims, or more fundamentally by adopting a war aims programme that posited any profound alteration in the European order. In the event the impact of the war on Russia did have a major impact on the European balance. Within a decade Austria had been defeated by France and lost the leadership of Germany to Prussia, the real beneficiary of the war.

4. Political weakness. The inability of Palmerston to create a cabinet consensus higher than the 'Four Points', allied to the weak parliamentary base of his administration, precluded the adoption of a more wide ranging war aims programme. Strategy was bent to wider aims, but only in certain areas, primarily those where maritime rather than purely military operations were required.

5. Outside the war the United States, Persia and India posed serious threats to British interests. They had to be countered, India by scarce troops. Persia by war and the United States by armed diplomacy. All three used up human and material resources.

Had the grand raid at Sevastopol been successful many of these problems would have been reduced, but not avoided. The fundamental error came when the allies adopted a war aims programme based on the 'Four Points', without appreciating what such terms would require of Russia. The allies wasted eighteen months fighting a limited war only to discover Russia would not surrender her position on the Euxine without some more powerful threat. Sweden would not join the allies until they made an unlimited effort. Austria was the first to realise that unlimited methods would have to be used to secure peace. The Ultimatum was an attempt to persuade the Czar to concede what he had already lost, before defeat in an unlimited struggle altered the balance of power, something that could only damage Austrian interests. When Palmerston realised what was being done he switched to the only unlimited operation open to

Britain, the naval assault on Cronstadt/St Petersburg. If the alliance had been in better health a combined attack, as sketched by Canrobert, might have been adopted, but time and confidence in the French were lacking. Instead the Great Armament was cobbled up into half a decisive strategy. Austria's *latent* threat, along with the enormous cumulative damage caused by two years of economic warfare and the attrition in the Crimea left Russia with no reserves to meet the new challenge. Swedish intentions, always uncertain, added further complications. This unlimited threat ended the war, secured the 'Four Points' and represented a major setback for Russian Baltic policy, despite the inherent weaknesses of the British position that precluded the adoption of any other method. Although the object of the war, even in Palmerston's grandest permutations, was never more than to place some barrier in the path of Russian expansion, this could not be achieved by limited means. Russian acceptance of the Austrian Ultimatum reflected her inability to win the war and the effect of the war on the state, rather than any victories won by allied arms. When the future held only more defeats it was sound policy to give way, recover, rebuild and start again.

British grand strategy had always relied on this cumulative, long term build up of pressure, wearing down the enemy: achieving results against land based powers, such as Russia, took a long time, much longer than any British statesman would commit himself too, publicly or privately. The public expected repeat performances of Trafalgar and Waterloo, having forgotten Bergen-op-Zoom, Coruna and Walcheren; they had no desire for a long war. Among the politicians Graham had both a sense of the cost of a long war, and the courage to attempt a solution. His strategy attempted to secure quick, largely naval victories against naval targets. This involved taking risks, particularly at Sevastopol, and the plans came unstuck. His colleagues realised it was politically impossible to start a public discussion of a long war, although several knew this was the only way to put pressure on Russia. Russell, like Graham, supported bold military action, because he feared the political consequences of a long drawn out war. French, Turkish and Sardinian troops permitted a battle of attrition in the Crimea which, allied to the strategic dislocation imposed by the Baltic campaigns and the economic warfare of which so little had been anticipated, brought Russia to accept the 'Four Points'. These developments were not the intended result of allied strategy; they flowed from the failure of the original war plans.

The Crimean campaign became the exact opposite of what had been intended by its projectors. This forced the allies to reconsider their strategy, although they had few options. The political impact of the initial failure made the capture of Sevastopol the overriding political imperative. Strategy was at a discount until it was taken. Only then were plans for Cronstadt, and wider campaigns in the Euxine, seriously considered.

Technology affected the war at every level. Steam battleships provided an unequalled strategic command of the Black Sea and the Baltic, despite the presence of powerful Russian sailing battlefleets. Russian seapower had become obsolete in the five years before the war, for although the allies could still use sailing battleships they required steam for every significant operation, from passing the Dardanelles to taking up their positions before Sevastopol on 17 October 1854, the day the steam battleship came of age with *Agamemnon*. Steam frigates and corvettes allowed the allies to exploit the command guaranteed by the battleships. In both seas an effective blockade depended entirely on the presence of steamers. They could not be driven off by adverse winds or evaded by skilful blockade runners. Steam-powered flotilla craft gave the allies command of the Sea of Azov and threatened Cronstadt. Steam transports allowed the allies to mount the grand raid against Sevastopol and kept their armies supplied so effectively that 3,000 miles from home they wore down a more numerous enemy in their own country during a year-long battle of attrition. Despite the enormous distance the allies possessed a logistics superiority over the Russians that, reinforced by the depredations of Osborn in the Azov, secured Sevastopol. Lacking railways Russia depended on coastal and riverine shipping; once this was broken the road network was unable to meet the demands. This made the Crimea an ideal theatre for a limited war, far better than the Baltic. On land the allied lead in technology allowed a limited effort to overcome an unlimited Russian defence. In the Crimea allied superiority in infantry firepower decided the battles of the Alma, Inkerman and the Tchernaya. Superior artillery, brought up from Balaklava by rail, wore down the defences. Behind those lay the superior technical and manufacturing base which enabled the allies to develop and introduce new weapons as the war progressed: ironclads, steam gunboats, long range rockets and guns. The Russians had no answer to this; they could only try to import rifles and steam engines, or make do with whatever was to hand. The technological lead that allowed the allies to dictate the direction of the war was at its height in the mid nineteenth century. In no other period could the invasion of the Crimea have been undertaken so lightly. Once Russia had rail connections with the peninsula the invasion would have been a very serious undertaking. Previously sailing transports would have been unable to keep up the supply requirements in winter. However it must be stressed the allies never intended to fight a battle of attrition in the Crimea; the failure of the grand raid forced them in to the attrition strategy. In the process they discovered new, hitherto unexploited forms of war power. In this sense the Russian War was the first modern conflict, one in which technology and productive capacity played a major part.

The fundamental lesson of the war, one that should have been obvious from the chastening experience of acting in concert with France, was that British power on the continent was of little account. Until she was prepared to create a continental army British naval and commercial power were only auxiliaries; the pathetic attempt to browbeat Prussia over the Danish Duchies seven years later brought the lesson home. The subsequent retreat into imperial isolation was in part reaction, in part understanding. The evidence had been available in 1856, but in the euphoria of victory such deeper insights were lacking. Even the pessimistic Graham did not realise how far the war had damaged British prestige; sixty years later continentals still gave her little credit for military power. Russia was more clear-sighted in defeat and in her naval, northern and strategic policies it is still possible to see the impact of the war. As if to demonstrate the degree of ignorance in Britain it was the sea, the one element where she had nothing to fear, that provoked the greatest alarm after 1856. Palmerston led an absurd campaign to spend vast sums of money on forts when the development of naval forces during the war had been all in Britain's favour, making more use of iron and steam, areas in which France still lagged behind. Furthermore the Grand Armament of 1856 was perfectly capable of demolishing any French naval arsenal, and the ships inside. However these new developments were ignored. The mortar vessels, gunboats and floating batteries were all paid off in 1856, and much money spent on forts. With an adequate flotilla French seapower could be attacked and destroyed at root. Battlefleet superiority was the key to British security, the 1856 flotilla could convert command of the sea into an offensive. The failure of politicians and later naval intellectuals to accept this stands in stark contrast to the energy expended on the development of the ironclad battleship. The major navies all considered the flotilla an inferior, degenerate, form of warfare. The need was for a a balanced fleet, capital ships and a flotilla; the two were not mutually exclusive. British policy makers had shown little enthusiasm for the flotilla before 1854, they evinced none after 1856. By contrast the Russians accepted the lessons of the war, adopting new weapons and tactics to suit their new defensive requirements.

Even if this new offensive naval power had been understood, the destruction of French, American or Russian seapower was not the same thing as defeating those nations in war. Without a reliable and pliable ally of continental stature, a highly unlikely situation, Britain could not defeat her enemies. In 1854 British statesmen attempted to 'win' the war against Russia with peripheral campaigns and limited means because those were the only means to hand. Russia, as a large land empire with vast reserves of manpower would not be easily defeated by such methods, as any contemporary student of Russian history could have informed them. Unfortunately the distorted 'Crimeocentric' view of the war soon linked the fall of Sevastopol with the end of the war and ignored the limited objects of the original raid. As a result diplomatic historians play down the role of military operations in resolving the conflict. They brush aside the Cronstadt plan, ignoring the massive concentration of Russian resources in the Baltic, to the detriment of the Crimea and the power of the Great Armament. A better understanding of the Baltic campaigns would have avoided the error, but none was forthcoming.

As the Baltic did not fit in with the agreed war aims of early 1854 it was left to Graham to cobble up a policy relying on the hope of Swedish alliance. His colleagues were never aware of the objects of this policy, and never agreed on any war aims programme for the Baltic. Without cabinet sanction there could be no realistic Baltic strategy. Similarly, in 1855 the Baltic had no role until Palmerston's diplomatic initiative, the fall of Sevastopol and the Austrian Ultimatum forced the adoption of a more ambitious strategy. The real failure of the two seasons in the Baltic was that of the politicians; without an agreed policy nothing could be done. Once Palmerston accepted the need for an assault on Cronstadt to bring Russia to accept allied terms, the fleet, no longer even in the Baltic, had, for the first time, a major influence on the war. As this was essentially a political success, not a spectacular operational victory, the influence of the Baltic fleet and the concept of a Russian War was soon lost. When Admiral Fisher floated his Baltic schemes in 1905 the War Office objected that Baltic operations had no effect on the 'Crimean War'.[1] No more powerful criticism of the label 'Crimean' can be made. The position is no better understood today.

Note

1 SCHURMAN, D., *Julias S. Corbett, 1854–1922* (London, 1981), p. 42.

Bibliography

Existing secondary literature on the Russian War is deeply flawed. Certain areas have been well researched, leading to extensive and authoritative works, elsewhere it remains little more than a travesty of scholarship. The diplomacy of the crisis and the conflict are, within the limits of the 'Crimean War', well known; the campaign in the Crimea has been subjected to a larger, if less rigorous, body of work. However the formation of strategy, pre-war planning, the Baltic theatre, wartime naval policy, the conduct of operations in the Black Sea before the Crimean operation, after the fall of Sevastopol and outside the Crimea have been neglected. The principal failure is summed up in the term 'Crimean War'. So long as historians begin their work from this premise it is hardly possible they can advance our understanding of the conflict. If this book has any purpose it is to posit an alternative view of the war, based on British strategy and operations.

The best evidence in support of this argument comes from the MS collections. Several have either not been used before, or have not been used in any published work. The most important of these are the naval and strategic correspondence of the two First Lords of the Admiralty, Graham and Wood. In both cases the collections have become divided, the latter into three separate parts. Neither have been exploited before, and they provide the basis of any new view of the war. Similarly the papers of Admirals R. S. Dundas, J. W. D. Dundas and Lord Lyons had not been used at all; the former were actually placed in folio while the author was consulting them. This failure can also be traced back to the Crimean label. It is otherwise difficult to imagine how such major collections, all of which are accessible, could be overlooked, particularly given the important roles of J. W. D. Dundas and Lyons in the Crimean campaign. The Royal Navy has been dismissed with a variety of contemptuous phrases without any adequate research, when existing material at the Public Record Office and in private collections provides a very different view.

Among the secondary literature there are some outstanding works. Henry Sulivan's life of his father, the Baltic surveying Captain, provides an invaluable, intelligent view of the campaigns, and of the development of plans for Cronstadt. The three volumes of official correspondence published by the Navy Records Society (the cabinet's printed record) demonstrate the scope and complexity of the war. However, they do not cover the pre-war period, or offer much on the policy of the Government. Used in conjunction with the Admiralty collection at the Public Record Office they provide a basic chronology. Real insight into the policy making process can only be acquired from the MS collections. J. S. Curtiss's *Russia's Crimean War*, for all the bias of the title and the text, provides invaluable coverage of the Russian dimension, including material which breaks down the view the title adopts. P. Schroeder's *Austria, Great Britain and the Crimean War* offers similar insight into the Austrian position, although he shares the bias of all academic studies, basing his work on the chancelleries and the Crimea. J. B. Conacher's *The Aberdeen Coalition, 1852–1855* provides an excellent introduction to the political problems of the British Government in the first half of the war, and offers more coverage of the Baltic than other works. His more recent volume, *Britain and the Crimea, 1855–56* is less satisfactory, giving no hint of the Baltic plans for 1856, less than one page on the 1855 campaign and a curious treatment of the Vienna conference. A. P. Saab's *The Origins of the Crimean Alliance* can justly exclude the Baltic, being the first scholarly work to make use of the rich Turkish sources. It is an essential corrective to the European slant of earlier works, and used in conjunction with Slade's book provides a new perspective. W. Baumgart's *The Peace of Paris, 1856*, once mastered offers a wealth of detail on the peace process not available elsewhere.

Primary sources

Public Papers held at the Public Record Office, Kew

Admiralty Papers: ADM
  1. Secretary's In letters
  2. Secretary's Out letters
  3. Special Minutes
 12. Digest
 50. Admiral's Journals
 84. Steam Department
 87. Surveyor's Department
 91. Material Department Out letters
 92. Surveyor's Submission Book
180. Progress Book

Foreign Office Papers: F.O.
 22. Denmark, In letters
 64. Prussia, In letters
 65. Russia, In letters
 73. Sweden, In letters
 78. Turkey, In letters

Hydrographer of the Navy Papers: Taunton

Private papers
ABERDEEN Held at the British Library
BAYNES Held at the National Maritime Museum, Greenwich
CLARENDON Held at the Bodleian Library, Oxford
CODRINGTON Held at the National Maritime Museum
COWLEY Held at the Public Record Office
DUNDAS, J. W. D. Held at the National Maritime Museum
DUNDAS, R. S. Held at the Scottish Record Office, Edinburgh
GLADSTONE Held at the British Library
GRAHAM Held at Cumbria Record Office, partly available on microfilm
GRIEVE, Lieutenant. National Maritime Museum
HALIFAX Held at the British Library (Naval Correspondence) Borthwick
    Institute, York (General Correspondence) and the India Record Office
    (Indian Correspondence)
HERBERT Held at the Wiltshire Record Office, Trowbridge
KEPPEL Held at the National Maritime Museum
LYONS Held at the Sussex Record Office, Chichester
MARTIN Held at the British Library, correspondence of Admiral Sir
    Thomas Byam Martin and his sons Admirals Sir William Martin and Sir
    Henry Martin
MILNE Held at the National Maritime Museum
NAPIER Held at the British Library, the Public Record Office and the
    National Maritime Museum
NEWCASTLE Held at the Univerity of Nottingham
PALMERSTON Broadlands collection consulted while at the National
    Register of Archives, now deposited at the University of Southampton
    Letter Books at the British Library
PANMURE (DALHOUSIE) Held at the Scottish Record Office
PARKER Held at the National Maritime Museum
RAGLAN Held at the National Army Museum
ROYAL ARCHIVE Held at Windsor Castle
RUSSELL Held at the Public Record Office
SPRATT Held at the National Maritime Museum
STRATFORD de REDCLIFFE Held at the Public Record Office
WALKER Held at the University of Capetown

Published documents

Parliamentary Papers, Great Britain
1847–8, vol. xxi
1852–3, vol. ix
1854–5, vol. ix
1856, vol. xi
1859, vols. xiv, xv
Further correspondence relating to the military expedition to the East (eight
vols.)

Hansard's Parliamentary Debates, Third Series

Collections
Aberdeen. *Correspondence*: nine volumes covering the years 1846–1862 edited by Lord Stanmore. Privately printed.
Argyll. *Autobography and Memoirs* (London 1906), two vols.
Baring. *Journals and Correspondence of Francis Thornhill Barin, afterwards Lord Northbrook* (London, 1905), two vols.
Burgoyne. *The Military Opinions of General Sir John Fox Burgoyne* (London 1859) ed. Captain G. Wrottesley.
Burgoyne. *The Life and Correspondence of Field Marshal Sir John Burgoyne* (London, 1873), two vols., ed. G. Wrottesley.
Cowley. *The Paris Embassy during the Second Empire* (London, 1928), ed. F. A. Wellesley.
Greville. *Memoirs* (London, 1938) eight vols., ed. Strachey and Fulford.
Loftus. *The Diplomatic Reminiscences of Lord Augustus Loftus; 1837–1862* (London, 1892) 1st series, two vols.
Palmerston. *The Palmerston–Sullivan Correspondence 1804–1863* (London 1979), ed. K. Bourne.
Panmure. *The Panmure papers; Being a selection from the correspondence of Fox Maule, 2nd Baron Panmure, afterwards 11th Earl of Dalhousie* (London, 1908), two vols., ed. Douglas and Ramsay.
Russell. *The Later Correspondence of Lord John Russell, 1840–1878* (London, 1925), two vols., ed. G. P. Gooch.
Stanley. *The Political Journals of Lord Stanley* (London, 1979) ed. J. Vincent.
Victoria. *The Letters of Queen Victoria 1837–1861* (London, 1907), three vols., ed. Benson and Esher.

Publications of the Navy Records Society
Bonner-Smith, D., *The Russian War 1854: The Baltic* (London, 1943)
Bonner-Smith, D., *The Russian War 1855: The Baltic* (London, 1944)
Bromley, J. S. *The Manning of the Royal Navy* (London, 1974)
Corbett, J. S. *Fighting Instructions 1530–1816* (London, 1905)
Corbett, J. S. *Signals and Instructions 1776–1794* (London, 1909)
Dewar, Capt. A. C. *The Russian War 1854: The Black Sea* (London, 1943)
Dewar, Capt. A.C. *The Russian War 1855; The Black Sea* (London 1945)
Hamilton, C. I. 'Selections from the Phinn Committee of Inquiry, 1855' in *The Naval Miscellany vol. V* (London, 1985), ed. N. A. M. Rodger
Hamilton, Adm. Sir R. V. *Letters and Papers of Sir T. Byam Martin* (London 1899, 1900, 1903), three vols.
Lambert, A. D. 'Captain Sir Henry Keppel's Account "Capture of Bomarsund – August 1855" ' in *The Naval Miscellany Vol. V* (London, 1985), ed. N. A. M. Rodger
Ryan, A.N. *The Saumarez Papers: The Baltic 1808–1812* (London, 1968)

Newspaper
The Times

Secondary sources

Books

Albion, R. G. *Forests and Seapower* (Harvard, 1925)
Anderson, O. *A Liberal State at War* (London, 1967)
Anderson, R. G. *Naval Wars in the Baltic in the Sailing Ship Epoch, 1522–1850* (London, 1910)
Anderson, R. G. *Naval Wars in the Levant 1559–1853* (Liverpool, 1952)
Andersson, I. *A History of Sweden* (London, 1956)
Bailey, F. E. *British Policy and the Turkish Reform Movement, 1826–1853* (Harvard, 1942 and 1970)
Banbury, P. *Shipbuilders of the Thames and Medway* (Newton Abbot, 1971)
Bapst, C. G. *Le Maréchal Canrobert, souveniers d'un siècle* (Paris, 1898–1913), six vols.
Barros, J. *The Aland Islands Question* (New Haven, 1968)
Bartlett, C. J. *Great Britain and Seapower, 1815–1853* (Oxford, 1963)
Baumgart, W. *The Peace of Paris, 1856* (Santa Barbara, 1981)
Baxter, J. P. *The Introduction of the Ironclad Warship* (Cambridge, Mass., 1933)
Bayley, C. C. *Mercenaries for the Crimea* (London, 1977)
Bentley, N. ed. *Russell's Despatches from the Crimea, 1854–1856* (London 1966)
Biddlecombe, G. *Naval Tactics and Sailing Trials* (London, 1850)
Biddulph, Lady. *Charles Philip Yorke: Fourth Earl of Hardwicke, Vice-Admiral R.N. A Memoir* (London, 1910)
Blake, R. *Disraeli* (London, 1966)
Bourchier, Lady. *Selections from the Correspondence of Sir Henry Codrington* (London, 1880)
Bourne, J. M. *Patronage and Society in Nineteenth-Century England* (London, 1986)
Bourne, K. *Palmerston: the early years* (London, 1982)
Bourne, K. and Watt, D. C. *Studies in International History* (London, 1967)
Brereton, Major General W. *The British Fleet in the Black Sea under the command of Vice Admiral Sir J. W. D. Dundas* (London, 1856)
Briggs, Sir J. *Naval Administrations, 1827–1892* (London, 1897)
Burrows, M. *Memoirs of Admiral Sir H. D. Chads* (Portsea, 1867)
Busk, H. *The Navies of the World* (London, 1859)
Carlyle, T. *On Heroes and Hero Worship* (London, 1840)
Case, L. M. *French Opinion on War and Diplomacy during the Second Empire* (Philadelphia, 1954)
Chamberlain, M. E. *Lord Aberdeen* (London, 1982)
Chevalier, E. *Histoire de la Marine Français* (Paris, 1905), five vols.
Clapham, J. H. *An Economic History of Modern Britain* (Cambridge 1926), vol. I
Clausewitz, K. *On War*, ed. Brodie, Howard and Paret (Princeton 1982)
Clowes, W. L., ed. *The Royal Navy* (London, 1903), vol. VI
Cobden, R. *Political Writings* (London, 1868), two vols.

Colomb, Admiral P. H. *Naval Warfare* (London, 1891)
Colomb, Admiral P. H. *Memoirs of Sir Astley Cooper-Key* (London, 1898)
Conacher, J. E. *The Aberdeen Coalition 1852–1855* (Cambridge, 1968)
Conacher, J. E. *The Peelites and the Party System, 1846–1852* (Newton Abbot, 1972)
Conacher, J. E. *Britain and the Crimea, 1855–56* (London, 1987)
Corbett, J. S. *Some Principles of Maritime Strategy* (London, 1911)
Craig, G. *The Politics of the Prussian Army, 1640–1945'* (Oxford, 1955)
Crauford, *The Russian Fleet in the Baltic in 1836* (London, 1837)
Curtiss, J. S. *The Russian Army under Nicholas I, 1825–1855* (Durham, N. C., 1965)
Curtiss, J. S. *Russia's Crimean War* (Ithaca, 1979)
Dasent, A. I. *John Thadeus Delane* (London, 1908), two vols.
Day, Admiral Sir A. *The Admiralty Hydrographic Service* (London, 1967)
Douglas, General Sir H. *Naval Warfare under Steam* (London, 1857)
Douglas, General Sir H. *A Treatise on Naval Gunnery* (London, 1861, sixth edition)
Eardley Wilmot, Captain S. *The Life of Vice-Admiral Lord Lyons* (London, 1898)
Earp, G. B. *The History of the Baltic Campaign of 1854* (London, 1857)
Echard, W. E. *Napoleon III and the Concert of Europe* (Baton Rouge, 1983)
Egerton, F. *Admiral Sir Geoffrey Phipps Hornby* (London, 1896)
Elers-Napier, General G. *The Life and Correspondence of Admiral Sir Charles Napier* (London, 1862)
Emmerson, G. S. *John Scott-Russell* (London, 1977)
Erickson, A. B. *The Public Career of Sir James Graham* (Oxford, 1952)
Fawcett, M. *Life of Sir William Molesworth* (London, 1901)
Fincham, J. *A History of Naval Architecture* (London, 1851)
Fitzmaurice, Lord E. *The Life of Granville George Leveson Gower, Second Earl Granville, 1815–1891* (London, 1905), two vols.
Fortescue, J. W. *A History of the British Army* (London, 1930), vol. XIII
Friendly, A. *Beaufort of the Admiralty* (London, 1977)
Giffard, Admiral Sir G. *Reminiscemces of a Naval Officer* (Exeter, 1892)
Gleason, J. H. *The Genesis of Russophobia in Great Britain* (London, 1950)
Gooch, B. D. *The New Bonapartist Generals in the Crimean War* (The Hague, 1959)
Gooch, G. P. *The Second Empire* (London, 196
Gorshkov, Admiral S. *The Seapower of the State* (Oxford, 1979)
Gosset, W. P. *The Lost Ships of the Royal Navy, 1793–1900* (London 1986)
Graham, G. S. *The Politics of Naval Supremacy* (Cambridge, 1965)
Greenhill, B. and Giffard, A. *The British Assault on Finland 1854–55* (London, 1988)
Hallendorf, C. and Schuck, A. *A History of Sweden* (New York, 1970)
Hamilton, Admiral Sir R. V. *Naval Administration* (London, 1897)
Hamley, General Sir E. *The War in the Crimea* (London, 1890)
Heath, Admiral L. G. *Letters from the Black Sea* (London, 1897)
Henderson, G. B. *Crimean War Diplomacy* (Glasgow, 1947)
Hibbert, C. *The Destruction of Lord Raglan* (London, 1963)

Hoseason, Commander J. C. *The Steam Navy* (London, 1853)

Hoskins, H. L. *British Routes to India* (London, 1928)

Imlah, A. H. *Economic Elements in the Pax Britannica* (London, 1958)

James, W. *The Naval History of Great Britain* (London, 1902 edn), six vols.

Jane, F. T. *The Imperial Russian Navy* (London, 1904)

Jane, F. T. *Heresies of Seapower* (London, 1907)

Jenkins, E. H. *A History of the French Navy* (London, 1974)

Kennedy, P. *The Rise and Fall of British Naval Mastery* (London, 1976)

Keppel, Admiral Sir H. *A Sailor's Life under Four Sovereigns* (London 1899), three vols.

King-Hall, L. *Sea Saga* (London, 1935)

Kinglake, A. *The Invasion of the Crimea* (London. 1877), nine. vols.

Kingsley-Martin, B. *The Triumph of Lord Palmerston* (London, 1924)

Krien, D. *The last Palmerston Administration* (Iowa, 1978)

Lambert, A. D. *Battleships in Transition: The Creation of the Steam Battlefleet 1815–1860* (London, 1984)

Lambert, A. D. *Warrior: Restoring the World's First Ironclad* (London, 1987)

Laughton, J. K. *Memoirs of the Life and Correspondence of Henry Reeve* (London, 1898), two vols.

Lewis, M. *The Navy in Transition, 1814–1865* (London, 1965)

Lincoln, W. B. *Nicholas I* (London, 1978)

Lloyd, C. and Coulter, *Medicine and the Navy, 1200–1900* (Edinburgh, 1963), vol. IV

Luvass, J. *The Education of an Army* (London, 1965)

McNeil, W. *The Pursuit of Power* (Oxford, 1983)

Mahan, Captain A. T. *Naval Strategy* (London, 1911)

Malmesbury, Earl of, *Memoirs of an Ex-Minister* (London, 1884)

Martin, T. *Life of the Prince Consort* (London, 1879), five vols.

Martineau, J. *Life of Henry Pelham, Fifth Duke of Newcastle* (London, 1908)

Marx, K. *The Eastern Question* (London, 1897)

Maxwell, H. *The Life and Letters of the Fourth Earl Clarendon* (London, 1913), two vols.

Mead and Juatinen, *The Aland Islands* (London, 1975)

Mitchell, D. *A History of Russian and Soviet Seapower* (London, 1974)

Mosely, P. C. *Russian Diplomacy and the Opening of the Eastern Question in 1833* (Cambridge, Mass., 1934)

Munsell, F. D. *The Unfortunate Duke: Henry Pelham, Fifth Duke of Newcastle, 1811–1864* (Missouri, 1985)

Napier, Admiral Sir C. *The Navy* (London, 1851)

Navy List, Various.

O'Byrne, W. *Naval Biographical Dictionary* (London, 1849) two vols.

Otway, A. *Autobiography and Journals of Admiral Lord Clarence Paget* (London, 1896)

Parker, C. S. *Life and Letters of Sir James Graham, 1792–1861* (London, 1907), two vols.

Parry, A. *The Admirals Fremantle* (London, 1971)

Pasley, L. *Life of Sir T. S. Pasley* (London, 1900)
Phillimore, A. *Life of Admiral Sir William Parker* (London, 1876–8), three vols.
Piggott, Sir F. *The Declaration of Paris, 1856* (London, 1919)
Poole, S. L. *The Life of Stratford Canning* (London, 1888), two vols.
Prest, J. M. *Lord John Russell* (London, 1972)
Preston, A. and Major, J. *Send a Gunboat* (London, 1967)
Puryear, V. J. *England, Russia and the Straits Question, 1844–1856* (Berkeley, 1931)
Ranft, B., ed. *Technical Change and British Naval Policy, 1860–1939* (London, 1977)
Read, E. J. *On the Modifications which the ships of the Royal Navy have undergone in the Present Century* (London, 1859)
Rich, N. *Why the Crimean War?* (London, 1985)
Richmond, Admiral Sir H. *National Policy and Naval Strength* (London, 1928)
Richmond, Admiral Sir H. *Statesmen and Seapower* (Oxford, 1946)
Ritchie, Admiral Sir G. S. *The Admiralty Chart* (London, 1967)
Rodger, N. A. M. *The Admiralty* (Lavenham, 1979)
Rolt, L. T. C. *Isambard Kingdom Brunel* (London, 1957)
Ross, Sir J. *Memoirs of Lord de Saumarez* (London, 1838), two vols.
Saab, A. P. *The Origins of the Crimean Alliance* (Virginia, 1977)
Schroeder, P. W. *Austria, Great Britain and the Crimean War* (New York, 1972)
Schurman, D. M. *The Education of a Navy* (London, 1965)
Schurman, D. M. *Sir Julian Stafford Corbett, 1856–1922* (London, 1981)
Scott, F *Sweden* (Minnesota, 1977)
Seaton, H. *The Crimean War* (London, 1977)
Seeley, J. R. *The Growth of British Policy* (Cambridge, 1922)
Semmel, B. *Liberalism and Naval Strategy* (London, 1986)
Seton-Watson, H. *The Russian Empire, 1801-1917* (Oxford, 1967)
Seton-Watson, R. *Britain in Europe* (London, 1938)
Shannon, R. *Gladstone* (London, 1982), vol. one
Sharp, J. A. *Memoirs of Rear Admiral Sir William Symonds* (London, 1858)
Shaw, Stanford J. *History of the Ottoman Empire and Modern Turkey* (Cambridge, 1977), vol. II
Slade, A. *Record of Travels* (London, 1833), two vols.
Slade, A. *Turkey and the Crimean War* (London, 1867)
Southey, R. *Life of Lord Nelson* (London, 1833)
Spiers, E. M. *Radical General* (Manchester, 1983)
Stanmore, Lord *Life of Sidney Herbert* (London, 1906), two vols.
Strachan, H. *Wellington's Legacy: The Reform of the British Army, 1830-1854* (Manchester, 1984)
Strachan, H. *From Waterloo to Balaklava* (Cambridge, 1985)
Sulivan, H. N. *Life and Letters of Admiral Sir B. J. Sulivan* (London 1896)
Sumner, B. H. *A Survey of Russian History* (London, 1947)
Taylor, A. J. P. *The Struggle for Mastery in Europe, 1848-1918* (Oxford, 1954)

Temperley, H. M. V. *England and the Near East: The Crimea* (London, 1936)
Van Crefeld, M. *Supplying War* (London, 1977)
Vincent, J. *The Formation of the British Liberal Party, 1857–1866* (London, 1966)
Ward, J. T. *Sir James Graham* (London, 1967)
Warner, P., ed. *The Fields of War* (London, 1977)
Waterfield, G. *Layard of Nineveh* (London, 1963)
Webster, Sir C. *The Foreign Policy of Palmerston* (London, 1951), two vols.
Wellesley and Sencourt, *Conversations with Napoleon III* (London, 1934)
Williams, H. N. *The Life and Letters of Admiral Sir Charles Napier* (London, 1917)
Wilson, K. M., ed. *British Foreign Secretaries and Foreign Policy from the Crimean War to the First World War* (London, 1987)
Wuorinen, J. H. *A History of Finland* (New York, 1965)

Articles

Brown, D. K. 'Shells at Sevastopol', *Warship*,, April 1979
Brown, D. K. 'Thomas Lloyd, CB', *Warship*, October 1981
Hamilton, C. I. 'Sir James Graham, the Baltic Campaign and war planning at the Admiralty in 1854', *The Historical Journal*, 1976
Hamilton, C. I. 'Naval hagiography and the Victorian hero', *The Historical Journal*, 1980
Knaplund, P. 'Finnmark in British diplomacy, 1832–1855', *The American Historical Review*, 1925, vol. 30
Lambert, A. D. 'Soviet seapower; the element of strategic continuity', *Warship*, October 1987
Lloyd, C. 'Dundonald's Crimean war plans', *Mariner's Mirror*, 1946, vol. 32
Herkless, J. L. 'Stratford, the Cabinet and the outbreak of the Crimean War', *The Historical Journal*, 1975
Osbon, G. A. 'The First Ironclads', *Mariner's Mirror*, 1964, vol. 50
Osbon, G. A. 'The Crimean gunboats', *Mariner's Mirror*, 1965, vol. 51
Ranft, B. 'Restraints on war at sea before 1945', in *Restraints on War*, ed. M. Howard
Saab, A. P., Knapp, J. and Knapp, F. 'A reassessment of French foreign policy during the Crimean war based on the papers of Adolphe de Borqueney', *French Historical Studies*, 1986
Stone, I. R. 'The Crimean War in the Arctic', *Polar Record*, 1983
Stone, I. R. and Crampton, R. J. 'A disastrous affair'; the Franco-British attack on Petropavlosk, 1854', *Polar Record* 1985
Strachan, H. 'Soldiers, Strategy and Sebastopol', *The Historical Journal*, 1978
Taylor, R. I. 'Manning the Royal Navy: the reform of the recruiting system, 1852–1862', *Mariner's Mirror*, 1959, 1960, vols. 44, 45
Temperley, H. W. V. 'The alleged violations of the Straits Convention by Stratford de Redcliffe between June and September 1853', *English*

Historical Review, 1934

Vincent, J. 'The Parliamentary dimension of the Crimean War', *Transactions of the Royal Historical Society*, 1981

Unpublished dissertations

Hamilton, C. I. 'The Royal Navy, Seapower, and the Screw Ship of the Line; 1845–1860' (Cambridge 1973)

Lambert, A. D. 'Great Britain, the Baltic and the Russian War; 1854–1856' (London 1983)

MacMillan, D. F. 'The Development of British Naval Gunnery; 1815–1853' (London 1967)

Roberts, S. S. 'The Introduction of Steam Technology into the French Navy; 1818–1852' Chicago 1976

Index